PE64.   67-9315
W5   Warfel
W3   Noah Webster
No
1966

Date Due

		JUL 2000	
		JUN 0 9 ANS	
		JUL X X 2015	

PRINTED IN U.S.A.

NOAH WEBSTER
SCHOOLMASTER TO AMERICA

Painted by S. F. B. Morse, 1823

NOAH WEBSTER

Aged 65

NOAH WEBSTER

SCHOOLMASTER TO AMERICA

BY

HARRY R. WARFEL

1966

OCTAGON BOOKS, INC.

New York

67-9315

Reprinted 1966
by special arrangement with Harry R. Warfel

OCTAGON BOOKS, INC.
175 FIFTH AVENUE
NEW YORK, N.Y. 10010

LIBRARY OF CONGRESS CATALOG CARD NUMBER: 66-28378

Printed in U.S.A. by
NOBLE OFFSET PRINTERS, INC.
NEW YORK 3, N. Y.

TO
RUTH FARQUHAR WARFEL
Wife and Colleague

TEN years ago I began a history of nationalism in American literature, but before proceeding very far I discovered that the basic studies necessary for so broad a survey had not been made. Chief among these was a good biographical and critical study of the achievements of Noah Webster. During my researches, fortunately, I made the acquaintance of William Chauncey Fowler, of Durham Center, Connecticut, a great-grandson of Webster. In his possession were letters to his grandmother, Harriet Webster Fowler, from her father and mother and sisters and brother. Not only did Mr. Fowler permit me to examine and use these materials, but he urged me to prepare a biography. I then communicated with Mrs. Roswell Skeel, Jr., a great-granddaughter of Webster; she, too, insisted that I write this book. For many years she has been engaged in preparing a definitive bibliography of the newspaper, magazine, and book publications of Webster in an effort to untangle the maze of hundreds of issues of his single works. When her three-volume work appears, it should be consulted for the indispensable background of minute details which I have been forced to omit or summarize. Mrs. Skeel gave me permission to examine some parts of her manuscript, and it is to her generosity that I owe the celerity of my independent investigations. She has enthusiastically encouraged me and has read my manuscript. My perversity alone, I hasten to add, is to be blamed for any errors which may have crept into the text.

Because Mrs. Skeel's bibliography will present all the facts in Webster's long career as an author, I have omitted footnote citations, substituting therefor a brief statement of my sources. Had I located every detail and had I argued my conclusions, as is so frequently done in footnotes, I would have doubled the size of the present volume. Where so much is new, as in this book, almost every sentence might be expanded or traced to a source. To aid any students who may wish to follow my footsteps, I have inserted in the text all relevant dates and locations, so that my sources may be consulted or my quotations verified.

If this book brings to light, as I think, a new character of first importance in the study of early national American culture, it is because our historians have been too preoccupied with political figures to see the creators of social forces at work in humble ways. Our educators, too, have been superficial in the investigation of the history of American textbooks. Fifty monographs, such as the admirable one by Dr. C.–E. A. Winslow on "The Epidemiology of Noah Webster," should have preceded the writing of this book, but for these I could not wait. The materials are here sketched for more patient hands to support or amend.

In tracing the growth of Webster's ideas and influence, I have occasionally brought him under comparison with other men, men more solidly established in history and in our prejudices. In every case, as with Alexander Hamilton for example, the comparison applies only to the given situation in which these men were comparable. I attempt to express a final judgment on no person other than my subject.

In extenuation of my approach to Webster's life and character, I can merely say that I, too, am a teacher, possessing a native share of my subject's crotchets.

Since the varying spelling forms of Webster may be interesting to some readers, I have followed the spelling of my sources in all quotations, but I have on occasion normalized the punctuation. The spelling of my text follows the rules of *Webster's New International Dictionary, Second Edition* (1934).

I am indebted to many librarians for their genial replies to my inquiries and for their assistance. Above all, to Andrew Keogh, Librarian, and Charles E. Rush, Associate Librarian of the Yale University Library, I owe many kind acts of friendly help which this statement poorly repays. Charles R. Green, Librarian of the Jones Memorial Library, Amherst, Massachusetts, and Albert C. Bates, Director of the Connecticut Historical Society, Hartford, lent their possessions and gave heartily from their rich stores of knowledge. In my statement of sources are listed the institutions and individuals who graciously permitted me to copy manuscript materials in their possession.

William C. Fowler has permitted me to reproduce the portraits of Webster and his wife. The Trustees of Amherst College have granted permission for the reproduction of Mrs. Orra White Hitchcock's painting of Amherst Church and Amherst College. G. and C. Merriam Company has permitted the reproduction of pages from the original manuscript of Webster's great Dictionary. The selections from Alice Morse Earle's *Child Life in Colonial Days* are used with the permission of The Macmillan Company. For these permissions I am very grateful.

This book was written while I held a Sterling Research Fellowship at Yale University, but most of the research was completed while I taught at my Alma Mater, Bucknell University. To the President and Board of Trustees of Bucknell University I express gratitude for unfailing interest in my work and for granting me leaves of absence to prosecute my studies.

Norman Holmes Pearson, J. Orin Oliphant, and Edgar F. Long enriched the manuscript by their careful reading. My wife assisted me daily; her limitless good cheer brightened every moment of my long task.

HARRY R. WARFEL

University of Maryland
        College Park
February 28, 1936

CONTENTS

ILLUSTRATIONS

NOAH WEBSTER
SCHOOLMASTER TO AMERICA

PROLOGUE

On his seventieth birthday, October 16, 1828, Noah Webster lifted his eyes from the last proof sheet of the scholarly Introduction to his Dictionary. Slowly he wiped the ink from the quill, laid it down, and methodically capped the inkwell. His moist eyes blinked. He turned to his wife and colleague, caught her hands. Together they knelt by the desk and prayed tremblingly in giving thanks to God for His providence in sustaining them through their long labor. Since June 4, 1800, when the project was first publicly announced, Webster had dandled his book on his knee to the tune of a public lullaby of jeers, insults, and misrepresentation. Every opprobrious epithet in the vocabularies of calumny and abuse had been showered upon him. Undeterred by it, he had completed, single-handed, America's first monumental work of scholarship. *An American Dictionary of the English Language* was immediately acclaimed, in England and Germany as well as in America, the best work of its kind ever prepared.

Today, *Webster* and *dictionary* are synonymous terms in our language. No tribute can surpass this one.

Yet, curiously enough, although the name *Webster* is on the tip of every person's tongue who wants to consult that indispensable reference book, the dictionary, few can give the lexicographer's first name. When asked the question, the average informed person looks blank a moment, then hesitantly ventures, "Daniel, I guess." Thus Noah Webster, who eminently deserves a niche in the Hall of Fame, not only is not memorialized in that pantheon, but has suffered an even worse fate: his name has coalesced with that of the famous orator and statesman who was not even his kinsman.

Like Dr. Samuel Johnson, whose dictionary lost ground as Webster's gained, Noah Webster was more than a "harmless drudge," a writer of definitions. Before announcing his dictionary at the age of forty-two, Noah Webster had become the pivotal figure in American education and literature. As the author of a series of primary school textbooks and as the expounder of a nationalistic theory of education, he had become the young nation's first schoolmaster. As an itinerant propagandist for a Constitution, he had done more than any other single individual to prepare a climate of opinion in which a Constitutional Convention could be successful. As a clear-visioned economist, a humanitarian, a magazine and newspaper editor, a historical scholar, and a moralist, he ceaselessly drove his pen in furthering the best interests of his country. Although he completed the Dictionary in 1828, he never surrendered work until death called him in his eighty-fifth year, May 28, 1843.

Something of the many-sided intellectual quality of Benjamin Franklin reappeared in Webster. Both possessed astonishing versatility and delved into every area of knowledge, leaving marks of influence in almost every field of activity developed in their times. It was fitting that Franklin, in his old age, befriended the young schoolmaster and tutored him in simplified spelling. But Webster, unlike Franklin, did not permanently slough off the iron mantle of New England Calvinism. And Webster never sought or obtained high political position. Essentially a scholar and publicist, Webster wielded his pen as a weapon in the perennial warfare against social injustice, scientific error, mental torpor, and national instability. Early in life he called himself The Prompter, the man who sits behind the scenes to correct errors or assist the memory.

Webster became our greatest schoolmaster. He passed successively from the desk of a Connecticut log schoolhouse to the lecture platform, to the editorial chair, and finally to the home library table as the arbiter of every English-speaking reader's and writer's diction. His schoolbooks were carried from the hills of New England across the Alleghenies; his were among the first books printed in every new settlement. Across the prairies and over the Rocky Mountains his carefully marshaled columns of words marched like warriors against the ignorance that tended to disrupt the primitive society of thinly spread and localized culture of America. Dialect variation disappeared from our writing and spelling, and to his blue-backed Speller, of which nearly one hundred million copies were sold before it went out of general use, America owes its remarkable uniformity of language. No other book, the Bible excepted, has strained so many heads, or done so much good. It taught millions to read, and not one to sin. And today the monolithic "Webster" on every school teacher's desk, on the reference tables of libraries, at the elbow of the justice, and on the study table of the scholar, bears silent testimony to Noah Webster's enduring labors and superb genius.

Patient, indefatigable laborer for American cultural advancement that Webster was, he yet never won the warm personal sympathy of his countrymen. A pugnaciousness in propagating his own strongly phrased ideas, a gesture many people considered egotistic, rendered Webster socially unattractive. His tall, spare, Yankee form stiffened under opposition. His massive head grew rigidly upright in an inflexible ambition to do good. The mountainous forehead, crowned with a forest of autumn-tinted hair, sloped to beetling crags of eyebrows. Deep set, as in a cave, small gray eyes flashed lightning warnings of intense mental operations. A massive square jaw and a jutting nose persuaded opponents that here was one endowed by nature to hold his own against any and all opposition. The narrow, thin line of lips held taut a tongue ever ready to castigate error.

"If my name is a terror to evildoers," Webster once wrote, "mention it." In this respect, too, Webster was the typical schoolmaster, the man who is more concerned to have lessons well learned than to secure the adulation of shirking, fawning ignorance.

CHAPTER I

LIFE's ABC's

NOAH WEBSTER, JUNIOR, was born in West Hartford, Connecticut, on October 16, 1758, a descendant of a long line of sturdy democrats. The name Webster, meaning a female weaver, of early English origin, is derived from a trade, and therefore bearers of the name are not necessarily related. No connection between the families of Noah and Daniel Webster has been found, nor indeed between these two and the other eight main groups of Websters in America.

John Webster, the founder of this branch of the family in America, emigrated about 1630–1633 to Massachusetts Bay Colony from Warwickshire, England. Settling near Boston, he joined the church of the Reverend Thomas Hooker, whose stubborn democratic spirit rebelled against the reactionary theocracy of John Cotton, John Winthrop, and Governor Haynes. With Hooker's little band of dissenters, in 1635–1636, John Webster moved to New Towne, now Hartford, Connecticut, where we first find his name among the extant colonial records. In wealth Webster surpassed most of the party, for only four took up more land than he, and only two took up as much. In 1638 he was made a member of the Court of Magistrates, and continuously until his death he served in this or other governing bodies. He became Deputy Governor of the Colony of Connecticut in 1655 and Governor the following year.

When Mr. Hooker died in 1647, his successor, the Reverend Mr. Samuel Stone, deviating in doctrine and procedure from the beloved founder, altered the democratic structure

of the Church. Stone stood for "a speaking aristocracy in
the face of a silent democracy," and refused to allow the
congregation to vote upon the selection of a new pastor. A
conflict flared between the supporters of opposite principles
of ecclesiastical order; during ten years the fire of controversy
burned increasingly brightly. A church council, composed
of Connecticut pastors, in June, 1656, convened at the
request of Webster and others, and vindicated the opponents of the pastor. Stone, refusing to yield, sought political interference by the Massachusetts Council and tried
to unseat dissenting magistrates like Webster. One charge
against Webster grew out of an exegetical, if not lexicographical, disagreement, the Governor refusing to yield to
the pastor's interpretation of "submit" in Hebrews, XIII, 17.
Obstructionist tactics restrained the remonstrants from leaving the parish until April 18, 1659, when fifty-nine men,
headed by John Webster, agreed to move out of the juris-
diction of Connecticut into Massachusetts. Some forty of
them purchased and settled Hadley, which then included
the present towns of Hadley, South Hadley, Granby, and
Amherst on the east side of the Connecticut River, and Hat-
field and a part of Williamsburg on the west side. Shortly
after his settlement in Hadley, Webster became a judge of
the court in Hampshire County. He died on April 5, 1661,
"an exile for conscience sake from the infant city which he
helped to found." In 1818 Noah Webster erected a modest
slab tombstone over the pioneer's grave.

The eldest of John Webster's sons, Robert, was probably born in England and was brought to America by his
father. A man of ability, he served the community in many
ways. He settled in Middletown and upon the organization
of the town in September, 1651, was chosen recorder, a position he held again in 1656 and 1657. In 1654 he was a
lieutenant in the Connecticut forces raised to repel Indian
invasions; from 1653 to 1658 he was the representative

for Middletown in the colonial parliament. Although his name was on the list of those who served intention of moving to Hadley, Robert evidently moved to Hartford in 1659, for he was a selectman in that town in 1664 and 1673. In King Philip's War, when the Indians approached Hartford, Webster was appointed to arrange the defenses of the Town, October 11, 1675. He died as a result of a severe illness about May 31, 1676. Suzannah, his wife, was a daughter of Richard Treat, Sr., of Wethersfield, one of the patentees in the Royal Charter of Connecticut, framed in 1662.

The annals of the family now became scant, for there were no indefatigable diarists of the Sewall or Mather type in Connecticut settlements. John, the eldest son of Robert and Suzannah Webster, was born in Middletown, November 10, 1653, and he died on December 8, 1694. He and his wife, Sarah Mygatt, had seven children, four sons and three daughters. The youngest son, Daniel, was baptized on October 1, 1693. He married Miriam, daughter of Noah Cooke, of Northampton, and widow of Abram Kellogg of Hartford. Daniel Webster was a captain in the fourth company or trainband of Hartford in 1736, and in the Spanish war of 1745 he commanded a company. He died on December 21, 1765, three of seven children surviving him: Noah, Miriam, and Daniel.

Noah Webster, Senior, named for his maternal grandfather, was born at Hartford on March 25, 1722. He became a rugged Yankee farmer, whose intelligence, able counsel, and wise administrative ability helped to guide the West Hartford parish through his active life of ninety-one years. He served as a soldier during the troublous period of the French and Indian Wars, rising to the rank of Lieutenant. In the Revolution, although exempt by age from military service, he commanded the local alarm list, marching with his three sons to Ticonderoga in September, 1777, to repel the invasion of Burgoyne. He filled numerous positions of importance in the parish, then called the Fourth Society of Hartford. In 1757, when Asa Merrill had accused the pastor, the Reverend Mr. Benjamin Colton, of imbibing thirteen and a half gills of brandy, Webster served as one of a committee to "use all means to bring him to repentance" and "make gospel satisfaction." On April 3, 1775, he was elected Deacon, an office testifying at once to the dignity of his character, the strength of his moral influence, and the friendly regard of his neighbors. In later years Webster was chosen treasurer, rate-maker, and moderator of the Society. From 1781 until 1796 the Connecticut Legislature appointed him annually a Justice of the Peace. Thus he reached in the town the two highest offices which the Church and State could confer, and he was variously known as Deacon Webster and Squire Webster. The depreciation of Continental currency straitened his finances during the War, but the age of sixty was no time to surrender to misfortune. He vigorously continued his labors and achieved a modest competency before his retirement. He died, aged ninety-one, on November 9, 1813.

On January 12, 1749, Noah Webster, Sr., married Mercy Steele, a great-granddaughter of William Bradford, Governor of Plymouth Colony from 1621 until his death in 1651. She was baptized on October 8, 1727, probably a short time after her birth. "A woman of great intelligence and energy," Mrs. Webster was "a gentle, loving mother and caretaker, looking well to the ways of her household. She carried on the farm quite successfully while her husband and sons were in the War of the Revolution." She died October 5, 1794.

Five children were born to this couple: Mercy, born November 8, 1749; Abraham, born September 17, 1751; Jerusha, born January 22, 1756; Noah, born October 16, 1758; and Charles, born September 2, 1762. The girls,

bright religious women, married early. Charles entered
business, and Abraham became a farmer in New York State
near Utica. The Webster children, trained to severe and
unremitting industry in the employments of the farm, acquired habits of early rising, strict temperance, and vigorous
exercise in the open air, habits which gave them hardihood
of constitution and which prolonged their lives. Both daughters lived to be seventy; Charles, fifty-five; Abraham,
eighty; and Noah, eighty-five.

The birthplace of Noah Webster still stands in West
Hartford on South Main Street. From its slight eminence
it affords an eastward view of the towering structures of
Hartford, and a magnificent westward vista over undulat-
ing hills and fertile farms. Renovation by recent owners
has not destroyed the familiar old New England lines. It
is severely plain, and its dark red color blends into ever-
greens now thickly planted around it. The main part of
the house is two stories high. On each side of the front
entry on the first floor is a large room. The chambers above
correspond to the rooms below. In one room the large un-
sheathed beams appear, evidence of the solidity with which
the house was built. The rear portion of the house is one
story high, the roof sloping unbroken from the ridge. In
the center of the house rises a huge stone chimney. To this
are connected three fireplaces and a brick oven on the first
floor, and two fireplaces on the second floor. The unpre-
tentious comfort of the house, with its old-fashioned pine
walls and fireplaces, testifies to its builder's democratic simplicity.

Connecticut boyhood in the years before the Revolution
knew few advantages except the assured dignity of toil. As
soon as a boy could call a dog, he was sent in seasonable
weather to keep the cattle from straying, to pick berries, and
to help clear the stony fields. A stouthearted lad of twelve

drove a team or even walked behind the plow. Milking became a chore morning and evening. Carrying in wood and splitting it were winter activities. Butchering, with its pleasant neighborly gathering, required the carrying of hot water, the whetting of tools, and the preparation of sausage skins. Every day had its grist of duties, for a farm was almost a self-sufficing community, dependent only on the blacksmith, the miller, and the general storekeeper for occasional services. A farmer was of necessity a jack-of-all trades, calling into use his Yankee ingenuity.

Games and sports were not unknown, but except on election day and at the husking bee, the barnraising, harvesting, indoor bees, and skating, a boy had few opportunities for companionable play. Houses were not numerous in either West Hartford or Hartford in 1765, so that the country boys, who seldom could be spared on pleasant days for a visit to the more populous districts, snatched from their toil their minutes for play.

The citizens of Connecticut were practical democrats who early decreed that their children should be given the advantage of common schooling. A state law required that elementary schools be conducted eleven months each year under the control of the church societies. "It was the glory of the fathers of New England that they placed their social and political fabric upon the foundation of Religion and Education." The church and the schoolhouse stood side by side; the former held the adult population rigid in the faith of the fathers, while the latter trained children in the Congregational way of life. All instruction had a religious tone, as if preparation for the eternal life were more important than a knowledge of the life at hand. Since a boy followed his father about as helper or companion, he picked up practical knowledge sufficient to support him in like situations. The school subjects, therefore, consisted merely of the three rudimentary R's: reading, writing, and arithmetic, a curriculum designed to eradicate illiteracy and to place the student upon the bottom rung of the ladder of learning.

Children did not attend continuously during the eleven months that school was in session. Abecedarians of four to six or seven years attended during the summer, when a woman generally had charge; older children, as long as they or their parents believed the time was spent profitably, attended during the winter periods when work was not pressing at home. Little differentiation in studies was made, each class using the same books. Webster recalled late in life that in the common schools in which he received his earliest instruction, "the books used were Thomas Dilworth's Spelling Book, a Primer, and a Psalter on the Bible. I do not recollect any other book for reading. Fenning's Spelling Book was in the country, but was not used in my neighborhood. . . . The grammar in Dilworth's was the only one I knew, till [Bishop Robert] Lowth's appeared. This was printed by Robert Aitkins of Philadelphia in 1775." The study of geography was not introduced into the schools until after Dr. Jedidiah Morse published his first work in 1784, and Webster devoted a brief section of his Reader (rev. ed., 1787) to this subject.

The only textbook for a half-century after 1690 had been *The New-England Primer*, and it still in 1765 introduced children to the alphabet and to their first steps in reading. Little rhymes illustrated each letter, as

> *A: In Adam's fall*
> *We sinned all;*

and
> *Z: Zaccheus he*
> *Did climb a tree*
> *His Lord to see.*

The children imbibed Calvinist religious principles from A to Z, without quite the pleasure that youngsters today derive vitamins and learning from alphabet soup. A set of questions and answers on the Bible prepared the way for the last item, the most important, the Shorter Catechism, which contained one hundred and seven questions and answers. Cotton Mather had called it a "little water pot" to shed good lessons, and had begged mothers to "continually drop something of the catechism on their children, as Honey from the Rock." The little prayer, "Now I lay me down to sleep," first circulated through the medium of the *Primer*.

This book determined the catechetical method of American colonial instruction. This question and answer process was perfectly mechanical: the students came up to the teacher, who asked the set questions and waited for the proper reply. Failing to get correct answers, he sent the students back to their seats, generally with a lash of a birch rod to stimulate renewed activity. Success depended upon the retentive power of the memory, a system capable of rendering learning laborious and irksome. Spelling lessons were graded in the *Primer* from *a-b ab* to five-syllable words like *abomination*, and *mortification*.

Thomas Dilworth's *New Guide to the English Tongue*, first published in London in 1740, had attained by 1765 a universal adoption in New England schools. This book contained a series of spelling and reading lessons, and a short grammar. Ten fables, "adorned with proper Sculptures," that is, wood engravings, served as incentives for students to reach the end of the book. Like the *New-England Primer* Dilworth's textbook was a handmaid to religion, its first reading lesson, consisting of words not exceeding three letters, being,

> No Man may put off the Law of God.
> The Way of God is no ill Way.
> My Joy is in God all the Day.
> A bad Man is a Foe to God.

Nearly all the sentences, and the fables as well, turn upon religious duties, and the words, God and Lord, recur hundreds of times. Dilworth wanted to rescue "poor creatures from the Slavery of Sin and Satan" by setting "the word of God for a Lantern to our Feet and a Light to our Paths."

The Psalter or Bible was the only other book used in Webster's earliest school. Herein was tested one's proficiency in reading, emphasis being placed always on loudness and clearness of enunciation and not on a knowledge of the contents. Students reread the Bible, as they did the *Primer* and the *New Guide,* until every syllable grew as familiar as the local landscape. J. T. Buckingham stated in his *Memoirs* that he read the Bible through at least a dozen times before he was sixteen years old. Some portions, especially Revelation, filled him with unspeakable terror, and he called the enforced reading "a piece of gratuitous and unprofitable cruelty." However unpleasant this exercise may have seemed, it is apparent that the King James' version of the Bible maintained a unity of language between England and her American colonies and added a rich store of allusions to speech and writing.

The colonial fathers, despite the democratic idealism which inspired them to nurture each New England child in an elementary school, failed to make adequate provision for instruction. The buildings were generally shabby affairs, maintained under defective regulations; the houses were inconvenient and ill adapted to answer the end for which they were intended. Thin walls, leaky roofs, and earthen floors comprised most of them, wretched shells in which the largest fire could not keep the children comfortable during extremely cold weather. If the master held them at their business at a distance from the fire, they sat shivering with cold and never looked on a book; and if he permitted them to crowd around the fire, they pushed and abused each other, and the master's ears were stunned with the din of endless complaints. Such buildings required an extraordinary quantity of wood, the expense of which in a few years equalled the cost of a good brick building.

The equipment was as faulty as the buildings; at low tables, made to fit the abecedarians, the growing country lads had to take their places. Legs crowded the aisles and shoes soiled the clothes of the boys in the rows ahead. "When I was a school-boy," Webster wrote in 1781, "the greatest part of the scholars did not employ more than an hour in a day, either in writing or in reading; while five hours of the school time was spent in idleness—in cutting the tables and benches to pieces—in carrying on pin lotteries, or perhaps in some more roguish tricks." It was taken for granted that children would misbehave, destroy property, and waste time; consequently, few schools possessed maps, globes, library, or apparatus.

Slates were not known in Webster's school, although their adoption as early as 1752 has been noted. Pencils were quite unknown; goosequill pens, ink, and paper alone recorded the students' writing. Lockers or drawers did not exist, so that, because of petty thievery or bullying by the elder boys, the poorest materials always were given the children for school use. Penmanship and mathematical exercises, dictated by the master, filled many manuscript books, neat examples of which are still commonly seen.

With such equipment and in such surroundings students made whatever progress the master might inflict upon them, for it was a continuous warfare between the two, the children dragging along under the lash of the master's rod. Often the master could not inspire the respect of his pupils, because of his temper, his ignorance, or his baseness. Drunkenness was so universal among schoolmasters, says Alice Morse Earle in *Child Life in Colonial Days*, that a chorus of colonial "gerund-grinders" might have sung in Goldsmith's words:

Let schoolmasters puzzle their brains
  With grammar and nonsense and learning,
Good liquor I stoutly maintain,
  Gives genius a better discerning.

Salaries were small, and teachers frequently boarded around among the families of the parish. Here and there a brave pedagogue, trusting to the high worth of his calling and not to his salary for reward, built bright fires of learning in these country schoolhouses and transmuted dull lads into eager scholars.

As little Noah Webster trudged to school, his bright eyes studied the flowers, trees, and sky. In childhood and youth one must take all knowledge for one's province, because all things are new and need to be understood. Events occurred of startling nature, the meaning of which he may have grasped in part from the talk of his father. On February 10, 1763, the Seven Years' War came to an end with the Treaty of Paris, and immediately thereafter Parliament proposed to quarter troops in America at the colonists' expense and to place a tax upon sugar and molasses. James Otis asserted that this attempt to enslave America should be repelled, and R. H. Lee declared, "we cannot be deprived of English liberty." *The Connecticut Courant,* founded in 1764, led the attack in Connecticut against the unpopular parliamentary decrees by denouncing the men who took or sought the position of tax collector: " 'Twould be prudent for those that are gaping and begging for the Office . . . to consider whether the gain of their servile employment will compensate for the Reproach and Contempt they are likely to incur." A serial "Journal of Occurrences" recorded the unpleasant events at Boston resulting from the alleged bestial conduct of the soldiers, the unpatriotic conduct of money lovers, and the rising anger of the populace. The die was cast; succeeding events merely

rallied American opposition to England and prepared the
way for the Revolution.

Local matters, too, came to the boy's ears. The New
Lights in the Congregational Church, as well as members
of other sects, "spewed out invectives" against maintaining
ecclesiastics by taxation. Asa Merrill's long controversy
with the West Hartford Church over the parson's drinking, and the founding of an Episcopal church, aroused
storms of unpleasantness, the thundering of which frequently reverberated in the Webster home. Tragedies, too,
brought home the awful truths of gospel promise. On May
23, 1766, an overheated stove exploded in the Hartford
brick schoolhouse, killing several children. Lightning struck
the steeple of the First Church in Hartford, June 14, 1767;
falling timbers killed one young woman and injured several
others. Unseen forces lay behind man and nature, forces
the boy tried to understand.

Benjamin Franklin's lightning rods had found little favor
in Hartford before the steeple crashed. Objections against
the invention had been urged "by many strong anti-elec-
tricians; and some of them from religious principle had
censured the erection of 'sharp points' as a presumptuous
meddling with heaven's artillery, and that instead of drawing down safety wished it might not be a means of drawing
down the divine displeasure." The Society voted to recon-
struct the steeple and to place a rod upon it. The erection
of rods, first on the church and then on barns and dwellings,
aroused a new line of inquiry for the boy, for it seemed that
man could control the great careless strength of nature, even
of that fleet warrior, lightning.

Except such other materials as the boy may have found in
a nearby library or in the homes of his relatives and pastor,
young Noah Webster probably had few books to help him
answer his questions about nature and man. Books were
available through the Librarian Company, a not overly ac-

tive Hartford association, and through purchase from
Hezekiah Merrill, whose drug store "a few rods south of
the Courthouse" held (May 11, 1773) a sizeable stock of
belles lettres and professional books, as well as "a great
variety of small books for children." What use Webster
may have made of these opportunities we can only surmise.
The pastor was often the sole man of learning in a rural
Connecticut community; his small collection of books, sometimes no larger than Chaucer's Clerk's, could not hold for
many hours a boy entering his teens. Novels and drama,
part of the devil's armory, were shunned like poison. Since
Webster expressed orthodox antipathy to this form of reading in his own textbooks and essays, it is not likely that he
sinned in youth by reading fiction.

In 1772, when the youthful Reverend Nathan Perkins
was settled as pastor of the West Hartford Church, Webster seems first to have taken seriously the thought of his
life work. Perkins, a Princeton graduate who had a passion
for stimulating boys to enter upon advanced studies, may
have found in the bushy-haired, voluble Webster the right
stuff of scholarship, and may have led the boy to understand
his proper vocation. The pastor's interest was well repaid;
Webster showed an eager love for study and books. He took
his Latin grammar into the fields, stopping under the apple
trees to con his paradigms and to translate. His father,
according to Eliza Webster Jones, "was a wise man, and,
finding Noah stretched on the grass forgetful of his tasks,
he decided to permit him to follow his inclinations." For a
time, it is said, his father opposed his wishes, for the small
farm had produced merely a sufficient income to feed the
family of five children. The boy's persistence won even
then, as it was to win many times in later life.

Three influences, his work, the government, and the
church, shaped every Connecticut man's thinking. First, in
fact, if not in importance, was the Yankee philosophy of

work, deeply ingrained in the Puritan character. Idleness
was frowned upon. Every boy learned many trades, not
forgetting the art of growing wooden nutmegs. Idle hands
served the devil; busy hands served God. And so the Yankee
farmer, his crops in, gainfully employed the winter in making tinware, silverware, cutlery, harness, needles, thread,
and cloth. These articles, as well as the treasure trove of
knickknacks imported by the East India captains, were
loaded on wagons and peddled through the less indus-
trialized regions of the South. A Yankee peddler became
the synonym for a cheat. Virginia and Carolina women were
warned by angry husbands to keep the doors locked against
itinerant merchants. But insinuating ways, story-telling deceit, and ingenuity for circumventing objections gained them
admittance. Even at home this "school of dishonesty" was
frowned upon as a pernicious evil. "It has injured, if not
ruined, the morals of a large proportion of young men in
many of our towns," wrote "A Real Patriot." "The object
of the Pedlar is to get money: it is his interest to deceive
and impose on his customers, and to practice all the arts of
knavery. . . . He learns to lie and cheat as that branch
of his profession on which his success principally depends,
and to drink, swear, and gamble by the company he keeps."

The Yankee peddler brought home news from the other
states, particularly distasteful items concerning life in the
South. The Negro slave became an object of pity, because
his animal docility and ignorance had made him the dupe
of lazy white men. More menacing was the danger of slave
work destroying the lucrative trade of the peddler by the
development of unpaid, skilled hands. The seeming idleness of the southern planters annoyed these energetic
Yankees, whose philosophy of work could not approve the
southern economy. The hearty response of Connecticut to
the pleas of abolition societies in part finds its explanation
in this personal experience of its merchants. Rugged, busi-

ness individualism developed the humanitarian, democratic strain in the Yankee philosophy.

Connecticut merely altered the phrasing of its old laws when the Declaration of Independence was promulgated. A Constitution was not adopted until 1818, the State continuing its business to that time under the Colonial Charter much as if the Revolutionary War had not taken place. Freemen were admitted to the right to vote upon proof of the possession of a freehold estate to the value of seven dollars a year, or a personal estate of $134, and upon certification that they were "persons of a quiet and peaceable behavior and civil conversation." This legal provision effectually retained the control of the government in the hands of a minority, and against this law the Democrats waged a bitter fight. Equally effective was the method of election. To each society was presented a list of candidates for office; these names were arranged in order of seniority of service and nomination. As each name was called, the elector passed in a slip of paper to vote for that candidate or held his paper. This law, permitting every man to see how his neighbor voted, guaranteed the election of the leaders on the list and blocked rotation of officers. Until the adoption of the State Constitution nearly every major official, once elected, remained in office until death or infirmities removed him. No one dared announce his name or solicit an office; in due Calvinistic manner a man waited until the people were pleased to elect him. This government by old men, sage and experienced counselors, gave Connecticut a stable government, the virtues of which Noah Webster extolled throughout his life.

The town meeting form of government, still practiced in small communities in Connecticut, was of great personal importance to every freeman. Here he deliberated every year on the measures of local policy; he raised his voice in approval or objection; he exercised personally his share in the legislative and executive departments of government.

The Congregational Church, established as the state church at the foundation of the colony, dominated the community. The parish meeting preceded the town meeting; often it was difficult to distinguish between them, for many matters of discipline, ratemaking, and all matters pertaining to education were settled by the society. Frequently the preacher directed the discussion, acted as final arbiter in disputes, and prepared the written records. The vicar of God, he called his parishioners to support the fundamental tenets of the Church and the laws of the State. In many communities he was a virtual dictator, using his frown or the dignity of his office to prevent innovations.

The case-hardened doctrines of Calvinism were supported by ancient law. Any person would be disfranchised, it was decreed, who, having made profession of the Christian religion, "shall deny the Being of a God; or any one of the Persons of God in the Holy Trinity to be God; or shall assert and maintain that there are more Gods than One; or shall deny the Christian religion to be true, or the Holy Scriptures of the Old and New-Testament to be of Divine Authority, and be thereof lawfully convicted before any of the Superior Courts of this State."

This organization of church (and school) and state developed the peculiar quality of Connecticut's "steady habits." Strict discipline prevailed everywhere. Silence and subordination to age marked a child's life at home and at school, and, as he grew older, at the town meeting. The quiet decorum of Sunday behavior repressed in the conscientious any desire for sport or gaming. In Deacon Webster's home one can be certain the children sat laced to ladder-back chairs while Abraham played the flute and the family sang Watt's Psalms, or while the Deacon read the Bible.

Such training from youth to age gave a Pharisaical twist to Connecticut comments on other American states. Even

Noah Webster, Junior, when thirty-eight, saw that his old neighbors were not "turbulent subjects," but "good republicans," because of these steady habits which "are formed by a singular machinery in the body politic, which takes the child as soon as he can speak, checks his natural independence and passions, makes him subordinate to superior age, to the laws of the state, to town and parochial institutions—initiates him in the business of government by making him an active party in local regulations, and in short moulding him into a peaceable citizen, an intelligent man, and an independent, but rational freeman."

Each county was required by state law to operate an academy in which were taught Latin and the other subjects required for entrance into college. At Hartford, the Hopkins Grammar School, founded in 1665, had degenerated into a poverty-stricken primary school. Between 1765 and 1767 new regulations for "promoting and advancing good literature" were adopted, so that in 1774 the institution was a fairly respectable one. Webster passed from the tuition of Dr. Perkins to the Grammar School, but, finding that his pastor gave the more able instruction, he completed his preparatory training at West Hartford, and secured from his pastor a certificate of his character and attainments.

As he left home to start his collegiate career at Yale, Noah Webster bore with him a sweet remembrance of parental affection in a religious home, and he frequently recalled the benediction with which his father and mother blessed him on parting: "We wish to have you serve your generation and do good in the world and be useful and may so behave as to gain the esteem of all virtuous people that are acquainted with you and gain a comfortable subsistence, but especially that you may so live as to obtain the favor of Almighty God and his grace in this world and a saving interest in the merits of Jesus Christ, without which no man can be happy."

CHAPTER II

Education of a Radical

AMERICAN colleges in the last quarter of the eighteenth century were little more advanced than our preparatory schools today. In an atmosphere of restricted, prisonlike control, with fines or rustication as threatened punishment for indiscretions no more serious in nature than youthful horseplay, a group of boys came together for the benefits of the old fortifying classical curriculum. The Latin and Greek languages, philosophy, mathematics, and theology comprised the tasteless curriculum. Little natural science was taught, even the soda water chemistry of Priestley being unheard of. But unexciting as this program may seem to an age when college "courses" are "offered" and "taken" for cash register "credits" by students trading with no intellectual capital, its rigorous content developed minds that wrestled courageously with the greatest problems of humanity and of scholarship.

Yale differed from the eight other American colleges in 1774 only in its depressed condition. Three dingy buildings comprised the physical plant, nicknamed "Brick Prison" by the students who objected to the rigid watch placed over their movements. A brick chapel, fifty feet by forty, with a steeple one hundred and twenty-five feet high, contained in addition to the auditorium a dusty library of old and infrequently consulted books and a museum crowded with moth-eaten stuffed birds and animals, fossils, stones, and philosophical apparatus. Connecticut Hall, the dormitory in which Nathan Hale had lived during his attendance at

Yale, still stands, a wistful memento of Yale's early, simple Americanism in architecture. Webster roomed in this building. The third building, a rickety, blue-colored recitation hall, razed in 1782, housed the dining hall and buttery. The latter supplied students with candy, baked goods, beer, cider, and metheglin. The college porter, who held this concession, paid rent by furnishing the chapel with candles. The dining room had a high table for the faculty members, who from this eminence frowned upon bread throwing and upon loudly voiced objections to the quality of the food. The income of the endowment, all invested in land, was small, so that the student fees paid most of the running expenses of the institution. Friends had not yet come forward to purchase new books and laboratory equipment, or to endow professorial chairs. If Harvard, as Henry Adams remarked, "resembled a priesthood which had lost the secret of its mysteries, and patiently stood holding the flickering torch before cold altars, until God should vouchsafe a new dispensation of sunlight," Yale resembled a youth's convention to which came aspirants for worldly honor in the hope that four years of congenial association, some study, much social activity, and an imitation of courtly ways, would prepare them for successful labors in business, medicine, law, and statecraft. It was becoming a matter of concern that so few Yale students chose divinity for a career.

The institution entered upon the dark days of the Revolution without a duly elected presiding officer, the Reverend Dr. Naphtali Daggett having served as President *pro tempore* since October, 1766. Strong-framed but corpulent, slow and clumsy in movement, he could not discipline the wild colts under his charge. His sermons, though orthodox and uncontroversial, were delivered in a drawling, unanimated way. The students resented his inadequacy, and Webster's class petitioned for his removal in 1776.

President Daggett, himself Professor of Divinity, was

assisted by one professor and three tutors. Professor Nehe-
miah Strong, Puritanic preacher and almanac maker, taught
mathematics. Each class was in the direct charge of a tutor,
who, conducting all recitations in all subjects, usually remained with his class during its four years. Joseph Buckminster directed the studies of Webster's class, that of 1778, continuing in charge until Dr. Ezra Stiles accepted the Presidency of Yale in April, 1778. Buckminster, who worried
more about his charges' souls than their brains, was an amiable, friendly man with a passion for accuracy which the
romantic boys like Barlow disliked. Webster became one
of Buckminster's pets.

In addition to Webster the Class of 1778 numbered on
its roll many who in later life made distinguished contributions to American life: Joel Barlow, the poet and Minister
to France; Alexander Wolcott and Abraham Bishop, each
active in Jefferson's democratic movement; Zephaniah Swift,
Connecticut's greatest jurist; Oliver Wolcott, Jr., successor
to Hamilton as Secretary of the Treasury; Uriah Tracy, a
United States Senator; Josiah Meigs, President of the University of Georgia; and thirty-two others. As a Class it
became Yale's most distinguished up to the Civil War.

This Class felt the quickening impulses of both local and
national dissatisfaction. Timothy Dwight, tutor in charge of
the Class of 1777, continued the work he and John Trumbull
had begun in 1771 to liberalize the curriculum and substitute English composition and the study of English literature for a portion of the work in ancient languages. Trumbull had expressed his dissatisfaction with Yale academic
standards in his verse satire, *The Progress of Dulness*
(1772): "Ignorance wanders unmolested," he stated in the
Preface; "Examinations are dwindled to mere form and
ceremony, and after four years' dozing there, no one is ever
refused the honors of a degree, on account of dulness or insufficiency."

Dwight, who had already begun his epic, *The Conquest of Canaan,* summoned about him a band of young intellectuals. They admired his derisive criticism of his superiors and his ability to inspire students to Icarian poetic flights. Joel Barlow began *The Vision of Columbus* under Dwight's tutelage, and even the prosaic Webster, ticking out heroic couplets, penned verses, one of which he proudly reprinted in his *Lessons for Youth* to the end of his life. On September 5, 1777, Barlow and Tracy, serving as a committee of the Class of 1778, unsuccessfully petitioned the Corporation to assign Dwight to them as Senior Tutor. Dwight awakened in these youngsters a sense of their high personal and social duties, and the love they bore him to his death arose from his dynamic, magnetic power.

The revolutionary educational stirrings at Yale arose not only as a protest against the incompetency of the management, but also against a barren imitation of the collegiate forms of Oxford and Cambridge. In procedure and in curriculum Yale was fifty years behind her sister institutions across the Atlantic. Professors wore black robes, white wigs, and high cocked hats. Tutors appeared in silk gowns with chevrons, an ornament setting them apart from the graduate students. The three upper classes were distinguished by camlet gowns, the freshmen alone appearing hatless in undignified street dress. These barbarians were required by college rules to act as slaveys to the faculty and upper classmen in order that a just subordination to superiors might be learned. This silly traditionalism gained little respect from hardy country boys who felt the stirrings of ambition in their minds.

But if Yale students seethed with dissent at the pettiness and insufficiency of their college, they felt equally the national unrest in those days following the Boston Tea Party when the Continental Congress firmly resisted unpopular English demands. As early as September, 1770, six months after the Boston Massacre, Yale's chapel rang with stirring calls to independence. John Trumbull's master's oration, for example, contained the following paragraph:

America hath a fair prospect in a few centuries of ruling in arts and arms. It is universally allowed that we very much excel in the force of natural genius: and although but few among us are able to devote their whole lives to study, perhaps there is no nation in which a larger portion of learning is diffused through all ranks of people. For as we generally possess the middle station of life, neither sunk to vassalage, nor raised to independence, we avoid the sordid ignorance of the peasants, and the unthinking dissipation of the great. The heroic love of Liberty, the manly fortitude, the generosity of sentiment, for which we have been so justly celebrated, seem to promise the future advancement and established duration of our glory. Many incidents unfortunate in themselves, have tended to call forth and sustain these virtues. Happy, in this respect, have been our late struggles for liberty! They have awakened the spirit of freedom; they have rectified the manners of the times; recalled to our minds the glorious independence of former ages, fired us with the views of fame, and by filling our thoughts with contempt of the imported articles of luxury, have raised an opposition, not only to the illegal power, but to the effeminate manners of Britain. And I cannot but hope, notwithstanding some dangerous examples of infamous defection, that there is a spirit remaining in these colonies, that will invariably oppose itself to the efforts of usurpation and perfidy, and forbid that Avarice should ever betray us to Slavery.

President Daggett enunciated similar sentiments in his sermons and helped to fan to white heat the enthusiasm of his students for American independence. When the War came, he declared he was willing to sacrifice all his sons in the great cause, and he himself at the invasion of New Haven rode his black mare directly into a company of British soldiers. From the wounds sustained on this daring assault, he died. To his son, Henry, he wrote in 1778: "When I considered the controversy to be truly and simply this, whether this large and fertile country, settled with infinite toil and dangers by our fathers, should be our own free possession or at the disposal of a bankrupt prodigal State in Europe, I could not hesitate a moment, and I cannot but view it in its probable, or rather certain, consequences the most important contest that hath taken place on the globe for many centuries past. . . . Under this view of the justice and high importance of the controversy, I feel willing to risque my temporal all in support of it."

Tidings of the Battle of Lexington reached New Haven on April 21, 1775. The students, although exempt from military service, formed a company and drilled on the Green with the New Haven militia. Webster, who had learned to play the flute, paced the marchers with "Yankee Doodle" and other popular airs. News of the battle of Bunker Hill intensified their zeal.

When General Washington and Major General Charles Lee reached New Haven on their way to take charge of the American Army at Cambridge, they were escorted out of the city on the morning of June 29 by the two local uniformed companies and by a company of students. Their handsome appearance and expertness in military exercises gained them the approbation of the generals. "It fell to my humble lot," Webster wrote in his old age, "to lead the company with music." Two weeks later Congress set "forth the causes and necessity of their taking up arms."

The alarms of preparation for war disturbed the college routine; students felt it was impossible to pursue their studies with profit. Barlow wrote his mother, July 6, 1775: "The students are sensibly affected with the unhappy situation of public affairs, which is a great hindrance to their studies." Many achingly desired to join Washington, and some did. Tory sentiments evoked quick warnings, as in the case of Abiather Camp, a sophomore. Asked to declare himself on June 13, 1775, Camp insulted the committee and vowed to join the British troops and kill a number of the damned rebels, as he called them. His Tory sentiments were advertised on the hall-door, and he was treated with the "utmost neglect," as the college officers euphemistically reported.

Classes under Tutor Buckminster dragged along. The six o'clock rising bell summoned the freshmen to Cicero's orations, the Greek testament, logic, and arithmetic. All students devoted Saturday to the study of divinity. On Tuesdays and Fridays original essays in English, Latin, Greek, or Hebrew were prepared and declaimed. The manuscript of one of Webster's sophomore Latin efforts, a comparison of youth and old age, is preserved in the Yale library. Another essay, this one in English and written in his sophomore or junior year, he kept by him until 1790, when he sent it to *The Gazette of the United States,* where it appeared as "The Tablet, No. LXXXII," on January 23, with this motto: "The importance of female education is evident from the influence that women have over the manners of civilized society." This—probably his first—essay on education shows that even as a boy of eighteen Webster had formed definite ideas on the subject which would engage his attention for sixty-five years. Webster joined Brothers in Unity, a literary society which offered the advantages of a library of several hundred books. Underclassmen were not permitted to draw books from the college library, then containing about twenty-five hundred volumes.

The studies of the second year, in addition to divinity, were Latin, Greek, rhetoric, geometry, and geography. But the progress of the hostilities interested the students more than their lessons. Thomas Paine's fiery essays incited them to nourish thoughts of military glory. When the Declaration of Independence was published in New Haven, the Corporation met in special session and granted the seniors their diplomas on July 24, 1776. On the following day Dwight pronounced the Valedictory Address; in stirring terms he demanded heroic qualities of the first War Class:

You should by no means consider yourselves as members of a small neighborhood, town or colony only, but as being concerned in laying the foundations of American greatness. Your wishes, your designs, your labors, are not to be confined by the narrow bounds of the present age, but are to comprehend succeeding generations, and be pointed to immortality.

You are to act, not like inhabitants of a village, nor like beings of an hour, but like citizens of a world, and like candidates for a name that shall survive the conflagration. These views will enlarge your minds, expand the grasp of your benevolences, ennoble all your conduct, and crown you with wreaths which cannot fade. . . . Remember that you are to act for the empire of America, and for a long succession of ages.

In August, when an epidemic of typhoid fever caused the dismissal of the college, Webster rushed to West Hartford. His brother Abraham, who had been a member of the expedition to Canada, was at home convalescing from an attack of smallpox. After his health was restored, he, with Noah as a companion to take home his horse, returned to his company, then stationed at Whitehall, at the head of Lake Champlain, New York. On this trip Noah first experienced the unpleasantness of a soldier's life. He spent one night along a mosquito-infested lake, where the tents had to be filled with smoke to permit sleeping. At Mount Independence "half the soldiers were sick with dysentery and fever, so that the very air was infected." On the homeward journey he slept one night on the floor of a newly built house. These impressions remained indelibly on his mind; of this cost of independence in human suffering he always reminded his later political enemies.

November of 1776 found Yale so crowded that four students were required to lodge in each large room in Connecticut Hall and two students in each small room; thus the normal capacity was doubled. Through this overcrowding the effect of war upon society was a lesson learned more quickly than the stated junior recitations in Latin, Greek, natural philosophy, astronomy, and divinity. Provisions were scarce; with difficulty the commons secured sufficient food. On December 10 the students were dismissed, the Corporation confessing its inability to secure adequate food supplies. On January 7, 1777, the students again assembled, but, the same problem recurring, they were dismissed on March 29. Webster recalled that during this time "the farmers cut cornstalks, crushed them in cider mills, and then boiled the juice down to a syrup, as a substitute for sugar."

During this vacation Webster suffered an attack of smallpox, but his fresh, fair skin, bright with color until his oldest age, showed no trace of the disease. From this time on Webster frequently complained of illness; it may be that his vigorous pursuit of study and the infirm state in which he was left by this disease united to weaken the stout frame of the country lad.

The drums of war sounded nearer and nearer to New Haven, a port of entry to one of the most populous districts in New England. In April General Tryon, approaching from Peekskill, New York, where he had arrived on ships, advanced to Danbury and burnt valuable Continental stores. Generals Wooster, Arnold, and Silliman drove the British troops back to the Hudson, but this threat of invasion, as well as the limited supplies, led the Corporation to seek new quarters for the College. The students were ordered to reassemble on April 30 at places in Connecticut not far distant from New Haven where provisions were more bountiful. The seniors under Dwight were stationed at Wethersfield; the juniors under Buckminster and the sophomores under Professor Strong, at Glastonbury; and the freshmen under Abraham Baldwin, at Farmington. Webster, who resumed his studies late in May, roomed with Ichabod Wetmore at Asa Talcott's. Before the classes came to a close on September 10, the petition to secure Dwight as tutor during the

senior year was prepared. Webster supported the document with a personal poetic tribute to Dwight:

Those views extensive, that exalted mind;
That manly firmness, and that zeal refin'd;
That sacred fire, which, like the electric blaze,
Darts thro' each state and beams enlivening rays,
Glow in your breast; you reach a fostering hand
To nourish science and adorn the land.

If Dwight reached a fostering hand to science, Webster
wished equally to lend a helping hand to his country. The
British threat in the spring seemed like a raid on a barn-
yard compared with the terror General Burgoyne spread in
June throughout northeastern New York and Vermont. He
planned to move down the Hudson to Albany and there to
meet the British army from New York City. Together
these two groups would establish a line of posts from New
York to Canada and prevent intercourse between New England and the southern states. General Burgoyne came down
Lake Champlain from Canada, bringing seven thousand
men, besides Indians and Canadians, and laid siege to Ticonderoga. The Americans, in danger of being completely
surrounded, withdrew to Skeensborough, leaving their heavy
guns and a great part of their baggage and stores behind.
On the retreat an action took place in which the Americans
were defeated, and Colonel Francis, a valuable officer, was
killed. In August General Burgoyne sent a force of soldiers
and Indians to Bennington to seize the military stores there,
but the marauders were met in two actions and defeated.
These victories revived hope in the Americans and renewed
recruiting zeal.

In each Connecticut town the militia organized, and prepared to join the troops along the Hudson River. At West
Hartford Noah Webster, Sr., now a Captain, drilled the

alarm list, men over forty-five, and a little band of volunteers, among whom were his two sons, Abraham and Charles. Noah, Jr., returned from college in time to volunteer, and a few days later the father and three sons marched off toward the scene of action. The regiment advanced along the east bank of the Hudson River just as Kingston, which had been fired by a detachment of British troops, burst into flames. The militia hurried northward, but before they reached Albany, a courier rode by, waving his sword in triumph and crying out as he passed, "Burgoyne is taken, Burgoyne is taken." He had been bottled up near Saratoga; the army from New York City had failed to arrive; and surrender alone was open to him. This, Webster thought, was the most eventful crisis of the War, and "well might every American who had shared in the conflict, or who was hastening to meet the foe, exult in such a victory."

Late in November, 1777, Webster, now a veteran of the War, joined the seniors at New Haven for his last year's work, which included a study of Locke's "On Human Understanding," a work which, though read to be refuted, gave rise to many ideas hostile to orthodox Calvinism. The other three classes remained in the country. Exigencies of wartime again caused the dismissal of the students, this time for the long period between February 24 and June 23, 1778. Meantime Buckminster resigned when Dr. Stiles was elected President. The favor Dwight enjoyed irked the Tutor, and he wrote Webster of the pain caused by "the disagreeable circumstances that attended the close of our connexion." Buckminster viewed his association with the Class of 1778 "with particular satisfaction," while regretting "the independent spirit" which had marked the students' attitude.

Dr. Ezra Stiles, now fifty years of age, electrified the seniors with his vast erudition in Hebrew, his zeal for learning, his catholic views in both religious and political matters, and his shrewd ability to control the students, whom he likened to a "bundle of wild fire." "At best," he meditated, "the diadem of a President is a crown of thorns." He had served as a tutor from 1749 to 1755, and like Dwight he had large ideas of the duties of a college. Under his leadership Yale grew in strength and numbers, laying a foundation upon which the future greatness might be adequately built. Stiles knew how to temper criticism with praise and did not hesitate to say whether his students disputed "inimitably well" or unsatisfactorily. For the first time the Class of 1778 met a superior mind; their response was unanimous, and their friendship abiding, even though their association lasted only three months.

At the Commencement, September 9, 1778, Webster pronounced the Cliosophic Oration in English, an honor which placed him high in the first quarter of the class. In accordance with ancient custom each recipient of a degree gave the President a gift of money. Stiles carefully noted the contribution of each—Webster's was ten dollars,—figured the total against an estimated average, and complained that he lost £25 on his first class.

Little is known of Webster's college life. None of his letters has survived, nor does his name figure in the extant college records. He enjoyed the respect of his classmates, and with only one or two exceptions neither politics nor religion could destroy the early affection these boys developed for each other. Zephaniah Swift, writing an Addisonian epistle on December 13, 1776, remarked on the difficulty of becoming at once a man of letters and a man of the world, but he assured Webster, "Your opportunities and the time you spend with the Ladies will enable you to reach both." Sophomores at this time, these lads could take time in the first terrible winter of the Revolution to assay calmly the dross and gold in their own characters. Webster, though delighting in parties and dances, was a conscientious, obedi-

ent student, cheerfully following the assignments from day
to day. Latin and Greek he mastered thoroughly, so that in
his old age he could write Latin letters to his favorite granddaughter, Emily Fowler. The construing of ancient texts
must have been a pleasant game to him. But Webster did
more than play games. He absorbed the contents of his
books, and he learned from them to delve into original
historical sources. He left Yale with a tolerable education
which he energetically proceeded to complete by private
study.

CHAPTER III

COUNTRY SCHOOLMASTER

WHILE he was at home in West Hartford after graduation, at a loss which way to turn for employment, yet desiring to engage in the study of law, Noah was called aside one day by his father. The farm had been mortgaged to raise funds for Noah's college education; no other resource remained. His father put into the young graduate's hands an eight-dollar bill of the depreciated Continental currency, then worth about two dollars in silver, and said, "Take this; you must now seek your living; I can do no more for you."

Noah, disappointed and yet grateful, retired to his room; here he spent three days in study and meditation. The stern moralizing of Dr. Johnson's "Rambler" calmed his mind and quickened his self-confidence; one sentence he burned into his memory: "To fear no eye, to suspect no tongue, is the great prerogative of innocence, an exemption granted only to invariable virtue." This statement, he remarked fifty-five years later, had no inconsiderable influence in regulating his moral conduct.

Soon after this conversation with his father, Webster left home, his duties lying clearly before him. The untoward times need not embarrass or dishearten him. Joel Barlow, one of his bosom friends of college days, felt this way too. "You and I," he wrote, "are not the first in the world to have broken loose from college without friends and without fortune to push us into public notice. Let us show the world a few more examples of men standing upon their own merit and rising in spite of obstacles." Barlow added cheeringly, "I have too much confidence in your merits, both as to greatness of genius and goodness of heart, to suppose that your actions are not to be conspicuous."

Webster, having asked help from no one, went first to Glastonbury, where he had spent part of his junior year in college, and there secured a school for the winter term. His name is not on the list of public school teachers; if he taught in the Academy, was his experience like that of his classmate, Shubael Breed, who complained:

I have taken upon me the important office of a schoolmaster—about 30 scholars, one third Latin, who by their continual clamour open a scene of unbounded torment and eternal vexation. Had the Devil had wit enough to set Job to keeping school, instead of giving him the itch, he had cursed his God and Lord. It's a poor business, the wages not equivalent to a support, & the knowledge gained by it, not worth a farthing. I shall soon dismiss it.

In the spring of 1779 Webster moved to Hartford, where he taught in the Brick School House and resided with Oliver Ellsworth, later Chief Justice of the United States. He studied law in the large library of that eminent jurist and assisted in the conduct of the office. Simeon Baldwin, in a similar situation, complained of exhausting toil. He entered school at nine, finished the morning recitation at eleven and the noon recitation at twelve, and conducted an afternoon session from two to five. Then he read languages and law until eleven at night. Webster was probably similarly occupied, and the double duties of teaching and study took prompt toll of his frail body; he contracted a nervous affliction, which for two years distressed him.

Something of the noble plans Webster formulated at this time appears in Tutor Buckminster's reply (October 30, 1779) to a letter from Hartford: "The resolutions you form in your letter are good; to obtain a knowledge of your own country, of the genius, manners and policy of our fellow citizens is commendable. . . . Your resolution of making yourself master of every evil passion and propensity is an exceeding good one." Buckminster also congratulated Webster on his connection with Ellsworth and on the opportunity he had of acquiring an acquaintance with men and manners from those who had long experience in this "perverse world."

That winter Webster returned to his father's house and engaged to teach a school in his native parish. Teachers received one pound to a pound ten shillings a month for their services, a sum insufficient to repay any of Webster's college bill of £120. But he was now self-supporting, whatever his brothers might say about the prodigal's return. The winter of 1780 became a memorable one for extremity of cold and depth of snow. For three months Webster walked to his school—nearly four miles a day—through drifts of snow which completely covered the adjoining fences. This experience, as well as his daily routine, sharpened his criticism of the public schools. Remembering his own inadequate elementary training, he penned four essays to point out "the most usual defects of our country schools." The motto he chose for the first was: "People never misapply their economy so much, as when they make mean provision for the education of children."

"The general institution of schools in this country," he wrote, "is full proof that the inhabitants are convinced of their utility and importance." But a false economy, or carelessness, or ignorance placed the schools under such defective regulations that the wishes of the parents, "to give their children the best education with the least expense," were defeated. The schoolhouses remained in the same ill-favored status they had been in before the War and gave disgraceful evidence of neglect. More reprehensible was the failure of parents to secure books: "Nothing but the absolute impossibility of obtaining books will render negligence in this respect excusable."

A new point of view towards American elementary education emerged in these essays. In opposition of the age-old motto of "Spare the rod and spoil the child," Webster proposed the very modern principle, "The pupil should have nothing to discourage him." The school should be equipped properly, special care being taken to give each student a comfortable desk so that his posture would be correct both in reading and writing. This emphasis on pupil health was new in America.

Although Joseph Lancaster's monitorial system of education did not become popular in the United States until the 1820's, Webster had thought about this method. Many schools contained fifty to seventy pupils, a number too large for a single instructor to manage, especially since the children ranged in age from six to sixteen. But the inexpensive device of employing older scholars to teach younger ones did not satisfy the critical young teacher. "These subordinate guides," he wrote, "assume an haughty air of authority, and teach the children to hate the instructor much faster than to love or learn the lesson." Webster wanted trained teachers in each room, teachers who had, to use the recent term, professional interests and enthusiasm. With such men at the desk, "children will be educated cheaper, if there are never more than twenty or twenty-five pupils under the charge of one instructor."

Such teachers would lay aside the vain and fruitless flogging method of stimulating study and substitute for it the kindlier device of offering an alluring object to reward attainment. Books would be made a pleasure: the master would have an easy task; the child would make rapid improvement. "Some trifling gratuity on quarter-day," Webster declared, would "do more to engage children to be diligent and make them fond of books than all the reasoning in the world or ten thousand rods of correction."

In these turgid essays lies the origin of Noah Webster's lifetime battle for improved public schools. Only a year

out of college and barely twenty-one, he laid down a program of reform that a half century could not bring to
fruition. Yet Webster never wavered in his assault upon
the old order. He knew that thousands of persons, who
had grown up to a state of manhood without ability to read
or write, fervently wished their parents had left them less
estate and a better education. At this time the humanitarian
and economic aspects of the school problem impressed him
most; later he would add both the religious and democratic
ideals to motivate his reform.

In the summer of 1780 Webster moved to Litchfield,
Connecticut, whither he was invited by Jedidiah Strong, a
Justice of the Quorum and Recorder of Deeds for Litchfield
County, who had been laid up by "an inveterate complica-
tion of nervous disorders." Here Webster renewed his study
of law, either under Strong or Tapping Reeve, founder of
the famous Litchfield law school, and assisted Strong in the
duties of his office during the winter. To Litchfield, already
well known as a center for the study of law, many young
men came to study. At the March term of court Webster
and nearly twenty others, it is said, applied for admission
to the Bar. All were examined on the same evening by the
local committee and all were refused recommendation. The
reason for this surprising action is not known, but it may be
surmised that fear of overcrowding the profession caused
the wholesale refusal. Webster proceeded at once to Hartford, where, examined and approved, he was admitted to
practice on April 3, 1781.

In becoming a counselor at law, Webster joined an ancient but no longer honorable profession. Public hostility
had arisen, partly because poor debtors found themselves
driven to distraction by dunning tactics or suits in court. One
critic wrote of lawyers:

They foment more wrath, evil speaking and bitterness among
neighbourhoods than their reverend fathers could heal, if they should

attempt it. And if sin be, as some clerical wiseacres have asserted, for the glory of God, these lawyers work day and night for his glory. Without dignity of manners they blacken the courts and clients and witnesses and each other most unmercifully. They consider the receipt of fees as justifying them in pursuing to utter destruction an honest family by a claim which they know to be unrighteous.

Now Webster, having studied two or three years, was dubbed *Esquire.* Physicians used the title of Doctor, and clergymen used the title of Reverend. Approved an attorney, why should he not append Esquire to his name? He felt that way, a bit proud of the progress he had made. He liked the sound of his name. Doubtless he looked in his steel mirror and often repeated: NOAH WEBSTER, JUNIOR, ESQUIRE, ATTORNEY AT LAW.

The continuation of the War threw a dark cloud over his hope for professional employment. Miserable were the prospects, even in so litigious a state as Connecticut, for the causes were petty, the fees small, and there was a multiplicity of needy lawyers. Wisely Webster decided to return to schoolmastering, an occupation for which he was adapted by interest and temperament. Determined to establish his own academy, he moved to Sharon, Connecticut, a town in Litchfield County on the eastern border of New York State. Several Whig refugees had fled there from New York when that city was captured by the British. Among them were the families of Robert Gilbert Livingston and Mrs. Theodosia Prevost, who afterwards became the wife of Aaron Burr. Webster published the following advertisement in *The Connecticut Courant:*

The subscriber, desirous of promoting Education, so essential to the interest of a free people, proposes immediately to open a school at Sharon, in which young Gentlemen and Ladies may be instructed in Reading, Writing, Mathematicks, the English Language, and if desired, the Latin and Greek Languages—in Geography, Vocal Music, &c. at the moderate price of Six Dollars and two thirds per quarter per Scholar. The strictest attention will be paid to the studies, the manners and the morals of youth, by the public's very humble servant,

NOAH WEBSTER, Jun.

P.S. If any persons are desirous of acquainting themselves with the French Language, they may be under the instruction of an accomplished master in Sharon.

Sharon, June 1, 1781.

The school opened on July 1, probably in the spacious attic of the Governor John Cotton Smith home. Livingston sent three daughters, Cornelia, Catherine, and Helen, and two relatives named Hake. Frederick and Barton Prevost, Jonas Platt, and Laura Canfield, among others, also attended. This excellent patronage should have assured him of success as long as he wished to stay.

Webster, lawyer and teacher, carried himself with the proud dignity of his honors. In September, at the annual commencement of Yale College, he had been admitted to the degree of Master of Arts. His "dissertation in English" took the schoolmaster on to the second main point in his educational philosophy, "On the universal diffusion of literature as introductory to the universal diffusion of Christianity." In the ebb and flow of words, "literature" has lost its eighteenth-century meaning. Then the term meant "learning, reading, skill in letters and books," or more distinctively it embraced all the liberal arts as well as belles lettres. In this essay, which unfortunately has not survived, Webster probably formulated the second main point in his battle for universal public education: the truths of religion could push aside the clouds of superstition only in minds capable of intelligent discussion. In reaching this conclusion, Webster followed the precedent of the first settlers in New England, one of whom said, "unless school and college flourish, Church and State cannot live."

Among those in Sharon who smiled at this strutting schoolmaster were several pretty young ladies. At singing

school, which he conducted in the evening, and at the meetings of Juliana Smith's literary society, Webster sought them
out, talked earnestly of his ambitions, and looked for re-
sponsive throbs. At Yale Webster and Barlow courted New
Haven girls, Barlow winning pretty Ruth Baldwin and
secretly marrying her shortly after graduation. As a college
junior Webster had penned an essay on the importance of
female education in which he berated the negligence of those
who have the care of their instruction. Here in Sharon,
therefore, he courted brains as well as beauty. He met his
match in the nineteen-year-old Juliana Smith, sister of John
Cotton Smith, later to be Governor of Connecticut. She
edited "The Clio, a Literary Miscellany," a manuscript
magazine, composed of contributions by the members of the
society. To the issue for October, 1781, Webster contributed a stilted fable with just such a hackneyed moral lesson
as a self-conscious schoolmaster would be expected to write.
His other writings she snubbed. In her diary she put her
haughty disdain:

Mr. Webster has not the excuse of youth, (I think he must be
fully twenty-two or three), but his essays—don't be angry, Jack,—
are as young as yours or brother Tommy's, while his reflections are
as prosy as those of our horse, your namesake, would be if they were
written out. Perhaps more so, for I truly believe, judging from the
way *Jack Horse* looks 'round at me sometimes, when I am on his
back, that his thoughts of the human race and their conduct towards
his own might be well worth reading. At least they would be all *his
own*, and that is more than can be said of N.W.'s. In conversation
he is even duller than in writing, if that is possible, but he is a painstaking man and a hard student. Papa says he will make his mark; but
then, you know that our dear Papa is always inclined to think the
best of every one's abilities, *except* his own and MINE, of which
last, I grieve to say, his opinion seems to be sadly low.

Joel Benton, in a romantically indefinite essay, stated
that Webster suddenly closed his school on October 9 and
left Sharon because Rebecca Pardee, a very beautiful girl,

had another lover, a Major in the Army, whose unexpected return from military duty upset the girl's mind so much that she could not decide whether to accept Webster's or the Major's marriage proffer. A family council failing to solve the dilemma, it was placed before the church elders. Their decision favored the Major; he had a prior claim. No contemporary record of the incident survives. Whether it was Rebecca Pardee or Juliana Smith who drove the young attorney and schoolmaster from Sharon, it cannot be known today, but I suspect the latter's sharp tongue more than a broken heart. More likely, Webster had overtaxed his strength and could not continue teaching.

To his onerous school duties, he had added an ambitious program of study. Under the Reverend Mr. John Peter Tetard, a learned Genevan Huguenot pastor, Webster began studying French. The fascination of comparative modern grammar took hold of him, and soon the German, Spanish, and Italian tongues unlocked their mysteries. History, law, and the wartime polemical literature kept him stooped over books late into the night. Tom Paine's stirring essays, *The Crisis*, took on new meaning when Webster received from Tetard a copy of Rousseau's *Social Contract*. Unexplored vistas opened before him; his vague humanitarian longings received philosophic form and unity. The doctrine of the social compact clarified his concepts of governmental rights and obligations, of the basis of social union in conventions, of the invalid status of slavery, of the inalienable and indivisible nature of popular sovereignty, of the marks of good government, and of the unwisdom of an established church.

These ideas swirled in Webster's brain, animating him to lend his contribution to the American cause. What could an impecunious country schoolmaster do? When the report of Cornwallis's surrender on October 19, 1781, brought assurance of final victory and independence for America,

Webster felt that a nation of freemen, possessing property but unable to read and write, could not wisely exercise popular sovereignty. Untutored in the simplest principles of personal rights and governmental procedure, they would become slaves to ignorant passion, or to demagogues, or to a self-perpetuating aristocratic minority. A national system of education, reaching into every home and teaching fundamental precepts of morality and patriotism, Webster determined, alone could give stability to a new government. With faith born of idealism, Webster initiated his plan, knowing that one physically unable to endure the rigors of march and battle, might do as much as a soldier for his country.

As he worked over his study table, startling challenges to American independence guided him to drop his book temporarily and to write the first of his many statements in defense of our country, "Observations on the Revolution of America," published in *The New-York Packet*, Fishkill, beginning January 31, 1782. Sir Henry Clinton had published a "Declaration to the Inhabitants" on December 29, 1780, in which he had announced that Great Britain had repealed the tax on tea and had exempted the insular colonies forever from parliamentary taxation. These "affectionate and conciliatory intentions," he wrote, had removed the "pretended grounds of discontent. . . . The door is thus again thrown open . . . for commencing negociations which may instantly terminate the miseries" of America. An immediate settlement, he thought, would rescue the people from "being delivered over to Popish and arbitrary nations." This "Declaration," printed by Rivington in the *Royal Gazette* for six months, produced neither action nor alarm.

But in October, 1781, Rivington began publishing a series of letters, supposedly intercepted, from Silas Deane, American agent in Paris. Deane had had a checkered career in official positions, his careless bookkeeping having led Thomas Paine to accuse him of profiteering in war supplies, and yet his influence, buttressed by friendships with Franklin and Robert Morris, was great. His eleven letters, dated Paris May 10–June 15, 1781, addressed to his brother and to American officials, accused the French government of duplicity and intrigue, asserted the unwisdom of prolonging the war, advised a return under British rule in accordance with the terms advertised by Clinton, and in general attempted by pessimistic views to undermine the spirit of freedom.

Webster believed that these letters were a British trick, that British propaganda was replacing musketry as an offensive weapon. "Great Britain," Webster wrote, "having experienced the inefficacy of fleets and armies to support her illegal claims, . . . is making use of sophistry, fraud, and bribery to disunite the Americans and overturn our independence. We are harassed with manifestos, proclamations, foreign letters of disappointed courtiers, and a thousand fugitive publications of mercenary printers, generals, governors, and anonymous scribblers. The attempt is really glorious; and perhaps for depth of invention . . . never was equalled except by another plan of the same statesmen and generals, the counterfeiting of depreciated continental currency."

Webster took particular umbrage at the attempts to distort *The History of the Revolution in America* by Abbé Raynall, who, he said, was "a friend to mankind and a most reputable philosopher." "The Abbé's history," he continued, "abounds with the most accurate ideas of political liberty, with a very pathetic representation of the miserable state of Europeans; and with a philanthropic sense of the felicity of America in its disconnected situation." In explanation of the Abbé's enthusiasm, Webster stated, "A philosopher like the Abbé . . . must see that the astonishing opposition of America to the attacks of Great Britain cannot be the fortuitous ebullition of popular frenzy, but the effect of design, the calm result of daring zeal, tempered with reason and deliberation." Further, the events in America will be studied by a thousand philosophers; the result will not only be "a full vindication of America," but also the Revolution will have "considerable influence in unfettering the shackles which are so generally rivetted on the human race." Thomas Paine had begun a rebuttal of the garbled English version of Raynal's pamphlet as early as November 30, 1781, but the finished article was not published until September, 1782. Paine argued the fundamental assumption of Raynal, as if to keep the history of the Revolution free from gratuitous oversea inferences. Webster, however, with his thoughts on the total effect of the pamphlet, stressed Raynal's approval of the Revolution and disapproval of a return to vassalage. *The Salem Gazette* reprinted Webster's essay, giving it currency in Boston as well as in New York.

In his second article Webster explained the legal principle upon which Americans justified the Declaration of Independence, stating "that the King of Great Britain, having attempted to impose some unconstitutional and oppressive laws upon the colonies, having withdrawn his protection and confiscated their property, had thus forfeited all right to their allegiance." In developing this argument, Webster leaned heavily on Paine, and, almost quoting from the Firebrand of the Revolution, Webster declared, "Had there never been any provocation on the part of Great Britain, the moment our dependence became irreconcilable with our real interests as a nation and we arrived to strength adequate to our own defence, a separation from the parent state would have been justifiable." Webster also pointed out the fallacious logic in the statements that Americans are "children and brethren of England" and that "a separation of such relations is unnatural." "Children" and "brethren" as well as "rebel," he explained with lexicographic precision, were terms appropriated improperly, because England's treatment of Americans had severed all filial ties. "America is now an independent empire," he insisted; "She acknowledges no sovereign on earth, and will avow no connexions but those of friend and allies, in which characters all nations are invited to her commerce."

The third article refuted the general idea that "America can never be happy under any other than British government." "A dependence on foreign government," he wrote, "is incompatible with the tranquillity of America." Economically no fears need arise. Britain, he argued, cannot refuse to trade with us; France will be sincere in her alliance; Russia will not rival us; and America within twenty years, so great is the commercial and enterprising spirit, will have "more tons of shipping in traffic than any power in Europe." As a prophet, the young schoolmaster was far from being wrong.

The attack on American independence by inflaming moral and religious prejudices was repelled in the fourth essay. "They tell us," he wrote, "that a separation from Great Britain will introduce and accelerate the progress of luxury, and that the protestant religion will lose ground, if not be totally extirpated, through the influence of a popish ally. To liberal minds," Webster snarled, "these dangers are phantoms, mere illusions of a distempered imagination." In Luther's day protestant hostility to catholicism had been inspired by the "resentment roused by a violation of the rights of conscience," but the cause of that enmity had long since disappeared. The Pope no longer holds temporal power; fear of his intervention in government now is a chimera. Believing that the great danger to popular rights arises from an established religion, against this form of tyranny Webster, a sturdy son of "steady habit," Congregational Connecticut, wrote his most pungent paragraphs:

The very idea of a system of religious principles and a mode of worship, prescribed and established, by human authority, is totally repugnant to the spirit of christianity. Every establishment is only a milder term for tyranny. . . . It is an insult to humanity, a solemn mockery of all justice and common sense, to assume the right of entailing our opinions and formalities of devotion upon posterity, or to exclude them from the protection or emoluments of government for a non-conformity dictated by conscience. . . .

An established church, he declared, not only checks improvement "by making it the interest of knaves, fools, and rascals to embrace it for the sake of emoluments," but also produces jealousies out of which arise "tumults and massacres which have deluged kingdoms in blood and filled the christian world with rancor and animosity. All the dangers to which any government can be exposed by sectaries, must arise wholly from intolerance; and the Roman Catholics, when indulged the free exercise of their religion, make as good subjects, as peaceable citizens as any sect of protestants." The truth of this assertion found verification in the long tranquil history of Pennsylvania, "an illustrious example of the happy effects of toleration" and "a living burlesque upon all establishments and restrictions," including New England's. Until the Deity publishes to the world a prescribed system of principles to direct our faith, Webster continued, "that civil magistrate who ventures in the least punctilio to abridge a man's liberty of thinking or worshipping according to the dictates of his conscience, encroaches upon the prerogatives of heaven, and impiously attempts to wrest the scepter from the hand of Jehovah." Webster concluded with rapt prophecy:

America sees the absurdities—she sees the kingdoms of Europe, disturbed by wrangling sectaries, or their commerce, population and improvements of every kind cramped and retarded, because the human mind like the body is fettered "and bound fast by the cords of policy and superstition": She laughs at their folly and shuns their errors: She founds her empire upon the idea of an universal toleration: She admits all religions into her bosom—She secures the sacred rights of every individual: and (astonishing absurdity to Europeans!) she sees a thousand discordant opinions live in the strictest harmony of friendship. This privilege of an unprecedented toleration must incite nations into her dominions; preserve a tranquillity in society, that must cast a shade upon all the Hierarchies of the earth—it will finally raise her to a pitch of greatness and lustre, before which the glory of ancient Greece and Rome shall dwindle to a point, and the splendor of modern Empires shall fade into obscurity.

This credo of a young liberal carried the full freight of Rousseau's and Raynal's radical ideas. Webster, alert to the renovating doctrines of the old world, unhesitatingly demanded that the newly won independence be more than a mere removal of the seat of governmental authority from London to the United States. The bright hopes of our future glory could come to fruition only when the age-old fetters on the human spirit were unshackled. The time to remodel mankind was now. Enlightened concepts should replace old superstitions and misunderstandings; justice should replace tyranny over body and mind. What better aid to this end, was there, Webster asked himself, than a national system of education?

In the spring of 1782, after a winter spent in an unsuccessful attempt to secure mercantile employment, Webster returned to Sharon with the purpose of re-establishing his school. He published the following advertisement, which is interesting because it describes the curriculum of an early national secondary school and because it gives evidence of Webster's progress in developing his system of education:

On the first of May will be opened at Sharon in Connecticut, a school, in which children may be instructed, not only in the common arts of reading, writing, and arithmetic, but in any branch of Academical literature. The little regard that is paid to the literary improvement of females, even among people of rank and fortune, and the general inattention to the grammatical purity and elegance of our native language, are faults in the education of youth that more gentlemen and ladies have taken pains to censure than to correct. Any young gentlemen and ladies, who wish to acquaint themselves with the English language, geography, vocal music, &c., may be waited

upon at particular hours for that purpose. The price of board and
tuition will be from six to nine shillings, lawful money per week,
according to the age and studies of the Scholar; no pains will be
spared to render the school useful.

Sharon, April 16, 1782   NOAH WEBSTER

N.B. The subscriber has a large convenient store in Sharon for
storing articles of any kind, where they may be secured at a moderate expense.

There is no record that the school ever opened its doors,
although Webster had left behind the reputation of a "good
and thorough teacher." Doubtless most of his former pupils
had been placed in satisfactory schools by parents who were
unwilling to disturb these arrangements to assist a more or
less itinerant schoolmaster.

Downcast, in May he left for the South. After crossing
the Hudson River at Newburgh, the resting place of the
American army while awaiting disbanding, Webster proceeded westward to Goshen, Orange County, New York.
Here, among strangers and with only seventy-five cents in
his pocket, he became a teacher in the local high school, The
Farmers' Hall Academy, to which Henry Wisner, a signer
of the Declaration of Independence, the Reverend Dr.
Nathaniel Kerr, and a Mr. Wilkins, among others, sent their
children. From the attendance of Jonas Platt, who had
been in Webster's school at Sharon, we can infer that the
young schoolmaster effectively satisfied his clientele. Here
for the first time he received his pay for tuition in silver,
and not in depreciated Continental paper, which was the
general currency of the country. His income was small, a
mere pittance which hardly furnished him the means of
support. He studied and wrote after school hours, filling
page after page of manuscript with notes toward his system of education, so humbly begun at the abc's with a spelling book.

CHAPTER IV

THE BLUE-BACKED SPELLER

THE victory over British arms did not complete the Revolution. America's dependence on England, despite the sundering of political ties, continued unchanged in manners, education, literature, science, philosophy, and religion. Samuel Seabury begged the Archbishop of Canterbury to appoint an Anglican bishop in America. His request refused, Seabury bowed before nonjuring bishops of Scotland who performed the service of consecration. This act, requested immediately after the Peace of Paris, symbolized America's reverence for all things British. The Methodist church likewise drew its inspiration from English leaders. Aspiring physicians studied in Edinburgh or London, and many southern boys completed their collegiate educations in Oxford or Cambridge. The theater depended on British actors and British plays for successful operation. The comedies of Congreve, Farquhar, and Keefe taught lessons in polite seduction, while the actors' cockney accent brought in an affected pronunciation. English books crowded the scant shelf space of libraries and stores. Shakespeare, Milton, Addison, and Johnson were in every good library, along with the standard works on religion by Watts, Doddridge, and others. Americans feebly imitated the periodical essay of Addison and Steele, and the jingling couplets of Butler or Pope. The few exceptions are not worth noting. An original American novel, *The Power of Sympathy*, appeared in 1789, and our first native play of any importance, containing an American character, was Royall Tyler's *The Contrast* in 1787. As late as 1820 Sydney Smith could fling his taunt: "Who reads an American book?" and grin at the universal answer, "No one."

What elementary education American children received, tied them to the leading strings of England. The textbooks originated in England, contained sentiments of respect to royalty, and dealt with British customs and geography. The organization of schools did little to shake America's attachment to Great Britain. A general public school education was required by law in several states, but only in Calvinistic Massachusetts and Connecticut were effective measures taken to give each child an elementary training. No advance was made, however, on the practices already in vogue for more than a century. The other northern states, Rhode Island excepted, developed elementary schools in the years before 1795, and by the same time pauper schools at public expense were created in Pennsylvania, New Jersey, Delaware, Maryland, Virginia, and Georgia. Rhode Island established public elementary schools in 1800. North Carolina, South Carolina, Kentucky, and Tennessee took no action until 1830 or later.

Every effort was made to provide schools at public expense with masters who would instruct youth at low salaries. Against the viciousness of this economy, Webster had directed his earliest educational criticism. Teachers frequently hired out to school committees for brief periods, so that continuity of instruction was improbable, and uniform quality impossible. Often, too, the instructors were worthless characters, men of no breeding and in some cases infamous for detestable vices. Before the War, convicts, who had been transported for their crimes, were employed as private tutors in families. Under these conditions teaching ranked lower than the menial services, and college graduates hesitated to demean themselves in such an employment. At best, as with Webster, teaching served as a stop-gap, a temporary employment during a time when other positions were not available.

Without a system of our own and without the means of developing a system, it was inevitable that in manners and fashions America should remain attached to Europe with iron hoops. A hundred and fifty years have served only to weaken, not to destroy this dependence. The ambition of Americans was to imitate the dress and to introduce as fast as possible the fashionable amusements of the European courts.

Another Declaration of Independence needed to be promulgated, a declaration ending American servility to European modes of thought, fashion, and manners.

Noah Webster made that Declaration. Not an engrossed parchment, solemnly attested by duly elected representatives of the people, but a little fourteen-penny Spelling Book carried the thrilling message of independence. A country schoolmaster and attorney without portfolio became in a moment of magnificent egotism, Schoolmaster to America and attorney in defense of America's latent possibilities for self-sufficient nationality. In reply to charges of egotism, he replied:

However detestable personal pride may be, yet there is a national pride and a provincial, that are the noblest passions of the republican patriot. . . . For my own part, I frankly acknowledge, I have too much pride not to wish to see America assume a national character. I have too much pride to stand indebted to Great Britain for books to learn [sic] our children the letters of the alphabet.

No other secular book has reached so many minds in America as Webster's Spelling Book, and none has played so shaping a part in our destiny. In looking for guiding impulses in history, students examine great causes, famous names, or learned books. Seldom are correct answers found, for obscure, unheralded individuals send their thoughts among their common fellows with the result that a veritable wave of unified sentiment soon produces the amazing impulse that changes our social behavior. Noah Webster had a genius for many things, not the least of which was to lead common men to a rational understanding of their needs. He became our greatest schoolmaster, not by pontificating from a chair in a great university, but by teaching simple fundamentals—in language, morals, economics, politics—to the masses.

This little book had a long background, as common textbooks go, to prepare for its glorious history. Webster conceived his idea of a new system of American education while teaching at West Hartford in 1779–1780, but active preparation awaited a full study of the problems involved. The writing was probably begun in 1781 in Sharon; as his materials grew, he enlarged his plan to two volumes and then to three. The Spelling Book, first in the series of three volumes under the title *A Grammatical Institute of the English Language,* was not completed until early in 1783. At Goshen he first ventured to test his idea by talking with the parents of his scholars. Their uniform approval exhilarated him. And yet in August, 1782, he wrote despairingly of his prospects and misfortune. The book was a child of personal sufferings as well as of national necessity. In January, 1783, after a winter of indefatigable work, he wrote: "I have sacrificed ease, pleasure, and health in the execution of it, and have nearly completed it. But such close application is too much for my constitution. I must relinquish the school or writing grammars."

Late in August, 1782, Webster carried his manuscript to Philadelphia, Princeton, New York, and New Haven to invite criticism and to secure for his work the protection of copyright. In accordance with the custom of the time, he bore with him letters of recommendation, epistles introductory and commendatory. One of them illustrated almost humorously America's need for such a simple compendium as he proposed to publish. Happily an amanuensis prepared this letter for Henry Wisner's signature, so that that sturdy patriot's orthography and grammar do not fall under our reproach:

Goshen: 26ᵗʰ August 1782

The Bearrer Mʳ Noah Webster has taught a grammer School for sometime past in this place much to the Satisfaction of his Employers   he is now doing some business in the liturary way which will in oppinion of good Judges be of Service to postarity   he being a Stranger in philadelphia may Stand in need of the assistance Some gentleman with whome you are acquainted   he is a young gentleman whose morral as will political caracter is such as will render him worthy of your notice   any favours which you may do him will be Serving the public and Accepted as a favour done your friend

and very humble Servant
HENRY WISNER

The Honourable
James Duane
Robert R Livingston } Esqʳˢ

Duane smiled as he read this letter, looked hard into Webster's face to see if a hoax were being perpetrated on him, and then wrote letters to Thomas Jefferson and other men able to judge the merit of the manuscript. Jefferson passed the schoolmaster along to James Madison, then in Philadelphia. The short, stout Virginia legislator surveyed the manuscript perfunctorily; but, recalling his college collaboration on an epic poem with Philip Freneau and Hugh Henry Brackenridge, he approved Webster's ideas for copyright legislation. At the University of Pennsylvania the work was examined in detail; at Princeton Professor Samuel Stanhope Smith, later to be President of the University, suggested the printing of *-tion,* *-sion,* and *-cion* terminations as one syllable. Dr. Smith also wrote a testimonial approving Webster's plans and supporting his application for copyright:

Mr. Noah Webster having shown to me a plan of reforming the spelling book of Mr. Dilworth, associating with it an abridgment of Mr. Lowth's Grammar and other articles of knowledge, very proper for young persons in the country; and having shown to me a part of the execution; I do conceive that he proposes many useful improvements in a book of that kind; and that he has executed with judgment that part which he has already finished. Every attempt of this nature undoubtedly merits the encouragement of the public; because it is by such attempts that systems of education are gradually perfected in every country, and the elements of knowledge rendered more easy to be acquired. Men of industry or of talents in any way, have a right to the property of their productions; and it encourages invention and improvement to secure it to them by certain laws, as has been practiced in European countries with advantage and success. And it is my opinion that it can be of no evil consequence to the state, and may be of benefit to it, to vest, by a law, the sole right of publishing and vending such works in the authors of them.

SAMUEL S. SMITH.

Princeton, Sept. 27, 1782.

The legislatures of Pennsylvania and New Jersey were not in session at the time of Webster's visit, and his mission in behalf of copyright seemed a failure. At Trenton Webster inquired of Governor William Livingston whether a copyright law could be obtained in New Jersey. The Governor replied that if Webster would wait until noon, the question would be put to the Council, then in session. At the time appointed Webster called again, only to hear that the Council gave very little encouragement.

In New Haven Dr. Ezra Stiles examined the plan with care, but he did not approve Webster's tentative title for the work, "The American Instructor," a name that was attractive, short, and indicative of the author's nationalistic ardor. Stiles supplied, in keeping with his character, the ponderous title Webster adopted, "A Grammatical Institute of the English Language," a title probably drawn by analogy from John Calvin's *Institutes*. Whether Stiles pressed the analogy and urged Webster to become the great lawgiver in language, we cannot know, but powerful suasion must have operated to cause the alteration of the name. Webster's own choice was better as he soon realized, for the inclusive title laid him open to the charge of vanity. In 1787 he subordinated this title to others, two of the books, the Spelling Book and the Reader, acquiring the indispensable adjective, "American."

Webster's first excursion into the world of affairs among men of national consequence depressed him. It was just such a tour as he had planned in 1779, but the expense depleted his small store of cash, and the trip seemed almost fruitless. Some men thought the idea too trifling to discuss; others expressed a settled prejudice in favor of Thomas Dilworth's *New Guide to the English Tongue*, the work in universal use which Webster sought to supplant. His general design was approved by several teachers, but, although he brought home a few testimonials, he had no assurance his work would be protected by law. He had not yet learned to penetrate beneath politeness and carry his point; as a lawyer at the bar of public opinion he failed to win his own case.

But he persisted in spite of public apathy and discouragement, for his observant eye everywhere detected the same faults he deplored in the schools of Connecticut. What seemed a trifle to others, this matter of infant education, loomed large in his own thinking. He held in his mind the solution to all the problems of the nation, the cure for all social and political ailments. With the conviction of the discoverer of a panacea, he pressed forward, demanding legislative recognition of his book:

I must think that, next to the sacred writings, those books which teach us the principles of science and lay the basis on which all our future improvements must be built, best deserve the patronage of the public. An attention to literature must be the principal bulwark against the encroachments of civil and ecclesiastical tyrants—and American Liberty can die only with her Mæcenases. A folio upon some abstruse philosophical subject might, at first thought, appear to be the work of some consequence and attract the public attention. But this would be read only by a few and its utility seldom reach further than the philosopher's head. While a little fifteen penny volume, which may convey much useful knowledge to the remote, obscure recesses of honest poverty is overlooked as a matter of trivial notice. The former, like a taper, gives light only in chambers of study. The latter, like a star, casts its beams equally upon the peasant and the monarch.

This impassioned plea was sent to John Canfield, Esq., a Sharon lawyer, whose daughter Laura had studied under Webster. Canfield presented to the January, 1783, session of the Connecticut Legislature Webster's petition for a copyright law to protect his books for a term of thirteen years.

An Act was passed. A similar memorial to the New York Assembly, meeting at Kingston, was prepared, but a motion by General Philip Schuyler later produced an Act and superseded the necessity for the petition. Massachusetts in March, 1783, and Maryland in April, 1783, provided protection. In May, 1783, Congress passed an Act, on Madison's motion, recommending to the several states to secure to authors or publishers a copyright for fourteen years on books not before printed. New Jersey accordingly passed an Act on May 27, 1783, and New Hampshire and Rhode Island in the same year. Webster made personal application to the legislatures of other states in the succeeding years, and in each of them, Vermont excepted, largely through his vigorous crusade, laws were passed. He asked Madison, "from the small acquaintance I had with you in Philadelphia and the recommendation of Mr. Jefferson," to propose a bill in the Virginia Legislature in 1784. Webster unquestionably is the father of copyright legislation in America. For more than fifty years he agitated for improved laws for the protection of the rights of authors in the ownership of their writings.

In his petitions Webster briefly stated the reasons why he laid claim to governmental protection. First, his books would be useful in simplifying and unifying the language. The many improvements of his three volumes were

calculated to extirpate the improprieties and vulgarisms which were necessarily introduced by settlers from various parts of Europe; to reform the abuses and corruption which, to an unhappy degree, tincture the conversation of the polite part of the Americans; to render the acquisition of the language easy both to American youth and foreigners; and especially to render the pronunciation of it accurate and uniform by demolishing those odious distinctions of provincial dialects which are the subject of reciprocal ridicule in different States.

Second, his books would offer moral and religious instruction: "The exercises are such as to inspire youth with a contempt of the unmanly vices of mankind, and a love of virtue, patriotism, and religion." "Some remarks upon the vices of mankind [are] designed to inspire youth with an abhorrence of vice and a love of virtue and religion." Third, his books would incalculate patriotic feelings: "Your memorialist, ever ambitious to promote the interest of literature and the honor and dignity of the American empire, designs the above mentioned work for the general benefit of the youth of the United States."

To Canfield he wrote: "America must be as independent in *literature* as she is in *politics*—as famous for *arts* as for *arms*,—and it is not impossible but a person of my youth may have some influence in exciting a spirit of literary industry." Webster's intense national feelings received clearer expression in the preface to his Spelling Book:

The author wishes to promote the honour and prosperity of the confederated republics of America; and chearfully throws his mite into the common treasure of patriotic exertions. This country must in some future time, be as distinguished by the superiority of her literary improvements, as she is already by the liberality of her civil and ecclesiastical constitutions. Europe is grown old in folly, corruption and tyranny—in that country laws are perverted, manners are licentious, literature is declining and human nature debased.

For America in her infancy to adopt the present maxims of the old world, would be to stamp the wrinkles of decrepid age upon the bloom of youth and to plant the seeds of decay in a vigorous constitution. American glory begins to dawn at a favourable period, and under flattering circumstances. We have the experience of the whole world before our eyes; but to receive indiscriminately the maxims of government, the manners and the literary taste of Europe and make them the ground on which to build our systems in America, must soon convince us that a durable and stately edifice can never be erected upon the mouldering pillars of antiquity. It is the business of *Americans* to select the wisdom of all nations, as the basis of her constitutions,—to avoid their errours,—to prevent the introduction of foreign vices and corruptions and check the career of her own,—to promote virtue and patriotism,—to embellish and improve the sciences,—to diffuse an uniformity and purity of language,—to add superior dignity to this infant Empire and to human nature.

In these remarks we see the earliest statement of the fundamental tenets in Webster's philosophy. He desired to develop a simple system of elementary education by which the speech and language of the United States would be rendered uniform, moral and religious truths would be propagated, and a love of country would be developed. At a moment when popular opinion was forgetting the acrimony of a seven-year war and when America was again turning to Europe for all its supplies, Webster demanded that we develop a system of our own. Not the least gift of Webster to his country was this insistence that America choose its own course, unhampered by the maxims of the old world.

Webster sought in vain for a publisher for his *Institute.* So dislocated was business and so uncertain was the stability of the new nation, no printer would risk the expense, nor would a friend underwrite publication. In June, assured of copyright protection in his own and several other states, he went to Barzillai Hudson and George Goodwin, publishers of *The Connecticut Courant* in Hartford, and made a contract by the terms of which they would accept his note for the printing bill if he would grant them sole privilege to print succeeding editions of the book. An edition of 5000 was struck off; on October 7, 1783, advertisements offered the book for sale at the price of fourteen pence a single copy or ten shillings a dozen. The title was: *A Grammatical Institute, of the English Language, Comprising, An easy, concise, and systematic Method of Education, Designed for the Use of English Schools in America. In Three Parts. Part I. Containing a new and accurate Standard of Pronunciation.*

This little book of 119 pages looked suspiciously like the well-known spellers of Dilworth and Fenning, for the serried columns of words at first seemed identical with the older books. The reading lessons "of easy words to learn [*sic*] children to read and know their duty" began with Dilworth's first sentence, as if to keep the old text, but the others were new:

> No man may put off the law of God.
> My joy is in his law all the day.
> O may I not go in the way of sin.
> Let me not go in the way of ill men.

Fenning's familiar "Story of Tommy and Harry" appeared on page 113, but Webster rewrote and shortened it, because "in the original the language is flat, stale, and puerile." Much material, indeed, was lifted from Dilworth and Fenning, but all of it was organized on new principles. And Webster added many pages of his own. Essentially it was a new book along the lines of a familiar pattern.

Dilworth's *New Guide*, "the nurse of us all" as Barlow remarked, had held almost undisputed command in the teaching of orthography in American schools since 1750. To supplant its use seemed an impossible task, so rooted was prejudice in its favor. Printers threw off vast editions, and the book passed like currency, its sale with each reopening of school being as certain as day and night. Its fables and maxims were known as well as Poor Richard's proverbs.

But it was a British book, bursting with loyalty to the king and the British Isles; its geographical section listed villages and shires in England, names unfamiliar and unnecessary to an American student. Robert Ross in *The New American Spelling Book,* published several years later, echoed Webster: "Dilworth's Spelling Book, recommending Subjection to a foreign Power, has a Tendency to promote Disaffection to the present Government, and must therefore be very improper for the Instruction of the *Freeborn* Youth of *America,* since we have become an INDEPENDENT NATION." Dilworth's section on grammar held up in Barlow's estimation, "a scarecrow in the English language, and lads once lugged into it when young are afraid of all kinds of grammar all their days after." It was defective also in syllabication and orthoepy.

Webster launched his book and an attack upon Dilworth at the same time. He pointed out the weaknesses and insufficiencies of the *New Guide* in newspaper advertisements and in an Introduction. He called it "the most imperfect guide" in use in schools, even though its authority had become as "sacred as the tradition of the Jews or the Mahometan Bible." "One half of the work," he added, "is totally useless, and the other half, defective and erroneous."

Webster jettisoned most of Dilworth's religious materials, especially the many passages containing the name of the deity. For these he substituted precepts of the Poor Richard type, brief exhortations to lead good lives and proverbial phrases, counsels, and maxims. This type of wisdom, clinging to the mind like a burr in the hair, lent to the Spelling Book an attractive value which kept it a favorite among children and an object of sentimental interest to these same children when they were grown. Webster's Speller was a worldly book by comparison with Dilworth's, whose thoughts always dwelt upon sin, death, the grave, and eternal damnation. Webster planted seeds of practical wisdom, such as

When wine is in, wit is out.
A good cow may have a bad calf.
You must not buy a pig in a poke.
Let not your tongue cut your throat.
He that lies down with dogs must rise up with fleas.

Much good advice was given to children on the management of their time in school, on the development of good habits, and on the means to success. This example of monosyllabic wisdom reads like a children's "Poor Richard":

A wise child loves to learn his book; but the fool would choose to play with toys.

Sloth keeps such a hold of some clowns, that they lie in bed when they should go to school; but a boy that wants to be wise will drive sleep far from him.

Love him that loves his book, and speaks good words, and does no harm, for such a friend may do thee good all the days of thy life.

Be kind to all as far as you can, you know not how soon you may want their help; and he that has the good will of all that know him, shall not want a friend in time of need.

If you want to be good, wise and strong, read with care such books as have been made by wise and good men; think of what you read in your spare hours; be brisk at play, but do not swear; and waste not too much of your time in bed.

A spelling book affords little opportunity for flag waving; Webster's introduction, however, called for an American language, and his innovations on every page symbolized the new national spirit animating the author. Dilworth's catalogues of English place names and abbreviations were replaced with similar lists suitable to America. Shrewdly Webster included a complete list of Connecticut towns, accompanied by tables of their population and distance from Hartford. This appeal to local pride effectively won skeptical teachers to use the book in Connecticut. As the sphere of influence widened, suitable alterations were made. The book closed with a chronology of important American dates.

The most notable improvements were made in syllabication and orthoepy, the general principles of which Webster not only retained in his later publications, but which have become standard in American and English usage through his influence.

In Dilworth such words as *cluster, habit, nostril,* and *bishop,* had been divided as *clu-ster, ha-bit, no-stril, bi-shop.* Webster divided them as we do today, *clus-ter, hab-it, nos-tril, bish-op,* so that the smallest child could not mistake their pronunciation nor fail to spell them correctly. This alteration was made "with deliberation and diffidence, but with a full conviction that both necessity and utility demanded an alteration." One change provoked great hostility. The psalter required two syllables in pronouncing the suffixes *-tion, -sion,* and *-cion,* but Webster correctly welded the letters into one spelling and pronouncing unit. The prejudice against this innovation is humorously exemplified in an anecdote related to Webster respecting an old Scotch Presbyterian elder in Western Pennsylvania. "When the *Spelling Book,* under the teaching of some Yankee adventurer, had made its way into a small valley of the Allegheny mountains, where the good man lived, and the heresies it contained began to spread among the people, the storekeeper at the Four Corners saw the elder riding down furiously one morning and calling out as he drew up to the door: 'Have ye heard the news, mon? Do ye ken what's gaen on? Here's a book by a Yankee lad called Wobster, teaching the children clean agenst the Christian religion!' 'Oh, how so?' 'Why, ye ken ye canna sing the psalms of David without having *salvation* and such words in four syllables, *sal-va-ci-on,* and he's making all the children say *salvashun.*' "

English sounds, in respect to spelling, remain the most chaotic and unsystematized of any language. Pronunciation is capricious and irregular, following no spelling rules. *Cough, tough, slough* look alike, but the vowel in each is pronounced differently. Similarly *rove, move,* and *dove* tantalize the beginner. Different vowels, singly or in combination, receive the same sound, as *a, ai, ei,* and *e* in *bate, laid, vein, there.* Yet these and fifty other problems had passed unnoticed by authors of spelling books and dictionaries. They lamented the disorder and dismissed it without a remedy. "Thus," scornfully exclaimed Webster, "the pronunciation of our language, tho' the most important and difficult part of grammar, is left to parents and nurses—to ignorance and caprice—to custom, accident or nothing. Nay, to something worse, to coxcombs, who have a large share in directing the *polite task* of pronunciation, which of course is as vicious as that of any other class of people. And while this is the case, every person will claim a right to his own fancy, and the language will be exposed to perpetual fluctuation."

To remedy this defect in pronunciation, Webster devised a single system of notation by which he hoped, with the aid of such a standard universally adopted in schools, to "demolish those odious distinctions of provincial dialects which are objects of reciprocal ridicule in the United States." To each distinct vowel sound he gave a number, and this figure, placed above the proper letter in each word, directed the reader's pronunciation.

Webster's standard of pronunciation was "general custom" or, to use the more recent phrase, "standard usage." In this choice of current speech, rather than the university, dictionary, or stage, as his source of correctness, Webster anticipated by nearly a century and a half the innovations of The National Council of Teachers of English. In choosing between two or more common pronunciations, Webster adopted the standard New England form. His short experience in traveling and his opportunities to hear the English speech of visitors from settlements other than those in which he lived, had been small; of necessity he corrected in later editions some of the provincialism into which he had fallen unconsciously. But, it must be said, Webster was not a skilled phonetician; at no time in his long career did he record spoken English very accurately.

Among Webster's idiosyncratic, but permanently held, opinions in this book, one may invite a smile. He omitted the name of the Deity from his reading lessons for an "important and obvious" reason: "nothing has greater tendency to lessen the reverence which mankind ought to have for the Supreme Being than a careless repetition of his name upon every trifling occasion." He objected, too, to the frequent use of the Bible as a textbook. Fifty years later he prepared his own—the first American—version of the Bible as a crowning monument to his plan for the improvement of American literature and language. In 1783 he already held fixed ideas on this subject.

In view of his later crusade against the inclusion of *u* in words like *honour* and *favour*, his defense of this older form shows that all his ideas were not fully formed in 1783. "Expunging the superfluous letters," he wrote with characteristic vigor, "appears to arise from the same pedantic fondness for singularity that prompts the new fashions in pronunciation." Even more surprising is his statement that innovating authors "have omitted the letter that is sounded and retained one that is silent, for the words are pronounced *onur, favur.*"

Among the footnotes sharp warnings cautioned children not to pronounce *negro* as *neger, spirit* as *sperit, quoit* as *quate, confiscate* as *confisticate;* nor to drop the final *g* in participles; nor to adopt the cockney sound of *a* for *e*, as *marcy* for *mercy, parson* for *person*, etc. This last, he said, was vulgar, the result of "a vicious drawling habit contracted by carelessness."

A virago is a turbulent, masculine woman.

An orator makes orations.

The Bad Boy, illustrating the famous fable of the
apple thief.

These pictures are from *The Pictorial Elementary
Spelling Book*

The woodcuts and fables, so prominently mentioned in all discussions of the Speller, were a later addition. Woodcuts were expensive and engravers scarce. Whether pictures formed a part of the original plan cannot be known, but as soon as he could, Webster procured the now famous cuts of the boy stealing apples, the crestfallen milkmaid, the partial judge, the entangled fox, the crafty cat, the patient fox, the cowardly friend, and the dog which unwisely kept bad company. Additions and changes in content and spelling were made from time to time in the Speller, but the Fables were never altered.

The great favorite among the fables has always been the first, which was lifted from Fenning's Spelling Book:

OF THE BOY THAT STOLE APPLES

An old man found a rude boy upon one of his trees stealing apples, and desired him to come down; but the young sauce-box told him plainly he would not. Won't you? said the old man, then I will fetch you down; so he pulled up some turf or grass and threw at him; but this only made the youngster laugh, to think the old man should pretend to beat him down from the tree with grass only.

Well, well, said the old man, if neither words nor grass will do, I must try what virtue there is in stones: so the old man pelted him heartily with stones, which soon made the young chap hasten down from the tree and beg the old man's pardon.

MORAL

If good words and gentle means will not reclaim the wicked, they must be dealt with in a more severe manner.

In 1788 the title became *The American Spelling Book: containing an easy Standard of Pronunciation. Being the First Part of a Grammatical Institute of the English Language.* A clause in the contract executed for this and all succeeding editions, required the use of a blue paper cover. Here is the origin of the "blue-backed speller." To this and

succeeding editions for some years a portrait woodcut, said
to have been made without Webster's knowledge, decorated
the inside front cover. Different engravings appeared in the
Hartford and Boston imprints; one of them gave Webster
the appearance of a porcupine. A hostile reviewer in the
Monthly Anthology said the likeness was so badly executed
"as to frighten children who use it from learning to read."
In 1794 a "Moral Catechism" and a "Federal Catechism"
were added. In 1804 a revised edition, retaining all the
popular features was marketed. Twenty-five years later it
was altered to bring its spelling into conformity with the
great Dictionary, the title becoming *The Elementary Spelling Book*. After 1843 *The Pictorial Elementary Spelling
Book* simultaneously carried on the Webster tradition, although it is doubtful whether Webster would have sanctioned the alteration of the engraving of the youthful apple
thief so as to portray him thumbing his nose at the remon-
strating farmer.

The reception of the first part of the *Institute* cheered and
fortified Webster. With characteristic local pride nearly
every Connecticut worthy affixed his name to a testimonial
in behalf of the book. Webster travelled from town to town
to secure signatures and to urge the adoption of the *Institute*.
He sent copies to college libraries for preservation as an
earnest of America's literary independence. Harvard has its
fresh, unmutilated, calf-bound copy, a precious rarity housed
in the Treasure Room. He sent copies to his friends and
classmates. Joseph Buckminster, his Yale tutor, bubbled
with delight, because he had "been honored as an instrument of assisting so many young Gentlemen to acquire the
rudiments of human literature, who bid fair to act so distinguished a part on the American Theatre." How much
stir this little volume created, Webster learned only in part,
for few men grow lyrical enough over spelling books to
write letters home about them.

At least one such letter emanated from the camp at New-burgh, New York, where the American army awaited orders to disband. Colonel Timothy Pickering, Quartermaster General, worried much about the proper education of his son, John, a youngster growing up at home without a father's guidance. Pickering, having heard of the *Institute*, ordered a copy, and waited impatiently. When it came, October 30, 1783, he read it through—some tables excepted,—spending a long wakeful night in its perusal. On the next morning he lauded it to his wife, and paid this tribute to Webster, whom he did not know: "The author is ingenious, and writes from his own experience as a schoolmaster, as well as the best authorities; and the time will come when no authority, as an English grammarian, will be superior to his own. It is the very thing I have wished for."

Not every reader echoed Pickering's satisfaction. An old Litchfield schoolmaster by the name of Hughes grumbled his dislike of the young upstart who besmirched dependable Dilworth. When the second edition was published in June, 1784, Hughes could no longer contain himself. To the recently founded *Freeman's Chronicle* he sent a long, punning, denunciatory letter over the signature, "Dilworth's Ghost." He chided Webster for plagiarism; for poor judgment; for a style that "is not only inaccurate, but inelegant and bombastick"; for inconsistency; for teaching a vicious pronunciation; and for spleen, ambition, avarice, arrogance, and want of candor. He sneered also at Webster's securing a copyright as "truly a very laughable affair."

A dextrous reply on July 5, 1784, answered none of the objections, merely suggesting that only signed and grammatical publications would be noticed. Obviously Webster wished to prolong the controversy to secure free publicity, for the original article had already been copied by other papers. Hughes did not rise to the bait. Webster, therefore, on July 22, 1784, prepared a detailed answer, in which he defended his auctorial honesty and motives. In regard to his style, he wrote:

> If this be too plain and pointed, it must be ascribed to the feelings of a man, who, after he had spent years in the study of language, found that he was totally unacquainted with the elements of his own; that he had been learning errors himself and teaching them to others. . . . But so blind was my respect and veneration . . . that in the first edition I adopted many things as right, which I since find to be wrong.

Not until November 1, 1784, did an attack come which led to a prolonged exchange of inelegant remarks and to publicity. "A Learner of English Grammar" disagreed with Webster's rule in the pronunciation of vowels. At once "Entity" and "Ghost" joined the newcomer. Waiting until the flurry was over, Webster egged them on: "I defy all the Ghosts of Pedants in the invisible world and all the Pedagogues and smatterers of this, to discredit the system or prevent its prevalence." In February, 1785, accused of trying to stop the printing of critical articles, Webster replied that he wished every printer on the continent to publish any remarks whatever, unfavorable as well as favorable, on the *Institute*, for had he not confessed on January 18, 1785: "I am under ten thousand obligations . . . for [the Ghost's] spiteful attempt to depreciate my publications. Had not his scurrilous remarks appeared, people would have taken less pains to examine the design, the plan, and the merit of the *Institute*. The result of a critical examination into the work has generally been in its favour."

Indeed, the quarrel drew the attention of Benjamin Edes of Boston to the work. A contract followed. Booksellers from Maine to Maryland laid in supplies. Webster owed, not only increased business to his enemies, but also a national prominence which made him an object of curiosity, if not of celebrity.

A few statistics may indicate the acceleration of the book's adoption. The first edition of five thousand copies sold out in nine months. Second and third editions appeared in 1784, the latter of which contained a fulsome dedication to President Stiles. Edes of Boston brought out an impression in 1786, William Young of Philadelphia and Samuel Campbell of New York in 1788, John Carter of Providence and Thomas and Andrews of Boston in 1789. Other printers in later years bought rights and supplied the back-country regions. More than fifty impressions, some of them of 25,-000 copies each, appeared before 1800, one hundred by 1814, and one hundred fifty by 1829. This is a conservative estimate, for Webster stated that two hundred editions had appeared by 1810. Not all of these editions have been located by Mrs. Roswell Skeel, Jr., Webster's great-granddaughter and bibliographer, many whole impressions having been thumbed to shreds by their youthful readers. A full count is made difficult, too, by the frequent appearance of bootleg issues and by the distribution of stereotype plates. One and a half million copies were sold by 1801, twenty million copies by 1829, and at least seventy-five million by 1875, when a million or more copies were sold annually. A grand total of one hundred million copies, before it was supplanted, appears quite within reason. Several thousand copies are still sold annually by the present publishers of *The Elementary Spelling Book*.

A gold mine opened at Webster's door. A penny royalty for each copy would have given him a large income. Edes gave £5 10s per 1000 for 5000 copies, September 16, 1786. But Webster, wanting ready cash, threw away a fortune for a few pounds. To Samuel Campbell unlimited rights for selling in New York, New Jersey, North Carolina, South Carolina, and Georgia for five years were granted for £80 New York money or $200 cash. Campbell turned out 20,000 copies a year, and before the termination of the contract trickily stocked up with a printing of 100,000 copies. By this arrangement Webster lost upward of £1000 or $2500 in five years; yet he was willing to sell the same right for eleven years for $1000 or for $150 a year. These offers were grasped promptly, so that for a few pence he sold pounds. Many printers lied in their returns, paying only a fraction of the royalty. Others, like Nathaniel Patten of Hartford who bound Campbell's issues, took thousands for themselves and threw the copies into competition with authorized editions. Suits were instituted against infringements, and Webster recovered small damages several times. But proof of wrongdoing was difficult to secure: journeyman printers moved from town to town with sufficient frequency, so that an employer could change hands often enough to prevent any one from tattling. How much Webster secured in royalties cannot be known, but it is evident that only a small fraction of the possible sum ever reached his hands.

Many irksome problems constantly kept Webster in a ferment. Careless proofreading allowed hundreds of errors to creep into each new printing. For a time Webster watched over the presses, but it was an impossible task to read proof in a half dozen cities at once. His troubles with faulty texts ended only with the development of the stereotype process. The haste with which printers threw off editions led to unsatisfactory press work, a fault Benjamin Franklin alluded to thus: "Your Spelling Book is miserably printed here, so as in many places to be scarcely legible, and on wretched paper." Campbell and Young in 1788 used a portrait of Washington as a frontispiece. Webster thought this act not right: "It is using the General disrespectfully to make him a passport for spelling books." On May 10, 1790, Nathaniel Patten, who had been successfully sued for violating the copyright act, broadcast "A Proposal to save three hundred and thirty pounds six shillings and eight pence, annually to the inhabitants" of Connecticut. Claiming that editions of 20,000 could be printed at 2¾ pence a copy and bound at 1½ pence, Patten demanded that the price be reduced or that he be allowed to print and sell at a lower figure than the established fourteen pence. Public sentiment did not support this assault on the copyright law; he therefore printed a huge edition of Dilworth, which he sold for ten pence, four pence under Webster's speller. In 1792 Campbell asserted his edition was "the most correct"; Webster scented a scheme to stir a quarrel among the publishers. In a letter to the public he wrote: "I find it the most incorrect edition I have ever seen. There are in it between two and three thousand errors in printing. . . . I utterly disclaim it." Campbell responded violently, calling Webster a "pedantic grammarian . . . full of vanity and ostentation." The upshot of the controversy was the severing of relations between the two, but not until Campbell printed 100,000 copies for sale after his contract expired. Similar sad tales of deceit, masked by controversy, emerge from Webster's papers.

Not less annoying were the many infringements of his copyright by other authors. Every disgruntled printer issued his own Spelling Book, generally a slight variation from Webster's. Robert Ross's *The New American Spelling Book*, published by Thomas and Samuel Green, New Haven, was probably the earliest of a long line of imitators. These lifted whole sections, even copying the fables verbatim. American schoolmasters' lack of originality showed patently in their inability to find new methods of presentation or new reading selections. New and better books were needed, but none really challenged the supremacy of Webster until the Spelling Book War of the 1820's, and none dislodged Webster's until twentieth century educational research provided scientifically graded volumes.

The great vogue of the book was in the country districts. In some schools Webster remained standard for more than a century. The Reverend Mr. A. M. Colton, recalling his childhood experiences with the Speller and speaking of the long history of the book, said, "It is an institution, yes, a university. It has trained and strained more heads than any book of the kind ever did, or perhaps ever will." Whittier, seeking a simile to indicate the modern Yankee's loss of superstition and terror at the unknown, told how all nature now was as "familiar" as "Webster's Spelling-Book." The city teachers, partly because of their dislike of the rural quality of Webster and partly because of their desire to use books of local composition, supplanted *The American Spelling Book* with one of several dozen imitators. Webster decried the hostility evidenced toward his book, and asserted that the introduction of new books would inevitably lead to linguistic chaos.

The South remained loyal to Webster longest. Even today recent editions still may be found in an occasional school. Despite the abiding hatred of all things from New England, Southerners took this Yankee Speller to their hearts. Fitz-Greene Halleck described the Connecticut schoolmasters as

Wandering through the Southern countries, teaching
The ABC from Webster's Spelling Book;
Gallant and godly, making love and preaching
And gaining, by what they call 'hook and crook,'
And what the moralists call overreaching,
A decent living. The Virginians look
Upon them with as favorable eyes
As Gabriel on the devil in Paradise.

Not even the Civil War could break the hold of the Speller. J. W. Burke of Macon, Georgia, revised an edition to suit the sentiments of the Confederate States, because the book was "as essential to the mental existence of the South as hog and hominy to their physical needs." In Raleigh a revision "adapted to Southern Schools" appeared in 1863. The publishers naïvely remarked that since they had removed the Puritan element and had added "a few Southern touches," the book was "perfectly suited to the wants of our population." Robert Fleming brought out an edition of 40,000 in Atlanta, "adapted to the youth of the Southern Confederacy." He added scriptural texts in support of slavery to replace omitted sentiments respectful to the North.

The book was carried into the West as part of the cultural equipment of the emigrant preacher and teacher. Editions were printed without Webster's knowledge and without permission. As each village was established, the Speller laid the foundation of education and encouraged national unity. In the 1840's, as pioneers pushed across the Rocky Mountains to claim the whole breadth of the continent for the United States, the Spelling Book helped to inspire an enduring national spirit. An unexpected link in the chain of Webster influence was forged at this time when an edition of the Spelling Book was printed in the Oregon Country. North and South, East and West, Webster dominated American elementary education.

The unparalleled success of Webster's Spelling Book under its various titles may be explained, not only by the merits of the book, but by the shrewd publicity devices of the author. He rode horseback from village to village, visiting preachers, teachers, lawyers, and school committees. He gave copies to printers with the injunction, "Hereafter spell according to this book." He secured testimonials by the hundred, even asking Washington, Jefferson, and Franklin for statements, which, by the by, they graciously refused to make. He wrote constantly under various pseudonyms newspaper puffs, and he answered every criticism. He kept controversies alive, publishing somewhat erratic criticisms on Gibbon, Johnson, and Walker, so that he might exhort the public to support its first schoolmaster in scholarly tasks.

He pleaded poverty with as long a face as a begging friar, insisting that the meager royalties of his little book alone "sustained a numerous and growing family and made possible the compilation of his great Dictionary." He donated books to charity societies, and gave portions of his royalties for the support of missions, of schools, of prize essay contests. He lectured audiences on every possible occasion. During the rapid population of the West in the 1830's, he placed his blundering son William at Lafayette, Indiana, to capture the western market. His sons-in-law wrote, at his goading, favorable reviews of his books. Webster knew the arts of publicity and practiced them with a Yankee cunning combined with the fervor of an evangelist. Webster knew, and profited by the knowledge, that an author is known by what he writes—about himself.

A whole volume might be devoted to the history of the Spelling Book, to its author's numerous maddening experiences, and to the many testimonials of its contribution to American life and education. Only a few items in the long catalogue, however, can be mentioned here. The spelling bee, still a favorite evening exercise in Grange meetings, demanded a uniform arbiter throughout a county and even a state. Webster's book early was given this position, and although other books printed *publick* and *honour*, the contestants spelled the words *public* and *honor*. The fun of the social gathering was quite unlike the tedious drill tactics of the average schoolmaster, who literally pounded correct spelling into the human anatomy with about the same type of brutality by which cattle are branded. Many children, like cattle, "got their letters," but they did not approve the method. The fetish for spelling accuracy is well illustrated by the following notice of a Danbury, Connecticut, school:

The advantages that small children obtain at this school may be easily imagined when the public are informed that those who spell go through the whole of Webster's spelling book twice a fortnight.

A generalized description of class-room procedure with the book is given by Alice Morse Earle in *Child Life in Colonial Days:*

The teaching of spelling in many schools was peculiar. The master gave out the word, with a blow of his strap on the desk as a signal for all to start together, and the whole class spelled out the word in syllables in chorus. The teacher's ear was so trained and acute that he at once detected any misspelling. If this happened, he demanded the name of the scholar who made the mistake. If there was any hesitancy or refusal in acknowledgment, he kept the whole class until, by repeated trials of long words, accuracy was obtained. The roar of the many voices of the large school, all pitched in different keys, could be heard on summer days for a long distance. In many country schools the scholars not only spelled aloud but studied all their lessons aloud, as children in Oriental countries do today.

If a certain amount of barbarity, a kind of animal trainer's repetitive drill, appeared essential in the teaching of this old book, let it not be forgotten that in our impoverished schools, manned by unlettered masters, the book was successful, and not even floggings could destroy students' affection for it. Mark Sullivan in Volume Two of Our Times gives much testimony of this type.

Other pictures can be drawn too, pictures radiant with the light of knowledge first dawning in shadowed places through the influence of the Spelling Book. James Lane Allen has recounted a touching incident of an ex-slave and the Spelling Book in "Two Gentlemen from Virginia." Even more amazing is the story of Sequoyah, the Cherokee Indian, who with only a Webster's Spelling Book as a guide, reduced his language to written symbols and taught that orthography to his fellows.

No other book, the Bible excepted, played so unifying a part in American culture; it fixed the speech habits of the older English settlers and brought into linguistic harmony with theirs the usage of millions of immigrant children. To Webster's Spelling Book belongs much of the credit that in forty-eight states, each populated with a people of un-English origin numerous enough to destroy the supremacy of the American-English language, a basic pattern of written and spoken language prevails everywhere. From Maine to California and from Oregon to Florida, each American uses the same words in the same way and pronounces them, slight dialect variations excepted, similarly. National speech unity in a great nation never before had been achieved, and exists nowhere else. The dream of a country schoolmaster named Noah Webster has come true.

CHAPTER V

AN AMERICAN SYSTEM OF EDUCATION

THREE subjects perennially provoke argument: politics, religion, and grammar. Not the least of these is grammar, for nothing appears more sacred than the established teachings in the field of language. It seems not known that language is a set of human habits, not an object of fiat creation. "Ain't," a harmless, useful contraction, arches every schoolmarm's back within hearing. "It is me," with its supposed violation of the law of case, upset the whole country when Chicago's superintendent of schools granted his teachers permission to accept it as a correct locution. Early highway signs warning autoists to "Go Slow" occasioned many petulant letters to the newspapers. Recently The National Council of Teachers of English placed its stamp of approval upon more than a hundred items of disputed usage, such as "Who were you with," "I ain't," and "It is me." But public opinion lags. Modern degeneracy nowhere appears so blatant as in our imputed disregard of old grammar rules.

The fact is, English grammar has long been fettered to Latin, and many textbooks are mere translations into English of Latin grammars. Our students worry over the gender and case of nouns, the subjunctive and potential modes of verbs, and many other sticks of academic lumber. For hundreds of years lore has been taught that long since disappeared in fact. Stupid traditionalism, blind to the true facts of English language, brands the new descriptive grammarian as an innovator and a radical. In no field of study has progress been so slow as in the teaching of English grammar.

Noah Webster may not have been the first American to
prepare an English grammar, but, country schoolmaster that
he was, he was the first to discern the folly of teaching English as if it were Latin. In his own schoolroom he learned
the futility of teaching by rote rules unsubstantiated by actual
usage. In vain he tried to test sentences by the rules of
Dilworth and Lowth. In vain he sought for actual subjunctives, actual nouns in the objective case, actual passive
verbs or neuters. When his common sense investigation
proved the inadequacy of earlier books, he prepared his
own.

With that painstaking thoroughness which later marked
his investigations in etymology, he diligently compared his
findings with those of his predecessors, and then reluctantly
but "with the fullest persuasion that [he] was warranted by
the nature and idioms of the language," he sent forth his
little book. Published at his own expense by Hudson and
Goodwin, the little thin volume of 139 pages was ushered
into the world in March, 1784, with a title page more en-
cumbered than that of the Spelling Book: *A Grammatical
Institute, of the English Language, in Three Parts: Part II,
containing, A Plain and comprehensive Grammar, founded
on the true Principles and Idioms of the Language; with
an analytical Dissertation, in which the various uses of the
auxiliary signs are unfolded and explained: And an Essay
towards investigating the Rules of English Verse.*

Like the Spelling Book, the Grammar followed an older
pattern and appeared at a casual glance no different from
other grammars. The Preface, however, quickly carried the
reader into the realm of controversy. Dilworth's grammar
in *A New Guide* was denounced as "a mere Latin grammar,
very indifferently translated"; its author, who knew nothing of the principles peculiar to English, was said to have
erred on every page. Other grammarians were equally bad,

for they held the "stupid opinion" that the only way of acquiring a knowledge of the English tongue was by first learning Latin.

Having dismissed the older grammarians from consideration, Webster proceeded to demonstrate the new principles upon which his book was framed. He clarified the subject of gender, showing that "neuter" cannot properly be called a gender, but rather a destitution of gender. Verbs were divided into transitive and intransitive, instead of the older threefold division, active, passive, and neuter. Chaos was reduced to some order in the discussion of the auxiliary verbs, although he confessed he found more difficulties than he could remove. The subjunctive mode he thought obsolescent, and he prophesied that in time the doubtful tenses would be banished from books. In these matters, only Joseph Priestley, whose book Webster had not seen, agreed in principle.

One innovation of Webster, it is to be profoundly regretted, has not been adopted, although its recognition would have been a boon to society and to schoolteachers. Even yet the form persists in popular speech and stands high in the list of so-called common errors. This is the form *you was* in the second person, singular number, past tense, indicative mood of the verb *to be*. Throughout the English literature of the eighteenth century and in the letters of learned men this form was preferred. Usage certainly sanctioned its adoption. Logic, a poor criterion in language, sanctioned its adoption. But "schoolmarm English" has boasted in this instance one of its few pyrrhic victories over Webster's common sense. The world of American education would have been saved one of its greatest laundering tasks had Webster prevailed, for a century and a half of teaching have only slightly altered the conditions he described: "The compilers of grammars condemn the use of *was* with *you*— but in vain. The practice is universal, except among men who learn the language by books. The best authors have given it their sanction, and the usage is too well established to be altered."

From a modern point of view, Webster's grammar is surprisingly sane and adequate for the objects proposed. The pioneering consisted not so much in adding new materials to the study of grammar, as in shearing away the useless Latinate terminology and in describing, not prescribing, actual grammatical usage.

Webster's Grammar sold well, because the replacement of Dilworth's *New Guide,* which had combined under one cover a speller, grammar, and reader, forced teachers to secure a second book. The first edition was exhausted within a year, and others followed immediately afterward. In 1787 alterations were made in response to criticism of some of the definitions, and the section on punctuation was enlarged.

In 1790, as a result of six years of linguistic study, he revised many passages. He had compared the King James version of the New Testament with the original Greek, and he had taken notes on the best English writings of the seventeenth and eighteenth centuries. With this huge mass of evidence collected from research, he unhesitatingly rejected older, erroneous conclusions. But he himself had been beguiled by Horne Tooke's *Diversions of Purley,* an amazing compend of philological pioneering and political nose-thumbing. Webster adopted the name "Abbreviations" for the particles, including under this one category the conjunctions, prepositions, interjections, and adverbs, because Tooke derived these forms etymologically from verbs. This was a bit of new-found knowledge which Webster, in his eagerness to prove the older grammarians wrong, adopted too hastily, as he later admitted.

Experimenter and unsettler of tradition though he was, Webster yet had his feet more firmly on the rock foundation of truth than his occasional idiosyncratic pronouncements would seem to warrant. He tested all disputed points in usage by "the genius of the language," insisting that errors had crept into grammars because "our *own language* and its *peculiar idioms*" had not been examined. Pugnaciously he reiterated this idea, while insisting, for example, that in the phrases *very cold, full sweet, most excellent,* the words *very, full,* and *most* are adjectives. Perhaps, he wrote, it will be said these words are used adverbially: "This is a pitiful substitute for truth. The truth is, the Saxon idiom was to use one adjective to qualify another; and this idiom stands its ground in the Saxon branch of the language; but the Latin idiom, that an adjective is qualified by an adverb, had been introduced with the derivative from the Roman tongue. Both idioms are good in English; both are derived from the highest antiquity, and stand on the immovable basis of *general undisputed practice,* the foundation of all languages on earth." Webster's method of inductive investigation was correct, but unhappily he proceeded to draw his conclusions from the forms and not from the uses of the words. He argued that *very* has an adverb *verily; full, fully; most, mostly;* therefore, the forms without -*ly* were adjectives. This conclusion, of course, failed to account for the loss of inflectional endings in the adverb. In other matters, such as a resolution of the problems involved in *I feel badly (bad), I had rather, I had as lief, He need not go, averse from (to),* he did good service to students by his original investigation. He agreed with Joseph Priestley, an innovator in grammar as well as in religion and science, that *It is me* and *Who is she married to?,* though not strictly grammatical, should be admitted as anomalous forms because of their prevalence.

Two common teaching devices, inherited from the Latin grammars, were advocated and illustrated. First was the "False Construction" or "False Syntax" lesson: "It was agreeable to him and *I*, that we and *them* should study together." Footnote corrections guided the student to accurate answers. Second was parsing, the explanation of the grammar and syntax of each word in an involved sentence. Webster's footnote comment suggests that the method had not become popular in America: "This method of parsing the English Language, which has been hitherto very little practiced, is the only way to obtain a thorough knowledge of it." He added that a pocket dictionary might be of assistance to the children in determining the parts of speech.

One novel device in this book was the inclusion of Latin equivalents of English conjugations, the purpose of which was "to assist foreigners in acquiring the true signification and force of our verbs."

Webster's *Grammar* was a learned, pugnacious book, beyond the reach not only of the children for whom it was designed, but also of most schoolmasters, who, Webster averred, were "illiterate men" with "no instruction in grammar." His reforming zeal outran his judgment, and he lost the field to Lindley Murray, whose *Grammar* (1795) leaned heavily on Webster but avoided novelties, experiment, and argument.

In 1807 Webster revamped the whole book, convinced that he had been led into many errors by earlier compilers. The new work, *A Philosophical and Practical Grammar*, never took hold, and only a few editions appeared. With that fondness men show for their less successful ventures, Webster declared this work to be the one he was most satisfied with. It is a good book, despite the belligerent retention of his new terminology and erroneous conclusions with regard to adverbs; it is the first English grammar based upon a thorough investigation of usage, and its illustrations alone make the work a sourcebook on disputed points of English style.

Grammar, unlike spelling, was an unpopular and greatly

disliked subject. Pupils who could read, speak, and write with fluent accuracy, often could not dissect out the subject or object in a Miltonic sentence, nor parse correctly idiomatic sentences like "He was elected President," or "Starch makes cloth stiff." Since passive verbs cannot take a direct object, according to the textbooks, what case is "President"? Starch, of course, does not make cloth; nevertheless, what part of speech is "stiff" and in what case is "cloth"? These questions are still asked in school today. English Grammar still is a hateful subject.

Reading, however, was the one subject which drew lads willingly to school. Spelling could be a game full of fun on occasion; grammar was torture; geography and history were suppliers of uninspired facts about places or events too far away ever to affect the student's life. But reading added imagination to dull reality, clothing the world in beauty and sentiment. The cold facts of the Revolution took on new meaning while Patrick Henry's bristling defiance rolled off a slippery tongue. Love, gallantry, virtue, industry, sobriety, honesty—all the moral and intellectual virtues—became understandable when phrased by Addison, Shakespeare, or Washington.

Webster's priority in the field of American readers has not been disputed, nor can it be denied that his Reader determined the form and content of this type of instruction for a century. This book, Part III of the *Institute*, was published in February, 1785, by the firm of Joel Barlow and Elisha Babcock, printers of *The American Mercury*, a Hartford weekly newspaper. Its unwieldly title ran: *A Grammatical Institute, of the English Language, in Three Parts: Part III. Containing, The necessary Rules of Reading and Speaking, and a Variety of Essays, Dialogues, and declamatory Pieces, moral, political and entertaining; divided into Lessons, for the Use of Children.* With this 186-page book Webster completed the system of education he had proposed for the improvement of American elementary instruction.

The Preface began modestly with the author's statement that he desired "to furnish common English schools with a variety of exercises for reading and speaking at a small expence." The lack of such anthologies had led to the use of the Bible as a textbook, a reprehensible practice for two reasons. First, the uniform, antique style prevents the acquisition "of a complete knowledge of words and of the modern manner of writing." Second, "such a common use of the Bible is a kind of prostitution of divine truth to secular purposes." Familiarity breeds disgust, levity, and wickedness, which lead to a profanation of the "awful solemnities of inspiration." Dr. Benjamin Rush, among others, was shocked by this statement, the feeling having been general that too much study of the Bible was impossible. Webster slid out of the controversy over this point by eliding this passage from future editions. The statement had been unnecessary, but it followed the Webster pattern of prefacing each new book with a denunciation of all competitors.

The guiding principle in the choice of his selections has become classic in discussions of American nationalism:

In the choice of pieces, I have not been inattentive to the political interests of America. Several of those masterly addresses of Congress, written at the commencement of the late revolution, contain such noble, just and independent sentiments of liberty and patriotism, that I cannot help wishing to transfuse them into the breasts of the rising generation.

Yet the book in its first edition was not a predominantly nationalistic one. It opened with four simple rules for reading and speaking, brief hints for proper articulating, pausing, accenting, and gesturing. Thirty-one pages of short prose and verse selections followed, the first of which Webster might have adopted for his own motto: "To be very active in laudable pursuits, is the distinguishing characteristic of a man of merit." Proverbs, aphorisms, and sententious statements from the writings of Swift, Shakespeare, Johnson, Pope, Bacon, Dryden, Addison, and Franklin, radiate piety, patriotism, and virtue. The thoughts in these briefer statements were developed at length by three sentimental tales lifted from *The Mirror,* and by three original characterizations by Webster, one of which may have described Juliana Smith of Sharon:

> Juliana is one of those rare women whose personal attractions have no rivals, but the sweetness of her temper and the delicacy of her sentiments. An elegant person, regular features, a fine complexion, a lively, expressive countenance, an easy address, and those blushes of modesty that soften the soul of the beholder; These are the native beauties, which render her the object of universal admiration.
>
> But when we converse with her, and hear the melting expressions of unaffected sensibility and virtue that flow from her tongue, her personal charms receive new lustre, and irresistibly engage the affections of her acquaintance.
>
> Sensible that the great source of all happiness is purity of morals and an easy conscience, Juliana pays constant and sincere attention to the duties of religion. She abhors the infamous, but fashionable device of deriding the sacred institutions of religion.
>
> She considers a lady without virtue as a monster on earth; and every accomplishment, without morals, as polite deception. She is neither a hypocrite nor an enthusiast; on the contrary, she mingles such cheerfulness with the religious duties of life, that even her piety carries with it a charm which insensibly allures the profligate from the arms of vice. . . .

These sugary-sweet compositions with the hectic flush of Richardsonian sentimentality were followed by selections from the unpublished epics of Barlow and Dwight, by a portion of Trumbull's *M'Fingal,* and number of dramatic scenes from *The School for Wives, False Delicacy, The Merchant of Venice, Venice Preserved, Tale of a Tub, Cato, I Henry IV, Henry VIII, Hamlet,* and *Julius Caesar.* Two addresses of Congress, a brief extract from Thomas Paine's

Crisis, No. V, and Thomas Day's letter on Negro slavery concluded the volume.

This Reader was constructed more to illustrate Webster's faith in dialogue reading as a teaching device than to implant patriotic principles. In his Preface Webster explained the purpose of including so many dramatic selections by saying: "It is found by experience that Dialogues, as bearing a near resemblance to the common talk of children, are the best calculated to prevent or break the ill habits of reading, and to teach them an easy unaffected pronunciation."

In 1787, while Webster was teaching in the Episcopal Academy in Philadelphia, he revised Part III of the *Institute,* exactly doubling the size to 372 pages and altering the title to indicate its new content: *An American Selection of Lessons in Reading and Speaking. Calculated to improve the Minds and refine the Taste of Youth. And also to instruct them in Geography, History, and Politics of the United States. To which is prefixed, Rules in Elocution, and Directions for expressing the principal Passions of the Mind.* Patriotism radiated from the new selections, these having been collected to spread enthusiasm for the new government for which a Constitution was being framed while the book was in press. Here were Warren's and Hancock's orations on the Boston Massacre, four addresses of Congress, the Declaration of Independence, Washington's Farewell Orders to the Army and Circular Letter, and equally stirring selections from the speeches of Governor William Livingston, Hugh Henry Brackenridge, Governor Edward Rutledge, and Joel Barlow. Two poems by Philip Freneau, "Columbus to Ferdinand" and "On General Washington," replaced the selections from Dwight's and Barlow's epics, then published. Among the dialogues added was "Hunks and Blithe," a comic skit on the problem of parental dictation in marriage, written by Mr. Andrus of Yale in 1776.

Webster wrote more than fifty pages of new material for the book. He prepared histories of the discovery and settlement of North America and of the Revolutionary War. To the latter he added "Authentic Accounts of the Principal Battles" from Bunker Hill to the capture of Cornwallis. For the first time in the United States a school book recorded the history of the events which led to the formation of the nation.

Another innovation was the inclusion of a brief section on the geography of the United States. After the terms of science, such as island, cape, bay, strait, gulf stream, etc., were defined, Webster described the geography of the thirteen states. Jedidiah Morse, a graduate of Yale in 1783, had imbibed a nationalistic ardor equal to Webster's, and when Part I of the *Institute* appeared, Morse began the compilation of a small *Geography;* this book was published in 1784. In no sense was Webster competing with Morse; if anything, the pages in *An American Selection* served to call attention to the imperfect geographical accounts in atlases and gazetteers of British origin, and to the superior merit of Morse's work. Evidently the latter felt this way about it, for in 1789 in *The American Geography* he used a thirty-six-page History of the United States by Webster. When Morse's school Geography attained almost universal adoption in 1795, Webster removed the geographical passages from his Reader.

Webster also included in *An American Selection* his lecture, entitled "Remarks on the Manners, Government, Laws, and Domestic Debt of America," a forceful argument on the importance of developing national manners and a national language.

Few books for school use have carried quite as heavy a burden of patriotic precept as *An American Selection* (Philadelphia, 1787); at no other time, probably, has it been as important that such a doctrine be taught. Realizing fully what he was doing, Webster placed on the title page a motto from Mirabeau: "Begin with the infant in the cradle; let the first word he lisps be Washington." Webster knew these books would be taken home by the children, whose parents would listen patiently and well while these sentiments were pronounced in study and practice. Their wholesome effect would never be erased.

An American Selection was too obviously prepared to meet an emergency; as the years passed, each bringing new problems, the enthusiasm for the war thoughts waned. New books, culling the flowers of poetry and sentiment, replaced Webster's Reader, which lost the field by 1800, although it was reprinted as late as 1816. Caleb Bingham's *American Preceptor* (1794) forged to the front and maintained undisputed sway for a generation. Webster's affection for his book must have prevented his making alterations, for in 1835 he reprinted it, with some changes, "to instruct our youth in what belongs to this country." Here illustrated is the sincerity with which Webster labored in advancing the interest of his country.

Between 1786 and 1790 Webster prepared abridgments of or introductions to the three parts of the *Institute,* little kindergarten works designed to help children over the rough and thorny path to correct spelling and grammar. The first of these, a new edition of *The New-England Primer,* that earliest of our textbooks, was seen through the press by Timothy Pickering in Philadelphia in 1786. This homely, pious pamphlet, with its grotesque woodcuts and doggerel illustrations, had remained a favorite textbook since its first printing in 1690. Webster's revision involved almost a whole new text and new selections, and, although he wished to "instruct youth in the knowledge of reading and religion," he softened or removed many of the harsh Calvinistic doctrines of the original book. Thus, for the customary illustration of the first letter of the alphabet,

Title page of Webster's edition of *The New-England Primer*.

Two pages from Webster's edition of *The New-England Primer*.

In Adam's Fall
We sinned all,

he substituted

A   Was an Apple-pie made by the cook.

This succulent beginning must have invited every youngster
to proceed through the other letters, illustrated with equally
unorthodox sentences:

B   Was a Boy that was fond of his book.
N   Was a Noddy, as dull as an ass.
S   Was a Simpleton, ready to cry.
T   Was a Tell-tale and hiss'd out of school.

Four little stories taught just such morals as Juliana
Smith had disdained. A boy went into the water at Goshen,
nearly drowned, and when withdrawn, "He said he was
sorry he had not minded his parents." Another boy fell
asleep in a field while weeding beets and a mouse bit his
toe. "He remembered his father had told him that a mouse
would never bite a boy when he was at work." The other
stories illustrated the wickedness of truancy and the blessed
rewards of industry. The Shorter Catechism, Watts's Cradle
Hymn, and prayers concluded the thirty-six-page book. No
copy of this issue has been found, but other editions, as late
as 1801, can be seen.

The second little book was *An Introduction to English
Grammar*, an abridgment of the *Grammar*. Early in 1790
Webster revised this primer and gave it the title, *Rudiments of English Grammar*. Except for his wise injunction
to teachers that children must learn their native tongue by
ear and by use and not by rules, this booklet might seem
no different from any other small grammar. But at the
end he added "A Federal Catechism," the first simple explanation for the use of schools of the newly adopted American Constitution and of the working of our government.

By virtue of this work, Webster became the first American teacher of civics.

Later in 1790 Webster compiled *The Little Reader's Assistant*, the backbone of which was the *Rudiments*. He included also twenty-two short narratives, tales simply written in explanation of incidents from American life and history, or illustrative of humanitarian motives. Here were included the stories of Columbus, John Smith and Pocahontas, the first settlers of New England, and two anti-slavery tales. At the end he placed "A Farmer's Catechizm," in which he stated in a familiar style the most general and most important rules of husbandry, "the *first*, the *best*, and the most *necessary* business of life." Webster's attitude supported that of his time, as his first two questions and answers show:

Q. What is the best business a man can do?
A. Tilling the ground, or farming.
Q. Why is farming the best business?
A. Because it is the most necessary, the most healthy, the most innocent, and most agreeable employment of men.

These six small textbooks, the three parts of *A Grammatical Institute of the English Language* and the three introductory pamphlets, played so formative a part in the development of a unified American culture and national spirit, that it is difficult to overrate their contribution. As it has been stated, Webster was first to insist upon nationality in language, manners, and education, and first to prepare books to teach children these principles. In the course of his work, he was first to prepare a system of education, and first to write and teach American history and civics. This contribution alone would merit a position of primacy in our educational history. But Webster's influence was more far-reaching.

During the infant years of our national existence, European ideology laid a strangle hold upon our political action. America tetered between England and France, our leaders wondering with which nation, both diplomatically friendly but actually hostile to our shipping, might best serve our needs. During this shuffling indecision the American merchantmen were harassed, seamen were impressed into foreign service, and whole cargoes were rifled or taken. Voices cried loudly for alliances, Hamilton leading the Anglophiles and Jefferson the Francophiles. Webster stood with Washington between the two antagonistic groups, demanding neutrality and a self-assertive independence. Without intruding his opinions upon students, Webster cleverly included in his Reader such passages from the Addresses of Congress or from the writings of Washington, Jefferson, and Barlow as would establish his point. Even in the Grammar and Speller, where opportunity might seem to have been lacking for nationalistic propaganda, Webster managed to slip in footnotes or prefatory statements.

This unified series of textbooks effectually shaped the destiny of American education for a century. Imitators sprang up by the dozen, and each echoed Websterian nationalism. The word "American" became indispensable in all textbook titles; all vied in patriotic eloquence. Jedidiah Morse, whose nationalistic teachings are second only to Webster's, adopted the tone of his mentor, and for a time they worked together, adopting as their motto an American interpretation of Middleton's remark, "The children of ancient Rome were obliged to learn the laws of the twelve tables by heart." Nicholas Pike prefaced his *Arithmetic* (1788) with a typical Websterian statement: "As the United States are now an independent Nation, it was judged that a System [of Arithmetic] might be calculated more suitable to our Meridian, than those heretofore published."

In belles lettres the effect of these books was no less electrical. Webster first published selections from budding epic writers, first gave rules of versification to children, and first let it be known that genius did reside on the western shore of the Atlantic. Bright-eyed youngsters formed ambitions for literary excellence as they conned Webster's pages. Juiceless as these six little books may seem to have been, they formed the wellspring of our rising national literature.

Webster believed his great gift to America was his successful fostering of a consciousness of nationality. Every school child who used his books felt that America was a unique land, capable of going its own way and of achieving primacy among nations. This idea Webster stressed in his lectures and other books, and it is true that he did more than any other man to unify America.

But most important was Webster's contribution to America's feeling of democratic idealism. He early saw the relationship between popular education and popular sovereignty. With logical democratic reasoning he argued that popular speech and idiom were correct and should be the basis of textbook instruction. Just as the popular will should rule in speech, so should it rule in Church and State. Although Webster's later conservatism led him to modify the doctrine of popular sovereignty, his first books fostered the idea both by implication and by direct statement. Our first teacher was our first democrat.

CHAPTER VI

STEADYING THE SHIP OF STATE

HARTFORD, CONNECTICUT, in 1783 was a little village of three hundred houses, sprawling along the west bank of the Connecticut River. Ancient trees, like the gigantic "Charter Oak," shaded the streets and lanes. Farming was still the chief occupation of the twenty-five hundred residents, although shipping, manufacture, and trading busied many men. As the gateway to the upper reaches of the Connecticut Valley, Hartford did a thriving business with the people of Western Massachusetts and Vermont, and with the thousands of immigrants who at the close of the War moved up the river, stopping at Hartford for supplies, and who pushed deep into the northern wilderness. Unexpected wealth poured into the city; businessmen like Colonel Jeremiah Wadsworth, who imported ship loads of merchandise and cattle, developed large fortunes. A boom town, Hartford quickly grew self-conscious, drawing tight social lines between the traders and the farmers, and creating an aristocratic class feeling. An animated program of social activity kept high heels clicking every night of the week. Buckram as these burghers were, they held memories of a noble past and treasured their Revolutionary heroes.

In returning to his home community from Goshen, Webster rented a room with John Trumbull, now profitably busy in the practice of law. The author of *M'Fingal* took pride in the young pedagogue and helped him become established. Together they worked over mutual plans, Trumbull collaborating with Webster to the extent of writing a chapter on versification for the Grammar. Webster begged Trumbull to compose an epic, but the jealous mistress, law, left the satirist too weary for extended poetic composition. Oliver Wolcott, Jr., classmate at Yale, introduced Webster into the younger, fashionable set. Together they traveled about to dances, courting beautiful, aloof young ladies. The farmer lad, profiting by his experiences at Sharon and Goshen, affected the dandy, paying much attention to sartorial splendor.

Hartford was a friendly town. Everywhere Webster found a pleasant welcome awaiting him. At the literary clubs, and at the meetings of the young lawyers, who perfected themselves in speaking or discussed hypothetical cases while awaiting business, Webster served as guest critic. He looked in at the courts, watched the work of the Legislature, took part in the town meetings, and quietly made his presence felt in the community. Bumptious as he was supposed to be, he restrained any inclination to shine or to push himself forward.

Anxiously he questioned whether he should attempt to establish himself in the law. Litigations were numerous, but fees small. Only those young men who could depend upon support from home or from another business, managed to appear successful. Joel Barlow, now settled with his pretty wife in Hartford, was trying his hand at many things, at versifying, psalmody, business, publishing, and law, but, cheerful as he was, he could not encourage Webster to hope for gainful professional employment.

Teaching alone offered an opportunity for an income. But he, the author of "the best standard of pronunciation" and a member of the Bar of Connecticut, could not return to a country school. Hopkins Academy, though disgracefully run down, was fully supplied with instructors. Acting upon the advice of his young lawyer friends who needed guidance in speaking, he determined in January, 1784, to open for adults and children an evening Rhetorical School, in which he would offer instruction "in the most elegant modern pronunciation, from the simple sounds that compose words to a just and graceful elocution." Thirty scholars, the required number, failed to turn up, although he stated that "children whose parents are in necessitous circumstances, and especially orphans, shall be instructed gratis."

Undaunted by this failure, Webster used his time to advantage in reading language, law, and history. Books were his passion; while occupied with them, his unemployed state was forgotten. His own textbooks, still in the process of preparation, took much time and gave him the satisfaction of having a kind of settled occupation. Public questions, too, invited his pen and frequently relieved the tedium of study. To *The Freeman's Chronicle,* a Hartford newspaper owned by Bavil Webster, his cousin, he contributed (September 22–November 10, 1783) his "Observations on the Revolution of America," adding to the original four papers two more to condemn established religion and to assert "that the purity of the religion and the peace of society depend on giving an unlimited indulgence to all sectaries." At the next session of the Legislature, a toleration act was passed, granting each Connecticut citizen the right to prove his affiliation with a nonestablished church and thereby to secure release from paying rates to the Congregational Church. As a publicist Webster early learned the art of proper timing; no doubt these articles contributed much to the legislators' desire to grant this type of toleration.

For six months, from August, 1783, to March, 1784, he wrote the substance of a volume in a successful effort to put down a dangerous faction.

In the summer of 1783 the thrifty inhabitants of Connecticut began to count the cost of the War; certain expenditures seemed exorbitant, and some unnecessary. Particularly dis-

tasteful was the grant to the officers of the American Army,
a pension intended to indemnify the losses they sustained
while receiving pay in depreciated currency. Congress made
a grant of half pay for life in 1778, but uneasiness among
some of the northern states led the officers to propose
settling for a certain sum in gross or full pay for a term of
years. Congress consented to make the exchange and gave
five years' full pay; the army accepted these conditions just
before disbanding.

As soon as the dangers of war were over, some persons,
suspicious characters who had been silent in the contest or
had opposed the Revolution, declaimed against Congress
and the grant. A general campaign of defamation aroused
the populace; town meetings assembled to pass denunciatory
resolutions. Congress and the bold patriots of the state
were represented as tyrants, and the people as in danger of
slavery. The real purpose of the agitators was not to procure a redress of grievances so much as to change the per-
sonnel of the Connecticut Senate, then named the Council.
A list of nominees was secretly handed about, in which the
best men were omitted and doubtful characters put in. In-
flammatory publications, distributed throughout the state,
called on the people to send representatives to a convention
and to appeal against the law.

The first convention assembled at Middletown on September 8, 1783. Although a majority of towns sent representatives, the meeting was adjourned until September 20,
when more than fifty towns, representing five-sevenths of
the state, sent remonstrants. The burden of the complaint
fell chiefly on Congress, but a discussion of local dissatis-
factions evoked condemnation of the Governor and Council.
The efficient and wise Governor was Jonathan Trumbull,
whom Washington affectionately addressed as Brother
Jonathan, a term even now used to denominate any "steady
habit" Yankee. Trumbull's long, unmarred record of service

did not exempt him from virulent abuse. Malcontents attempted to storm the citadel of government.

Webster, quick to scent trouble and facile with his pen,
addressed through *The Connecticut Courant* a series of
letters, under the pseudonym "Honorius," to "the discontented people of Connecticut." In the first, August 26, 1783,
he carefully explained the nature of the debt occasioned by
the War, the amount of annual interest, and the small proportion commutation would bear to this expense. A week
later he supported, as a plan of finance which would discharge the whole public debt without burdening the people, the proposal of Congress that a national impost be
placed upon imported articles, and that this income be
ticketed specifically for the payment of the interest and principal on bonds issued to cover the whole war debt. Such
action would pool the states' debts and remove inequalities
created in Connecticut, New Jersey, and North Carolina,
states which did not enjoy much direct international trade.

The dissatisfaction of the people arose not so much from
the probable expense of commutation, Webster thought, as
from relaxed morality and industry, and from hot-headed ignorance. Of the last type of mind, he wrote: "Nay should
God Almighty place Gabriel at the head of our affairs, they
would find fault with his administration, especially if it
were rigorously just—they would wrangle him out of office
and choose some unprincipled demagogue." Expensive habits,
a sham morality which closed its eyes to gambling and dishonesty, and a lack of public virtue—these qualities, Webster said, characterized the remonstrants. He hurled the
old taunt at them: "The inhabitants of New England have
the character of being knaves and hypocrites." He ridiculed
the complaint against lawyers, saying that the number had
increased not because of the baseness of that profession,
but because of the people's unwillingness to pay debts until
duns, writs, lawyers, and courts forced them to do it. In

one year six, seven, and even eleven hundred actions, ninety-five percent of which were for only five or six pounds, had been brought in one county court. Webster reprobated such "vile, impolitic manners."

In January, 1784, Webster again busied himself "combating the Convention, a nest of vipers, disturbing the tranquillity of government to answer selfish purposes." To the *Courant* he wrote: "I am no friend to the half-pay establishment. I wish the idea had never been started in America. At the same time, I conceive that the securities given to the army, however they may amount to great sums on paper, are scarcely an equivalent for their services, or a just discharge of the original contract." And he added, "Every attempt to keep alive the present jealousies, to foment divisions and create new animosities, must be treason against the State."

A third meeting of the Convention was adjourned and a fourth called for March 16. Webster in February again returned to the contest, this time obliquely with a series of four articles under the title, "Policy of Connecticut," an elucidation of the political and commercial interests of Connecticut and a renewed plea for a national impost. In these he retraced his earlier arguments, designed to end discord, promote harmony, and inculcate the idea that Congress and the State officials had done the best possible under the circumstances. The debt had become the great political question of the day. The value of the confederation as a band of union among thirteen independent states was involved in it. The failure of the proposal by Congress would be, in effect, the failure of the confederation. A new note, therefore was sounded in these essays, a unifying idea which Webster would develop and stress during the coming years.

Danger lay ahead for the nation in these civil commotions; the shocks of repeated assaults upon Congress would inevitably lead to a breakup of the Federation, for the loose compact of States allowed Congress authority only to request and not to compel united action. Not a weaker tie, but a stronger one was required. "The dignity, safety, and happiness of America," Webster asserted, "are inseparably connected with a union of all the States." At first he thought that nothing was wanted to secure our perpetual union but "a strict adherence to the spirit of the confederation," and "wisdom and policy in calling forth the resources of the country." This general proposition, obviously inadequate, led him to formulate a clearer theory of union. Needed was "a federal head, vested with powers sufficient to compel any particular State to comply with the measures that are adopted by the majority of States." Rhode Island had passed a State impost law, while refusing to authorize a national impost; this act practically nullified the union, for Congress could advise but not compel action. From this incident Webster drew his conclusion that a stronger federal government was essential to the political success of the American states. Practical wisdom, not theory, determined his political and economic, as well as his educational, ideas.

Webster inveighed against State imposts because they placed Connecticut in an unfair position. Most of its foreign purchases were transferred to coastwise and inland carriers at Boston, Newport, and New York. Consequently, Massachusetts, Rhode Island, and New York secured an income from Connecticut, a state denied this revenue. But other prudential considerations demanded a single national impost. Western land could be purchased only by co-operative effort on the part of all the States or by the Federation, and coast guards, whose general usefulness would equal that of the soldiers acting as frontier guards, could only be employed and paid by the national government. The ruinous state of American trade arose not so much from a post-war

business recession, he thought, as from unwise local legislation.

In comparison with greater national problems, commutation dwindled to an almost unimportant matter, and Webster
concluded (March 16, 1784):

> Commutation is an evil—but weighed against the consequences of
> refusing to comply with the recommendations of Congress—weighed
> against the importance of the union—the importance of securing the
> friendship of other States—the importance of fulfilling our engage-
> ments—the importance of regulating and extending our commerce
> —weighed against these considerations, *commutation* dwindles into
> nothing, a mere *cypher* that stands for nothing.

The convention of March 16, through William Worth-
ington, clerk, circulated a summary statement of grievances
(commutation, excessive power claimed by Congress, exorbitant salaries of national officers, and the Cincinnati)
and called on Mr. Policy [Webster] to explain why other
states had done nothing on the general imposts. Webster
gratified their wishes by heaping ridicule upon their statement, answering it (April 6, 1784) point by point with facts
and with remarks like "What a vile mixture of misrepresentation and falsehood is this!"; "What an insidious attempt to play upon the ignorance, the passions and the interests of the multitude"; and "Rogues only dread the
execution of justice."

Although one critic had called Webster "a sneaky, snaky,
fainthearted Whig," and another had written that Web-
ter's "dirty squibs will avail . . . no more than spitting
against the north wind," the clamor ceased, and the convention men were defeated. In the next election, although
Governor Trumbull retired from public life because of his
great age, the Council and congressmen favorable to commutation were returned to office; and the Legislature on
May 19 passed a bill empowering Congress to lay and collect an impost as had been requested. So highly were Web-

ster's efforts regarded that the Governor thanked him in
person, and a member of the Legislature, Stephen Mix
Mitchell, declared that Webster had "done more to allay
popular discontent and support the authority of Congress
at this crisis than any other man."

Webster's joy in the passage of the Impost Act found
expression in a note to the *Courant*, May 25, 1784, in which
he reiterated the need for an effective union of the States.
"Every well wisher to a *Continental* union," he wrote, substituting "continental" for the usual "Federal," "must feel,
every hour, the necessity of a *continental* head—The necessity of a harmonious concert in *continental* measures—the
absolute necessity of *unanimity* and *vigour* in all our federal
operations." He reprobated the "paltry jealousy" manifested toward Congress and the selfishness of the States
refusing to comply with salutary national measures, because these two manifestations of disunity would "end in
the creation of some compulsory power on the continent
which shall oblige the States to act in concert; or what is
more to be dreaded, terminate in a total dissolution of our
federal government." Webster would reiterate this argument many times, knowing that the art of teaching has for
one of its principles, "Repeat your leading idea often."

Most teachers, even so-called "born teachers," excel in
digesting, clarifying, simplifying, and restating the ideas
of others; originality and insight are not their endowment.
Webster, unlike these useful catalytic agents, saw the problems of society, formulated his own conclusions, and proceeded to teach the public what to think, knowing that an
aroused public will compel a democratically elected legislative body to follow its wishes. The pen was his natural
weapon, and when he touched it to paper, a clear flow of
fact, united with a vein of vitriolic sententiousness, attracted
attention and wore down opposition. It was against the
rock wall of prejudice that Webster successfully flung his

strength; his textbook prefaces, his early essays on education, and his writings on politics followed the formula of combating opposition by calling it "prejudice." In this latest article on the need for "continental union" he added the Cassandra quality: he became a prophet of misfortune, insinuating that evils would result from a failure to follow his advice. Not until Bache and Cobbett taught America the art of making prose crackle and flare like lightning, did Webster have an equal in polemic writing. Heavy-handed as he was at times, he managed with dexterity the tricks of Swift and Junius.

Webster was always teaching the public something, an editorial, monitorial urge crowding his brain and forcing his pen to write articles on every conceivable subject. Thus, when the objection to new taxes was at its height, Webster investigated means by which Connecticut could increase its income. The Convention over, he added two papers to the "Policy of Connecticut" to show how Connecticut's extensive imports might be balanced with exports, and how, as a result, specie might again come out of hiding and prosperity spread its cheer through the whole state. The first article (May 18, 1784) advised the union of merchants into bodies corporate, by which means an extensive capital could give superior advantages in purchasing and in marketing produce. The second, published a week later, stressed the need for the development of home-owned carriers and for the inauguration of a vigorous business policy of exporting native products: pine for masts, flaxseed, potash, meat, and fish. On this excursion into practical economics Webster entered congenial territory, for business and law are inextricably intertwined. Adam Smith's *Wealth of Nations* had become one of his most frequently reread books.

Although Webster was engaged in serving the best interests of the State and the Confederation, his mocking criticisms had embittered the members of the Convention. Few secrets could be concealed successfully in Connecticut; a system of petty snooping in the mail and spying in printing offices made public to interested persons all that was written in confidence or under the shield of anonymity. Suspicion pointed to John Trumbull first, and then to Webster. Immediately the truth was ascertained, attacks appeared against Webster's *Institute* with the object of ridiculing it out of existence. In a published letter, dated Hartford, July 22, 1784, Webster ascribed the origin of "Dilworth's Ghost" to the anti-convention articles, which had made him "some personal enemies, who acknowledge my influence by seeking revenge. But," he concluded, "if I have been in the least degree instrumental in effecting a revolution of sentiment in a single state that was embroiled with faction, the thought will give me happiness on the verge of eternity— while the sacrifice of a few friendships and the loss of pecuniary advantages will be deemed trifles beneath the notice of . . . your most obedient humble servant."

Webster had got his name before the public now as an author of textbooks and as a political writer; he was making his presence felt in Hartford and in the state at large. Glimpses of his numerous activities become clear after January 1, 1784, because on that day he began jotting into a brief diary his daily activities. He had removed to the residence of Captain John Skinner, but on July 8 he took rooms with Dr. Fish in order to be nearer Trumbull, with whom he began to review the principles of law. Parties enlivened his evenings. In February he "rode to Wethersfield with the Ladies, who reminded us of the mile-stones and bridges." The next evening, on a ride to East Windsor, "Mile-stones and bridges almost totally neglected." There is no need to say why. Later he wrote of "a multitude of pretty faces," but he added jauntily, "My heart is my own." His diary contains a census of the eligible maidens of Hartford, but there is no indication that he seriously thought of marriage.

He had turned Philosopher, as he called himself, and he occasionally set down some of his observations. The warm beauty of spring occasioned this soliloquy:

> April 4 [1784]. At home. Read a little, had some company, and visited the Ladies in the evening as usual. If there were but one pretty Girl in town, a man could make a choice—but among so many! one's heart is pulled twenty ways at once. The greatest difficulty, however, is that after a man has made *his* choice, it remains for the Lady to make *hers*.

Three weeks earlier he had been quite unwell. His mind turned to the orthodox teachings of his youth for a plausible explanation of his miseries. Doubtful though he was of the Church, he found comfort in Calvinistic fundamentals:

> March 13th [1784]. At home very unwell. The little indispositions of life are essential to happiness. Uninterrupted felicity never fails to cloy; indeed there is very little pleasure without preceding pain. The author of the universe seems to have framed it with a view to give his creatures an opportunity to exert virtues, which could not exist without natural and moral evil. If it were impossible for mankind to sin, there would be no virtue in preserving their rectitude. If there were no pain, misery, misfortune, or danger to which they could be exposed, patience, humanity, fortitude, and prudence would be empty names. The result of this doctrine is to teach us a peaceable submission to the evils of life and calm acquiescence in the disposition of the divine providence which suffers no more evils to take place in the system than are necessary to produce the greatest possible good.

Two weeks later, however, he remarked on an excellent sermon, "It is easier to hear than to remember and practice." In April the "absurd institution" of the Half-way Covenant aroused his wrath: "Into what inconsistencies are mankind led by rigid, illiberal tenets! A *half member* of Christ's Church is an *oddity* in religion. Scripture knows no such thing, and common sense rejects the idea as the creature of superstition." On April 20, 1785, a day of fasting, he commented: "We must fast regularly every year, whether we are plunged in calamities or overwhelmed with the blessings of heaven! Strange superstition! the effect of custom."

The writings of Locke, Hoadley, Rousseau, Price, Priestley, and Furneax, who had ventured out of the beaten path of prejudice, had left Webster with scant sympathy for the hard traditionalism of the Congregational Church, its stranglehold on the government, and its uncompromising insistence on worn-out beliefs. He did not, however, relish the conclusions of the Deists, whose discoveries, he smilingly remarked, "had escaped all the divines from the apostles down to Mr. Hume." Webster's home training, his delight in attending church and in singing in the choir, kept him from straying from the faith in which he was educated; his intellectual dissatisfaction with New England Calvinism never dislodged the fundamental religious concepts he acquired as a child.

Webster opened a law office in the summer of 1784, but few clients entered his door. On August 21 he settled an action between J. Caldwell and Thomas Bird of Salisbury. Three months later he appeared in court, as defense attorney in an action for debt. On the next day, November 25, he successfully pleaded the case of one Bidwell against Abiel Wilson before Webster's father, who sat as Justice; both must have been happy in the son's first legal victory. In January, 1785, his eloquence at Wethersfield saved Isaac Mix an interest charge on a debt of twenty-eight years' standing. On February 1 he returned victorious in his first case before a jury. On April 15, 1785, he was admitted to practice in the Superior Court. Short, indeed, are these annals of a country lawyer, but Webster's ability was demonstrated.

Webster's brief experience at the bar brought clearly to

his attention the defective nature of Connecticut's judicial system. It was the custom to choose the judges of the courts annually and to elect the same men to positions in the legislative or executive departments of the state. Against these two "absurdities" and "gross errors" in government, Webster wrote a letter to the *Courant*, April 26, 1785, declaring that annual elections rendered judges "timid and cautious in executing the laws" and "unwilling to offend a jury even by a wise decision," and that the appointment of the same men to make and to execute the laws offered opportunities for the defeat of justice. Two thirds of the lower house and all the upper house at this time were magistrates or justices of the peace. These men had the right of making laws in General Assembly, and at home these same men were the principal executive officers of their own laws. "Of all absurdities," Webster jeered, "this is the greatest."

One commission came to the young publicist rather than to the lawyer. William Judd, General Parsons, Webster's father, and many other Connecticut citizens had formed a stock company for the development of the Connecticut claim to the land along the North Branch of the Susquehanna River at Wyoming, within the present bounds of Pennsylvania. In 1754 the native Indians sold their rights to the company, but, when settlers arrived the following year, the faithless savages drove out the newcomers. Pennsylvania also claimed the land, so that when a permanent settlement was made, a conflict arose as to the legitimacy of the Connecticut title. In 1784, after Pennsylvania had engaged in a series of illegal actions, including a barbarous use of military force, to dispossess the settlers, title in the land remained undetermined. Congress had intervened, but in a matter involving the rights of two States, safety lay in tabling the matter. Judd asked Webster to prepare a statement of Connecticut claims; this he did between November, 1784, and January, 1785. Seven articles, published concurrently

in the *Courant* and *The American Mercury*, beginning
January 3, 1785, presented the history of the grants, the
events in the controversy, and the larger problem of western
land involved in this dispute. So far as he could, Webster
restrained his pen, for he was writing to present facts and
not to arouse antagonism against Pennsylvania. Occasionally
a phrase slipped in, telltale of the animus he felt; of the
Pennsylvania Legislature's action in repealing in August,
1783, an Act of April, 1783, by which suits against the inhabitants of Wyoming were stayed, he wrote: "The foregoing resolution . . . must be considered a wanton sport-
ing with the sacred rights of men—a public mockery of law
and justice sanctioned by legislative formality."

Angry though he was at a state government which had
been duped by designing land-grabbers, Webster saw more
to the problem than his employers did. They wanted their
rights confirmed or their investment returned. This was
natural. But Webster, interested in the Union, asked himself several fundamental questions. If all the states rush
to claim the unseated lands within the limits of their over-
lapping, carelessly defined colonial grants, will not a civil
war arise on a greater, more terrible scale than that at
Wyoming? If a large state begins a campaign to extend its
borders, what power can stop the aggressor from conquer-
ing and absorbing its neighbors? The United States, then
spelled without the capitals, consisted of thirteen federated
republics, each of which denied the authority of Congress
to dictate in one or another matter. The Union was a cobweb
made by thirteen spiders who rent and tore it in jurisdic-
tional squabbles. Congress was debating its answer on the
Connecticut-Pennsylvania controversy. What, asked Webster finally, can happen to the Union in case the land question becomes acute?

The western lands, he answered (February 15, 1785),
might be apportioned among the states, and from the sale

or rental thereof might come the resources for the payment of the state and national debts, and the funds for the future support of government. But, he added, this act would perpetuate jealousies and produce dissensions between the states: "Such a separation of interests would eventually destroy our union."

He suggested as a remedy for this possible evil that all the states cede their claims to unlocated lands to the United States for the common benefit of all. A part of them might be sold to sink the domestic debt, and a part might be reserved as a demesne land or perpetual patrimonial estate to defray the necessary expenses of the national government. Since this endowment fund would be equally the property of every citizen, Webster thought it would form a strong, permanent bond of union.

The danger involved in a confederation of large and small states could be removed only by the resignation on the part of every state of all desire for superiority or dictatorship, for, said Webster sagely, "The safety and harmony of the whole depend on a proper equality in the several individuals." The Union could be preserved only if "some common interest" could "overpower the influence of the jealousies and clashing interests of particular states."

Noah Webster was not the first man to express the opinion that a union of the states was necessary under a compact more firm and compelling than that of the Confederation. As early as 1780 Alexander Hamilton pointed out defects arising from state sovereignty, and a year later he wrote "The Continentalist," advising the transfer to Congress of certain powers. In May, 1781, Pelatiah Webster published a pamphlet in which he urged the calling of a Continental Convention whose duty would be the formulation of a Constitution. The New York Legislature in the summer of 1782, at the instance of General Philip Schuyler, passed a resolution declaring that the Confederation was defec-

tive and that a general convention should be called to revise and amend the original articles. Alexander Hamilton,
in referring to the New York resolution, told Congress,
April 1, 1783, that he wished to see such a general convention take place. Meantime Pelatiah Webster had published in February, 1783, his pamphlet, entitled *A Dissertation on the Political Union and Constitution of the Thirteen
United States, of North-America: Which is necessary to
their Preservation and Happiness.* The author urged the
necessity of a more efficient national government, one which
would vest in Congress a power to control the several
states in general concerns, and to carry all their decisions
into effect. A bicameral legislature was proposed in this
pamphlet, the first published proposition for a more efficient
government. R. H. Lee and James Madison agreed in
correspondence that a convention was desirable. General
Washington, who had suffered from the cruel delays involved in the dependence of Congress on the voluntary and
simultaneous compliance of the States, as required in the
Articles of Confederation, remarked in his Circular Address
to the Governors of the States, June, 1783, on the need for
"a supreme power to regulate and govern the general concern of the Confederate Republic." Many men remarked,
but few did anything. Simeon Baldwin, a tutor at Yale,
expressed the popular opinion in a letter to James Kent,
dated April 24, 1785: " 'Tis dangerous meddling with constitutions; ripping up the foundation of Government is hazardous; it is better to experience many inconveniences than to
attempt it. . . . Our great study will be to preserve what
we have obtained; 'tis true it is capable of greater perfection,
but I have but little idea of its ever taking place."

Noah Webster disliked nothing more than supine acceptance of imperfect present conditions when a little thought
and action might bring improvement. In March, 1784,
he had demanded "a federal head, vested with powers

sufficient to compel any particular State to comply with the measures that are adopted by the majority of the States." During the succeeding months he tested that proposition by every problem facing the government; each time an unmistakable answer supported his opinion. He determined, therefore, to do for the nation what he had done for Connecticut: he would teach the people their duty and by popular demand secure mass action. This plan fitted into his educational ambitions, because his proposals for the adoption of a national standard in language depended for success upon a nationwide use of his textbooks. These he would have to take to the South, even as he had peddled them through New England, and explain their merits to schoolmasters, preachers, and government officials. With him he would take also, as a kind of *carte de visite*, a statement of his political opinions, climaxed with a plan for a strong national government.

These opinions were written in February, 1785, and published on March 9, 1785, in a forty-eight-page pamphlet, entitled *Sketches of American Policy. Under the following Heads: I. Theory of Government. II. Governments on the Eastern Continent. III. American States; or the principles of the American Constitutions contrasted with those of European States. IV. Plan of Policy for improving the Advantages and perpetuating the Union of the American States.* In later years Webster repudiated the first three sections, because they contained "many chimerical notions respecting a popular government which [he] had imbibed from the writings of Dr. Price and Rousseau." The fourth sketch, of which he always spoke with pride, contained his arguments for a new form of federal government and an outline of it.

Dr. Richard Price, an English nonconformist preacher, whose warm support of the American revolutionists had exposed him to much abuse and some danger, published late in 1784 a pamphlet, entitled *Observations on the Importance of the American Revolution,* in which he expressed the opinion that "next to the introduction of Christianity among mankind, the American Revolution may prove the most important step in the progressive course of human improvement. It is an event which may produce a general diffusion of the principles of humanity and become the means of setting free mankind from the shackles of superstition and tyranny." In vigorous language Price said that the powers of Congress should be enlarged; that "a system of perfect liberty, religious as well as civil" should be established, a system tolerant of all beliefs and opposed to any civil establishment of formularies of faith and worship; that "education ought to be an initiation into candour, rather than into any system of faith"; that large public debts, unequal division of property, foreign trade, imprecatory oaths, and the Negro trade should be feared as sources of public danger, and that these evils should be eliminated as soon as possible. Webster, who read this pamphlet just as he was about to write his own, remarked that many of his own observations, "particularly on religious tests and establishments, and on liberty of discussion," had been anticipated by Price. "If sound sense is to be found on earth," Webster wrote, "it is in his reasoning on this subject."

Webster's first Sketch, "Theory of Government," drawn largely from Rousseau's *Social Contract,* proceeds through a series of definitions to the conclusion that "a representative democracy seems . . . to be the most perfect system that is practicable on earth." The second Sketch briefly analyzes the governments of Europe for the purpose of forestalling the objection "that all kinds of government have been attempted by mankind, and that all the efforts of knowledge and virtue have proved ineffectual to preserve the rights of men from the grasp of ambition or from the gradual approaches of corruption."

The third Sketch shows that the American states, unlike
"the infant situation of all other nations," began their career
"in the most enlightened period of the world" and had "the
science and experience of all nations to direct them in forming plans of government." They had no "hereditary distinctions of rank." They enjoyed "a most liberal plan of
ecclesiastical policy," although "some of them retained
some badges of bigotry," requiring office holders to profess
the Christian religion or "to subscribe certain articles of
faith." This blemish on the state constitutions Webster
wished removed in the belief that, "if there are any human
means of promoting a millennial state of society, the only
means are a general diffusion of knowledge and a free unlimited indulgence given to religious persuasions, without
distinction and without preference." In the general education of youth "the American states are superior to all nations," the institution of schools having arisen naturally
from the genius of American society. Where schools flourish,
there is the firmest security of liberty, because "it is scarcely
possible" to reduce an enlightened people to civil or ecclesiastical tyranny. "Finally, the local position of the states, the
nature of their industry and their tendency to interchange
ideas, together with the freedom of each individual to choose
congenial employment, powerfully influence the American
people, making them more sensible and discerning than
their oversea cousins, forming them to the habit of knowing
and improving their advantages, and thus increasing their
capacity for self government."

The last Sketch, "Plan of Policy," outlines Webster's
"new principles in modeling" a union of the thirteen states
along the lines of the state governments. He reiterates
his earlier statement that "there must be a supreme power
at the head of the union, vested with authority to make
laws that respect the states in general and to compel obedience to those laws." Without such a head the states could

not unite nor could the confederation rise to more than "a ridiculous farce, a burlesque on government." Webster advocated the election of a President and a Congress to represent and govern the thirteen states, the power of the union to reside in Congress in such a manner that no individual state could control or defeat legislation in the way Rhode Island had refused to collect the national impost. Subordinate officers would be held responsible for their acts by higher officers, and the whole executive department would be headed by the President. The heart of Webster's plan lies in this paragraph:

Let Congress be empowered to call forth the force of the continent, if necessary, to carry into effect those measures which they have a right to frame. Let the president, be, *ex officio*, supreme magistrate, clothed with authority to execute the laws of Congress, in the same manner as the governors of the states, are to execute the laws of the states. Let the superintendent of finance have the power of receiving the public monies and issuing warrants for collection, in the manner the treasurer has, in Connecticut. Let every executive officer have power to enforce the laws, which fall within his province. At the same time, let them be accountable for their administration. Let penalties be annexed to every species of mal-administration and exacted with such rigour as is due to justice and public safety. In short, let the whole system of legislation, be the peculiar right of the delegates in Congress, who are always under the control of the people; and let the whole administration be vested in magistrates as few as possible in number and subject to the control of Congress only. Let every precaution be used in *framing* laws, but let no part of the subjects be able to resist the execution. Let the people keep, and *forever keep*, the sole right of legislation in their own representatives; but divest themselves wholly of any right to the administration. Let every state reserve its sovereign right of directing its own internal affairs; but give to Congress the sole right of conducting the general affairs of the continent. Such a plan of government is practicable; and I believe, the only plan that will preserve the faith, the dignity and the union of these American states.

Webster was not so much concerned with outlining a detailed form of government, as he was with imprinting upon the consciousness of his readers the absolute necessity for union. "The American states, so celebrated for their wisdom and valour in the late struggles for freedom and empire, will be the contempt of nations, unless they can unite their force and carry into effect all the constitutional measures of Congress, whether those measures respect themselves or foreign nations." The unpleasant alternative to an efficient union, Webster thought, was a monarchy, a type of government rendered distasteful to Americans by the war propaganda. Indeed, the pamphlet was written to forestall the monarchist movement initiated by some of the military leaders who, in view of the mobs and conventions opposing the half-pay grant, wished "to give a government to this country by force." Joel Barlow, "who was then ripe for the establishment of a monarchy," had been sent to Boston as an agent from Connecticut to formulate plans for concerted action. *Sketches of American Policy* effectively quieted the Connecticut monarchists and also started Joel Barlow on that democratic train of thought which lifted his political writing to an importance far exceeding his tin-plated epic, *The Columbiad*.

In his last pages Webster mentioned several other matters that might serve to confirm the union of the states: universal education; annihilation of local prejudices, particularly the hostility evidenced between the North and the South; removal of interstate taxation and commerce; abolition of slavery; uniformity in state constitutions; granting clergymen the privilege of elective office; and avoidance of servile imitation of the manners, the language, and the vices of foreigners. These ideas he developed in detail in lectures and essays during the next few years as he carried his doctrine from one end of America to the other. Finally, he pleaded for a national spirit: "We ought to generalize our ideas and our measures. We ought not to consider ourselves as inhabitants of a single state only; but as Americans; as the common subjects of a great empire. We cannot and ought not to divest ourselves of provincial attachments, but we should subordinate them to the general interest of the continent; . . . as a citizen of the American empire," an individual "has a national interest far superior to all others."

At the heart of Webster's nationalistic program lay the idea of constantly evolving institutions. Webster derided artificial, aristocratic "hereditary honors," "superiority of birth," and the "two instruments of despotism," a state church and a standing army; he favored popular control through a representative government, the will of the majority always to prevail. As conditions altered, the Constitution should be modified, because "government originates in necessity, and takes its form from the genius and habits of the people." National unity would be achieved through the social control of education in a system which would eradicate "dissocial passions" and prejudices, and through "a growing intercourse" which would "harmonize the views of all the citizens."

Noah Webster grounded his plea for a strongly centralized national government on a humanitarian, perfectionist philosophy. He differed greatly from Pelatiah Webster and Alexander Hamilton. The former wanted a "chamber of commerce" set up as a court of last resort in all matters pertaining to commerce; the latter urged that Congress be given powers of taxation, of disposing of the ungranted land, and of regulating trade. They pleaded for union because thirteen sets of state laws precipitated economic chaos. As a political philosopher Noah Webster defined more clearly than any other writer the American democratic ideal and laid down a practicable program for its attainment.

In the course of events Hamilton's economic argument, expressed no less forcibly and frequently by Webster, may have become more persuasive than Webster's fully rounded philosophical exposition, because the monetary question struck every citizen in his pocketbook; but during the long period of public apathy in 1785 and 1786 Noah Webster alone pressed for the necessity of union. He carried his pamphlet the length of the country from Charleston, South Carolina, to Portsmouth, New Hampshire; in whole or in part it was reprinted in Charleston, Baltimore, Philadelphia, and New York newspapers. He handed a copy to General Washington, who in turn showed it to Madison. Franklin approved it. Nearly every liberally educated American read it and felt the force of its argument. Madison, the prime mover of the Annapolis Convention and self-elected recording secretary of the Constitutional Convention, referred to it in the Preface to his *Debates* as one of the earliest statements he had seen.

Webster claimed as early as 1797 that he made the first written proposal for a form of government similar to that framed by the Constitutional Convention, and he never surrendered his claim to priority. William Cobbett seized upon the claim as a sample of Websterian egomania and made sneering references to it. Chancellor James Kent, however, supported Webster and frequently in conversation insisted on Webster's right to this honor. This question of priority, however, is beside the point, for Pelatiah Webster's pamphlet preceded Noah Webster's. What should not be forgotten is Noah Webster's continuous labor for a national language, a national spirit, and a national union, because in preaching the gospel of Americanism Noah Webster not only was first, but he was unsurpassed in excellent achievement.

CHAPTER VII

ITINERANT LECTURER ON NATIONALISM

THE South was the land of opportunity for Yankee intellectuals after the Revolutionary War, just as the West promised golden soil to the farmer tired of planting cornrows in fields of New England stone. Provision for public education was contemplated in the southern states immediately after independence was won, but the South itself was unable to supply teachers. The dispersed situation of the plantations had prevented the establishment of common schools in the rural districts; the majority of white children had never seen a school. In the larger towns excellent academies existed, but few children enjoyed training. William and Mary College alone kept alight the torch of higher learning in a state where a governor had once thanked God that there were no free schools. South Carolina founded three colleges in one day in 1785, and other states, attentive to the need for an educated leadership, set about developing academies and colleges. Teachers, lawyers, and physicians whose northern opportunities were inauspicious, found in the cotton and tobacco country a ready welcome. Abraham Baldwin, tutor to Yale's Class of 1780 and Joel Barlow's brother-in-law, quickly rose to eminence in Georgia, whose citizens sent him to the Constitutional Convention in 1787.

Webster had planned to go South as early as 1782, when he was unsuccessful in re-establishing his school in Sharon. Now that his textbooks were introduced generally in the New England schools, he determined to tour the remaining states with a view to encouraging the adoption of his

system of education and to securing copyrights. Doubtless
he intended to remain in each section of the nation for an
extended period, so that his enthusiasm for nationality
might appear to be grounded on experience.

On May 2, 1785, Webster left Hartford, a case of books
having been sent ahead to Baltimore. In his trunk he carried
copies of each of his publications for distribution among influential persons he might meet. Like the Yankee peddlers
he had his own type of notions to sell, and he went about the
business energetically. At New Haven he sold an edition of
the grammar to Fitch. In New York he called upon Mrs.
Aaron Burr, whose children he had taught in Sharon, and
from that moment until his return to Hartford thirteen
months later, he associated with the leading citizens in every
town he visited. His diary might serve as the first *Who's
Who in America.*

In Philadelphia he entered the *Institute* with the Prothon-
otary and secured a Pennsylvania copyright. Then he dined
with Pelatiah Webster, a distant kinsman and fellow alum-
nus of Yale, who examined the young schoolmaster's
Sketches with great care, pointing out with friendly interest
the radical tendencies of many passages in the first three
essays. On the thirteenth he set out for Baltimore by stage,
a two-day journey by way of Wilmington over a notoriously
bad road, in which chasms to the depth of six, eight, or ten
feet occurred at numerous intervals. Accidents were so common that the commissioners of the high roads were accused
of maintaining a private understanding with the practitioners
of surgery.

Baltimore in 1785 was a bustling city of nearly ten thousand inhabitants, the number increasing almost daily as ship-
loads of Scots-Irish immigrants hesitated whether to cross
the mountains into Western Pennsylvania or to remain.
John Pendleton Kennedy described the little town as "springing forward with elastic bound," an ambitious, "rollicking

young aspirant for municipal honors—growing rapidly, like a healthy boy, fat and frolicksome, and bursting incontinently out of his clothes in spite of all allowance of seam and selvage." Webster, critical investigator from the North with a full share of Yankee notions of propriety, thought the "healthy boy" lacking in decent behavior on Sunday, when "hundreds of blacks collected for pastime, cracking their whips, elevating kites into the air, breaking each others' heads with clubs, and alarming whole streets with their quarrels."

Unattractive as Baltimore was, compared with the white cleanliness of Hartford, Webster was persuaded that he might well make his southern headquarters here, since no other city equalled it in enterprise. Josiah Blakeley, a Hartford friend, made that point clear. After taking lodgings with Mrs. Sanderson, Webster began his tour of visits, calling first on the merchants to whom he offered the *Institute*, then on John Hayes, publisher of *The Maryland Journal*, to whom was given an advertisement for Webster's books and proposed school. Later he met the Reverend Dr. Patrick Allison, pastor of the "Two Steeple" Presbyterian church and friend of learning. Dr. Henry Moyes, the blind Scotch scientist, was lecturing four times a week in Baltimore at this time. Webster, who had heard of his appearances in other cities, immediately sought an introduction. On the sixteenth Webster listened to a lecture on light, a discussion the more remarkable because of the speaker's infirmity. As Webster listened, the thought came to him that he too might give his message to America in this manner. The idea was novel, but it was worth consideration.

On May 18 he set out for Alexandria, Virginia, but the stage wagon broke down on the rough corduroy road, and he was forced to return to Baltimore and hire a horse. On the following day he rode fifty miles to Alexandria and there laid before Dr. David Stuart, a member of the Vir-

ginia legislature, his wishes for a copyright law. On the
nineteenth he rode to Mt. Vernon.

General Washington greeted the itinerant schoolmaster
cordially, invited him to spend the night there, and to join
the family in playing whist. Webster handed the General a
copy of his *Sketches* and discussed subjects of mutual interest: the need for a strong federal government, abolition of
slavery, agriculture, and education. At dinner Webster
charmed the Washingtons with his witty and sensible remarks, making the general burst into laughter when a serving of molasses was refused with the remark, "We have
enough of that in our country." Later he asked Washington
to write a testimonial of the *Institute,* but the General, though
willing to lend his name to help introduce the work to public
notice, refused to give a certificate because he did not consider himself a competent judge. Washington admired Webster's straightforward manner, and, even though he did not
in this instance comply with Webster's request, he cherished
a pleasant memory of his visitor.

Back again in Baltimore, Webster prepared to visit
Charleston, South Carolina. An overland journey being
out of the question, he engaged passage on the sloop George.
Twenty-seven days were consumed in the voyage, a fa-
tiguing, disagreeable trip marked with alternating squalls
and calm. At Norfolk he went ashore long enough to sell
three dozen of the *Institute* and to learn that "little attention is paid to religion, education, or morals. Gentlemen
are required to send their children to the Northward for
education." He added this comment to his notation: "A
shame to Virginia." The long voyage brought hardship,
for the fresh food supplies were expended, and restrictions
were placed on the use of water. At last the weary passengers disembarked on Sunday, June 26.

Webster admired the beautiful homes and churches of

Charleston, as well as the civic pride which had prevented the erection of buildings along the water front. Thrice he went to church that first day; in the morning he attended St. Michael's, where his New England conscience was shocked by an announcement that Miss Storer would sing a part of Handel's Messiah after the services. "An odd affair this," he remarked, "for a woman to sing for her own benefit; but I put a quarter of a dollar in the plate. She sang well in the modern taste, but I cannot admire it." In the afternoon he went to White Church, where his heart was gladdened by the New England method of psalm singing. In the evening he heard part of a Methodist sermon. Everywhere he was politely received, and he noted with some slight surprise that the people behaved "with great decency in church." The attentiveness and decorum of the Negro worshipers interested him.

Samuel Baldwin took the visitor in hand; they called on General Gadsden, Mayor Hudson, and on the committees which had just founded three colleges. To the Mount Sion Society, sponsors of Winnsborough College, he presented two hundred copies of the Spelling Book and one hundred copies of the Grammar. In his letter of appreciation the secretary of the Society assured Webster that "the production of a native of America at so early a period after her arduous and successful struggle for freedom and independence, must reflect the highest honour on the ability and liberality of the author." The local newspapers carried an equally flowery tribute. The gift was a winning stroke, as Webster remarked to his astonished publishers, and made his books standard in South Carolina.

After an eight day voyage, Webster again was in Baltimore on July 15, anxious to learn how many inquiries had come from parents about his school. The advertisement had run:

To the Inhabitants of Baltimore

It is a very common and a very just complaint that no Branch of Education is neglected so much as the Study of our native Language. From what Cause this Neglect proceeds, it is needless to examine, as the Fact is generally acknowledged and lamented. It is a Fact equally to be regretted, that the Instruction of a School has in many Places been accounted a disreputable Employment, and of course committed to Men of indifferent Characters and Abilities. The Good sense of Baltimore seems to have prevailed over these Prejudices, and it is sincerely to be wished that a total Reformation may be wrought in our Method of Education. The Subscriber, having employed several years in improving the English Grammar, and with very unexpected Success, offers, at the Solicitation of his Friends, to open a School in Baltimore, for the Instruction of young Gentlemen and Ladies in Reading, Speaking and Writing the English Language with Propriety and Correctness. He will also teach Vocal Music in as great Perfection as it is taught in America. He expects as an indispensable condition that the School should be patronized by Families of Reputation, and he himself will be responsible for the success of the undertaking. For particulars inquire of the Subscriber, at his Lodgings at Mrs. Sanderson's, opposite South Street.

May 25, 1785   NOAH WEBSTER

The proposed school was not undertaken, either because an insufficient number of pupils appeared or because Webster decided to turn lecturer. On June 14 William Nixon advertised that he would begin a school; it may be that he balked Webster's school plans. On July 19 Webster, who had promised to "teach vocal music in as great perfection as it is taught in America," announced that he would open a school for teaching vocal music in "a regular scientific method." Dr. Allison had offered his church for the use of the school if the singers would serve as a choir. After six weeks of training and practice, the ten vocalists appeared in the church on September 4. All Baltimore was astonished at Webster's success, and many others joined the class. A notebook lists twenty-one members, each of whom paid twelve shillings for books and a dollar, or seven shillings six pence, for instruction. Rigid discipline caused an occasional rift in the harmony of the choir, a "miff" between a Mr. Hall and the instructor having been notable enough for record in the diary. But Webster had not forgotten the pleasurable stimulus of gratuities; on one occasion he banqueted the group and supplied them with three dozen bottles of wine at a cost of four pounds one shilling. Some of the tuition fee was taken in barter, for he credited Miss Jenny Boyd with three and nine for a pair of gloves and Samuel Owings with a pair of shoes at thirteen and nine, a pair of slippers at twelve and six, and a pair of silk stockings at one pound one shilling.

Meantime he had been attentive to his other interests, watching particularly the political and economic tendencies of the state. The scarcity of cash had become a general complaint throughout the nation; a clamor arose for the issuance of paper money as a relief. Congress had been authorized to coin money, but it had been given no power to purchase bullion. It devolved upon the states to remedy the situation, now made acute by the great amount of specie sent out of the country for foreign goods and by the rapidly increasing population. North Carolina had already issued paper, and Baltimoreans asked that a similar measure be taken in Maryland. Webster, on August 9, explained in an anonymous communication to *The Maryland Journal* the causes of the scarcity and laid down five propositions which "are generally, if not universally, true":

1. That the imports of a country should never exceed its exports.
2. That too great a quantity of cash in circulation is a much greater evil than too small a quantity.
3. That too much money in a commercial country will inevitably produce a scarcity.
4. That the wealth of a country does not consist in cash, but in the produce of industry, viz. in agriculture and manufactures.

5. That in a commercial country, where people are industrious, there can never be, for any long time, a want of cash sufficient for a medium.

These points Webster developed with a simple clarity, applying his principles of economics to the actual situation in Baltimore and counseling the disaffected merchants to cultivate the idle fertile soil where real fortunes lay untouched instead of demanding paper money. His mission to bring about a union of the states was not forgotten; and he used the present occasion, as he would use all others, to repeat his plea: "the want of a proper *union* among the states will render our commerce fluctuating and unprofitable. . . . We shall feel national abuse till Congress are vested with powers sufficient to govern and protect us."

Late in August, his preparation now complete, Webster began writing his dissertations on the English language and on American education. When they were completed, he took them to Dr. Allison and secured permission to read them in the church auditorium. An advertisement announced the five lectures at a price of two shillings each or seven and six for the series, the titles being History of the English Language, Pronunciation, Errors in Pronouncing, Errors in the Use of Words, and General Remarks on Education.

The objects of these lectures [Webster stated] are to point out and reconcile, on established principles, the most material differences of pronunciation and use of words in the American States; to check the errors and abuses which the fashion of another country is palming upon us for propriety; to prove that some of the received rules for the construction of our language are founded on erroneous principles; to show the defects of our present mode of education; to draw the outlines of a system better adapted to our forms of government; and to detach the Americans from that dependence on foreign opinions and manners, which is fatal to efforts of genius in this country.

These lectures, improved from time to time, became the basis of *Dissertations on the English Language* (1789) and to a lesser degree of *A Collection of Essays and Fugitiv Writings* (1790), two important, if neglected, American books. The first lecture on October 19 attracted thirty auditors, the number increasing each night thereafter. At the conclusion of the last he felt that the applause was sufficient to induce him to revise and continue reading the dissertations in other towns.

The lectures expanded, illustrated, and amended the principles enunciated in the three parts of the *Institute*. Webster had engaged in an arduous course of research, reading critically every available work on language. In Horne Tooke's *Diversions of Purley* he thought he found "the true theory of the construction of language," and with this as his yardstick, he measured the conclusions of other writers. He agreed with Tooke that English was a Teutonic language, not a Latin language as was erroneously supposed, and that an investigation of its principles depended upon a knowledge of all the Germanic dialects. With characteristic scholarly energy he studied, as far as American libraries could supply him with books, Anglo-Saxon, Chaucerian Middle English, Danish, and German. False, he discovered, were the conclusions of "the elders in lexicography," whose authority Dr. Samuel Johnson had accepted, and the prescriptive rules of Lowth and other grammarians. Believing it would be an act of folly to accept these erroneous guides, Webster demanded that Americans examine their own usage as the basis for textbook principles in the study of their language. He had listened to the popular speech of every state, and he had reached the conclusion that "the people of America, in particular the English descendants, speak the most *pure English* now known in the world." This statement did not emanate from a mind imbued with unballasted nationalistic enthusiasm; it was founded upon a scientific fact now thoroughly established by recent research. A people migrating from a homeland, insulated, as America was by a wide ocean, from contact with the evolving mother tongue, will preserve almost in purity the speech which was carried with them on their departure.

On this ground Webster maintained that popular usage and the established principles of analogy, not the mistaken guesses of dictionary compilers or the affected elegance of stage players or the pomposity of Johnson and Gibbon, should determine American standards of speech. In defending his choice of the common yeomanry as his standard of usage, Webster gave this eloquent tribute to the "divine average," as Whitman called our common people:

> Let Englishmen notice that when I speak of the American yeomanry, the latter are not to be compared to the illiterate peasantry of their own country. The yeomanry of this country consists of substantial independent freeholders, masters of their own persons and lords of their own soil. These men have considerable education. They not only learn to read, write and keep accounts; but a vast proportion of them read newspapers every week, and besides the Bible, which is found in all families, they read the best English sermons and treatises upon religion, ethics, geography and history; such as the works of Watts, Addison, Atterbury, Salmon, &c. In the eastern states there are public schools sufficient to instruct every man's children, and most of the children are actually benefited by these institutions. The people of distant counties in England can hardly understand one another, so various are their dialects; but in the extent of twelve hundred miles in America, there are very few, I question whether a hundred words, except such as are used in employments wholly local, which are not universally intelligible.

The great number of immigrants pouring into America from all parts of Europe, was creating a number of dialects, whose long continuance would undermine the perfection of American speech. The body of the people, Webster thought, would retain their native peculiarities of speaking, and, for want of schools and proper books, would fall into many inaccuracies and thus imperceptibly corrupt the national language. "Nothing," Webster declared, "but the establishment of schools and some uniformity in the use of books, can annihilate differences of speaking and preserve the purity of the American tongue."

"*Now* is the time," he said in concluding his plea, "and *this* the country, in which we may expect success, in attempting changes favorable to language, science and government. . . . Let us then seize the present moment, and establish a *national* language, as well as a national government. Let us remember that there is a certain respect due to the opinions of other nations. As an independent people, our reputation abroad demands that, in all things, we should be *federal*; be *national*; for if we do not respect *ourselves*, we may be assured that *other nations* will not respect us. In short, let it be impressed upon the mind of every American, that to neglect the means of commanding respect abroad, is treason against the character and dignity of a brave independent people."

A national language, the institution of schools, and a national government—these were the three essential unifying agents that America lacked in 1785. If Alexander Hamilton's narrow views of nationality grant him the title of "The Greatest American," what title can be given to Noah Webster, who, when only twenty-eight years of age and by profession a country schoolmaster, singing master, attorney without portfolio, itinerant lecturer, and philosopher, elevated the thoughts of the whole nation from a preoccupation with local pride and prejudices to the contemplation of the means of national solidarity?

To Timothy Pickering, who wrote a friendly letter approving the *Institute* on the very day Webster began his lectures, Webster defined his purpose in going before the public. He wished to oppose the corruptions introduced into English by the affected pronunciation of actors and by the errors of such scholars as Thomas Sheridan, compiler of a dictionary, and Bishop Robert Lowth, whose grammar Web-

ster had corrected in Part II of the *Institute*. "I shall prove
a troublesome critic," Webster wrote; "My criticisms are
new, and no person here is capable of disproving my remarks." And with that egotism that carried him to success,
he announced, "I have begun a reformation in Language."
But he realized that a country schoolmaster and textbook
maker, somewhat badly abused by critical articles in the
newspapers, had almost insuperable obstacles to overcome;
he put his situation thus: "As I am the first American who
has entered on such important plans, and a youth, as well
as a Yankee, I shall need the countenance of gentlemen of
your established character." He suggested that Pickering
insert a favorable item in the Philadelphia newspapers about
the first American itinerant lecturer and thus pave the way
for a triumphal entry into the City of Brotherly Love.

Virginia having not yet framed a copyright law, Webster
started for Richmond on November 4, this time with the
intention of succeeding. He stopped at Mt. Vernon for letters of introduction and a testimonial, knowing that General
Washington's approval would sweep aside any objections.
A slight petulance mingled with the ink as the General
penned the following note to the Governor and the Speakers of the two houses of the Legislature:

> Mount Vernon, 6th Novr. 1785
> SIR,
>   This Letter will be handed to you by Mr. Webster whom I beg
> leave to introduce to your acquaintance. He is author of a Gram-
> matical Institute of the English Language—to which there are very
> honorable testimonials of its excellence & usefulness. The work must
> speak for itself; & he, better than I, can explain his wishes. I am &c.
>   G. WASHINGTON

Again Webster spent the night with the Washingtons,
enjoying for many hours the conversation of the family.
One incident occurred which showed strikingly the mettle

of the visitor. At dinner Washington mentioned that he was about to dispatch letters to Scotland, where he sought a young man who might serve as his secretary and as a tutor to Mrs. Washington's grandchildren of the name of Custis. Webster's nationalistic ardor bristled. He inquired of the General what European nations would think, if, after the exhibition of great talents in the War for Independence and in the establishment of a new nation on entirely new principles, we should send to Europe for secretaries and for men to teach the rudiments of learning. The question was well received, and the General asked: "What shall I do? There is no person to be obtained here for my purposes." Webster answered that he believed any of the northern colleges could supply such a person. After dinner, walking in the hall, the General resumed the conversation and said that he would lay aside his letter if Webster could recommend a person who would meet his views. Webster could not name a candidate at that moment, but he promised to dispatch letters at once to the North.

A month later the thought struck Webster that the position might afford him an opportunity to continue his literary work. He wrote Washington, therefore, offering to take the place in return for room and board, after he had completed his lecture tour to the north, if he found himself "in tolerably easy circumstances" and if the General would allow the use of his letters and other papers in the preparation of a documentary history of the Revolutionary War. In commendation of himself Webster wrote that he could promise "faithfulness and industry" and this ambition: "I wish to be settled in life—I wish not for solitude, but to have it in my power to be retired. I wish to enjoy life, but books and business will ever be my principal pleasure. I must write—it is a happiness I cannot sacrifice; and were I upon the throne of the Grand Seignior, I feel as tho' I could take pleasure in the education of youth." Washington re-

gretted that his need was so pressing he could not await the
outcome of Webster's business; Webster concluded not to
accept the position, which soon was filled by Tobias Lear
on the recommendation of General Levi Lincoln.

In the interchange of correspondence Webster asked
General Washington to send for newspaper publication the
Sketches of American Policy with such passages marked as
would assist "in harmonizing the views of the citizens of
different states." Hitherto permission to republish had been
withheld because of the exceptionable passages which Pelatiah
Webster had pointed out. Washington replied that "the
publication of extracts therefrom would be pleasing, and
may be beneficial. All possible lights ought, in my opinion,"
he went on, "be thrown on subjects of this importance, for
it should seem that ignorance, or design, have too great a
share in the government of public measures." In subsequent letters to other correspondents Washington several
times alluded to the need for a more perfect union in language almost identical with Webster's.

At Richmond Webster met again James Madison, who
this time greeted the Yankee schoolmaster with great cor-
diality, speaking not only of their earlier meeting in Philadelphia and their correspondence, but also with enthusiasm
of the *Sketches*, which he had seen at Mount Vernon. Washington's letter and Madison's efforts succeeded in convincing
the Legislature of the necessity for a copyright law, and
an Act was passed at that session. Having completed this
business successfully, Webster secured permission to read
his lectures in the capitol, where an audience of about thirty
gentlemen faithfully listened to him.

At Petersburg, which he considered an unhealthy place,
an audience failed to appear, and so he moved on to the
beautiful city of Williamsburg, seat of William and Mary
College. Here he was cordially received by Professors Andrews and Wythe, who secured for his lecturing the use of

a room in the College. Two of General Washington's nephews attended regularly, although the audience numbered only six. Webster explained the public inattention thus: "I am a stranger and a Yankee, tho' well introduced; the Virginians have little money and great pride, contempt of northern men, and great fondness for dissipated life. They do not understand Grammar."

These uncomplimentary reflections on Virginians were confirmed by an experience he had several days later at Alexandria. General Washington's nephew, an imprudent lad, invited Webster to a ball, for which a great supper with liquor to the value of eighteen pounds was prepared. On the following morning Mr. Washington arose at two o'clock, pawned his knee buckles and other articles, gave the landlord a note for sixty dollars, and then rode off without paying his hair dresser. This, Webster remarked scornfully, was "Virginia hospitality."

The true quality of Virginia's hospitality to intellectual truth did not become manifest until several weeks later when *The Maryland Journal* (January 3, 1786) published an extract from a "Letter from a Gentleman in Virginia, to his Friend in this Town [Baltimore]," praising the *Institute* and the lectures:

Mr. Webster has paid us a visit. His lectures in support of his plan were delivered and much approved by the first characters; and had Mr. Sheridan, the British standard of pronunciation, been present, he would have blushed to have reflected that he would have expended so much time to have established anomalies in our language, which had their origin from mere affectation, or depraved taste of a group of illiterate stage-players.

I think it is high time to dispossess ourselves of prejudice in favour of Britain, so far as to act ourselves. With the harmless we are apt to imbibe the vicious fashions, which attend splendor and magnificence; for as soon as the mind is intoxicated with those glittering baubles, vanity madly assumes the empire and reason becomes an humble suppliant.

What a despicable opinion will Britain form, to see us flocking to
her as the only oracle! Mad infatuation! Surprising indeed that men
of sense should prostitute their reason to that tyrant—Custom!

The seeds of nationalism, though planted in few minds,
took deep root.

On January 1, 1786, Webster arrived at Annapolis,
Maryland, where he quickly met Governor Smallwood,
who invited him to dine with a company of senators. In
conversation with Senator Lloyd, "a sensible man from the
Eastern Shore," Webster learned that few white men in
Maryland or Virginia could write their own names. After
noting this horrifying fact in his diary, he exclaimed: "O
New England! how superior are thy inhabitants in morals,
literature, civility, and industry!"

Yet an eager audience, fit though few, listened to him in
the State House in Annapolis, one of whom wrote to *The
Maryland Gazette* (January 10, 1786) of Webster's original thought and uncommon clearness and accuracy. "The
elegance of his style, the energy of his reasoning, profound
knowledge of the subject, and especially the candour and
independent spirit with which he delivers his sentiments,
are well calculated for a reform." The correspondent concluded with the observation: "Great Britain will yet be
indebted to America for the last improvement in the language." These encomiastic remarks were picked up by the
newspapers in Philadelphia, New York, and Boston, so that
an increasing interest was aroused in Webster's books and
ideas. Meantime, too, the newspapers were reprinting the
Sketches, and thus giving the itinerant schoolmaster a national publicity and importance.

He proceeded to Frederick, Maryland, where another
small audience greeted him. On returning to Baltimore,
Webster was injured when his horse fell; for a week Webster was quite lame, but he had strength enough to hobble
about to see the ladies and to tell them "pretty stories."

While he was laid up, he wrote to Pickering that he would soon risk his reputation in the northern cities. "I shall make one general effort," he went on, "to deliver literature and my countrymen from the errors that fashion and ignorance are palming upon Englishmen. The question will then be, whether the Americans will then give their opinions and principles as well as their purses to foreigners, and be the dupes of a strolling party of players, who, educated in the school of corruption, have no profession but to make people laugh, and who, dependent on opinion for subsistence, must conform to caprice at the expense of every principle of propriety. . . . Two circumstances will operate against me. I am not a *foreigner;* I am a *New Englandman.* A foreigner, ushered in with titles and letters, with half my ability, would have the whole city in his train. But let my fate be what it will, I am convinced I am right."

Buoyed by this wholesome egotism, Webster moved on to Dover, Delaware, where the Legislature accepted his petition for a copyright law and promised—and took—action at the succeeding session. At Wilmington he lectured to increasingly numerous audiences, whose applause flattered him so much that he commented: "More taste for science in these states than below." Here he met John Dickinson, whose American Farmer letters had helped provoke the Revolutionary War, and the two held a pleasant, lengthy conversation. Dickinson approved Webster's *Institute* and suggested that he add as a sequel to it an anthology of the best religious pieces in prose and verse "calculated for improving the understanding, purifying the heart, and regulating the conduct."

On February 14, 1786, Webster reached Philadelphia, the metropolis of America and seat of science and literature. Here would be given the real test of his nationalistic ideas; he proceeded cautiously, therefore, making the acquaintance of most of the leading citizens before announcing his lec-

tures. First he called on Pickering, who in appreciation of
Webster's confidences gave useful advice. Then he visited
Dr. John Ewing, President of the University of Pennsylvania; Pelatiah Webster; Mr. Andrew Bradford, the Attorney General; Mr. Sargent, and Mr. Biddle. He again
met Dr. Moyes, who was lecturing in Philadelphia, and
also Elias Boudinot and Dr. Benjamin Rush. With Dr.
Rush he formed a lasting friendship, their conversation on
"harmony of taste" proving them to have many similar ideas
on education and nationalism.

Early, too, Webster called on Benjamin Franklin, then
recently returned from Europe, full of an old man's wisdom and anecdotes. Webster asked for permission to use
for his lectures a room in the University, of whose trustees
Franklin was President. In explaining his ambitious scheme
for an American standard of language, Webster intrigued
the old printer, who had once played with the idea of developing a phonetic alphabet and had even gone so far as to
procure types for the exemplification of his scheme. For
years, because of his many engagements at home and abroad,
the matter had lain dormant. With a gleam in his eye,
Franklin drew out the young schoolmaster, led him on to
avow an interest in simplified spelling, and then proposed
that they should converse further on the subject after Webster's own ideas matured.

Thomas Paine was exhibiting his model of an iron bridge
in Philadelphia at this time. Webster met him and pronounced the invention a success. David Rittenhouse, the
astronomer, proved to be "a plain, modest man," well worth
knowing. Mr. Adgate, the vocal teacher, tested Webster's
voice in a duet, and then they reached an agreement by
which Adgate's chorus would sing at the lectures.

The first lecture was read on February 28 to an audience
of about a hundred persons, "mostly literary characters,"
who expressed "their applause by silence and attention and

clapping." Except the second, when bad weather kept many people away, the other lectures drew more than a hundred auditors, and the series closed with great applause. Despite a stormy evening nearly three hundred appeared at a benefit lecture for the Pennsylvania Hospital. On this occasion he delivered his newly written remarks on his observations of the industry, morals, education, and climate of the United States. Far away in Boston *The Massachusetts Gazette* remarked that Webster "gave the greatest satisfaction to his audience, and proved himself by his just and learned criticisms to be a man of genius and science."

To his publishers, Hudson and Goodwin, Webster wrote, "I am just beginning to make a bustle. I am diffusing useful knowledge and supporting the honour of New England. Even the Philadelphians, who are much inclined to find fault, acknowledge that my remarks are new and my design laudable."

The criticism had come from Pickering, who had perfected the art of reading aloud, modulating his voice and simulating the emotions of an article so accurately that a generous or pathetic sentiment would choke his utterance and suffuse his eyes with tears. Webster's reading of poetry, particularly, was unsatisfactory, and he pitched his voice too high. In his manner he exhibited, along with "a competent share of good sense, a *quantum sufficit* of vanity," and Pickering advised him "that diffidence in a public speaker, especially in a young man, was essential to the art of pleasing." Yet Pickering thought the encouragement Webster had received "was less than he deserved."

At Princeton, whither he went next, Webster was entertained by Dr. Samuel S. Smith, soon to be president of the College. Only sixteen students having signed the subscription papers, although all had expressed a desire to hear the lectures, Webster refused to speak and proceeded to New York City, where he arrived March 25, 1786.

The Continental Congress was in session at this time, and Webster made himself known to Dr. David Ramsay, acting chairman during the illness of John Hancock, and to many of the members with whom he dined frequently. On one occasion he dined in company with P. Bail and five other Seneca Indians who had come on business to Congress. He took tea with Colonel and Mrs. Aaron Burr, Dr. Samuel Latham Mitchill, and many other leading citizens. With Connecticut friends he attended the theater to see *The Provoked Husband,* but the excellent acting of Henry and Wagnell could not make palatable "low scenes and indelicate ideas." With Puritanical earnestness he remarked that "every exhibition of vice weakens our aversion for it."

The lectures, now increased to six with the addition of one on Versification, attracted audiences of seventy, one hundred, and finally two hundred. Dr. Ramsay, Dr. William Samuel Johnson, President of King's [now Columbia] College, and many of the members of Congress attended regularly. "They fall in with my plan," Webster wrote (April 14), "and there is no longer a doubt that I shall be able to effect a uniformity of language and education throughout the continent."

A friendly, though witty, critic commented on Webster's stiff delivery much in the same terms as Pickering had done, stating that "his voice is clear and distinct, but not very flexible or harmonious. . . . The style is both concise and forcible, . . . and although divested of flowers of rhetorick, yet it may be considered as tolerably elegant." His pronunciation, however, contained several New Englandisms, such as *lecter* for *lecture* and *Edurd* for *Edward.* More exceptional was his reading of poetry: "Mr. Webster speaks too quick, too much in the same tone, and raises his voice and pauses too long at the end of every line. He appears to be enraptured when he speaks, but his raptures seem forced. The motion of his hands are [*sic*] rather unpleasing. When he repeats verses he should forget that it is rhyme, for the harmony of numbers does not consist in attaching a particular sound, however musical, to the end of every line." On the whole the critic thought Webster was engaged in "a very laborious as well as meritorious business" and deserved encouragement. Webster promptly hit back with a reply in which he pedantically corrected stylistic errors in his critic's comment.

Francis Childs, editor of *The Daily Advertiser*, puffed the "New England Grammarian" in the following editorial, an amusing example of early national attempts to enlist interest in native intellectual achievements:

It is strange that curiosity should be so dormant and partial to an American in his own country. The Lectures of Mr. Webster, although of much public and private utility, do not seem to meet the encouragement in this city they so evidently deserve. What a pity it is he has all his faculties about him! if he had glass eyes or wooden arms, he would not fail of meeting the most unbounded encouragement—men, women and children all would go to see the man with glass eyes and wooden arms—if he were to advertise that he would go into a quart bottle or dance a hornpipe upon the slackwire, his company would be numberless. Alas! what a misfortune it is to be endowed with genius! A man may trudge on through the common beaten track of humanity without an idea above the most vulgar—nay, he may acquire riches the summit of worldly happiness, and grow a great man; but if he should chance to be cursed with genius, and competent to instruct his fellow citizens he may pine in want, and die in obscurity. The ignorant brute in human shape, whose narrow soul is circumscribed by a purse, contemptuously shakes his dross at the man of science and laughs at his refinement. When we recollect what a crowd attended the lectures of Dr. Moyes, altho' unimportant to the far greater part of the audience, and a foreigner besides, we cannot but think it a great reproach upon the taste of our ladies and gentlemen, to neglect the truly valuable LECTURES OF MR. WEBSTER.

During his stay of five weeks in New York, Webster perfected his scheme of a phonetic alphabet and carried it to

Dr. Ramsay for inspection. They discussed the feasibility of such a plan with members of Congress, and it was agreed that if Franklin and Washington would endorse the plan, Congress might see fit to enact a law whereby the new alphabet would form the basis of an American manner of printing the English language. In the perfervid ambition to render America completely independent of England, no one device seemed quite so simple as this. Within a few years after the adoption of the reformed alphabet, all books would have to be reprinted in the American manner. English would in a sense become a foreign language as unintelligible as German, and Americans would create their own literature, unhampered by the competition of oversea authors. Shakespeare, Milton, Addison, and Pope would lose their strangle hold on the mind of the western world; the genius of the new empire, thus freed from effete, king-ridden thoughts, would burst forth with Minervan eloquence.

Webster sent his rough draft to Franklin on May 24, 1786, with the remark, "A few distinguished characters might give such weight to an attempt of this magnitude as to crush all the opposition that would be made by the enemies of our independence. The minds of the people are in a ferment, and consequently disposed to receive improvements; once let the ferment subside, and the succeeding lethargy will bar every great and rapid amendment." To Pickering, through whom he sent the letter to Franklin, Webster outlined the following "advantages expected from a reformation of the alphabet":

1. It will render the acquisition of the language easy both for natives and foreigners. All the trouble of learning to *spell* will be saved.

2. When no character has more sounds than one, every man, woman, and child who knows his alphabet can spell words, even by the sound without ever seeing them.

3. Pronunciation must necessarily be uniform.

4. The orthography of the language will be fixed.

5. The necessity of encouraging printing in this country and of manufacturing all our own books, is a political advantage, obvious and immense.

6. A national language is a national tie, and what country wants it more than America?

Franklin responded enthusiastically: "Our ideas are so nearly similar, that I make no doubt of our easily agreeing on the plan." He believed, too, that the reformation was "not only necessary but practicable"; but, having so much to say on the subject, he wished Webster to confer with him upon it, "as that would save much time and writing." Webster promised a visit as soon as he had completed his lecture tour, a measure Franklin approved, because "lecturing on the language will be of a great use in preparing the minds of people for the improvements proposed."

Having completed his lectures and his business in New York City, Webster proceeded up the Hudson to Albany, where he was advised not to come for "any pecuniary motive," because the Dutch inhabitants were prejudiced against the "disagreeable" English tongue. Here between May 11 and 18 he gave his lectures to small groups, the last numbering thirty. Returned to New York City, he dined with President Wheelock of Dartmouth College and conferred again with Dr. Ramsay. In company with Colonel David Humphreys, aide-de-camp to General Washington and jingoistic poet, he returned to Hartford on May 29.

Home again after a thirteen months' absence, Webster met his friends and family in joyful reunion. He took his accustomed place in the choir of the First Church on Sunday; on Monday he dined with Barlow, whom he chided for failing to correspond regularly; and in due time he called on all his old friends and the members of the Legislature. From the latter he received permission to read his lectures in the State House, if he desired.

The prodigal had returned home, but he received from

the populace the typical elder brother's greeting. His announcement that he would read his remarks on the state of the Union at the First Church on June 6, admission fee two shillings, provoked his old neighbors to wrath. Some of them had not forgotten the lashing he had given the Middletown Convention, and so, partly because he had given tickets to the members of the Legislature, a mob collected outside the church and interrupted the speaker by jeering remarks and by throwing stones through the windows. "Let it be remembered," Webster noted in his diary, "that in the year 1786 there are people so illiberal that they will not permit lectures to be read in a church because they cannot be admitted without paying two shillings!" The Governor and the Church withdrew their permission for the use of their halls, and Webster had to move to Collier's dancing room, where the series was completed before a small, silent, visibly unimpressed audience.

Speedily he shook the dust of Hartford from his feet and hurried to New Haven, where the kind words of Meigs, Simeon Baldwin, Roger Sherman, and President Stiles warmed his heart. Seventy hearers, "consisting of the best families in town," and a few Yale students, seemed more pleased with his lectures than any other audience he had had.

From New Haven he went to Springfield, Massachusetts, stopping at Hartford to dine with Colonel Jeremiah Wadsworth, but most of the time he remained in solitude because he was "oppressed with *vis inertiae*." At Springfield he called on Timothy Dwight, whose *Conquest of Canaan*, a Biblical epic poem into which many critics read jingoistic notions, had recently been published. At Worcester accounts were settled with Isaiah Thomas, and an agreement was reached whereby the latter would print the *Institute*.

On July 6 he reached Boston, then a city of about fifteen thousand population. One of his earliest acquaintances was

Dr. Nathaniel W. Appleton, an energetic member of the school committee; with him Webster met often to discuss mutually interesting questions. Appleton had married a daughter of William Greenleaf, Sheriff of Suffolk County at the outbreak of the Revolution and a man of considerable means as well as the father of several very pretty and as yet unmarried daughters. Whether Webster met Rebecca Greenleaf at this time is not known, but he certainly must have heard about her, her family, and particularly about the successful importer and land speculator, James Greenleaf.

Early, too, he was introduced to Governor James Bowdoin, who so admired Webster's talents that he invited the visiting lecturer to a dinner at which Samuel Adams and a dozen other notables were present. Bowdoin also listened to the lectures, given in Mr. Hunt's School House, an audience of thirty to sixty attending. At Cambridge, where he called on President Willard of Harvard College for a recommendation of the *Institute,* he was introduced at tea to the faculty.

Between August 1 and November 1, 1786, when he returned to Hartford, Webster lectured in Salem, Portsmouth, Newburyport, Boston (this time in Fanueil Hall with Samuel Adams and General Lincoln in the audience), Providence, Newport, New London, and Norwich.

Webster had completed a lecture tour from Richmond, Virginia, to Portsmouth, New Hampshire. He had spread the gospel of nationalism in language and politics, and had secured the approval of every governor, every college president, and many of the leading citizens in the communities he visited. On men of education everywhere he urged the support of these principles by demanding the adoption of his school books. His success is apparent in the rapid multiplication of the sales of his books, and the simultaneous printing of them in Boston, Hartford, New York, and Philadelphia in 1787. The lectures, as Pickering had remarked, were "never intended as a catch penny scheme, but they served to explain and recommend the principles on which his *Grammatical Institute* was founded."

This achievement in itself was a magnificent one, viewed merely as a feat of salesmanship. Within the space of a year a country schoolmaster elevated himself to the dignified level of Schoolmaster to America, with college presidents, governors, legislators, and clergymen as his most eager students. For the first time the thought was actively propagated that a provincial pride which served to hold the thirteen states apart was a source of political evil, and that a firm unanimity in language, manners, and politics, arising from national pride, alone could bring happiness and order to the United States. For the first time, too, a native investigator rendered a critical opinion on the political, moral, religious, and educational status of the new nation. Webster minced no words in lashing the absurdities he found; his reforming zeal included every manifestation of American life. He demanded perfection in all things, just as he had insisted on perfect spelling recitations in his country school.

While Webster was in Massachusetts, Daniel Shays gathered his ragged mob of disaffected citizens and prevented the Courts of Common Pleas from sitting in Hampshire, Worcester, and Middlesex counties. At Bristol the militia dispersed a mob of five hundred. Although the uprising did not develop into a civil war, it illustrated anew to Webster how inadequate or ineffective political measures quickly led to popular tumult. The question of taxes and the lack of cash precipitated the trouble; had Congress not been balked by the recalcitrant states, and had it been able to provide a uniform system of currency and taxation throughout the Federation, these unfortunate events would not have taken place.

With the same promptness which marked his entrance

into the Connecticut half-pay contest, he penned anonymous articles for the newspapers, denouncing the villainous legislatures and tutoring the people in methods of economy. To *The Essex Journal*, Newburyport, September 13, 1786, he sent a brief article "On Redress of Grievances," the conclusion of which follows:

Mr. Printer, I saw a man the other day, crying a bushel of flaxseed. Flaxseed is a cash article, and cash pays taxes. The man wanted cash to pay his taxes; he *must* have cash; but, Mr. Printer, half an hour afterwards I saw him half drunk, and his saddle bags filled with coffee. But, sir, coffee pays no taxes.

Another, a few days ago, brought a lamb to market. Lambs command cash, and cash pays taxes; but the good countryman went to a store, and bought a feather; five shillings for a feather, Mr. Printer, and feathers pay no taxes. Is it not a *grievance*, Sir, that feathers and ribbands, and coffee and new rum, will not pay taxes?

Now, Mr. Printer, in my humble opinion, there are but two effectual methods of redressing grievances; one depends on the people as individuals, and the other on the Supreme Executiv authority.

As to the first, let every person, whether farmer, mechanic, lawyer, or doctor, provide a small box, (*a small box* will be big enough) with a hole in the lid. When he receives a shilling, let him put six pence into the box, and use the other six pence in providing for his family; not rum or feathers, but good bread and meat. Let this box remain untouched, until the collector shall call. Then let it be opened, the tax paid, and the overplus of cash be expended on gauze, ribbands, tea, and New England rum. Let the box then be put into its place again, to receive pence for the next collector. This method, Mr. Printer, will redress all grievances, without the trouble, noise and expense of town meetings, conventions and mobs.

As to the other method, sir, I can only say, were I at the head of the Executiv authority, I should soon put the question to a decisiv issue. It should be determined, on the first insurrection, whether our lives and our properties should be secure under the law and constitution of the State, or whether they must depend on the mad resolves of illegal meetings. Honest men would know whether they may rest in safety at home, or whether they must seek for tranquillity in some distant country.

In this article Webster achieved a homely, direct style, based upon simple illustrations, which he used later in occasional essays and in *The Prompter*. The origin of this form of writing may be traced to the Reverend Nathan Hooker's "Self Tormenting," which was culled from *The Connecticut Courant* for Part III of the *Institute*. It will be observed that Webster's spelling reform extended in this article only to the dropping of final *e's* in syllables with short vowels.

In Providence, two weeks after the appearance of the article on grievances, Webster learned from the Governor of Rhode Island that the Legislature had been summoned in special session at the request of a convention. An issue of £100,000 in paper bills had been decreed in July, and now a tender law was proposed, requiring creditors to accept goods in lieu of cash in the payment of debts. The people were in confusion, and the state officials were embarrassed. This farce of mobs dictating to the government and of a legislature declaring old horses to be the coin of the realm, angered Webster. He sent off to *The United States Chronicle*, Providence, the most sarcastically pungent article of his career, "The Devil is in You."

Beginning with the suggestion that the political body is subject to violent diseases when it abuses its blessings, Webster asserted the paradox, "Too much liberty is the worst of tyranny," because, when all men attempt to become masters, most of them must become slaves in the attempt. The devil, if one interpret the word to mean the effects ascribed to the prince of evil spirits, showed himself in the luxury raging among the people, in the tender law, in the mobs and conventions, and chiefly in the weakness of the federal government. Again he harped on the need for national union, exclaiming at the end:

While you attempt to trade to advantage, without a *head* to combine all the States into systematic, uniform measures, the world will laugh at you for fools. While merchants take and giv credit, the world will call them idiots, and laugh at their ruin. While farmers get credit, borrow money, and mortgage their farms, the world will call them fools, and laugh at their embarrassments. While all men liv beyond their income, and are harassed with duns and sheriffs, no man will pity them, or giv them relief. But when mobs and conventions oppose the courts of justice, and Legislatures make paper or old horses a legal tender in all cases, the world will exclaim with one voice—*Ye are rogues, and the devil is in you!*

This article, published under the pseudonym "Tom Thoughtful," was immediately reprinted in all the leading New England papers and helped to stem the rising tide of insurrection; at the same time it taught the need for an effective union.

In New London Webster learned that the Connecticut people were clamoring for paper money to remedy the lack of cash. Again he insisted that in union, not in paper money, lay the redress of grievances:

Americans! you talk of a scarcity of cash. Well, the only remedy is, to enable Congress to place our commerce on a footing with the trade of other nations. Foreign States have nothing to do with Massachusetts or New York. They must make treaties with *United America,* or not make them at all. And while we boast of the independence of particular states, we lose all the benefits of independence. For fear that Congress would abuse their powers and enrich themselves, we, like the dog in the manger, will not even enrich ourselves. We complain of poverty, and yet *giv* the profits of our trade to foreign nations. Infatuated men! We have one truth to learn —*That nothing but the absolute power of regulating our commerce, vested in some federal head,* can restore us cash, or turn the balance of trade in our favor.

At Hartford, where the doctrine of states' rights was already preached, Webster discovered an active anti-federal party, fomenting jealousy, "the child of hell and father of all mischief." The anti-federal men supposed the federalists to be "ambitious, tyrannical men, who are aiming at power and office at the expense of the people at large." Webster believed both groups generally honest and well meaning, but, he declared, "the anti-federal men think as they have been bred: their education has been rather indifferent; they have been accustomed to think on a small scale; they can think on no other without an enlargement of their mind."

And so Webster, who had left Hartford in May, 1785, with a bundle of pamphlets espousing the doctrine of democracy, now on November 1, 1786, returned home convinced that he was quite wrong. The tumultuous elections in the South, the rising of mobs in Massachusetts, the farcical legislature of Rhode Island, and the anti-federalists of Connecticut changed his mind. "People," he wrote rather sadly to *The Connecticut Courant,* November 20, 1786, "in general are too ignorant to manage affairs which require great reading and an extensive knowledge of foreign nations. This is the misfortune of republican governments. For my own part, I confess, I was once as strong a republican as any man in America. *Now,* a republican is among the last kinds of government I should choose. I would infinitely prefer a limited monarchy, for I would sooner be the subject of the caprice of one man, than to the ignorance and passions of the multitude."

Hartford had lost its glamour; Webster's pride in Connecticut had ebbed. It was not the éclat of his tour, although the pleasant applause still rang in his ears, that turned Hartford into a bucket of ashes. Nor was it merely the rude reception he had received as a lecturer. Rather, the ideal picture he had painted of New England's superiority had been daubed by time's dust and by inevitable disparaging comparisons. He looked into the courts where he was eligible to practice; he talked with Lemuel Hopkins, Joel Barlow, John Trumbull, and Colonel Wadsworth; he spent long days with his parents and relatives. No one could convince him to stay. Moodily he went about settling his affairs, assigning to Hudson and Goodwin the copyright of the *Institute*, and saying farewells. On Thanksgiving Day, ironically enough, he left Hartford, "perhaps for life," as he wrote in his diary, "to seek a living."

CHAPTER VIII

DEFENDER OF THE CONSTITUTION

WEBSTER did not have a settled opinion on the matter of his life's work; his vacillation while corresponding with General Washington demonstrated that large philosophical goals delayed his acceptance of a steady, income-producing position. He had run his father ruinously into debt to secure for himself a college education; he had risked his own future in gambling on the success of the *Institute;* and he had amassed a debt by touring the country as a lecturer. He loved teaching, but teaching in the common schools and academies offered no reward commensurate with his needs or ability. College professorships and tutorships were given to correct divinity students or to elderly preachers. President Ewing of the University of Pennsylvania had offered the chair of oratory to Webster, but the work involved long hours of monitorial service, labor that would cramp his thinking and prevent original composition. Webster had to write or explode, there was no other way about it. But writing paid nothing. Newspapers were clipsheets, and American magazines were simply handsomely printed *omnium gatherums.* Original material, though eagerly requested, was looked upon as a freewill offering for which publication was sufficient reward. Original books seldom paid the printing costs; men like Jeremy Belknap doggedly pushed forward in their writing and publishing despite their mounting indebtedness to printers. And so Webster, in debt and without prospects of employment, tried to find a congenial nook in which to settle.

He had written to Franklin another of those peculiarly indecisive letters in which he manifested a pride that seemed quite at variance with his expressed needs of employment. His debts, he wrote, swallowed the royalties on his textbooks, so that he was without funds sufficient to carry him to Philadelphia to keep his appointment to discuss the proposed phonetic alphabet. "I wish for business—it is my life —it is my pleasure, as well as my support," he continued. "But I began a vast design without a shilling, and I know the world too well to ask pecuniary assistance from any person. I want none, I will take none but what I earn. I wish, if possible, to have business which will afford me some leisure, for my lectures must be prepared for the press as soon as possible, and my *Institute* stands in need of improvement." A notion had entered his mind that he might be able to open an oratorical academy or to give public readings after the plan of Thomas Sheridan in London; he asked Franklin to comment on the possibility of success in either of these ventures. Evidently the kindly old Doctor could not respond with encouraging words, the only ones he relished writing during his old age, for no reply came.

Webster's association with the leading statesmen, clergymen, educators, and men of wealth during his lecture tour had considerably affected his philosophy. Approved as a worthy associate and a truth-bringer, he yearned for a position of dignity and income which would make him the social, as well as the intellectual, equal of these men. His vanity suffered rude shocks as he contemplated his father's embarrassed finances and his own danger of sinking into obscurity through an inability to support himself in scholarly activities.

Despite his reputation for vanity, Webster was a good student, ready to gather the crumbs of wisdom at the tables of the great men he met. Or rather, he was a publicist, a

young man with a flair for writing. He had embraced the
broad democratic philosophy of the Revolution and he had
developed a comprehensive program of nationalism. As
he had moved from city to city, mingling with men who
demanded federal union for economic reasons, he was led
almost imperceptibly to tone down or omit the more radical of his doctrines. Pelatiah Webster and other men of
wealth asked him whether the rabble understood enough
law or economics to determine the policies of a commercial
nation. Established clergymen in the South and North
asked whether religious teaching, paid by the state, was not
as necessary to the well-being of humanity as state-supported
secular instruction. Governor Bowdoin asked whether the
rabble under Shays or the Adamses, the Cabots, and the
Lowells should rule Massachusetts. Dr. Lemuel Hopkins
and the little band of Hartford Wits, to whom Webster was
allied by friendly association, handed him their versified
hatred of democracy and love of aristocratic government.
These objections, seldom voiced to Webster in direct refuta-
tion of his own leveling views, coincided with his observations. Born a Christian democrat and philosophically inclined to support the views of Rousseau and Dr. Richard
Price, Webster yielded here and there a point until in a
moment of despair he found himself writing, "*Now*, a Republican is among the last kinds of government I should
choose."

To this opinion, so extreme as to be a virtual denial of
all that he had previously written, Webster could not adhere
wholeheartedly. When he arrived at New Haven two days
after leaving Hartford, he took time to rethink his position
in conversation with President Stiles, Roger Sherman, David
Daggett, and Professor Josiah Meigs. Each of these men
in his own forceful way explained that the popular discontent arose, not from ignorance and a seditious disposition,
but from a series of real grievances. The substantial yeo-

manry, whom Webster had so highly praised, filled the ranks of the remonstrants; their chief grievance, against the method of funding the debt, was correct in principle, even if the wrong method of seeking redress had been adopted by some insurgents. Webster had erred, they said, in laying the blame entirely upon the poor farmers, for "a people who possess the means of information are not ultimately and generally wrong." In the unwise economic policies of the states he was advised to look for the real source of popular discontent. These friends demanded, too, that Webster repeat his lectures. When he left New Haven, therefore, on December 8, 1786, he had recovered his faith in the essential correctness of the principles he had so heartily enunciated on his lecture tour.

After a four-day journey, on which he was forced to walk through snow much of the distance, he reached New York. For two weeks he looked about for employment in vain, visiting the booksellers and printers, dining occasionally with friends, and writing several essays on manners and government.

"Something is wrong," he wrote in these new essays restating his position. Everywhere disillusionment had set in, because the Revolution had not brought about the "perfect political tranquillity" which had been promised by statesmen and divines, and because the wartime enthusiasm for "public spirit, heroic virtue, and love of country" was degenerating into the pursuit of private interest. In their disappointment the Americans were taking "an insect view of things." Webster, climbing the hill of prophecy, insisted that on a larger view the Revolution must prove a fortunate event both for the people of America and for mankind in general. Vast improvements must occur in science, religion, morals, and government: "the philosopher will felicitate himself with the prospect of discoveries favorable to arts and happiness; the statesman will rejoice that there is a

retreat from the vassalage of Europe; the divine will bless
God that a place had been reserved for an uncorrupted
church; and the philanthropist, who compares the yeomanry
of America with the peasantry of Europe, will congratulate
himself on an event which has removed millions of people
from the ambition of princes, and from the participation
of the vices, which mark the decline of nations."

The fundamental mistake of Americans, Webster decided, was their notion that the Revolution had been completed when it had really just begun. The people assumed
that a new governmental foundation was enough; they
failed to note that a wholly new superstructure was also
required, not merely a ready-made social fabric of European
construction. Here lay the radical cause of the present political evil: Americans were adopting as fast as possible the
fashionable amusements, luxuries, vices, clothes, language,
and manners of Europe. "It is a singular phenomenon,"
he declared in regard to dress, "and to posterity it will
appear incredible, that a nation of heroes, who have conquered armies and raised an empire, should not have the
spirit to say, *we will wear our clothes as we please.*" Were
Americans to develop their own laws of fashion and adhere
to them, a new species of independence would be developed,
the wholesome effect of which would be an increase of local
manufactures and an annual saving of at least one half of
the interest of the federal debt.

The second great mistake of Americans was their failure
to recognize that "men are influenced more by habit than
by any abstract ideas of right and wrong." In the settlement
of the Wyoming controversy, in the issuance of paper money,
and in the methods of funding the debt, correct theoretical
principles were employed, but the effect in each instance
was bad, because the people's minds were not prepared for
these innovations, or because more evil than good resulted
from the application of the principle. Webster reiterated

his theory of the evolution of institutions: "all reformation should be left to the natural progress of society, or to the conviction of the mind." Not only had the theorists been confounded by the insurrection in Massachusetts, by the peaceable convention in Rhode Island, and by the popular remonstrance in the other states, but these closet philosophers had also been chagrined to see as a result of their acts, the rise of speculation, a growing disrespect for law and lawyers, and a fatal extension of credit. Webster demanded a government suited to the people, not one which imposed regulations from above in the monarchical manner.

And so Webster returned again to his faith in common man, knowing that the disaffected populace had been more sinned against than sinning. The correction of governmental evils lay in the hands of the legislators; theory should be replaced with a wise concern for the virtues of the frugal farmer and an obedience to the popular will. To the people as a whole he said, "The only way to become rich and respectable at home and abroad is to become industrious, and to throw off our slavish dependence on foreign manners, which obliges us to sacrifice our taste and our interest to the policy and aggrandizement of other nations."

It was inevitable that Webster should retrieve his faith in democracy, because his whole philosophy had been based upon the doctrines of the perfectibility of mankind and the social compact. Since his program of educational and governmental reform was predicated upon these beliefs, his whole career as a philosopher would have crumbled if he had surrendered to a momentary disillusionment. But Webster had found kinship with that group of men who later would form the Federalist Party; in the rapid turn of events during the year the Constitution was adopted, he supported the framers of that document, and in the following years he echoed the economic and political theories of these "Fathers," who originated the doctrine that "the three fundamentals of American law are life, liberty, and property; and the greatest of these is property."

On Christmas Day, 1786, Webster set off for Philadelphia, three months late for his promised conversation on the phonetic alphabet with Franklin. But the genial old philosopher, who often slipped back into his Poor Richard character in these days of his pain and garrulity, merely remarked to the apologetic schoolmaster, "Haste makes waste." In a matter of so great importance to the nation, much thought was necessary to anticipate and remove the objections that prejudice and lethargy would bring forward.

Webster and Franklin met frequently, trying to harmonize their views. Franklin proposed the adoption of his new alphabet and spelling, first published in 1768, by which each sound would have its own symbol. Webster considered this scheme too radical, because it contained a combination of English and cabalistic symbols, and because the strangeness of new letters would prevent popular acceptance. With unexpected conservatism and common sense Webster said: "It is not to be expected that an orthography, perfectly regular and simple, such as would be formed by a 'synod of Grammarians on principles of science,' will ever be substituted for that confused mode of spelling which is now established. But it is apprehended that great improvements may be made, and an orthography almost regular, or such as shall obviate most of the present difficulties which occur in learning our language, may be introduced and established with little opposition." He did agree, however, to accept Franklin's types and to publish a dictionary in conformity with Franklinian orthography, provided that public support might be engaged to defray the expenses. This book was never published.

Webster pushed forward with his own scheme. Franklin, ever willing to compromise to secure practical results, promised "the best support" he could give it. Webster's scheme was based on a tendency he had discovered in the English language by which it worked itself clear of anomalies. By encouraging and wisely directing this evolutionary tendency, he thought the desired end could best be accomplished. Exceptions could be thrown away, and varying forms could be harmonized on a broad basis of analogy.

Webster's plan involved three simple rules of procedure. First, he would omit all superfluous or silent letters. Thus *bread, head, give, breast, built, meant, realm, friend* would be spelled *bred, hed, giv, brest, bilt, ment, relm, frend*.

Second, a character that has a definite sound would be substituted for one that is more vague and indeterminate. Thus by putting *ee* instead of *ea* or *ie*, he arrived at *meen, neer, greev, speek, zeel*; similarly he achieved *greef, kee, beleev, laf, dawter, plow, tuf, proov, blud*, and *draft*. Likewise the *ch* in Greek derivatives, such as *character, chorus, cholic, architecture*, would be changed to *k*, and these words would be written *karacter, korus, kolic, arkitecture*. The *ch* in French derivatives would become *sh; machine, chaise, chevalier* would be written *masheen, shaze, shevaleer*. The *ch* in English derivatives has a soft sound, as in *cherish*, and therefore it would remain unaltered.

The third change involved "a trifling alteration in a character or the addition of a point" to distinguish different sounds. The voiced and unvoiced *th* would be distinguished by having a small stroke across one of them. A point over the vowels, as *å* or *ī*, might suffice for differentiating sounds, and diphthongs might be united into a single compound character. These, with a few other inconsiderable alterations, Webster thought, might render the orthography of English sufficiently correct and regular.

For a number of years Webster spoke and wrote in favor of his system, placing a defense of it as an appendix to his *Dissertations on the English Language* (1789) and in the *Rudiments of English Grammar* (1789). Somewhat incompletely he used the simplified spelling forms in *A Collection of Essays and Fugitiv Writings* (1790), the labor of re-writing having deterred his desired full exemplification of his system. The Preface and two short essays at the end, however, were in the new form. These examples illustrate his innovations:

The following Collection consists of Essays and Fugitiv Peeces, ritten at various times, and on different occasions, az wil appeer by their dates and subjects. Many of them were dictated at the moment, by the impulse of impressions made by important political events, and abound with a correspondent warmth of expression. This free-dom of language wil be excused by the friends of the revolution and of good guvernment, who wil recollect the sensations they hav ex-perienced, amidst the anarky and distraction which succeeded the cloze of the war. On such occasions a riter wil naturally giv himself up to hiz *feelings*, and hiz manner of *riting* wil flow from hiz manner of *thinking*.

It haz been said that coquetts often looze their reputation, while they retain their virtu; and that prudes often prezerve their reputa-tion, after they hav lost their virtu.

A man is pleezed with the deference hiz wife shows for hiz opinions; he often loves her even for her want of information, when it creates a kind of dependence on hiz judgment. On the other hand, a woman always despises her husband for hiz inferiority in understanding and knowledge, and blushes for the figure he makes in the company of men who possess superior talents.

It is obvious that Webster had not attained a perfect system; by analogy with *looze*, *prudes* should have been *proodes* and *despises*, *despizes* or *despizez*. In the follow-ing years, as his studies increased his knowledge, he with-drew from his early extremist position and focused upon anomalous forms. If he here sowed an orthographer's wild oats, it was to good purpose, for he continuously winnowed the freak or bad forms from his plan, developing in the end a uniformity on analogical principles which has been generally accepted as standard in America.

Franklin must have advised Webster to deliver a new series of lectures, for on January 8, 1787, he announced his forthcoming appearance on successive Saturdays at the University. "The design of the Lectures," he stated, "is to weed from our native tongue a luxuriant growth of corruptions and to prepare the way for some national improvements now in contemplation—to awaken public attention to the subject of education in this infant country, and to discover the sources of the depravation of morals, the loss of public and private confidence, and of the commercial and political embarrassments which have followed the American Revolution."

In the first, scheduled for January 20 but adjourned on account of bad weather, he proposed to read his essay on manners and fashion. A little haughtily he advertised that his lectures were "not designed for amusement. They are designed for people who have leisure and inclination to devote an hour to *serious* reflection, as their object is to unfold some of the less visible causes of our political embarrassments. They are designed for thinking men of every denomination, and the first is particularly calculated for ladies of sentiment, who are very influential in manners." Evidently the Philadelphians preferred the amusement to be found at the Theatre in South Street or at Mr. Peale's exhibition of Moving Pictures with changeable effects, for few came out to hear this second clear call to national duty.

Webster may have lost his drawing power as speaker, because the Annapolis Convention had adjourned in favor of a new convention to meet at Philadelphia in May. The popular discontent was muffled by the winter snow; business was reviving. The itinerant lecturer was no longer of utility, for his most important idea, the need for federal union, would soon be realized in fact. His other notions might well wait upon the deliberations of the convention.

But if Webster faded in importance as a lecturer, he did

not disappear from public notice. In fact, his name appeared so often in the Philadelphia papers that gossipers, kept in ignorance of the events in the secret national conclave, must have exercised their talents in dissecting his character. Andrew Ellicot, the surveyor, wrote to his wife (May 10, 1787) that Webster had entered into the spirit of the contending parties and had "already got his hands full." "These northern gentry," he added, "appear mightily pestered with a restless and uneasy spirit, which some good people who are now lodging with me suppose must proceed from the remains of that witchcraft which formerly prevailed in their country." Benjamin Rush, on the other hand, wrote: "There is a primness, a simplicity, a morality, and an intelligence in the New England character which I have always admired, and which I have often defended."

One bit of Philadelphia humor, peddled later if not originated by William Cobbett, illustrates the charge of vanity against Webster. When he entered Philadelphia, Dr. Rush met him and exclaimed: "How do you do, my dear friend. I congratulate you on your arrival to Philadelphia." "Sir," Webster replied, "you may congratulate Philadelphia on the occasion."

Webster's first entrance into the local party warfare was occasioned by the publication on March 21, 1787, of his letter on the domestic debt, addressed to Governor James Bowdoin of Massachusetts. One of the common grievances throughout the nation was the determination of the legislatures to pay the debt to the holders of certificates. Originally these certificates were accepted by rich men who loaned money or by poor men who were rewarded for military service in the Revolution. When it was found that the states made no provision for the redemption of these papers or paid the interest in depreciated paper currency, some of the holders, particularly the poorer ones, were obliged to part with their certificates to speculators at great loss in order to meet obligations. Since the alienations resulted from public delinquency, Webster believed that the government was bound by its honor to take into account the losses sustained by the original holders. "To pay the debt to the men who now hold the evidences of it," Webster wrote, "appears to me the most iniquitous measure that a legislature can adopt." He demanded that the original holders be paid in full, and then that these men pay the later purchasers the selling cost plus interest.

The debate on this subject had been vigorously conducted by newspaper writers when "a certain retailer of nouns and pronouns" advocated his "hell-born opinions," as "A Pennsylvanian" described the author and his essay. This rebuttal, said to have been written by President John Ewing of the University of Pennsylvania, by accusing Webster of being a "fomenter of rebellion," drew forth many other articles. Webster denied that he had had a hand in publishing the article, although he wrote to Bowdoin: "The sentiments contained in this letter will be communicated to the public, without my name." On May 8 he admitted the authorship, but not until Ewing's and his names had been bandied about in the billingsgate common to the lowest political quarreling. Two days later he gave the press a long letter over his own signature, explaining in detail how he had reached his decision on the matter of the debt and reiterating his good intentions. On May 16 he republished the "Tom Thoughtful" article to refute the "base insinuations" against his "patriotic character."

In April Webster had accepted a position as Master of the English Language in the recently established Protestant Episcopal Academy at £200 to be paid in paper currency. On the eighteenth the following squib from the pen of Thomas Freeman appeared in *The Freeman's Journal:*

The uncertainty of all human affairs never appeared more manifestly than in the case of NOAH WEBSTER, jun. esq, whose extraordinary abilities and unparalleled knowledge of the English language, have enabled him to write that masterpiece of instruction, his *Grammatical Institute*. His consciousness of his own great learning and genius, had justly led him to imagine, that, by his becoming an itinerant lecturer through the United States, he would, by this means, be one of the most valuable citizens of our new empire, and have his name ranked among the great men of this western world.— But, alas! all his well-digested plans and schemes have vanished into smoke, his *learned* and *useful lectures* have been neglected, and he himself suffered to starve, or to join one of the most Herculean pieces of labor that ever any poor man engaged in, *to wit*, that of a schoolmaster.

This learned man, whose extraordinary knowledge and abilities gave him good reason to expect at least *one thousand guineas* a year clear profit from his lecturing, is now obliged to accept of *two hundred pounds* a year of paper money, which at present, allowing for discount, is scarcely one hundred pounds sterling. But what is still worse—to aggravate the misfortune, he is to be under the Principal of the Protestant Episcopal Academy, a man whose temper has already sent off above half a dozen of teachers, and in a short time must break up the academy. This is surely a strange reverse of fortune on the part of Noah Webster, Esq. Would to God that he may have magnanimity of mind sufficient to bear all this.

SETH

Webster replied a week later. Far from being humiliated by taking this position, he felt honored, because teaching is "the first business in society." Since "ancient kings and nobles taught schools," why should he refuse, the descendant of colonial governors, the author of books, the friend of "the first characters" and "the greater part of the literary gentlemen in the United States," the author of political writings which "have been the acknowledged means of restoring tranquillity to a distracted state and of bringing about federal measures of great consequence," a lawyer, and the possessor of property worth more than two thousand guineas. In defense of the mild and amiable Dr. Andrews he said that that gentleman had erred only in not having discharged some of his incompetent teachers sooner.

Immediately a series of articles girded at Webster's vanity, his use of the title *Esquire* arousing the most caustic comments. "Lamech" advised him to adopt the maxim, "humility leads to honor," for "who in his senses ever used the appellation *Esq.* to a schoolmaster? A *flagellator anorum* to be called *Esq.!* fie! fie! Such a contradiction of terms!" "Seth" answered laconically: "I wish he would not bother us, nor slap his merits in our teeth."

The appearance of Philadelphia editions, published by Young and M'Cullough, of the three parts of the *Institute*, gave cause for a third volley of hostile articles. In *The Independent Gazetteer*, an anti-federal newspaper whose editors delighted in putting Webster on the rack, "A Country Schoolmaster," admitting "no great knowledge of this subject myself," criticized Websterian innovations in grammar. "James Kidd, Clerk pro tem. of Pedagogue Hall," simultaneously aired his grievances in ten lengthy articles in *The Freeman's Journal* between May 9 and August 8, 1787. Against Webster's "spurious production of an unlearned brain," Kidd sent in June an open letter to the Constitutional Convention, demanding that something be done about this "destructive, heretical grammar" which was spreading "disorder, confusion and error among the rising generation." In his later criticisms Kidd tempered his manner, so that Webster (October 24) acknowledged the learning of his antagonist and the correctness of many of his grammatical opinions.

Webster's throttling of his own penchant for caustic reply during the heavy barrage of a threefold enemy may have been occasioned by the fact that he had fallen in love finally and irrecoverably. Diminutive Rebecca Greenleaf, witty, sensible, sociable, was visiting her sister, Mrs. Duncan Ingraham. With them also was James Greenleaf, a gay young merchant whose Midas fingers dispensed largess with the same ease his wealth was acquired.

On March 1 Webster first met her; on the seventh she was "the sweet Miss Greenleaf," and on the ninth, "the agreeable Miss Greenleaf." By the twenty-second she had become "the lovely Becca." When she left for Boston in June, she and Webster had reached an "understanding," the fulfillment of which depended partly on her family's wishes and partly on his progress toward financial independence. Dr. Nathaniel Appleton, commenting on Webster's enthusiastic remarks, wrote: "She is a charming girl, and no wonder that her fine eyes and amiable deportment have made so much havoc among the beaux and gained her so many good acquaintances among the judicious and discerning."

Webster hobnobbed with James Greenleaf, joining his festive parties and also taking him on calls upon Pelatiah Webster, Franklin, and members of the Convention. They cemented a firm friendship, Webster serving as a *fidus Achates* and economic consultant. When Greenleaf was about to go to Europe to expand his importing business, Webster secured James Watson, later to be the Federalist leader in New York City, as a partner in the enterprise. Together Webster and Greenleaf rode in the trial run of John Fitch's steamboat. The Yankee schoolmaster shared in every activity in the bustling city.

Webster's sudden interest in his family history and the readiness with which he flaunted his merits in letters to the newspapers, may no doubt be explained by his hope of alliance with the rich and illustrious Greenleaf family. He wrote to his father for genealogical information, and at the earliest opportunity consulted George Wyllys, Secretary of State in Connecticut, "that living library of American history."

There was good reason for his pride and for his restraint,

too, in the fact that so many members of the Constitutional Convention acknowledged his friendship and his services in "bringing about federal measures of great consequence." The Convention held its first session on May 24, Washington being elected chairman. Behind closed doors the work of formulating a plan of government went on. At first the Articles of Confederation were amended in an effort to bring them into some harmony with the requirements of the times. Soon, however, acting on the suggestion of Washington that the Articles be probed to the bottom and a radical cure effected, an entirely new Constitution was written. It was just such a document as Webster had suggested in his *Sketches of American Policy* and in his lectures.

Washington, not unmindful of the young schoolmaster's visits to Mt. Vernon, called to pay his respects at Webster's rooms two days after the opening of the Convention. With Franklin, Webster was now on intimate terms, visiting or dining at the former's home frequently. In the brief notes of his diary Webster recorded visiting or dining in company with these other members of the Convention: James Madison, Rufus King, Abraham Baldwin, Edmund Randolph, William Samuel Johnson, Oliver Ellsworth, Roger Sherman, and William Livingston. On August 23, when the Convention was nearing the completion of its work, Webster noted: "Pass evening at Mr. Marshall's, with Convention Gentlemen." Webster's *Sketches* must have been mentioned often in these meetings, even if merely in the moment the author was introduced to one and another delegate. It seems quite improbable that he was not occasionally allowed to say a word in defense of his plan in spite of the strict covenant of secrecy. A guard was put on Franklin, it will be remembered, to hush the garrulous old statesman when he began reciting the day's procedure. But this act of caution does not indicate that the subject of the new form of government was taboo in all friendly meetings of the delegates at dinner or over a bottle of wine.

Webster certainly could have had little influence in affecting the progress of the discussion, but it cannot be denied that he alone had sounded the clarion call to continental union from Charleston, South Carolina, to Portsmouth, New Hampshire. He alone had phrased the fundamental concept upon which the Constitution must be founded. It cannot be doubted that his presence in Philadelphia and his association with the leading members of the Convention served in some small measure to call, again and again, attention to his "Plan of Policy." But even if we deny any credit to Webster as one who affected the work of the Convention, we cannot deny the efficacy of his labors in creating a public sentiment favorable to the success of the Convention.

Thomas Fitzsimmons, a delegate from Pennsylvania, evidently recognized Webster's earlier services, for on September 15, two days before the Convention adjourned, he wrote to Webster a letter, requesting, "from a conviction that your abilities may be eminently useful on the present occasion," the immediate preparation of an essay in support of the completed document. "It is already too evident," Fitzsimmons stated, "that there are people prepared to oppose it even before they are acquainted with its outlines. . . . If unreasonable jealousies are disseminated, its adoption may at least be protracted. In my mind to delay is to destroy."

On October 8 and 9 Webster, now released from his duties as Master in the Episcopal Academy, prepared in response to Fitzsimmon's request a pamphlet, entitled *An Examination into the Leading Principles of the Federal Constitution proposed by the late Convention held at Philadelphia. With Answers to the Principal Objections that have been raised against the System. By a Citizen of Amer-*

ica. A week later it was published and distributed throughout the city and nation. Dr. David Ramsay wrote from Charleston: "I have read it with pleasure, and it is now in brisk circulation among my friends. I have heard every person who has read it express his high approbation of its contents. It will doubtless be of singular service in recommending the adoption of the new Constitution."

After a short introduction in which the work of the Convention is extolled, the *Examination* explains and defends the division of the legislative branch of the government into two houses. Franklin, to whom the pamphlet was dedicated, had surrendered his objections on this greatly controverted point. Although Webster believed that "the opinions of the majority must give law to the whole state," a fundamental doctrine that might be construed as necessitating a single legislative house, he cites resolutions of the Continental Congress and several state legislatures to show that "a single body of men can be led astray."

A second section provides an extended comparison between the proposed form of government and the two best constitutions that ever existed in Europe, the Roman and the British. Superiority is found in the American Constitution in respect to the appointment, powers, and duration of office of the supreme executive; in respect to the appointment and tenure of judges; in respect to the representation of the people in legislation; in respect to the equal representation of the states in the Senate; and in respect to the happy discrimination between national and state sovereignty. On the last point the following comment is made: "However each state may be flattered by its independent sovereignty, we can have no union, no respectability, no national character, and, what is more, no national justice, till the states resign to one supreme head the exclusive power of legislating, judging and executing, in all matters of a general nature. Everything of a private or provincial nature

must still rest on the ground of respective state constitutions."
In the matter of popular representation in legislation, Webster states: "It is a false principle in the vulgar idea of representation that a man delegated by a particular district in a state is the representative of that district only; whereas in truth a member of the legislature from any town or county is the representative of the whole state. In passing laws, he is to view the whole collective interest of the state, and act from that view, not from a partial regard to the interest of the town or county where he is chosen."

A third section answers the objections made to the provisions of the Constitution by those who believed that the new government would be expensive; that two legislative houses were unnecessary; that the state legislatures would be annihilated; that the freedom of the press had been destroyed; that Congress would be able to levy unreasonable taxes; that Congress would quarter a standing army with the people; that trials by jury would be abolished; that federal courts would absorb the local judiciary; and that Congress would remove from the states the right to deal with Negro slavery. "Such," Webster concludes, "are the principal objections. . . . They are mostly frivolous, or founded on false constructions, and a misrepresentation of the true state of facts. They are evidently designed to raise groundless jealousies in the minds of well meaning people, who have little leisure and opportunity to examine into the principles of government."

In his last pages Webster discusses the question of liberty and tyranny, declaring that "the present state of our American states is very little better than a state of nature" in which it is possible for a powerful state to lay its weaker neighbor under tribute. In some states power rests on religion or military force. These errors, as well as the false notion propagated by Montesquieu that virtue is the basis of government, can be rectified only when it is universally agreed that "A general and tolerably equal distribution of landed property is the whole basis of national freedom."

Virtue, patriotism, or love of country [he continues] never was and never will be, till men's natures are changed, a fixed, permanent principle and support of government. But in an agricultural country, a general possession of land in fee simple may be rendered perpetual, and the inequalities introduced by commerce are too fluctuating to endanger government. An equality of property, with a necessity of alienation constantly operating to destroy combinations of powerful families, is the very soul of a republic. While this continues, the people will inevitably possess both power and freedom; when this is lost, power departs, liberty expires, and a commonwealth will inevitably assume some other form.

The liberty of the press, trial by jury, the Habeas Corpus writ, even Magna Charta itself, although justly deemed the palladia of freedom, are all inferior considerations, when compared with a general distribution of real property among every class of people. The power of entailing estates is more dangerous to liberty and republican government than all the constitutions that can be written on paper, or even than a standing army. Let the people have property and they will have power—a power that will forever be exerted to prevent a restriction of the press, and abolition of trial by jury, or the abridgement of any other privilege. The liberties of America, therefore, and her forms of government, stand on the broadest basis. Removed from the fears of a foreign invasion and conquest, they are not exposed to the convulsions that shake other governments; and the principles of freedom are so general and energetic as to exclude the possibility of a new change in our republican constitutions.

Further supports to the stability of the new government are the general institution of schools and that "principal bulwark of freedom," the right of election. "Let us then consider the New Federal Constitution," he concludes, "as it really is, an improvement on the best constitutions that the world ever saw."

Webster had swung over to views of the Federalist majority in the Convention, further altering thereby the concept of democracy which he had stated in 1785. He believed that popular sovereignty should be limited to the right of electing congressmen; that the electors should have no right to control the votes of their representatives; and that a magisterial senate, sitting in judgment upon the resolutions of the house, should prevent the "sudden and violent passions" of the populace from silencing "the voice of freedom." He abrogated his earlier belief in a bill of rights and substituted for it the doctrine of the property basis of government. Webster had become a republican, although he still thought of himself as a democrat. Like all men whose utopian thoughts are corrected by practical necessity, he was not able to harmonize the duality that continued to mark his thinking.

CHAPTER IX

EDITOR OF *The American Magazine*

"I HAVE been industrious—endeavored to do some good, and hope I shall be able to correct my faults and yet do more good." These were the sentiments Webster recorded in his diary on the occasion of his twenty-ninth birthday, October 16, 1787. He had been released from his duties at the Episcopal Academy, where for one quarter he taught mathematics and for another, English grammar. Early in his engagement he was busy enough in attempting to correct the bad habits engrained or permitted by "poor, low Irish masters." Although he had not lost his enthusiasm for "teaching the young idea how to shoot," he could not remain an underling in a struggling school and also wed Miss Rebecca Greenleaf. He had to strike out into a new field.

In Philadelphia his friends, Mathew Carey, the publisher, and Francis Hopkinson, the author of brilliant prose and verse satires, had begun *The Columbian Magazine*, a repository of a pastepot and shears assortment of English and American articles, together with an occasional original article by Jeremy Belknap, Dr. Rush, and Hopkinson. In New Haven Josiah Meigs, Webster's classmate, had founded *The New-Haven Gazette, and the Connecticut Magazine,* a paper now memorable for the publication of *American Antiquities*, the satiric thrusts by the Hartford Wits at the antifederalists. Boston had its magazine, conducted by Isaiah Thomas. But New York, where Webster found "the most favorable stand for a great commercial port in the

United States," was without a magazine. Believing that
this city would soon dominate the business of the new nation,
Webster conceived the idea of founding a magazine that
would embody his nationalistic ideas and thus, unlike the
other provincial monthlies, attain a national circulation and
influence.

After saying farewell to Franklin and to many other
friends, Webster left Philadelphia on October 24, 1787,
and went to New York City. Here he reached a tentative
agreement with Samuel Loudon, the printer, who, however,
refused to accept any financial responsibility for the ad-
venture. To Samuel Campbell, whose shady character he
suspected, Webster sold permission to print his three textbooks for a period of five years. With this cash in hand he
was able to proceed.

During the month of November he traveled through
Connecticut, securing promises of contributions and subscriptions from his old friends. The subscription papers
from New York, Philadelphia, Charleston, and Boston gave
the over-confident editor a promise of a circulation of 500,
a number sufficient to pay printing costs and a handsome
profit. On December 3, 1787, Webster signed the printing
contract and joyously went to work in preparing the first
number.

He was very moderate in his promises in his Introduction, because "The expectation of *failure* is connected with
the very name of a magazine," but he stated that "great
pains will be taken to render it in the execution both useful and amusing." He was "determined to collect as many
original Essays as possible; and particularly such as relate
to this country, and contain useful and curious discoveries
in the history or geography of America, or ingenious remarks on the science of Government and the peculiar and
interesting customs of the people in the different States."
He wished to appeal to every class of reader, and assured

his "fair readers" that "no inconsiderable pains will be taken to furnish them with entertainment." The arrows of wit, satire, and humor would not be poisoned with personal invective, ribaldry, or immorality. Although he conceded that Americans had a predilection for foreign works of this type, he insisted that "none of them can be wholly calculated for this country."

The American Magazine became Webster's new forum from which to address his fellow citizens. The original materials were largely from his pen. Trumbull's satire on education, *The Progress of Dulness,* was reprinted; Dwight sent in a few lines of verse, and Dr. Mason F. Cogswell wrote an occasional sentimental tale. A few selections, not too wisely chosen, were lifted from British sources. Occasional Gothic and sentimental stories and didactic letters to belles and beaus alone offered the reader relief from weighty thoughts. It was a learned magazine, crammed with ideas, information, and argument.

Webster arranged his materials under topical classifications, such as government, antiquities, miscellaneous essays, reviews of new publications, agriculture, theology, poetry, and news. The selections were brief, giving the publication something of the quality of a modern "digest," although many essays were run in serial form during several months.

In three respects *The American Magazine* attained an immediate superiority over all its predecessors and its rivals, a superiority which merits giving Webster credit for having first seen and realized the possibilities of a journal of discussion in America. Here were first presented a comprehensive theory of education, an able presentation of governmental problems, and, according to Lyon Richardson, "the first distinguished department of literary criticism."

As a literary critic Webster followed the manner of the reportorial school, overshadowing his own remarks with summaries, extracts, and descriptions. Often, too, his in-

terest in language drew him on to the length of columns in
the criticism of words and phrases. But when he pronounced
a judgment, his lucid analysis carried intellectual conviction. The most notable of his reviews lambasted Timothy
Dwight's *Triumph of Infidelity,* accusing the author of
padding his own ill-turned lines with plagiarized passages
from Pope, and of expressing harsh, illiberal thoughts. "The
author," Webster wrote, "appears to be a theological dog-
matist who has found the right way to heaven by creeds
and systems; and with more imperiousness than would become infinite wisdom and power, damns all who cannot
swallow his articles of faith. A man who can group together such men as Shaftesbury, Priestley, Chauncey, and
[Ethan] Allen and stigmatize these and many of the first
philosophers promiscuously as fools and knaves, can hardly
be a candidate for that heaven of love and benevolence
which the scripture informs us is prepared for good men."
In defending his review when newspaper critics assailed him,
Webster wrote in *The Daily Advertiser* (September 5,
1788): "I believe that all men are my brethren. I believe
in that religion which teaches *God is love,* and that men approach to perfection in proportion as they cherish the heavenly principle." Dwight, it is needless to say, contributed
nothing more to Webster's magazine.

In his political articles Webster supported the new Constitution and the ideas of the Federalist fathers. Jefferson's
Notes on Virginia was published and circulated in Philadelphia just as the Constitutional Convention was concluding its sessions. Among the harmless historical, geographical,
geological, botanical, and legal items, Jefferson had inserted, in Query XVII, the demand for a Bill of Rights
in the Constitution of Virginia: "The time for fixing every
essential right on a legal basis is while our rulers are honest,
and ourselves united." This statement, seized upon by the
anti-federalists, marked the beginning of Jefferson's leader-

ship of the opposition, although he did not return from France until 1790. John Dickinson had contended that a bill of rights could have no proper place in a federal constitution; and Dr. Rush had taken the extremist position that a bill of rights would have disgraced the document. "Would it not be absurd," he asked, "to frame a formal declaration that our natural rights are acquired from ourselves?"

While Hamilton, Madison, and Jay developed their legalistic arguments in support of the Constitution in the papers collected under the title of *The Federalist,* Webster in more vivid phrase continued the analysis of the objections to the new Constitution which had been hastily set down in the *Examination*. In December, 1787, he wrote an answer to the dissenting members of the Pennsylvania Convention, a group that had withdrawn from the meeting and had issued a blistering statement demanding a bill of rights. Webster called their arguments "declamatory nonsense," echoing Rush in undertaking "to prove that a standing bill of rights is absurd." Basing his case on the theory of the evolution of institutions, he said, "No constitutions in a free government can be unalterable. The present generation have no right to say what the next generation shall deem a privilege. . . . If our posterity are bound by our constitutions, and can neither amend nor annul them, they are to all intents and purposes our slaves." "For mercy's sake," he cried, "do not shut the door to improvements."

Webster opposed perpetual freedom of the press on the ground that the principle would be abused, even as was then evident by the publication of salacious stories and scandalous libels. The right of trial by jury, so unwise in the settlement of certain types of cases, he declared, could not be taken away so long as "the people remain attached to this mode of deciding causes." Scornfully Webster remarked in reducing their statements to absurdity: "As a supplement . . . I would suggest the following restriction —'That Congress shall never restrain any inhabitant of America from eating and drinking, at seasonable times, or prevent his lying on his left side, in a long winter's night, or even on his back, when he is fatigued by lying on his right.' "

The illiberality of the proponents of bills of rights was nowhere so apparent, Webster thought, as in their exclusion of clergymen from the right to hold civil offices. The common opinion that the business of the clergy is wholly spiritual is a gross error, he wrote, because it is their business to inform the people on all subjects and correct their morals. Thus "they have a direct influence on government." Since they are subjects of law, they "ought as freemen to be eligible to a seat in the legislature, provided the people incline to choose them." Webster had learned in his travels that inattention to religion had become general and that a complete relaxation of moral standards might follow the disestablishment of the various state churches. On practical grounds, therefore, he withdrew from his youthful position in respect to the relationship between the church and the state: "Without any regard to the compulsion over consciences or any reference to a future life, a legal provision for the moral instructors of men is as beneficial in society as any civil or literary institution whatever; and a commonalty who have not the benefit of such instruction will, I presume to assert, always be ignorant and of rough uncivil manners." At this time the homogeneous population in each state, with respect to ancestry and church affiliation, had created no religious problem; in Connecticut, for example, a Toleration Act had been passed, granting the members of any church other than the established church exemption from the payment of church rates. Webster's opinion, therefore, did not, in his own way of thinking, go contrary to the spirit of the times. In a sense the church is an adult school, a continuation of the elementary school and the academy. Since the evils of the European church, as well as the bigoted intolerance of the Puritan fathers, had not been suffered to exist in eighteenth-century America, no danger seemed likely to arise under this system of a popularly supported clergy. To Webster, who still opposed state religious indoctrination, the usefulness of this method of popular instruction overbalanced all objections.

In his writings on government Webster fell foul of Jefferson, interpreting the latter's objection to an ordinary legislature's power to alter the Virginia Constitution, to mean that Jefferson advocated a permanent, unalterable government. In an epistolary interchange on this point, Jefferson (December 4, 1790) explained that he had been misinterpreted; Webster, however, refused to be corrected, rephrasing firmly, if somewhat deferentially, his interpretation of the remarks in the *Notes on Virginia*.

Webster held that "theories and forms of government are empty things," and that the spirit of a government springs immediately from the temper and habits of a people. Since habits are continually changing, the frequent election of representatives in a republic will and should keep the government in accord with the wishes of the majority. It was on this right of election that Webster grounded his whole argument, insisting that "a union of interests between the rulers and the people, which union will always coexist with free elections, is not only the best, but the only security for their liberties which the people can wish for and demand." He summarized his speculative opinions thus:

That the power of a State is at all times equal; that neither the people themselves, nor a Convention of their Delegates, have either the power or the right to make an unalterable Constitution; that the power of creating a legislative body, or the sovereign right of election, is solely in the people; but the sovereign power of making laws is solely in an Assembly of their Representatives; that the people have no right to give binding instructions to their Representatives; consequently a distinction between a *Convention* and a *Legislature,* can be merely a difference of *forms;* that Representatives have no right to prolong the period of their delegation; that being taken from the mass of the people and having a common interest with them, they will be influenced, even by private interest, to promote the public good; and that such a government, which is a novelty on earth, is perhaps the best that can be framed, and the only form which will always have for its object, the general good.

Notable though Webster's contribution to the political discussion of 1788 was, he was writing in a field thoroughly canvassed by every lawyer and legislator, and his opinions no longer had novelty. Beside the monumental *Federalist* Webster's essays fade into unimportance, but the good effect of their barbed shafts of ridicule was frequently commented upon.

Possibly of most significance in *The American Magazine* were the editor's extended remarks on education. These essays refined and improved the tentative statements in his textbooks and lectures. In his journeys Webster had investigated the state laws on the subject of education, had visited schools, academies, and colleges, and had spoken with many schoolmasters, professors, and men interested in education. Everywhere south of New England he noted with regret that "no provision for public schools was incorporated into the original fundamental laws." Academies and colleges had been established, in some cases under state auspices, but a common school education was out of the reach of the poor child. Webster, practical philosopher that he was, attempted to formulate a program for the time, not an idealistic theory which would not "come home to men's business and bosoms."

Beginning with the idea that "the mode of education and the arts taught to youth have in every nation been adapted to its particular stage of society or local circumstances," Webster pointed out the goals to be reached by an American system and the existent errors which deferred the attainment of these goals.

The objects of education should be, in addition to diffusing a knowledge of the arts and sciences, to "implant in the minds of the American youth, the principles of virtue and liberty, and inspire them with just and liberal ideas of government, and with an inviolable attachment to their own country." By this means could be established a national character, unique in informed intelligence and ability to cope with the problems of state, church, and personal conduct. Since Webster believed in the evolving nature of institutions, already demonstrated by his objection to unalterable constitutions, he thought of the school as the one instrument by which the people might be brought both to an understanding of their immediate problems and to a wise determination of the inevitable changes they would be called upon to make. A people possessing full power over its own destiny could not go astray if its democratic right of election and ownership of property were exercised in the light of such an education.

One error of several of the states brought this idea to a focus. They had established academies and colleges where men of property might send their sons for education, but these same states had not made provision for elementary schools where children of the poorer rank might even learn reading and writing. This system, which had been transported from Europe and which had functioned quite well while the colonies were members of a monarchy, was a glaring solecism in America. "The constitutions are *republican*, and the laws of education are *monarchical*. The former extend civil rights to every industrious citizen; the latter deprive a large proportion of the citizens of a most valuable privilege." Obvious it was to Webster that, if youth were to be expected to grow into citizens capable of directing a democracy, it must be by means of an education suited to American principles and not to an ignorance similar to that which everywhere existed in monarchical governments.

Webster had begun his nationalistic educational program with a vague emotional ecstasy, but in his years of study and travel he had found a valid philosophical basis upon which to establish it.

"When I speak of diffusion of knowledge," Webster explained in illustrating this doctrine, "I do not mean merely a knowledge of spelling books and the New Testament. An acquaintance with ethics, and with the general principles of law, commerce, money and government, is necessary for the yeomanry of a republican state." To these subjects he added also: "A selection of essays, respecting the settlement and geography of America; the history of the late revolution and of the most remarkable characters and events that distinguished it, and a compendium of the principles of the federal and provincial governments, should be the principal school book in the United States." He wished children to acquire ideas, and therefore he objected to the dull routine of the rote method and the time wasted in learning subjects that would never be of practical value.

This emphasis on practicality led Webster to reiterate his objections to the study of the ancient and modern languages, except on the part of future professional men, and to the use of the Bible as a textbook. He objected, also, to the too early introduction of difficult sciences into the curriculum. His own experience as a Master of Mathematics in the Episcopal Academy made clear to him that this subject should be deferred until pupils possessed the power of comparing and combining ideas. He objected, also, to the uniformity of the academic curriculum, believing that boys planning to enter the learned professions and mercantile employment and agriculture "should be directed to pursue those branches which are connected more immediately with the business for which they are destined." This type of vocational training would prepare the way for improvements and would make the pursuit of this occupation a pleasure. "What is now called a liberal education," he declared, "disqualifies a man for business," because a long life in the study of books inclines a boy to a life of ease "which no efforts can overcome." The ingraining of good habits of work, one of the chief ends of Webster's system, could not be accomplished by turning out "smatterers" in languages and sciences or by leading boys through subjects in which they had no interest.

Along with good habits of work, Webster wished students to acquire "good principles," a predisposition for a virtuous life. "For this reason society requires that the education of youth should be watched with the most scrupulous attention. Education, in a great measure, forms the moral characters of men, and morals are the basis of government. Education should therefore be the first care of a legislature; not merely the institution of schools, but the furnishing of them with the best men for teachers. A good system of education should be the first article in the code of political regulations; for it is much easier to introduce and establish an effectual system for preserving morals, than to correct by penal statutes the ill effects of a bad system." On this point Webster was emphatic; he asserted: "The goodness of a heart is of infinitely more consequence to society than an elegance of manners; nor will any superficial accomplishments repair the want of principle in the mind. It is always better to be *vulgarly* right than *politely* wrong."

Under such convictions Webster naturally placed great emphasis upon the need for trained, upright teachers. In many communities, he had found, "the most important business in civil society," teaching, had been committed to worthless fellows, even convicts who had been transported for their crimes. "Gracious heavens!" he cried. "Must the wretches, who have forfeited their lives and been pronounced unworthy to be inhabitants of a *foreign* country, be entrusted with the education, the morals, the character of *American* youth?" With a passionate fervor he asserted: "The education of youth [is] an employment of more consequence than making laws and preaching the gospel, because it lays the foundation on which both law and gospel rest for success."

In view of the inadequate provision for elementary education in the middle and southern states, Webster asked that schools be conducted for four months each year, "when boys are not otherwise employed." This modest beginning Webster thought neither impracticable nor difficult; its importance was second only to the establishment of an efficient and permanent federal government. Without it, "mankind cannot know to what a degree of perfection society and mankind may be carried."

As the culmination of this system of education Webster advocated that "a tour through the United States ought now to be considered as a necessary part of a liberal education." Instead of sending boys to Europe where they may learn follies and vices, parents should see that their sons acquire a correct knowledge of the geography and people of the several states. From this experience would arise an informed national loyalty and understanding, the first effects of which would be the eradication of petty sectional jealousies.

In his college days Webster had expressed disgust at the stupidity which had withheld the benefits of education from women. Now he brought this theme within his broad nationalistic concept by showing that women's "influence in controlling the manners of a nation" was in some ways more considerable than men's. Mothers form the dispositions of their children by teaching precepts of conduct and morality. For this reason, "their own education should therefore enable them to implant in the tender mind, such sentiments of virtue, propriety and dignity, as are suited to the freedom of our governments." In social intercourse women set the tone of conversation and action; since education fortifies female virtue, every girl should be sent to school.

But Webster objected to modeling American female education along European lines. "That education is always wrong," he averred, "which raises a woman above the duties of her station." Sending mechanic's and shopkeeper's daughters to boarding school is unwise; these girls acquire false aristocratical notions which their husbands, probably their fathers' apprentices, cannot support. Female education should have utility for its aim, and the subjects of study should comprehend those usually associated with a liberal education, the emphasis falling upon geography, history, and poetry, and Addison's essays. Novels were objected to because they paint, as well as the social virtues, "the vicious part of mankind." In "An Address to Young Ladies" Webster enlarged upon the disagreeable results attendant upon a too great fondness for reading: "Learning, or acquaintance with books, may be a very agreeable or a very disagreeable accomplishment, in proportion to the discretion of the lady who possesses it. Properly employed, it is highly satisfactory to the lady and her connections; but I believe observation will confirm my conjecture that a strong attachment to books in a lady often deters a man from approaching her with the offer of his heart."

Quixotic as some of Webster's educational ideas may seem today, it must be remembered that he was dealing with a frontier society. The rough manners of the wilderness needed to be softened, and the principles of virtue and good behavior inculcated. Useful learning needed to be spread among the whole body of children; any attempt to educate a class or a sex above its station or in foreign manners would destroy the unity and simplicity that should mark a new nation at its origin. Webster's theory of the evolution of society was predicated on the fundamental assumption that the whole population should move ahead en masse, the schools preparing the advance through uniformly useful instruction.

There were other interesting materials from the pen of the editor in *The American Magazine*. While conversing with Franklin, Webster had learned that the old forts still visible on the Muskingum River might have been erected by Ferdinand De Soto. From all available printed sources, Webster supported this conclusion, writing three long letters to President Stiles on the subject. Jeremy Belknap, the pugnacious historian, disproved Webster's contention in an article in *The Columbian Magazine*. Although he erred in his conclusions in this instance, Webster was correct in arousing an interest in the antiquities of America. Here and there a few persons, like Belknap and Ebenezer Hazard, were collecting state papers, historical information, and traditions. But on the whole the people were not conscious of their past or of the value of preserving the records of their past. Webster called attention to this subject by printing abridgments of Captain John Smith's *History of Virginia* and William Roberts's *History of Florida*, and by asking his readers to assist in throwing every possible light on American antiquities. In this work Webster was a pioneer.

Webster continued in *The American Magazine* his campaign for copyright legislation, because many of his articles were being reprinted in newspapers. "A man who has devoted a most valuable period of his life to the acquisition of knowledge; who has grown 'pale o'er the midnight lamp'; who labors to decypher ancient manuscripts or purchase copies at three thousand per cent. above the usual price of books, is indubitably entitled to the exclusive advantages resulting from his exertions and expenses." No less imperative than a copyright law was a law protecting "the authors of useful inventions," and Webster declared that "the want of some regulations for this purpose may be numbered among the defects of the American governments." "The productions of genius and the imagination," he continued with a logic that has since been written into law, "are if possible more really and exclusively property than houses and lands, and are equally entitled to legal security."

Philological writings also took up some space in the magazine. These emanated from an organization Webster was instrumental in founding in March, 1788, the Philological Society. To his friends, Dr. Mason F. Cogswell, Josiah Ogden Hoffman, William Dunlap, Samuel Latham Mitchill, among others, Webster had carried the idea that an organization "founded for the particular purpose of ascertaining and improving the American tongue," might pave the way for future investigators in "ascertaining the force and beauty of our own language." Webster read several dissertations, Dunlap read his play, *The Modest Soldier, or Love in New York*, and the other members contributed remarks and criticisms. In July, when the Federalists massed their strength in a parade to honor the occasion of the adoption of the Constitution of the United States by ten state conventions and to speed the decision of the New York Convention, the Philological Society formed a company of marchers. Their uniform black dress, probably in imitation of the French Academy, "made a very respectable figure." To Webster, the leading Federalist writer in New York, fell the pleasant duty of preparing the official report of the procession, and hence we have from his pen this account of the nationalistic ardor to which he inflamed his associates:

THE PHILOLOGICAL SOCIETY

The secretary, bearing a scroll, containing the principles of a *Federal* language.

Vice-president and librarian, the latter carrying Mr. Horne Tooke's treatise on language; as a mark of respect for the book which contains a new discovery, and as a mark of respect for the author, whose zeal for the American cause, during the late war, subjected him to a prosecution.

Josiah Ogden Hoffman, Esq. the president of the society, with a sash of blue and white ribbons. The standard bearer, Mr. William Dunlap, with the arms of the society, viz.—Argent three tongues, gules, in chief; emblematical of *language*, the improvement of which is the object of the institution. Chevron, or, indicating firmness and support; an *eye*, emblematical of *discernment* over a pyramid, or rude monument, sculptured with Gothic, Hebrew, and Greek letters. The Gothic on the *light* side, indicating the *obvious* origin of the American language from the Gothic. The Hebrew and Greek, upon the reverse or *shade*, of the monument, expressing the remoteness and *obscurity* of the connection between those languages and the modern. The *crest*, a cluster of cohering magnets, attracted by a key in the centre; emblematical of *union* among the society, in acquiring *language* the *key* of knowledge; the clinging to their *native* tongue in preference to a *foreign* one. The *shield*, ornamented with a branch of the oak, from which is collected the *gall*, used in making ink, and a sprig of *flax*, from which *paper* is made, supported on the dexter side, by Cadmus, in a robe of Tyrian purple, bearing in his right hand, leaves of the rush or flag, papyrus, marked with Phoenician characters; representing the introduction of letters into Greece, and the origin of writing. On the sinister side, by Hermes, or Taaut, the inventor of letters, and god of eloquence, grasping his caduceus or wand. Motto—*Concedat Laurea Linguae*—expressive of the superiority of *civil* over *military* honors. The flag, embellished with the Genius of America, crowned with a wreath of 13 plumes, ten of them starred, representing the ten States which have ratified the Constitution. Her right hand pointing to the Philological Society, and in her left, a standard, with a pendant, inscribed with the word, CONSTITUTION. The members of the society in order, clothed in black.

The Society suffered competition with a legal club, a situation evoking from Dunlap a wretched verse play with the title, "Cuttgrisingwoldes," a word interpreted by the author to mean brotherquills. In a dark plot to break up the Society some of the lawyers tricked Webster into supporting them, but their efforts were frustrated. Most amusing in the farce is the picture of Webster, the schoolmaster of a set of old dunces:

> *When first I join'd them how oft did I hammer*
> *Night after Night, to teach the dunces Grammer*
> *My Rules, my lectures, ev'ry night repeated*
> *Began to talk sometimes ere they were seated*
> *To shew my zeal I ev'ry night held forth*
> *And deep imprest th' Idea of my worth*
> *Not soon forgot.*

After a good deal of lecturing and cajoling, Webster secured from his colleagues a testimonial of the merits of his Spelling Book, recommending it "to the use of schools in the United States, as an accurate, well digested system of principles and rules, calculated to destroy the various false dialects in pronunciation in the several states, an object very desirable in a federal republic." But they refused to endorse his heretical Grammar, despite their reverence for Horne Tooke or their association with Tooke's American disciple.

Webster evidently inculcated his notions with thoroughness, for when the Society disbanded in favor of the Friendly Club, nationalistic feelings still animated the members. Dunlap went forward in the preparation of patriotic plays, and Charles Brockden Brown won for himself a permanent place in the history of American fiction by enunciating a nationalistic critical theory.

From the beginning of his magazine enterprise Webster wanted to create a national paper, one which would reach every corner of the United States and derive its materials from every able pen. When promised original materials failed to turn up, he formulated a scheme of uniting the chief literary characters of every state in a co-operative venture. He proposed inviting Belknap, Hazard, Dr. Ramsay, Dr. Rush, Dwight, Trumbull, Barlow, and Madison to become proprietors. Hazard, disliking Webster because he

was "the Monarch" of the Philological Society, advised
Belknap to withhold his acceptance. Dr. Rush refused to
share in the business because he could not promise regular
contributions and because the proposed magazine was not
to be issued in Philadelphia, "the primum mobile of the
United States." Hazard and Belknap jockeyed with Webster until an agreement was made to publish a combined
magazine and register of historical documents. Although a
prospectus was issued in November, the whole matter came
to naught. Webster announced that it was not consistent with
his "interest and views in life to devote his whole time to
a work of this kind." Despite his early sanguine expectations, he had lost £250 in *The American Magazine;* he
could not wed Rebecca Greenleaf on such unfavorable
prospects.

On his thirtieth birthday, October 16, 1788, he commented in his diary: "30 years of my life gone—a large
portion of the ordinary age of man! I have read much,
written much, and tried to do much good, but with little
advantage to myself. I will now leave writing and do more
lucrative business. My moral conduct stands fair with the
world, and what is more, with my own Conscience. But I
am a bachelor and want the happiness of a friend whose
interest and feelings should be mine." With these sentiments guiding him, Webster was "happy to quit New
York."

The year in New York had given Webster ample opportunity to test his powers as an author; the superiority of
The American Magazine, so much of it being from his pen,
gave him the position of America's leading essayist, even
though his vigorous, vehement, pugnacious, assertive articles never enjoyed any of the compensating graces of
rhetorical expression. With a bludgeon in his heavy hands,
Webster attacked fiercely, repeatedly the errors of American thought and practice. With exemplary lore drawn from

NOAH WEBSTER, JUN. ESQ.

PORCUPINE PORTRAIT OF WEBSTER
from *The American Spelling Book.*

the whole bibliography of recorded history, he adduced parallel situations for every American event. This parade of learning from Greek, Latin, Biblical, English, and French sources aroused many mocking comments from those who were unable to meet the schoolmaster with similar weapons. Webster was wont to pontificate, to grow red in the face with the moral earnestness of a Puritan pulpit-thumper. His snarling wit lacked the salt of Franklin's good humor and of Francis Hopkinson's rollicking fun. He had taken the nation for his scholars, and he used old-fashioned brow-beating tactics.

This quality for a time rendered him popular with the small group of lawyers, physicians, and businessmen with whom he associated in New York. But soon they, as Dunlap represented in "Cuttgrisingwoldes," grew tired of the ever-lasting harangues and complained of weary ears. To Cogswell Webster wrote shortly after his departure: "I am happy to be remembered to you. It is a satisfaction to find a few friends whose attachment is not shaken by slight faults or popular opinion." Webster became an interesting incident in these men's lives, not a friend. He won respect, not affection. His introspective investigations led more frequently to a rearrangement of his prejudices than to an improvement in the manner or content of his action or thought.

After a short visit with his parents at Hartford in December, 1788, Webster went to Boston, reaching that city on the last day of the year. His first act was to put to press his *Dissertations on the English Language,* which Isaiah Thomas printed in lieu of the payment of royalties on the *Institute.* In writing to Cogswell, on January 31, 1789, Webster described his book as "full of criticisms, which some will call good sense and others nonsense. People who will take the trouble to read it will say I have a wonderful knack at finding faults where they before found beauties. I shall assert some strange things; some of them will be proved; and others, the world will say, are left unsupported. Men who are friendly will be inclined to believe me; those who know nothing and care nothing about me will care as little about my writings; and a host of adversaries, whose favorite authors I attack, will kick and flounce till they fall themselves or throw me. Apropos: Some great men with whose works I have taken liberties stand with their mouths open, ready to devour the child as soon as it is born. But an author's brats are doomed to be the sport of a mad world; I have treated others as I thought they deserved; and probably mine will fare as well."

In May it was completed, an octavo volume of 410 pages. Here were printed the five dissertations on language Webster had read during his lecture tour, with copious notes and an appendix setting forth the advantages of a reformed mode of spelling. Dr. Stiles acknowledged the gift of a copy to the Yale College Library thus: "We glory in a Son of this Alma Mater that can be the author of such a learned production." *The Massachusetts Magazine* praised "the depth of philological knowledge, justness of sentiment, and purity of style." Several passages were reprinted to illustrate Webster's "superior abilities, nice discernment, and correct taste." The book is a curious compound of good sense and prejudice, the latter particularly evident in the strident denunciation of the stylistic vagaries of Dr. Samuel Johnson and the historians, Robertson and Gibbon. Much of the linguistic matter, developed on the theory of Tooke, is quite wrong, but not nearly so far wrong as the etymological opinions of Dr. Johnson. At this time the study of comparative philology was in its infancy; Webster's book placed him in the forefront of the workers in the field. A nationalistic ardor quickens the dead facts of linguistics and renders the book still very readable. Most interesting was Webster's explanation of the circumstances which "render a future separation of the American tongue from the English necessary and unavoidable":

The vicinity of the European nations, with the uninterrupted communication in peace and the changes of domination in war, are gradually assimilating their respective languages. The English with others is suffering continual alterations. America, placed at a distance from those nations, will feel in a much less degree, the influence of the assimilating causes; at the same time, numerous local causes, such as a new country, new associations of people, new combinations of ideas in arts and sciences, and some intercourse with tribes wholly unknown in Europe, will introduce new words into the American tongue. These causes will produce, in a course of time, a language in North America as different from the future language of England as the modern Dutch, Spanish, and Swedish are from the German or from one another.

This theory took hold upon the American mind, Jefferson so late as 1813 echoing it in his correspondence. Anglophiles, of course, repudiated the notion. Over this idea was waged a continuous warfare for a century, Webster becoming the focal point in the battle.

With the fondness for titles that marked the first days of our new nation, Webster dedicated his *Dissertations* to his mentor in phonetic spelling thus: "To his Excellency, Benjamin Franklin, Esq., LL.D., F.R.S., Late President of the Commonwealth of Pennsylvania." He added a four-page tribute to Franklin as the philosopher who sought practical truths, the writer who did not sacrifice truth to embellishment, the statesman who had courage to change his opinions, and the man whose conduct was regulated by rules of moral and social virtue. The old printer was pleased with this mark of respect; despite his illness and pain he wrote (December 26, 1789) a long letter of appreciation and commentary, listing errors which had crept into the English language and suggesting that Webster "in some future publication" should "set a discountenancing mark upon them."

Webster was happier in Boston than he had been in New

York, for "the good girl," Rebecca Greenleaf, expressed
deep interest in his wishes. James Greenleaf had commended Webster warmly to his parents, brothers, and sisters. All took a friendly part in making his visit and wooing
pleasant. Dr. Nathaniel W. Appleton had found much to
admire in the young lecturer on an earlier visit, and now
Thomas Dawes, Jr., talented young lawyer and whimsical
humorist, helped to mine the vein of gold in Webster.
They had married Greenleaf girls and they counseled Webster not to delay too long. Nearly two years had passed
since the "understanding" had been reached. They thought,
no doubt, that marriage would settle the itinerant schoolmaster, lecturer, and editor, and place him in a position to
secure the rewards his talents deserved.

James Greenleaf, with whom Webster had discussed his
marriage plans, was now in Amsterdam, engaged as an ex-
porter. In his letters he urged delay, on the ground that
his sister had never known the want of the little comforts
of life, and it would afford him "a very painful reflection
were she ever placed in a situation to want them." At the
same time he offered to do what he could to help in establishing the couple when Webster had favorable prospects.
Webster replied that he would postpone marriage until he
could place her "in a genteel situation and spread a decent
table for her friends." But the longer Webster remained in
Boston, the more intolerable became the prospect of continued bachelorhood. He determined to relinquish forever
"all little projects" and to enter the profession of law as a
permanent business. Dawes advised him to return to Hartford where he was known and where his property would
go further than in Boston in supporting a family. Webster
preferred to remain in Boston so that Becca might be with
her friends, but she graciously acquiesced in going to Hartford to avoid the uncertainty of success. Webster's pride
was enlisted in this too; he feared that their humble home

might compare unfavorably with those of Dawes and Appleton.

In May, 1789, Webster moved to Hartford, took rooms with John Trumbull, and again tacked up his little sign: NOAH WEBSTER, JR., ATTORNEY AT LAW. Some little business came to his office, and he was flattered with the hope of success. His friends, Trumbull, Dr. Lemuel Hopkins, and Jeremiah Wadsworth, assured him that he should have no fears. Royalties on his books would bring between £200 and £300 during the next two years. His prospects seemed bright enough. He wrote to James, therefore (June 6, 1789): "I think it prudent and best to marry as soon as a house can be obtained and furnished. For this we depend wholly on your goodness; and the sooner you can make it convenient to assist your sister, the sooner you will make us happy. We have habits of economy and industry; but we are perhaps more ambitious to be *good* than *great*. It gives me some pain that Becca will have to leave her friends,—friends which can no where be replaced. But no consideration can separate us, and she will cheerfully go where my interest leads me. For this she is entitled to my warmest gratitude; indeed, I hardly know which she has the most of, my gratitude or my love."

On October 12, 1789, two weeks before the marriage, he explained his prospects to James:

It is of consequence to a man to be settled, to be known as an established resident and citizen, and to take an interest in society and business, before he can acquire the confidence of his countrymen, and confidence must precede employment. In law as in physic, a young man must make slow progress in business; his abilities must be *tried*, before he can be much *trusted* with important business. The progress of young lawyers is nearly ascertained in this town. The first year, they get but little business—the second, more—the third, may nearly support themselves—the fourth, perhaps make a little money, and after that they have generally pretty full practice and make one, two or three hundred a year. I have as good a prospect as my neighbors; better I cannot expect. I believe however my talents for speaking, notwithstanding Mr. Watson's opinion, are rather superior to most of our young men's. I judge from debates in our clubs, and the opinions my friends there form of me. Impute this not to vanity; for I am writing to a friend. Any opinion of this kind must be here suppressed. Yet I am confident, perseverance will accomplish any thing; and nothing but sickness and death shall check my efforts.

James had given Webster an order for $1000 with which to buy furniture. Rebecca, with more taste than an eye on the pocketbook should have dictated, bought chintz furniture, china, and looking glasses. The money was gone, although the "best room" and the kitchen remained unsupplied. Her wedding clothes and dresses cost a hundred dollars more, and this Webster had to pay from his own pocket, as well as other expenses. When he told her what she had done, "she cried as if to break her little heart."

On October 26, 1789, Noah Webster and Rebecca Greenleaf were married in her father's home in Boston. She was twenty-three years of age, eight years younger than Webster; she was born on May 27, 1766. In his diary he wrote: "This day I became a husband. I have lived a long time a bachelor, something more than thirty-one years. But I had no person to form a plan for me in early life and direct me to a profession. I had an enterprising turn of mind, was bold, vain, inexperienced. I have made some unsuccessful attempts, but on the whole have done as well as most men of my years. I begin a profession at a late period of life, but have some advantages of travelling and observation. I am united to an amiable woman, and, if I am not happy, shall be much disappointed."

CHAPTER X

The Hartford Prompter

On November 7, 1789, the Noah Websters began house-keeping in a large, convenient, elegant—to use the proud young husband's adjectives—house, recently erected by Colonel Jeremiah Wadsworth. The new furniture was arranged, and an elaborate housewarming was planned. But Mrs. Webster came down with a severe case of influenza and caused the postponement of the party for three weeks. Her sister, Priscilla, had come with her, so that she was not wholly without the accustomed ministering hands of her own family. This illness, in addition to the disagreeable autumn weather, frequently sent the young bride into fits of homesickness. One day, she confided to her brother, she "did nothing but baul the whole day." But there was work to be done, and there were friends to be entertained. These duties soon brought back the roses to her cheeks and the smiles to her face.

For the Thanksgiving season, for example, she proved her domestic virtuosity. She baked eleven pumpkin puddings, three plum puddings, and seven apple pies. In a few days the pumpkin puddings were gone, and Webster and Priscilla began to make a hue and a cry for more, but she refused to humor them until the other pastry was eaten.

On Thanksgiving Day Noah and Rebecca were guests at his father's home. His mother shed tears as she met Rebecca the first time. Most of the family were together, and the little children crowded around the new aunt and admired her clothes, for Rebecca was wearing a thick green brocade,

flowered with pink and red roses. The little Boston lady
with elegant manners seemed like a creature from another
world in the plain Connecticut Yankee home in West Hartford.

On the following day the newlyweds had, as Rebecca
wrote to her brother, "a large company of the most respectable citizens to dine. For the sake of mentioning their pretty
names, I will record them: on my left hand sat the Hon.
Jesse Root, [Chief Justice of Connecticut]; John Trumbull,
author of M'Fingal; Peter Colt, Esq., Treasurer of this
State; Ralph Pomeroy, Esq., Comptroller General; Enoch
Perkins, Esq., an Attorney at Law; James Watson, Esq.,
partner of our dear James; if we unite to the above names
that of Noah, Priscilla and Rebecca, I think they will make
a notable appearance for one table—but I forgot to mention
the Hon. Jeremiah Wadsworth, who was one of the company." Following the dinner, the men, who formed a legal
club, meeting fortnightly, discussed the question: "Whether
a woman can be bound by warranty of land, made under
coverture."

Trumbull, in writing to Oliver Wolcott, expressed as-
tonishment at the elegance with which the Websters began
their career: "Webster has returned and brought with him
a very pretty wife. I wish him success, but I doubt in the
present decay of business in our profession whether his profits
will enable him to keep up the style he sets out with. I
fear he will breakfast upon Institutes, dine upon Dissertations, and go to bed supperless."

There was, indeed, a furrow in Webster's forehead, for
his wife's lavish expenditure for furniture had consumed
the money he had saved for household expenses. His father
was in trouble, too, an attachment having been laid against
his estate. Since this debt had been occasioned by Webster's
college expenses, he felt deeply wounded at the thought of
his father's being forced to move to the new settlements in

New York in a reduced condition. "I want money," he confided to James Greenleaf, "not merely to live, but also to purchase a Law Library without which I cannot do business to advantage or arrive at eminence." With $200 borrowed from James, he purchased a library. In April he wrote: "I think my prospects are good. My business is increasing, tho small. Attorneys are multiplying, and the business is diminishing. So that *eminence* alone can ensure full success. This is a spring to emulation, and I shall have the advantage of a better law library than three-fourths of my competitors. Besides, you will recollect that I always believed my talent to lay in *speaking*. In this you differed from me. But while I acknowledge your better opinion in most articles that respect myself, in this I have some proof that I am not mistaken. I will only add that so far as I can judge, the world is upon better terms with me." But increased business did not come, and Webster cast about for a means with which to speculate in the state debt and western lands, not that he might be rich, but that he might do good:

I have lamented that in the general scramble for property, I had not a small capital to employ; as the purchase of paper was attended with no risk, and I wished to add a few thousand dollars to my means of living—it would have made more cheerful hours in my little family. But I am not discontented as it is; as I am convinced I shall never want, while I have my health. Had I more property, I should gratify some of the strongest desires of my heart in projecting and carrying into effect schemes of public utility; but which I cannot bring forward with advantage, because I have not influence enough. *Money gives that influence.* This circumstance of my life gives me more mortification than any regard to property from other motives. However I think my influence is growing, as it is; and I believe it best for a man to grow slowly. The trees which are long acquiring their full growth are firm wood and durable. Those of rapid growth make poor timber.

As an earnest of the good he would do with wealth, Webster generously donated to Yale College in February, 1790, a premium of one per cent on his royalties from the *Institute*, the income to be given as a prize for the best essay in ethics, moral philosophy, and belles lettres. There were other hopeful plans Webster had for improvements, but these he could not express. His cramped circumstances and the evidences of hostility to his ideas depressed him. Little comfort was there in Dr. Rush's letter on this theme: "That man will be egregiously disappointed who expects the rewards of patriotism or successful enterprises on this side of the grave. . . . Continue to do all the good you can by enlightening our country. *Expect* to be persecuted for doing good; and *Learn* to rejoice in persecution." And so, when writing to President Washington on agriculture, Webster asked that his communication be kept a secret, "not because I doubt the justness of the principles advanced, but because any doctrines I might advance, under the signature of my name, would not meet with the consideration they might deserve. Setting aside my youth, the prejudices of many men are against me. I have written much more than any other man of my age in favor of the revolution and my country, and at times my opinions have been unpopular. I wish now to attend solely to my profession, and to be unknown in any other sphere of life."

But Webster's pen scratched on. He could not stop writing the opinions that crowded into his mind, nor could his embarrassed finances prevent him from launching new books.

In December, 1789, he published anonymously a closely reasoned eighteen-page pamphlet, entitled *Attention! or, New Thoughts on a Serious Subject; being an Enquiry into the Excise Laws of Connecticut,* in which he "endeavored to prove to the satisfaction of every candid mind that any duty laid on articles of import . . . is really and substantially an impost . . . and contrary to the spirit and letter of the federal Constitution." Such assessments, Webster argued, would destroy the commerce of Connecticut and arouse popular resentment, since the tax, proposed to be levied by the Legislature, would fall unequally on the people. "Excise duties are in themselves odious to a free people, unfriendly to morals, and productive of infinite frauds," he concluded. The Whiskey Rebellion in Pennsylvania was more than four years in the future, but Webster knew the American people sufficiently well to demonstrate the folly of unwise economic legislation.

This essay on the excise, although a restatement of his earlier objection to state imposts, may have originated in the legal club, where he presented papers on these subjects: "An Inquiry into the Origin of the Words Domesday, Parish, Parliament, Peer, Baron, with Remarks, new and interesting"; "The Injustice, Absurdity, and Bad Policy of Laws against Usury"; "The Grounds and Extent of Allegiance, Natural and Local"; and "Explanation of Reezons why Marriage iz prohibited between Natural Relations, designed to determin the Propriety of marrying a Wife's Sister."

There was another club in Hartford, The Friendly Club, now memorable as the gathering-place of the Hartford Wits, that little band of intellectuals and aristocrats who turned their disdain of democracy into bristling heroic couplets. Webster, who had added much luster to Hartford as a literary center, immediately took his place as a member. Here were John Trumbull, a frail, nervous, impatient little man with a cutting wit; Dr. Lemuel Hopkins, with a long nose as a handle to his cane-like body, equally ready to strike at political as well as at medical quacks; Dr. Mason F. Cogswell, affable and goodhumored, addicted to the writing of oriental tales and Richardsonian epistles; and Theodore Dwight, brother of Timothy, prating of Yankee superiority. Colonel David Humphreys stopped in occasionally, with a bag full of poetry as mechanical as his woolen factory; and Dr. Timothy Dwight, nearsightedly peering at his listeners, brought to Hartford his campaign for the presidency of Yale College, the epic poetic urge having been supplanted by more worldly ambitions. Only Joel Barlow, the bright, particular star of the galaxy, was missing, a reprobate now in France, but possibly not beyond redemption by such a saint of Congregationalism as Dr. Nathan Strong, should the wanderer return. It was a tight, smug, opinionated, but withal brilliant, circle, the like of which America did not have until the Saturday Club arose in Boston.

Webster had tuned his lyre in college and occasionally dusted it in the years of his wanderings. Now he took it down again, the rusty strings tinkling a pizzicato obligato to the smooth harmony of the experienced orchestra. To the *Courant* and the *Mercury* he presented newsboys' addresses for 1790. The first, after a series of jigging lines, came to a pretty good finale, the purpose of the addresses being to persuade subscribers to reward the boys' faithfulness during the year:

> *For boys, like wheels, in constant toil,*
> *Will lag and creak, without the OIL.*

The second, unfortunately, has come down to us only in part, but this fragment shows with what enthusiasm Webster could hymn the French Revolution, despite his colleagues' antipathy to leveling doctrines. The Boston *Centinel* and New York *Gazette of the United States* copied this passage from the lost broadside, entitling it: "What Tones, when Genius strikes the Lyre!"

> *Fair LIBERTY, whose gentle sway*
> *First blest these shores, has cross'd the sea,*
> *To visit Gallia, and inflame*
> *Her sons their ancient rights to claim.*

From realm to realm she still shall fly,
As lightning shoots across the sky,
And tyrants her just empire own,
And at her feet submit their crown.

Webster was still a utopian dreamer of democratic thoughts, but, like so many of us, he took more delight in popular agitation at a distance than at home.

Shortly after the death of Benjamin Franklin, April 17, 1790, Webster published in *The American Mercury* the long letter he had received in commendation of his *Dissertations*, and followed this with a series of fourteen articles "on the corruptions and errors which prevail in the English language." He pleaded for a uniformity of meaning in words throughout the country, asking the legislatures, for example, to adopt the word "court" in its usual significance and not to confuse the term, as was done in Maryland and Virginia, by calling the Legislature the "Supreme Judicial Court." He asked for an elimination of erroneous or ambiguous expressions, such as "more inconsiderable" and "shop" for "store." He also insisted on the correctness of such idiomatic expressions as "Who did he see?" and "them horses."

Them [he declared] is properly in the nominativ as well as the objectiv. The people at large, who are seldom without the warrant of antiquity, say *them horses* are sold, or he has sold *them horses*. These expressions may be censured as *vulgar*, but I deny that they are ungrammatical. As far as records extend, we have positiv proof that these phrases were originally correct. They are not vulgar corruptions; they are as old as the language we speak, and nine-tenths of the people still use them. In the name of common sense and reason, let me ask, what other warrant can be produced for *any* phrase in *any* language? Rules as we call them, are all formed on *established practice* and on nothing else. If writers have not generally admitted these phrases into their works, it is because they have embraced a false idea, that they are not English. But many writers have admitted them and they are *correct English*. They ought however to have preserved, as they are in our parent language, the German: *in dem Himmel*, in *them* heavens.

Webster also anticipated a problem which distressed the learned Professor Lounsbury a century later, when that pundit arrived at the conclusion that *as*, in such a sentence as "He employed such men *as* were fully competent to his purpose," is "an elusive relative pronoun." Webster called *as* a pronoun, and wisely let it go at that, not adding a romantic adjective as did Lounsbury.

But Webster was "weary of trying to arrest the progress of error," because "it is an odious task to find fault; the man who undertakes to *reform*, however good his motives, is sure to meet with reproach, and this is the most of the compensation I expect for several yeers' labor." He could not refrain, however, from rebutting in his last article (August 30, 1790) the common charge made against him:

Much censure has been thrown upon the writer of these remarks by those who do not comprehend his design, for attempting to make innovations in our language. *His vanity prompts him to undertake something new*, is the constant remark of splenetic and ill-natured people. But any person who will read my publications with a tolerable share of candor and attention, will be convinced that my principal aim has been to check *innovations*, and bring back the language to its purity and original simplicity. In doing this I am sometimes obliged to call in question authorities which have been received as genuine and the most respectable, and this has exposed me to the charge of *arrogance*. I have however the satisfaction to find the ground I have taken is defensible; and that the principles for which I contend, tho violently opposed at first, have afterwards been believed and adopted.

No doubt these new comments on Webster's vanity had been aroused, not only by his series of articles, but also by his *Rudiments of English Grammar*, published on March 8, 1790, and *A Collection of Essays and Fugitiv Writings. On Moral, Historical, Political Subjects*, published by

Thomas and Andrews, Boston, on June 22, 1790. The latter had on its title page: "By Noah Webster, Esq., Attorney at Law"; but this little bit of self-advertising was not the cause of dismay. The articles, taken from newspaper publications during the lecture tour and from *The American Magazine,* were not the bearers of entirely unorthodox ideas. But the spelling! Final *e*'s had been dropped from all final syllables with short vowels, and the Preface and two essays had been printed in the new orthography. "I suspect," wrote President Stiles, "you have put in the pruning knife too freely for general acceptance." The ever scornful Belknap wrote to Ebenezer Hazard: "I join with you in reprobating the new div-is-ions of words, as well as the new mode of spelling recommended and exemplified in the *fugitiv Essays, ov No-ur Webster eskwier junier,* critick and coxcomb general of the United States." One kind word came, however, from Daniel George of Portland, Maine, who was so "pleasingly astonished" that he asked Webster to compile a dictionary on the new principles. Webster, "doubtful whether the public mind is prepared," admitted he had "thought of a plan for the purpose," but opined that his youth and lack of influence precluded any thought of engaging in it.

On July 19, 1790, was published another book through the generosity of the impecunious lawyer. It was the first printing of Governor John Winthrop's journal, the manuscript of which Webster had seen in the possession of Governor Jonathan Trumbull in 1786. Although several historians had drawn freely from this work, none had either the vision or the enterprise to publish the whole. Webster engaged John Porter, secretary to the Governor, to decipher and transcribe the crabbed Elizabethan handwriting at a cost of £7. On giving the completed work to Webster, Porter asked and received twenty shillings more. For this laborious task he received a total of $26.66. Webster did not sign the title page, nor indicate that he had had a part in the work. He lost money on the edition, but he had the satisfaction of initiating the good work of publishing source materials in American history.

The Little Reader's Assistant, for which Webster had written several narratives, was published on October 18, 1790. This method of inculcating wholesome lessons by means of moralizing tales gave Webster a new means of reaching his fellow countrymen. He had taught school, had written pungent essays, had lectured, had conducted a magazine, and had published learned volumes. Another way, the way of Franklin, remained. And so he sat down and dashed off a series of pithy, homely, attractive, didactic essays, which *The Connecticut Courant* ran, beginning in December, 1790, for twenty-eight weeks. The whole group was collected under the title, *The Prompter.* Editions sold off rapidly in Hartford, Boston, and Albany, but Webster refused to let his name go on the title page; "should it be known among my enemies," Webster told Pickering, "that Noah Webster wrote it, I am confident both the writer and the book will be abused." If Webster was vain—this one adjective was used to describe him for sixty years from 1783 to 1843—he certainly knew the value of subordinating that vanity to the good of the people.

The Prompter was an entirely original work, granting the inspiration Webster may have received from Nathan Hooker's "Self Tormenting," an essay in Part III of the *Institute.* In its aim *The Prompter* copied Cotton Mather's *Essays to do Good,* and in its manner it followed Franklin's "Sayings of Poor Richard," with which work it is not unworthy of being united. The essays abound in humor, good-natured satire, and excellent moral precepts. Editions to a total of nearly a hundred were printed as late as 1849, even the British printers pirating the work under its original title and under new titles. Its influence was immense, both in the correction of men's thoughts and of literary style. Joseph Dennie, who has been puffed as "the American Addison," wrote to Webster (September 8, 1796): "The simplicity and ease of that little volume taught me the value of the Franklin style. If there be any merits in the short essays of 'The Lay Preacher,' consider the author as your debtor." *The Prompter* helped to put a stop to the imitation of Johnson and Gibbon, and gave a new emphasis to simplicity, even homeliness, of statement.

"A Prompter," says Webster, "is the man who in plays sits behind the scenes, looks over the rehearser, and with a moderate voice corrects him when wrong, or assists his recollection when he forgets the next sentence. A Prompter says but *little*, but that little is *very necessary* and often does much *good*." He had cast about for a method of writing "calculated to do the most general good. He wanted to whip vice and folly out of the country." He thought of imitating *Hudibras* and *M'Fingal*, but "he found this would not do; for like most modern rhymers, he is no poet, and he always makes bungling work of imitation." He thought, too, of trying the grand style. But that he relinquished for these reasons:

At length he determined to have nothing to do with a brilliant flow of words; a pompous elegance of diction; for what have the *world* to do with the sound of words? The Prompter's business is the world at large, and the mass of mankind are concerned only with *common* things. A dish of high-seasoned turtle is rarely found; it sometimes occurs at a gentleman's table, and then the chance is, it produces a surfeit. But good solid roast beef is a common dish for all men; it sits easy on the stomach; it supports, it strengthens and invigorates. Vulgar sayings and proverbs, so much despised by the literary epicures, the Chesterfields of the age, are the roast beef of science. They contain the experience, the wisdom of nations and ages, compressed into the compass of a nut shell. To crack the shell and extract the contents to feed those who have appetites, is the aim of this little book.

The following essay illustrates Webster's use of the Yankee vernacular and method of taking a proverb and then illustrating it by a variety of incidents from everyday experience.

He Does Not Work It Right

What a vulgar saying the Prompter has selected for his text in this number! Yet these vulgar sayings are often of good sense.

I knew a young man who left the army with an invincible attachment to gambling. He followed it closely till he had lost most of his wages; he then purchased a shop of goods, mostly on credit; he had his nightly frolics; *he kept it up;* he was a blood of the first rate; his goods were soon gone and not paid for; his creditors called and he began to cry *peccavi;* in fact, *he did not work it right.* But his friends helped him out of six scrapes, yea out of seven. At length necessity broke his spirit; it tamed him; he married, became a man of business; recovered his lost credit; and now *he works it right.*

I often say to myself, as I ride about the country, what a pity it is farmers *do not work it right.* When I see a man turn his cattle into the street to run at large and waste their dung, during a winter's day, I say this man does not work it right. Ten loads of good manure at least, are lost in a season by this slovenly practice; and all for what? For nothing indeed, but to ruin a farm.

So when I see cattle, late in the fall or early in the spring, rambling in a medow or mowing field, poarching the soil and breaking the grass roots, I say to myself, this man *does not work it right.*

So when I see a barn yard with a dreen to it, I say the owner does not work it right; for how easy is it to make a yard hollow, or lowest in the middle, to receive all the wash of the sides, which will be thus kept dry for the cattle. The wash of the yard, mixed with any kind of earth, or putrid straw, is the best manure in the world; yet how much do our farmers lose! In fact they *do not work it right.*

When I pass along the road and see a house with the clap-boards hanging on end by one nail, and old hats and cloths stuffed into the broken windows, I conclude the owner loves rum; in truth, *he does not work it right.*

When I see a man frequently attending courts, I suspect he *does not work it right.*

When I see a countryman often go to the retailers with a bottle, or the laboring man carrying home a bottle of rum, after his work is done on Saturday night, I am certain the man *does not work it right*.

When a farmer divides a farm of 100 acres of land among five or six sons, and builds a small house for each and sets them to work for a living on a little patch of land, I question whether *he works it right*. And when these sons are unable to live on these mutilated farms, and are compelled by a host of children to go to work by the day to get bread, I believe they are all convinced that they *have not worked it right*.

When a man tells me his wife will not consent to go from home into new settlements, where he may have land enough and live like a nabob, and therefore he is obliged to sit down on a corner of his father's farm, I laugh at him, and some time or other he will own, *he has not worked it right*.

A man in trade who is not punctual in his payments, certainly *does not work it right;* nor does the man, who trusts his goods to *any body* and *every body*.

Whether in Congress or a kitchen, the person who *talks much* is *little regarded*. Some members of Congress then certainly *do not work it right*. A hint to the *wise* is sufficient; but twenty hints have not been sufficient to silence the clamorous tongues of some congressional spouters.

Family government gives complexion to the manners of a town; but when we see, every where, children profane, indelicate, rude, saucy, we may depend on it their *parents do not work it right*.

I once knew a young man of excellent hopes, who was deeply in love with a lady; The first time he had an opportunity to whisper in her ear, and before he had made any impression on her heart in his favor, he sighed out his sorrowful tale to her, in full explanation: The lady was frightened; she soon rid herself of the distressed lover; she said, *he did not work it right*.

Other proverbs illustrated are Every one to his notion, It will do for the present, It is better to borrow than to buy, Come, we'll take the t'other sip, Any other time will do as well, When a man's name is up, he may lie abed till noon, What is every body's business is no body's, When a man is going down hill, every one gives him a kick, I told you so, Take time by the forelock, She carries the bell, He is

sowing his wild oats, He would have his own way, A stitch
in time saves nine, He has come out at the little end of the
horn, and Stolen waters are sweet. There are essays, too,
on A Bellows, A Nose, The Fidgets, and The Underlip.

These essays lacked the polish and architecture of Franklin's "The Whistle," but they reached the minds of rude
frontiersmen who needed to be instructed with a laugh
rather than with a sermon or a treatise on domestic economy. Although *The Prompter* may not be worthy of a place
in history as a work of literary art, it is memorable as a
kind of prose satiric cartoon.

Webster's desire to project and carry into effect "schemes
of public utility" could not be restrained permanently by the
notion that he lacked influence. He had assumed the role
of a Prompter and he continued to play his part. With a
Franklinian sense for seeing and doing the obvious, he engaged in many activities for the improvement of the social
and economic conditions of Hartford.

Congress had established a national bank in Philadelphia;
its beneficent effects upon trade were immediately notice-
able within the trading area of the nation's capital. But
in remote cities like Hartford the old problems of the management of finances, particularly the difficulty in raising
sufficient funds for the purchase of cargo lots of rum and
sugar, remained. Ship owners or importers found themselves selling single hogsheads of rum or sugar to individuals
who could pay only in produce. This system of barter delayed voyages and required resale of produce. Importers
posted bonds for the payment of duties, and these could be
taken up with difficulty when produce and not specie had
been paid for foreign articles. Since Connecticut at this time
was "the soul of the West India trade," the want of a bank
was sensibly felt by the business men. Webster took up his
pen, therefore, and wrote three articles in March, 1791, for
the *Courant* "On the Utility of Banks," setting forth the

above observations and urging the establishment of a bank in every state.

Under the general title, "The Patriot," Webster added five more articles on the economic conditions of Connecticut and on the imperative requirement that a national policy in respect to commerce, manufacturing, and agriculture be adopted. He pleaded for the "necessity of encouraging home manufactures," stressing the need for better breeds of sheep and finer strains of hemp and flax. He thought Congress should compel owners of ships to use suits of sails made from American duck. That Connecticut might take the leadership in manufactures he thought possible, if the Legislature would give a moderate subsidy to every new industry. By this means America might become independent of British goods. "Those politicians," he declared, "who deride the idea of Connecticut's becoming a manufacturing country should never be considered as friends to the state, or as wise and useful statesmen." British writers had declared that America by nature was designed for an agricultural society, but Webster scoffed the idea.

Two suggestions were offered for the development of American manufactures. First, there should be a society instituted for promoting arts and sciences, husbandry, and manufactures, for furthering whose purposes the government should appropriate, annually, a certain sum of money to defray the expenses of publishing short, authoritative treatises on these subjects and to reward enterprise with premiums. Second, since there were available more hands than could be usefully employed in husbandry, Webster suggested the apprenticing of these people to manufacturers. "Examine the situation of most of the large towns in this state," he wrote, "and you will find an abundance of poor children wandering about the streets, clothed in dirt and rags, illy educated in every respect." These gamins might be trained to usefulness, both for themselves and the community, by placing

them in linen, woolen, or cotton factories. In the light of our
present child labor laws, this suggestion may seem cruel
or at least at variance with Webster's educational ideals; in
1791, it must be remembered, when children were given less
attention than calves or shoats or chicks, it was a humanitarian act to place them in an environment free from the
distresses of vagabondage or unkempt poverty.

Again Webster harped on his nationalistic idea: "We are
not in reality independent whilst we are obliged to look to
[Great Britain] for our necessary clothing, or even superfluous ornaments." In anticipation of the type of criticism
he suffered so often, he prophesied: "British merchants,
British agents, and those Anglofied Americans who turn up
their noses at everything which is not British, will affect to
turn my projects into ridicule and treat 'The Patriot' as a
lunatic, or at best a well meaning but weak, visionary pro-
jector."

A new series of eight "Patriot" papers, "A New Year's
Gift," began in the *Courant* on January 2, 1792. These
rephrase the earlier essays in an attempt to indicate what
could be done to make Hartford a place of greater commercial enterprise. Webster's leading idea is that Hartford by
its position ought to control the wholesale trade of the Connecticut Valley as far north as Haverhill, but that it does
not because local jealousies have prevented the formation of
large trading companies, the dredging of the Connecticut
River for unobstructed navigation to Hartford, the building
of a Cape Cod canal, and the construction of post roads with
stone foundations. The lack of a bank also is remarked
upon, as well as "that bane of all regular trade, and that
curse to the trade of Connecticut, *barter*." Infamous reports
had been spread about the dishonesty of Connecticut merchants, and these, Webster said, were "not all groundless."

Connecticut merchants were engaged in petty retail business, fighting over pennies, when large profits awaited en-

terprising projectors who could form extensive wholesale
establishments. A system of good roads, "with a hard,
impenetrable foundation, to admit the transportation of loads
at any season of the year"; a canal on the north reaches
of the Connecticut River and a canal from Buzzard's Bay to
Boston Bay; and a bank in Hartford—these three useful
aids to business, if immediately entered upon, would bring
to Hartford merchants and farmers, Webster thought, rich
rewards in increased business, higher produce prices, and
enhanced land values.

Among the errors of investors, Webster pointed out, were
a fondness for sinking money into land and a hesitancy in
risking loans to business. The reverse, he thought, should
be true, for commerce brings immediate rewards, while land
rises in value only as nearby trading centers increase the
prices of farm produce.

In his plea for a bank, Webster explained the use of such
institutions as depositories, as sources of loans at established
rates, as government depositories, and as aids in destroying barter. "For want of specie," he explained in reprobating this odious business practice, "articles in market must
be bartered—and barter is a public and private calamity.
The scarcity of money enhances its value and gives it too
high a preference over other commodities. The consequence
is that those who come to market will often undersell an
article to get specie for it. Then the man who has money
takes advantage of this eagerness to obtain it; overreaching
follows. Articles acquire two prices, a cash price and a barter price. . . . Barter is the father of fraud and the instrument of knavery."

Webster's articles were so successful that, when a meeting
was called in March, 1792, for organizing the Hartford
Bank, he was empowered with John Trumbull and Chauncey Goodrich to prepare and present to the Connecticut Legislature a petition asking for an act of incorporation. In

the long and explicit articles of association it was set down that 250 shares of stock should be issued with a par value of $400. The Legislature granted the petition and produced an Act. Webster, though too poor to purchase stock, had the satisfaction of knowing that this project of his had become reality.

Partly in recognition of his services to the community, Webster's name was placed in nomination for the Hartford Common Council. On March 26, 1792, he was duly elected, and the following year he was re-elected. He had now entered upon the lowest rung of Connecticut's ladder of political preferment, on the steps of which John Trumbull had already risen to the office of District Attorney, and soon would rise to a judgeship. Chauncey Goodrich, also on the Council, would soon go to Congress.

In this humble body Webster made his presence felt immediately. He instigated an investigation of the town records to ascertain the encroachments upon city property by private persons, and effected a return to the city of valuable riverside property. He secured ordinances by which new streets, pavements, gutters, and canals were constructed. He secured adequate meer stones to determine property lines. Like Franklin he was active in practical reforms.

With the members of his law club Webster solicited funds for the erection of a new state house. Together they raised £743; on May 17, 1792, they petitioned the Legislature to grant the sum of £2500 for carrying the project through.

Other projects animated Webster. One, suitably emanating from Hartford, arose from the pathetic deaths of two laboring men while engaged in their occupations. Each left a large family. Workmen then assumed all risk of injury, and no provision was made by law for reimbursing a bereft widow or family. The poor laws provided only for families in distress; injured or ill workmen received no compensation, and their families suffered great want. At times pride or modesty prevented the acknowledgment of adversity. For the relief of such persons Webster proposed the organization of "A Charitable Society," whose object would be "to give relief to honest, industrious, and frugal people, especially mechanics and other laborers who may be suddenly reduced to want." In support of his project, Webster presented the following argument (October 1, 1792):

The merchant can insure his ship and goods against the hazards of the sea, and the citizen can insure his house and furniture from the risk of fire; but no insurance is found for the poor man who climbs the shrouds in a gale of wind, who risks his limbs and life upon a plank or scaffold in the air, or who exposes himself at the bottom of deep wells or trenches. Yet the poor *must* live, and to furnish the means, they *must* labor; not only so, but they cannot always choose their employment—they must do such work and in such places as their employers direct, and the price of hazardous occupations is not always, perhaps not generally, proportioned to the danger. The soldier's compensation is very little above that of the common laborer in the field, but nations think it just to maintain their disabled soldiers for life. The mechanic, on the other hand, whose occupation on the whole may be as hazardous as that of soldiers in an army, finds no such provision made for him, in case he loses a leg or an arm; nor *for his family,* when he loses his life by falling from a building or a ship's round-top, or by being buried by earth in digging a well.

Webster's plan, probably the first which looked toward a system of unemployment insurance, involved general membership with annual payments of one dollar or more. The number of needy cases then was not large, and a modest organization could have been of great value. Had this society succeeded in its object, Hartford might have become even earlier than it did an important insurance city.

In line with his humanitarian interests, Webster became very active in the Hartford antislavery society, serving as secretary in 1792. At the annual meeting on November 19, 1792, Webster was one of a committee appointed to notify the public that the law requiring the registration of Negro children born after March, 1784, would be enforced. Such persons were assured their freedom on attaining the age of twenty-five. At the annual meeting of the society, May 9, 1793, Webster read an oration, later printed under the title, *Effects of Slavery, on Morals and Industry.*

After his tour through the South, Webster had met in Philadelphia, Anthony Benezet, the Quaker pioneer in slavery agitation. The unhappy plight of slaves, as well as his reading of history, convinced Webster that slavery was not only an intolerable infraction of human rights, but also an economic absurdity. For years he had meditated an essay on the subject, but it was not until the society called him forth that he actually wrote his opinions.

There was much of Rousseau left in Webster, despite his revolt at the mobbing tactics of Shays's followers. He asserted that every man, black or white, has a sacred right of freedom: "No time, no circumstances, no human power or policy can change the nature of this truth, nor repeal the fundamental laws of society by which every man's right of liberty is guaranteed." The holders of slaves, compelled by powers of reason to abandon their right to own human beings, had taken refuge in asserting the policy or necessity of the traffic. And so Webster, attacking these premises, showed that slavery, since oppression is the mother of crimes, renders slaves cruel, deceitful, perfidious, knavish, and lazy, while the masters become savage in their insensitivity to suffering. No less deplorable than this deterioration of human character, is the destruction slavery works on national industry. Many men do the work of one, and production mounts only under the whiplash of an overseer. Washington had remarked to him, "that from the northern to the southern states, the agricultural improvements are in an inverse proportion to the number of slaves." In developing this thesis, Webster said that slaves as tenant farmers on short leases impoverish the soil and waste its substance.

The poverty of these wretches prevents them from purchasing manufactured products, and thus industry is hampered. No one gains by such methods. On the contrary, "there is not an owner of slaves in Europe or America, the value of whose estate might not be doubled in a few years by giving liberty to his slaves and assisting them in the management of their farms."

This freedom Webster would not give by a sudden striking off of chains or by exportation or by the colonization of blacks in Africa. These schemes, so beloved by some of the reformers of the time, Webster thought impracticable and destructive of the best interests of America. Only one plan appeared expedient to him: "this is, to raise the slaves by gradual means to the condition of free tenants." Each slave would cultivate his patch of soil and purchase it with the profits of his industry, or the slaves might be placed as responsible tenants on farms. Each would thus become an independent farmer, testing his skill and industry in competition with his neighbor. The gain in increased production, proper care of the soil, and enhanced sense of human worth, would quickly compensate for the small loss occasioned by manumission.

In discussing slavery, Webster had divided the subject into two forms, political and civil. His marshaled array of historical evidence inevitably led him to a discussion of the French Revolution, which had begun just after he had settled in Hartford. He responded enthusiastically to the cries of the populace and supported the aims of the revolutionists. "France," he wrote in this pamphlet, "has now an opportunity of making a distinguished and glorious experiment in favor of national industry and public happiness." He apologized for the riots and outrages of the French people by referring to "the treachery and perjury of their perfidious domestic foes." In briefer statements in the *Courant* he went even further in his defense of the rights of the French peo-

ple to form a republic and put an end to the tyranny under
which they suffered.

It was this right of self-determination which led Webster to write, with John Trumbull and Chauncey Goodrich,
an "Address from the Inhabitants of Hartford to the President of the United States," supporting Washington in his
Proclamation of Neutrality of April 22, 1793. "Warmly attached to our government, both by interest and affection,"
they wrote on July 29, "we take the liberty to assure you, that
we shall ever stand ready by our utmost exertions, in every
legal and constitutional way, to support the just measures of
your administration; and to lend our assistance in maintaining the peace and harmony of the States, and in opposing
the insidious designs of those persons, if there be any so
deluded, who may wish to subject the country to foreign
influence, and involve it in the horrors of war." This one
calm statement, rising above the clamor of a hysterical faction, gave President Washington much comfort.

Many robberies of the mail having been committed, at or
between the cities of New York and Hartford, Webster offered to inspect the mails and to form a plan for capturing the
thief. Commissioned by Timothy Pickering, Postmaster General, Webster mailed marked letters and trailed them
through the post offices. The robber, an employee of the
New York office, knew of the scheme and escaped detection
for two years. By this service Webster became, probably,
the first American postal inspector.

Webster had attained in a measure that influence in Hartford and Connecticut which he lacked when he first settled
there in 1789. He had taught many wholesome lessons to
the public, lessons in humanity, economics, and law. But
his business had not kept pace with his ambition or needs.
In July, 1793, he found himself still in debt to the extent
of $1815, a clear loss of $400 on the *Dissertations* having
increased the sum he owed for his college expenses and lec-

ture tour. This sum, it might be said, did not include the gifts, for so the loans became, of James Greenleaf. Webster's assets included debts to him of $680, a law library worth $300, and his copyright, for which he had been offered $1250. In the general decay of legal business he had suffered with the other young lawyers. He had to look about for a new business.

Dr. Appleton had suggested that Webster enter into partnership with Childs, the Boston publisher, or take over the Boston Book Store. Mrs. Webster vetoed these projects, because she feared she could not live as fashionably as her sisters. Webster wanted to enter business or to write—he would take a farm as a second choice. He asked James Greenleaf, who had returned from Holland, for advice and for assistance. "All I ask (or ever wished)," he wrote on June 24, 1793, "is *business*, and whether on a large or small scale, I will be satisfied with it. To renounce all my literary pursuits, which are now very congenial with my habits, would not be altogether agreeable; but it would not make me unhappy. There are many pleasures in agriculture, and if our plan of book-selling upon a pretty large scale should fail, my second wish would be a farm. A man with a just mind and moderate talents may be respectable in almost any department of business."

In July Greenleaf went to New York, and there in consultation with James Watson arrived at the conclusion that Webster might undertake a newspaper. Alexander Hamilton, Rufus King, John Jay, and other supporters of Washington, wished a sound Federalist paper conducted in that city and were willing to advance money for its establishment. John Fenno had moved his *Gazette of the United States* to Philadelphia along with the national government. The field was held now by Thomas Greenleaf, publisher of the Jeffersonian *New-York Journal*, a paper which had been hostile to the Constitution and to President Washington.

Fenno's paper offered poor resistance to the Jeffersonians, who had Philip Freneau and Benjamin Franklin Bache in Philadelphia, as well as Greenleaf in New York. Webster's known talents and Federalist sympathies made him the logical choice for the task of supporting the government.

In August Webster consulted with the principals, agreeing to their proposition. In September he formed a partnership with George Bunce for the creation of a printing company. In November he moved to the city, eager to begin *The American Minerva*.

It was not easy for Webster to break the ties which bound him to Hartford by birth and association. His mother was growing very feeble, her death being but a few months in the future. His father's straitened circumstances gave him much sorrow; to leave seemed the act of an ingrate. And yet there was no other choice. When a man marries, he must look to his own family first.

Little feet were now pattering on the Websters' floor. Baby hands fondly clasped a loving father. Thin, piping voices daily drove Webster and his wife to consider plans for a more promising business. When the newspaper and printing business appeared certain, she insisted that he move.

They had been happy in their Hartford home, with its small garden where Webster experimented with soils, fertilizers, and seeds. He recorded meteorological data. He made investigations of dew, its source and its relations with damp and dry soil, wood and brick walls, wet and dry cellars. His inquiring mind passed carelessly over no single iota of knowledge. Although his early training had been in languages and law, he broadened with time, becoming an ardent agriculturalist and medical historian. An epidemic of smallpox broke out in Hartford in 1792, and the Town Council, of which he was a member, authorized three physicians to inoculate willing subjects. In the spring of 1793 Webster's children became ill of scarlet fever. Somewhat like Pasteur, his ignorance challenged by the terrible thought of his children dying while he stood impotently over them in silent prayer, he began a thorough course of reading, seeking an explanation of the then inexplicable phenomena of the transmission of diseases. The call to New York was imperative; his "schemes of public utility," his scientific, political, philanthropic, and humanitarian activities, and his friends —all had to be dropped for the time being.

From the Hartford friends, the poets, lawyers, and physicians, Webster now took leave, his regret chastened by the thought that in the amassing of worldly goods they had all surpassed him. From the quietness of a rural town, he plunged into the arena of embroiled national politics. The Hartford Prompter became the "Colossus of Federalism."

CHAPTER XI

Colossus of Federalism

New York, August 12, 1793: one of the most excited days in the history of the metropolis, then a little city of thirty thousand people. For four days Edmond Genêt, Minister Plenipotentiary of France to the United States, had been fêted, toasted, cheered by a whirling mob of fanatics who sang *Ca Ira* and the *Marseillaise,* who set off more powder in fireworks than was shot in the Revolution, and who paraded belligerently before the homes of members of the Chamber of Commerce. The "swinish multitude," as they called themselves, thus defined "democracy."

Genêt, thirty, handsome, brilliant, headstrong, self-assured, had ridden amid plaudits from Charleston, South Carolina, to Philadelphia, where he was privately encouraged but publicly snubbed by that master of tergiversation, Thomas Jefferson, Secretary of State of the United States. Along the route the mobs, hailing the Minister of our ally in the Revolution, demanded that Washington carry out the provisions of the Treaty of 1778. Instead, Jefferson wrote for Washington the Proclamation of Neutrality of April 22, 1793; nor could Genêt break through the firmness of Washington, the duplicity of Jefferson, the pomposity of Knox, the cunning of Hamilton.

Angry that the Minister of an ally should be treated as an underling, Genêt ranted and snarled in public, and sent haughty letters to Washington. Jefferson answered them evasively. Genêt moved on to New York, where renewed enthusiasm welcomed him.

The mobs were Jefferson's creatures, formed by disaffected politicians and hireling editors. The nucleus was the Democratic Society—in New York it was Tammany; most of the members were recent immigrants, men without the ballot. Their avowed purpose was to prevent the alleged monarchists—Washington, John Adams, and Hamilton— from establishing a hereditary executive, whose golden crown would symbolize the fetters of oppression worn by the people. "Wigwam," for example, commented in *Greenleaf's New-York Journal*, August 28, 1793, on Adams's alleged attempt to subvert American republican institutions in these elegant terms: "Was he to embrace a stinking prostitute, and endeavor to palm her on the people of America for an unspotted virgin, he would not, in my opinion, act a more infamous part than he has done."

The huzzas and addresses of these societies led Genêt to persist in fulfilling the letter of his commission. He yielded nothing; he compromised no whit; he believed the people ruled America, and that the mobs expressed the national will. He did not know the serenaders could not vote. But they could talk and write: "Americans love you. Americans are your brethren. Americans are ready to mingle their most precious blood with yours. . . . Our city swarms with enemies of freedom's cause—ignorant, ancient and modern tories—French aristocrats—British placemen and pensioners—royal slaves and hirelings." Gênet answered: "The strict performance of treaties is the best and safest policy."

To accede to Genêt's demands meant war. War would have meant ruin, so Washington believed. France's depredations on American shipping had made her inimical to the commercial interests of America. England sinned as did France. Between the two there was no choice. The Barbary Corsairs similarly looted American vessels or held them for ransom. The whole world, it might be said, was hostile to

America. It would have been madness to engage in war
under such circumstances.

Genêt's triumphal progress had to be stopped. Alexander
J. Dallas had remarked to Jefferson, who told Washington,
who told Hamilton and Knox, who told John Jay and
Rufus King, that Genêt "would appeal to the people from
certain decisions of the President." Hurrying to New York,
Jay and King caused to be inserted in Loudon's *Diary* on
August 12 a brief statement to this effect.

It was a bombshell. But Genêt thought it a firecracker
and smiled it away. The mobs hooted. The Jeffersonian papers catcalled K——g J——y [King Jay], called them liars,
libelers, and hirelings in the pay of Britain. Fiery orators
blazed at the government, showering the hot lava of invective on Washington, the Cabinet, the Senate, and the Supreme Court. For Jay was Chief Justice, and King was a
Senator.

It was on this day, August 12, 1793, that Noah Webster
entered New York, and threaded his way through a mob to
become a fellow lodger with Genêt at Bradley's Tavern on
Maiden Lane. The country squire suddenly became one of
the centers of importance in the continuous squabbling. He
dined with the Minister and his party, drew them out, raged
at their madness—"I cannot with propriety state all I said
myself," Webster told Wolcott. Genêt lost his temper under the blistering attack of Webster and blurted out that
"the officers of our government were in the British interest," and in severe language condemned the measures of government. Webster asked whether the Cabinet were "fools."
Genêt answered, "Jefferson is no fool." Pascal snarled
something in French to Bompard and Genêt, thinking Webster could not understand. Webster did, and he dashed off
a letter to Wolcott on the conversation. It was passed along
through Hamilton to Washington. The President requested
an affidavit, which Webster prepared to help send Genêt

home. Jefferson wrote the letter demanding that Robespierre recall Genêt, and recall meant, of course, another head for the guillotine.

James Greenleaf meantime had been talking for Webster. James Watson broached the subject of a progovernment newspaper, an enterprise most necessary now that the opposition controlled the press in New York. Jay and King fumed as they read Thomas Greenleaf's daily invective. On August 16 Webster dined with Jay. The matter was settled at once. Webster should establish a newspaper, the cost of which should be paid by temporary loans of $150 each from a group of Federalists: Jay, King, Watson, Greenleaf, Hamilton, and four or five others. Publicly Webster let it be known that he was moving to New York to superintend the printing of his textbooks which now had become valuable. Freneau had caused Jefferson no end of trouble, because he was avowedly a hireling editor, a government clerk while opposing the government for which he was employed. Webster would be a freelance, his recognized dignity as an author and lecturer preserving him from any aspersions of this kind.

On Monday, December 9, 1793, *The American Minerva*, "The Patroness of Peace, Commerce, and the Liberal Arts," a four-page sheet, made its first daily appearance, its "director" promising to preserve his paper "chaste and impartial." This initial issue is worthy to take its place beside *The American Magazine* as a compendium of nationalistic idealism and intellectual discussion. Webster set down his faith in the United States, in its future glory, in the importance of neutrality, and in the value of preparedness. He favored the French Revolution, but he deprecated the mild lunacy of Genêt, who, Webster said, had been misled by the sentiments of the city; the country people were not moved by "intrigue and undue influence," and they repudiated "demagogues of the street." It was good advice, but

Genêt's doom, although he did not know it, was sealed.

At no time did Webster descend into the low name-calling tactics of his opponents—Thomas Greenleaf in New York, Thomas Adams in Boston, and Benjamin Franklin Bache in Philadelphia. Freneau had dropped his paper, no doubt unable to keep the fires of hate burning when he saw Jefferson desert Genêt and vacillate in the French cause. But Bache and Greenleaf, with a mendacious audacity unparalleled in American journalism, insinuated and lied, distorting every possible word and act of Washington and his supporters. They pursued their continuous campaign of vilification relentlessly until they died in the yellow fever epidemic of 1798.

Bernard Faÿ, the apologist of Bache, has stated that Webster "had plenty of erudition, but he did not digest it himself, and his public never digested it at all." This sounds like one of Bache's many tirades. Bache himself wrote: "I look upon Noah Webster, Jun., Esq., . . . as the colossus of the faction." And Jefferson, unable to find a penman to rebut Webster, begged Madison to give "a fundamental reply" to Webster, whom he confused with Hamilton, as "a colossus to the anti-federal party."

Webster holds priority among notable American editors because he never surrendered his independence to a man or a party. Although he supported Washington with the fervor of a son upholding his father's reputation, he did not blindly espouse Federalism. James Thompson Callender called Webster "the pitch-pipe of Hamilton," but if so, Webster sounded the note; he did not echo it. William Cobbett gauged the quality of Webster within two weeks of the establishment of *Porcupine's Gazette*, and denounced him as a hireling in the pay of France. Obviously Webster could not serve two masters, France and England, who were tearing at each other's throats. With a rigidity of moral and patriotic fiber, the unmelted iron of his Puritan training upholding him, he pursued a dignified course, daily giving his widening audience a learned interpretation of world news and the substance of volumes in economic, historical, philanthropic, and medical lore.

Although Freneau and Bache have been extravagantly praised as editors, neither equaled Webster in learning, fairness, just interpretation of events, or useful influence. Webster was a liberal in these years, but not a blind zealot. In addition to fostering Americanism in language, education, manners, and politics, he proposed unemployment insurance, city planning, cleansing of city streets, improvement of penal laws, investigation of diseases, collection of statistics, forest conservation, organization of charity societies; he advocated the government's purchase and freeing of slaves; he developed a fuel-saving fireplace; he wrote a history of commerce and the first pages toward a history of epidemics. He was active in all good causes. No other newspaper of the time recorded so fully America's striving toward complete independence nor suggested so many means for attaining it. Benjamin Franklin would have recognized Webster as an editor after his own heart.

But the leading problem of the times was uppermost in Webster's mind: Should America accept the hegemony of England or France, or should America go alone? No other American newspaper devoted more space to a discussion of this problem. Webster estimated that he alone wrote more than enough matter to fill twenty volumes, much of it worth reprinting today. In addition he translated hundreds of columns from French newspapers. From foreign correspondents, like the learned German historian, Christopher Daniel Ebeling, or from Jay and King and Ellsworth when they were in Europe, Webster secured first-hand comments on the progress of events. In authentic correspondence, too, Webster took priority among editors. Although it was charged that he was unfair in his choice of materials and

biased in his opinions, a reading of the yellowed pages of
the *Minerva* will show that he held successfully a detached
point of view, and that, if he sinned at all, he erred only
in placing first the rights and prerogatives of the United
States.

On the French Revolution he wrote most frequently and
at his best. At the outbreak of the Revolution in 1789
Webster had exulted over the acts of the States General by
which the government was to be reformed and the people
raised from their degraded state of vassalage to the rank of
freemen. His faith in the goodness of the cause and the
purity of the reformers' intentions continued unabated for
nearly five years. The annexation of Avignon in 1791, and
the conquest of Savoy and the attacks upon Geneva and the
Netherlands in 1792, aroused his fear that the independence
of other states was being attacked unwarrantably. Yet
neither these acts nor the decree of November 19, 1792,
destroyed his belief in the utility of the Revolution. He
apologized for sanguinary measures and even condoned the
execution of Louis XVI. Webster believed firmly that, although the French were "creating some evils to correct enormous abuses," they would finally produce "an improved system of government."

It was not until Webster had come to New York that he
was impressed with the quality of French intrigue. His
personal encounter with Genêt shook his faith in the French
leaders. But he retreated slowly from his position. Believing that our friendliness to France had been misjudged and
that Genêt was engaged in unnecessary, if not hostile, activities, he addressed an open letter to the Minister (December 26, 1793): "British influence in America is extremely
limited and feeble. Almost every man who espoused the
cause of America in her struggle for independence is now
friendly to the Revolution in France. It is a general wish
in America that the Revolution might be effected and a *free*

Republican government be established. There is a general abhorrence of the combination of tyrants against France, which is intended to crush the rising genius of freedom in Europe, and which aims to establish the feudal despotism and tyrannical hierarchies of the 12th century."

The continuation of Genêt's bold and insulting movements, as well as the tide of events in Europe, compelled Webster to abandon his faith in the French leaders. The conclusion seemed inevitable, in view of the French treatment of other European nations, that a controlling influence was sought by force or intrigue over this country. Our status as an ally and as a republic granted us no security. One of Webster's cardinal political tenets required our nation to remain free from European entanglements. He exulted when Genêt was recalled, because immediate danger of conflict was avoided.

Since Webster disbelieved in foreign intervention in the United States, he logically applied the same doctrine to Europe. In many editorials he advised the allied powers to withdraw from France and allow the French people to solve their own problems. If their doctrines were dangerous and subversive of order, religion, and morals, it was even more important to withdraw, because opposition merely served to spread these heresies: "Remove your armies, and the people of France will soon remove the Jacobins." Webster insisted on the right of France to alter its form of government, and he denied the right of one country to control the internal arrangements of another independent society. He asserted (March 20, 1794): "the present war against France is an outrage on human nature, and can never prosper."

By the spring of 1794 American enthusiasm in support of the French had waned. The mounting toll of execution during the Reign of Terror sickened the hardiest liberal. Our commerce suffered depredations at sea by the belligerent powers and by the Algerines. Washington's wise policy of neutrality seemed best. The Democratic Clubs, leaders in arousing sentiment favorable to the French, lost prestige, many leading members withdrawing. The Whiskey Rebellion in Western Pennsylvania, said to have been fomented by these societies, stirred active hostility against all subversive doctrines and associations. While continuing to espouse the French cause, these societies discontinued their attempt to direct the international policies of the United States and centered their criticism upon President Washington and the Federalist Party. The first act to draw violent action was Jay's Treaty, but their plan for direct political action was formulated at least a year earlier. Webster saw the Machiavellian hand of Jefferson behind these organizations; to the end of his life the lexicographer never forgave Jefferson for this association. In 1800 the whole weight of his papers opposed the Virginian's election to the presidency "because the French wished him elected."

Webster was alert to the changed popular opinion. Fear of our entrance into the European conflict altered to a fear that the Democratic Clubs would precipitate in the United States a revolution as bloody as that in France. Henceforth he examined the acts of the French Revolution, not so much as a series of events of possible danger to us, but as the pattern we would inevitably follow if one self-seeking faction gained control of our government. He gathered his articles on the Revolution, and in March, 1794, shuffled them into a pamphlet, entitled *Revolution in France, considered in respect to its Progress and Effects*. Reiterating his faith in the necessity and justness of the cause of the Revolution, Webster analyzed the origin and progress of that struggle. A single Jacobin society in Paris had radiated its influence throughout the nation and had seized the government. The ends of that "amazing" Revolution he cherished: he foresaw improved agriculture, arts, and sciences; he believed a future legislature would substitute religion for "chimerical reason"; and he thought France would need a more energetic government than that provided by the Constitution. But the "Application" of his remarks was directed against the clubs: "The most important truth suggested . . . is that party spirit is the source of faction, and faction is death to the existing government." From this time forward Webster's *bête noire* was party spirit, the French Revolution serving as the awful example to point his diatribe. Webster predicated his remarks on the distinction "between the regeneration of the government of France, an object desirable to all good men, and the factious, violent means of conducting the Revolution."

Space does not permit a full examination of Webster's extended remarks on the events in France during the next five years. He early recognized the parallel between revolutionary France and ancient Rome, and he brought his vast historical knowledge to bear on the subject. From December, 1796, to March, 1797, he wrote a series of eleven articles "To the People of the United States," in which he traced the history of the French Revolution to prove that the Roman plans of aggrandizement were being imitated. Like the Romans, the French flattered conquered nations with the idea of being allies, "and this honorable appellation almost reconciled the vanquished people to a state of vassalage." Webster also noted that the French had adopted the Roman policy, "divide and conquer," a device which boded ill for the United States.

Webster indulged in several prophecies; with remarkable precision his Cassandran utterances proved correct. In 1794 he predicted that "the combined powers would never conquer France," a prophecy almost immediately fulfilled by the withdrawal of Prussia and Spain from the coalition. He declared that Robespierre's head would fall under the guillotine as had Danton's. On July 4, 1797, he predicted that the prospect of peace was chimerical and that a general or durable peace was not possible. The end of hostilities could come only, Webster thought, if "some popular man, who can attract around him a military superiority, [should] say to the perturbed ocean of anarchy, 'hitherto shalt thou come, and here thy proud waves shall be stayed.'" The man arose, but Napoleon Bonaparte chose to secure personal fame through war and not peace. When asked the source of this ability to foreshadow events, Webster replied: "The exact fulfillment of the prediction indicates nothing more than an ordinary share of historical knowledge, united with a candid comparison of all the circumstances and events that have marked the progress of the Revolution."

The formation of the Directory is often said to have ended the Revolution late in 1795. The continuation of hostilities, however, left no doubt in Webster's mind that the principles of the Revolution, no matter what the form of leadership, still directed the course of action. Although he had suspected the French of enmity to America at the time of Genêt's visit, he did not have specific evidence until the announcement in 1797 of the decree on contraband, by which all enemy property found on American vessels was made liable to seizure and condemnation. "This cool and infernal act of barbarous vengeance" enraged Webster, and he wrote: "The man who attempts to justify it merits the reward of a traitor." Hitherto French attacks on American shipping had been excused as assaults upon England. Now the Federalists, former supporters of a policy of peace, begged for war. But Webster, a political realist, saw that the United States was unimportant in international affairs, and that our wisest policy, like that of a bear cub scenting trouble, was to lie low. "We firmly believe," he wrote, "that the question of peace or war depends mostly on events in Europe, not on the measures or mode of negociating adopted by the United States. Our duty is within a narrow compass—to be firm and undaunted towards France without giving her just cause of offense; and to be united among ourselves in whatever measures shall be pursued."

Webster now investigated the dangers imminent from possible French aggressions on our continent. Looking into the treaties with France and at a map of her American possessions (which we had guaranteed to defend in the Treaty of 1778), he saw the possibility of the erection of a new republic in the southern parts of the United States, in the Spanish provinces, and in the western territory. The Treaty of 1778 guaranteed to France the West Indian islands, and the Treaty of 1783 sought to prevent the growth of a formidable American power. France wanted our western country; now the time seemed ripe to take it. By planting a colony at the mouth of the Mississippi, she could detach all the country west of the Alleghenies from the United States and prevent our development of a powerful nation. The Spanish possessions in Mexico and South America could be taken, and then the States would fall easy prey. Although this outline may read like the nightmare of a jittery spirit, anyone familiar with the French policy would recognize the effectiveness of the French strategy. Webster hoped "some miracle [might] intervene to prevent this," but he gloomily remarked that the influence of the French in this country was so great that "the union and patriotism of American citizens" could not be depended upon to defeat such a scheme.

This doubt arose especially from the actions of three prominent leaders. Early in May, 1797, Webster was first to publish Jefferson's letter to Mazzei, that "treasonable letter" in which our national officials were said to be under the influence of the English. Here Webster found the origin of France's enmity to us, for the circulation of such misrepresentations by former holders of high office "must convince the Americans that the differences between the government of that country and the United States have proceeded mostly from the arts and treachery of our own citizens." Similar degradation of national honor appeared in the recall of Monroe and his subsequent admission that he yielded France the merit of effecting the treaty with Algiers. Even more shocking was the attitude of his college chum and bosom companion, the poet Joel Barlow, who stated that the United States was "in danger of ruin from a rupture with France."

When three great leaders surrendered to America's palpable enemy, and when a large number of people continued blindly to believe in the good faith of a nation which had sent a Genêt and an Adet to beguile them and which had asked a bribe in return for a new treaty, Webster lost patience. His labors seemed fruitless. "I am fatigued," he wrote, "with narrating the absurdities of man." "We have found [the friendship of France] dangerous to our peace and prosperity," he declared; "I am persuaded that the Treaty of 1778 was an evil instead of a good; and in subsequent years it became the greatest scourge ever inflicted on our country, not excepting the plague . . . Her enmity alone can save us from ruin." From this opinion Webster did not recede; his later writings repeated this unhappy refrain.

In his comments upon England's acts of aggression on the United States, Webster took the same attitude that he did toward the French. He admitted that had France not sent Genêt and had not seized our vessels, entrance into the war as her ally would have been inevitable. But always Webster maintained that a policy of neutrality was wisest, even when he loudly denounced Britain's folly in antagonizing the source of three fifths of her foreign trade.

One incident overshadowed all others in 1795. Chief Justice Jay reluctantly accepted the responsibility of framing a new commercial treaty with Great Britain. The voyage exposed his life, by the nature of his constitution; and the mission committed his character, from the difficulty of executing it to popular acceptance. As soon as he sailed, late in 1794, the Democratic Clubs began their campaign of defamation, seeking through attacks on Jay to undermine the reputation of Washington. When Senator Thomas Stevens Mason handed Bache a garbled version of the treaty in July, 1795, the Democrats let loose a flood of billingsgate and vituperation, most of it founded on ignorance, on misrepresentation, or, at best, on party animosity. Webster pleaded for delay of judgment until the complete document was before the people. Then, with the assistance of James Kent who wrote two articles, Webster prepared twelve essays of "Vindication" under the pseudonym, "Curtius." Hamilton, with the aid of a noted Philadelphia lawyer, Mr. Lewis, published thirty-eight articles under the title, "Defence." Hamilton had originally chosen the title, "Vindication," but altered this at Webster's request. In his essays Webster explained in simple language the nature of the treaty, assured the public it was the best possible under the circumstances, and requested that party hatred should not be allowed to destroy the gains accruing from this compromise. Hamilton's essays, like those of *The Federalist*, were more learned, but they dragged out to a wearisome length.

Rufus King told Jay that "the papers of 'Curtius' had operated more powerfully than any other publication in calming the public mind and restoring confidence in the administration, being from their style and structure peculiarly adapted to the comprehension of the great body of the people." Jefferson had the same opinion, for he wrote to Madison: "I gave a copy or two, by way of experiment, to honest, sound-hearted men of common understanding, and they were not able to parry the sophistry of Curtius. I have ceased, therefore, to give them. . . . For God's sake, take up your pen and give a fundamental reply to Curtius and Camillus."

The fundamental replies came from Greenleaf and Bache; each devoted column upon column to undermine the character of Webster. Their lexicon of abuse was ransacked for every belittling epithet imaginable. Some of them were: "most learned Stultus," "self-exalted pedagogue," "rancorous," "base and uncandid," "utter enemy of the rights and privileges of the people," "quack," "mortal and incurable lunatic," "pusillanimous, half-begotten, self-dubbed patriot," "this scribble of a British faction, this ephemeron of literature, this petite maitre of politics," "dunghill cock of faction," and "Domine Syntax, alias Squire Webster." Always they referred to Webster as "the sapient editor of the immaculate paper." One writer threatened Webster with a "coat of tar and feathers." Had Webster been so harmless an editor as Faÿ alleges, Bache and Greenleaf would not have devoted hundreds of columns of space to him.

When Cobbett began his *Porcupine's Gazette* in Philadelphia in 1797, he attempted to curry Webster's favor and to win over the *Minerva* to monarchical ideas. Within two weeks Webster told Cobbett, "I know no party, but that of my country," and he denounced the bullying tactics of the many-quilled hog. Cobbett responded with a series of "dressings," emitting such phrases as: "this maniac anticipating newspaper writer," "wonderful Noah! amazing prophet!" "this sea-saw, cameleon-like editor," "prophetical, political, and dictatorial newsman," "spiteful viper," "base creature," "toad in the service of sans-culottism," "rancorous villain," "contemptible creature," "political hypocrite," "demagogue coxcomb," "a most gross calumniator, a great fool, and a barefaced liar," "this prostitute wretch," and "disappointed pedant."

Webster restrained his own sharp tongue, maintaining a

"chaste and impartial" newspaper by refusing to descend to the cat calling of his adversaries. Several times he drew apologies from Thomas Greenleaf and others, but never wittingly did he permit personal invective or scurrility to besmirch his paper. The opposition was the more incensed at this, having hoped to drag him into a free-for-all fight and to butcher him. Even Alexander J. Dallas became a party to the "get Webster" movement, for late in December, 1797, he sued Webster for libel as the result of a statement alleging that Dallas had overdrawn his bank account. Webster corrected the error, reported to him by Thomas Eddy, a reputable Quaker merchant in Philadelphia, but Dallas, the undoer of Genêt, relentlessly proceeded in order to give Bache basis for insulting remarks. Webster accepted sole responsibility for the item and said that he had no objection to be the subject of prosecution.

In the discussion of national affairs, although that subject engaged less editorial attention then than later, Webster maintained the same detachment he evidenced in his consideration of foreign affairs. His remarks on the clubs were generally elevated in tone and frequently eloquent in pleas for constructive, instead of destructive, criticism: "If instead of writing for party purposes, our ingenious men would now turn their attention to the improvement of our country, by establishing useful institutions for education, by extending and securing our commerce, by cultivating our soil, founding manufactures and correcting our laws and morals, it is probable the virulence of party-spirit would soon subside the distinctions of aristocrat and democrat, created for the most nefarious purposes, and which has converted innumerable friends into cold jealous party men and enemies, would soon give way to returning confidence and social affection. Union and harmony are our true interest, and those who would disturb these, must be unfriendly to the happiness of their country."

A good example of Webster's temperate manner is found in his comments on Edmund Randolph's resignation from the Cabinet, occasioned by a scandal involving the Secretary with Fauchet. Instead of lambasting the Democrats, as Bache and Greenleaf had slandered President Washington on this event, Webster asked the reading public to suspend judgment until Randolph's pamphlet of "vindication" could appear. When that document showed unmistakably Randolph's indiscreet conduct, Webster wrote: "It is a most gratifying circumstance that by the publication of Mr. Randolph's book and other disclosures, the President has recovered the confidence of his opposers. The tongue of calumny is struck dumb." His further remarks quite good-humoredly rebuked Bache's and Greenleaf's "lies," but Webster did not seize this opportunity, as he might have, to conduct a long campaign of abuse. The truth having been published, Webster was satisfied. He let the matter drop with that.

Only occasionally did Webster speak out directly in defense of President Washington, because he assumed that the noble service and inflexible integrity of that patriot required no apologist. With President John Adams it was different; he was assailed by enemies without and within the Federalist Party. The Democrats accused Adams of being a monarchist, an aspersion Webster rebutted by exhibiting Adams's leading rôle in the War of Independence and by giving publicity to the influence of Adams's *Defence of the American Constitutions* on the French Constitution. For a time the courtly ways of Adams were defended, but when Hamilton broke with the President over the raising of an army, Webster sided with Hamilton. Thereafter Webster seldom animadverted on the acts of the Executive, but in 1800 Webster vigorously denounced Hamilton's apostasy. Meantime, too, Webster became conscious of the disloyalty of Pickering and Wolcott in the Cabinet, but he set forth his criticism in personal letters and not in his papers. The absurdity, not to say the treachery, of their conduct nauseated the upright editor; he preferred public silence to an internecine internal party war.

Webster's wholesome desire for a peaceful government, as well as his magnanimity of mind, appeared in his attitude toward the election of Jefferson as Vice President:

Nor can we omit to express a firm hope and belief that the choice of THOMAS JEFFERSON to the second place in the government, will be productive of the most salutary consequences. His attachment to his own country and to its honor and independence, is universally acknowledged; nor can it be believed that any undue preference for a foreign nation will lead him to sacrifice the peace, the interest and the happiness of his own. That his bias towards the interests of France, in opposition to those of Great Britain, has been very visible in his commercial system, is believed in the northern states, and his ideas have been considered as hostile to the trade of those states. But it is not to be believed that Mr. Jefferson would, if in his power, consent to sacrifice any of our substantial interests, and a difference of opinion will yield to the public voice.

On the whole, the result of the election may prove, contrary to the views and expectations of both parties, the means of reconciling discordant opinions, of moderating the asperity of party, and uniting, in the administration, the confidence of men of different political opinions.—Such is our sincere wish and we believe it to be the wish of every uncorrupted patriot in the American Republic.

One looks in vain for a similar broadmindedness in the other newspapers of the day. Certainly a man who could write these paragraphs was no mere party hack, all the bluster of Bache and Cobbett to the contrary notwithstanding.

Webster was plagued not only by opposition editors, but he also suffered from inefficient and dishonest employees. George Bunce, taken into the firm as printer, turned out a wretched, incorrect, ill-printed sheet, so that on May 1, 1796, Webster dismissed him. George Folliott Hopkins and Joseph D. Webb became the new partners in the firm of Hopkins, Webb and Co., but Webb soon proved to be a petty peculator of cash and had to be dropped, July 13, 1797. He refused to surrender his contract, and the firm was dissolved; a new organization was effected with Hopkins as publisher. On June 4, 1794, Webster had founded *The Herald, A Gazette for the Country*, a semi-weekly paper made up without recomposition from the daily editions, the advertising being omitted. This device was an innovation of great utility, because country subscribers were freed from the payment of heavy postage on uninteresting advertising. *The Minerva and Mercantile Evening Advertiser* (the new name was adopted on May 2, 1796) became on October 1, 1797, *The Commercial Advertiser*, and *The Herald* became *The Spectator*. At this time the papers had a circulation of 1700, one third larger than any other New York newspaper.

On April 1, 1798, Webster withdrew from the active direction of the papers, disgusted at the personalities he endured and dissatisfied with Federalist bungling and self-seeking. The papers occasionally carried articles by Webster, who retained the political department. But the old life and energy departed. They became clipsheets, unoriginal as a rural weekly. Hopkins withdrew on July 1, 1799, and Webster placed his nephew, Ebenezer Belden, in charge. In 1801 Hamilton brought William Coleman to New York as founding editor of *The New York Evening Post*. Webster employed Samuel Bayard to give Coleman competition, but *The Commercial Advertiser* continued to lose subscribers. The papers that had boasted a circulation from Georgia to Montreal now were of importance only as local advertising sheets. In 1803 Zachariah Lewis became editor and then owner. He found the accounts deranged, Belden having shamefully abused his trust, so that Webster cut the original price of $5000 to a fraction of that amount. The integrity of Webster appears to advantage in this willing surrender of his profits when the sad tale of a neglected office and poor management came to his attention. Webster's paper later became *The Globe*, which died in 1923 when Frank Munsey merged it into the *Sun*.

Little is known of Webster's life in New York beyond his engagements as an editor and publisher. In the latter capacity he undertook to assist in preparing and to print Jedidiah Morse's *Gazetteer*, but after proceeding through several letters, illness forced Webster to surrender this work. Indeed, illness frequently confined the editor. His eyes, weak when he undertook his new business, frequently failed him, and one friend described them as "lined with red ferret." The long hours of unrelaxed work in translating and writing so taxed his strength that twice he sank under illnesses from which the physicians offered no hope of recovery.

In moving to New York, Webster took the commodious house formerly occupied by Thomas Franklin. James Greenleaf had rented this so that he and his friend, Charles Lagarenne, a French dandy and royalist, might have congenial quarters. Both were of a boisterous, bibulous nature, and their frequent appearance at dinner with unannounced guests so distressed Mrs. Webster that peremptory orders were given to Greenleaf to mend his ways. A breach was thus occasioned which time never healed.

In 1796 the Websters moved to Corlear's Hook, then a mile in the country from the city. Here they continued to receive their many friends. James Kent, who assisted Webster with the "Curtius" articles, came most frequently, full of good talk about classical literature of which he was a master. He was in the New York Legislature at this time, and he supplied Webster with running comments on the progress of political events. Dr. Elihu Hubbard Smith, Dr. Samuel Latham Mitchill, Dr. Edward Miller, the Reverend Mr. Samuel Miller, among others, enjoyed Websterian hospitality. Dr. John W. Francis, the eminent physician, late in life wrote this description of the editor: "He was in person somewhat above the ordinary height, slender, with gray eyes, and a keen aspect; remarkable for neatness in dress and characterized by an erect walk, a broad hat, and a long cue, much after the manner of Albert Gallatin, as depicted in the engravings in Callender's *Prospect before Us.*"

With all of the leaders of the Federalist Party Webster was on intimate terms, Jay and King supporting him in his dictionary venture years later. But with the dictatorial Alexander Hamilton, Webster kept an "off and on" friendship. They had many traits in common: both were journalists and pamphleteers, trained to the law and to the devices of convincing reluctant jurors; both were profound thinkers and exhaustive students; both were systematic in pursuing their work and their opinions; and both possessed inflexible determination to make their opinions prevail. On the last point they split. Webster could not forgive Hamilton's sordid affair with Mrs. Reynolds, an impeccable moral life having given Webster's large nose an instinctive upward twist at the nearest approach of fetid odors of scandal. But less could he forgive Hamilton's double-dealing with President Washington and with President Adams. Both Webster and Hamilton were ambitious for glory and honor, but, whereas Hamilton pursued narrow, tortuous ways for his own aggrandizement and for the salving of wounded pride, Webster looked steadily upon himself as a servant of his nation, a schoolmaster, born to counsel, to prompt, to instruct. Twice, when his investments yielded too small an income to support his family, Webster asked Wolcott and Madison for a petty clerkship to tide him over the lean season. Neither seems to have responded to Webster's letters. The humility of a great scholar, a great teacher, shines resplendently against the dark background in these incidents. But a scholar's humility develops giant power when pretended friends sully long-established ideals or intellectual truths. This great power Webster wielded against Hamilton, finally in 1800 bringing the quarrel into the open with a scorching pamphlet. Hamilton, with his customary indirection, hired William Coleman to establish *The New York Evening Post* and to ruin Webster financially by destroying the value of his newspapers. And Coleman, goaded on with secondhand hate, ridiculed every activity of Webster. "The little giant" deserves the adjective in more ways than one.

Somewhat like Milton, Webster considered himself "a member incorporate of that truth, whereof he was persuaded." In this quality lay his strength, but in it also lay his weakness as a candidate for preferment. He did not know how to file and smooth, cut and chisel his opinions to fit a man or a season. Forthrightly he announced his conclusions, and like the Rock of Gibraltar he maintained his ground. One must come down to the time of Horace Greeley for an adequate parallel to Webster, the newspaper editor.

With a sense of defeat Webster left New York for New Haven, where he made his residence on April 1, 1798. He had acquired financial independence, but he had become weary of narrating "the absurdities of man." He had lost his health. He had again become the target of malicious detractors and calumniators, because he placed patriotism above party, America above Europe. His one great happiness, beyond his joy in his wife and children, lay in his great, new humanitarian project: he would teach the truth about the origin of epidemic fevers.

CHAPTER XII

HISTORIAN OF EPIDEMIC DISEASES

NEXT to his own stupidity, man's greatest enemy is disease. But no one seems quite able to tell, even yet, what the relationship between the two is or which brings the other. In the last decade of the eighteenth century stupidity and disease carried on together their dreadful work of destruction; it was as easy to make reason prevail in a discussion of the yellow fever epidemics as to teach the mobs a judicial attitude toward France and England. Indeed, Alexander Graydon thought the plague a grim visitation of God to purge foul hearts because of their French enthusiasm. Graydon was almost as correct in his diagnosis as were the physicians, so pitifully ignorant was mankind of the origin and nature of diseases. Not until 1900 did Lazear and Walter Reed discover that only the mosquito could transmit yellow fever; not until 1913 did Noguchi capture the minutest of bacteria and develop yellow fever serum. In our three-day chick-like wisdom, we must not sneer too much at our grandfathers and great-grandfathers. Our stupidity and barbarism are only slightly different from theirs: ours are more refined and more cruel.

Epidemics of influenza in 1789 and 1790 and of scarlet fever in April–May, 1793, had come under Webster's observation, his children having been ill with the latter disease. "I attended night and day to its symptoms," he wrote about scarlet fever with the precision of a physician, "which were a catarrhal affection of the throat, attended with slight external discoloration about the neck and breast, and a fever whose exacerbations were violent, but the remissions regular, attended with profuse perspiration." Webster had been dabbling in scientific experiments, had gathered meteorological and thermometrical statistics, and had numbered physicians among his best friends. With a quenchless curiosity for a knowledge of the truth, he now attended to the collection of information on the subject of diseases.

Terrifying news from Philadelphia accelerated his investigations. Oliver Wolcott on September 19, 1793, told Webster of the dreadful yellow fever epidemic in Philadelphia, the deserted streets, the sad faces, the panic. One in every ten had died. In two weeks 517 were buried in Potter's Field, the total registered deaths in the season being 4,044. Everyone who could afford it fled to the country; even physicians turned tail, some of them scurrying out at night. Others remained, heroic figures fighting a phantom they could not grasp. Dr. Benjamin Rush treated as many as eighteen hundred patients in a week, while five of his students and family fell beside him. Stephen Girard and Peter Helm took charge of Bush Hill, the hospital where intolerable conditions had prevailed. Regardless of their lives, not knowing whether the disease was contagious, they changed the sheets, tinged with yellow and foul with gangrenous or black vomit. They swabbed the floors with vinegar and water, blew tar smoke through the halls, and spoke comforting words to the dying.

The physicians bickered over the causes and the treatment, whether the disease was local in generation or imported from the West Indies. Rush, disagreeing with his colleagues, withdrew from the College of Physicians and organized the Academy of Medicine. Freneau versified the situation thus:

Doctors raving and disputing,
Death's pale army still recruiting.

What a pother,
One with t'other,
Some a-writing, some a-shooting.

Dr. William Currie, sneering at Rush as a blood-letter and a charlatan, told the public in *The Federal Gazette* (September 17) that the disease was merely the fall fever, operating only on those who had had influenza. Rush gave blow for blow, reporting that he had cured himself by two copious bleedings and two doses of mercurial medicine. The quarrel initiated a pamphlet war in which every literate American physician took part. Dr. John B. Davidge of Baltimore, with Johnsonese affectation, told why he rushed into print: "Jurare in verba magistri is the motto of unthinking hebetude, but a master's nod ought not to block up the avenues of research."

In 1794 epidemics recurred in Philadelphia and appeared with fatal malignity at New Haven. In 1795 New York, Baltimore, and Norfolk were stricken. In 1796 Newburyport, Boston, and Charleston suffered. New York and Philadelphia were again stricken in 1797. The disease had come to Webster's very door. From the day the *Minerva* was founded, he made a running commentary on the epidemics, noting "something singular in the appearance and progress of putrid diseases" on April 11, 1794.

"The world is a book of instruction," Webster wrote; "and he who will not profit by the lessons before him, must be unfaithful to himself and his fellow-citizens." Later he wrote: "No sober reflecting man can cast his eye over the world, and see the miseries of man, without a humane wish to alleviate them." To this humanitarian motive Webster added his nationalistic zeal; America had contributed no new discoveries to medicine beyond the Indian's herbal lore. It was high time that something should be done. With customary energy he threw himself into the raging controversy. He asked for facts: "Theories are of little use, but facts are of infinite importance; and we conceive every new fact or observation on the subject of pestilential diseases to be well worth attention."

To get these facts Webster invited the physicians of America to send him accounts of their observations, experiences, remedies, and any other pertinent data. This circular letter, October 31, 1795, promised that the articles would be combined in a volume, to be printed at the expense of the editor. The rancorous party spirit immediately burst out in Bache's *Aurora*, "A Fellow of the College of Physicians" addressing an open letter to "Noah Webster, Esq., *Author and Physician General* of the United States," to assure him that his request, "couched in such *modest* terms and so complimentary to the faculty of medicine, ought not to be treated to silent contempt. When men of your eminence condescend to turn bookmakers for Physicians; when a man in whom all the rare qualities of human nature centre; when a man who can recite the etymology of words with as much facility as a child can recite its alphabet, deigns to step forward in behalf of the faculty, it would be the extreme of rudeness and brutality not to lend an attentive ear to him, and to furnish him a ladder to mount to fame and guineas. . . . To the author of the *Institutes*, the Editor of the *Minerva*, and to that omnipotent arm, which has 'dashed whole conspiracies with his single pen,' is reserved the honor and glory to triumph over a malady, dire as the conspiracies which he vanquished."

Webster's reply, November 10, stated that "the object of all [his] publications had been uniformly for the public good"; he explained further: "Humanity is a common cause and one that should level all distinctions of party. The investigation of the causes of diseases and the means of alleviating the calamities of life, is the business of every good citizen, whatever be his profession. In doing this, I

encroach not on the proper business of medical gentlemen.
I undertake only the part of a Compiler and Publisher; and
no man, whose heart is not hardened by party prejudices,
can wish to throw cold water on the undertaking."

In July, 1796, the information collected in response to
Webster's letter was published in a volume, entitled *A Collection of Papers on the Subject of Bilious Fever, prevalent
in the United States for a Few Years Past*. Webster had become convinced that the disease was of local origin and not
of a contagious nature. The essays by Dr. Valentine Seaman
and Dr. Elihu Hubbard Smith present the arguments in
support of this point of view. Webster, who wrote a Preface and Summary, used their evidence to buttress his plea
for improved city planning and sanitation. If the people
could be convinced that diseases may be of local generation,
"that sources of disease and death may be found among
themselves created by their own negligence, it is a great
point gained; for until they learn this, they will never
attend to the means of preserving life and health. They
will still wallow in filth, crowd their cities with low dirty
houses and narrow streets; neglect the use of bathing and
washing; and live like savages, devouring in hot seasons
undue quantities of animal food at their tables, and reeling
home after midnight debauches." Dr. Rush had been a firm
believer in the contagion theory, but through his correspondence with Webster and his reading of this book, he became
a convert to anti-contagion.

Incredible must have been the filth of American cities.
The Reverend Mr. Henry Channing of New London could
not tell whether the disease arose in his community from
the putrid effluvia of fifty barrels of rotten codfish, spread
out on the wharf to be dried and then to be sold for human
consumption; or of a great quantity of whale oil; or of
overflowing privies. He finally chose the fish, since they
were the most productive of offensive odors. Dead animals,

kitchen refuse, lees of fermented liquors, animal and human excrement lay scattered about so commonly that mayors
and town councils could not be prevailed upon to pay the
cost of removal.

In editorial after editorial Webster begged for sanitation,
for the introduction of channels of water for the cleansing
of New York's streets, and for the filling in of low, marshy
lots. As a result, new sanitary laws were passed in 1796;
Webster declared (October 14, 1797): "The cleansing of
the city has diminished the mass of autumnal diseases of a
lighter kind, and therefore cleansing has had a great and
obvious influence in lessening the number and severity of
autumnal fevers." Even if the idea were not true, Webster
thought it would be wise to propagate it as "a pious fraud"
in order to prove that "our public health depends on ourselves."

The bickering of the physicians continued. All sorts of
new theories were set forth. Dr. Joseph Browne, drawing
on Hippocrates for a clue, declared the cause of yellow
fever to consist in heat and a deficiency of *oxygenous air*,
or as he called it *animal vital air;* or a surplusage of *azotic*,
which he called *vegetable vital air*. The atmosphere is composed, he said, of these two airs, the *animal vital air* being
"the grand corrector of putrescency." Freedom from disease might be obtained by cleanliness, by abstention from
meats, by the avoidance of crowds, and by "the planting of
trees to absorb vegetable vital air and to evolve animal vital
air." Dr. Alexander Hosack proposed applying camphor
freely to the nose, but Dr. Samuel Latham Mitchill opposed this preventive measure because it "stimulated the
absorbents of the nostrils and promoted the ready inhala-
tion of the morbid effluvia." Dr. Rush prescribed frequent
bloodletting; Dr. Hosack declared that "the promiscuous
use of the lancet was very injurious and unsuccessful." Immediately came the irrefutable answer: "The abuse of a

remedy is no argument against its use," nor "is the fatal event of the case in which it was used any proof of its inutility or that it was pernicious." As excellent treatment Dr. Hosack recommended the evacuation of the bowels with emitics, the relaxation of the surface of the body with showers of cold water, and the inducing of a free perspiration. An objector noticed that the "general and pleasant coolness . . . over the whole system" was followed by "heat, fever and pain . . . till, at length, they became more severe and intolerable than at first." Well might the editors of *The Medical Repository* report: "In respect to the cure of yellow fever, generally speaking, we seem not to have attained, as yet, to that clear, decisive, and prompt method, which shall be always unequivocally safe and certain. The subject is still embarrassed with doubts and difficulties."

But these warring physicians were not embarrassed. Dr. William Currie continued to make rude aspersions on the practices and beliefs of Dr. Rush and other physicians, calling their conclusions "absurd and untenable." Webster wearied of this fruitless haggling; he remarked (October 24, 1797): "It has often been noticed by medical gentlemen that the yellow fever and plague have a most powerful effect on the brain. Is not this effect very visible in the violent contentions among the faculty in Philadelphia? Is not a partial delirium discernible in their writings and challenges? It seems to be nearly time for the police of the city to think of the strait-jacket for some of them." Webster wrote a grimly humorous piece three weeks later, touching on the speculation mania: "It is said by physicians that when a pestilence prevails, they can discover the persons infected before they are taken ill, by a certain *wildness of the eye*. I wish to have this remark well founded, because it explains all the phenomena of scrip and Georgia lands. It certainly must be an epidemic state of the atmosphere, which spreads the yellow fever, and the same pestilential air must disturb the brains of men—converting men of sober senses and sound discretion into maniacs, who run raving about streets, buying bubbles and selling them for cent-percent profit—and who never discover that they are dealing in bubbles————till they have been well bled and blistered ——in their pockets!——Surely Dr. Rush is right—*depletion* is the only effectual cure!"

The physicians having failed to establish truth, Webster determined to settle the question. Dr. Currie had published in October, 1797, three letters to Mr. Benjamin Wyncoop of Philadelphia, in which he declared that "*vegetable* effluvia from low marshy grounds produce intermitting and remitting fevers, and that these fevers are never contagious; but that *human* effluvia produce continued fevers of a nervous or putrid kind, which may be and usually are contagious." Between October 26 and December 23, 1797, Webster printed twenty-five letters to Dr. Currie. Without attempting to intrude into the province of the faculty, for he had read only three or four medical books, Webster controverted Dr. Currie's theories, denounced the baseness of trifling with truth and with social confidence and happiness, and demanded facts instead of theories. "Yes, Sir," Webster concluded his nineteenth article, "it appears to me that philosophers and physicians and most other men have treated malignant epidemics, just as children conduct [themselves] respecting mischief in the family: They are forever casting off the censure from themselves upon their neighbors." These papers were received with great approbation everywhere but in Philadelphia, and even there, according to Dr. Rush, "they have made a greater impression upon our citizens than anything that has even been published in Philadelphia on that subject." *The Medical Repository*, approving Webster's "forcible and manly reasoning," urged him to publish his papers in a book.

But Webster was not satisfied with them. They "were begun without previous preparation, and have been prosecuted amidst other incessant employments. They doubtless want correction and are certainly deficient in arrangement; but they have been written with a strong sense of the importance of the subject and an honest *zeal* to serve my country." The patriotic motive again! The warfare of opinions, renewed with near fury by Webster's letters, was "ridiculous," as Webster averred; therefore he would amend, augment, and publish his conclusions to achieve "a degree of unanimity of opinion and measures."

When he moved to New Haven on April 1, 1798, Webster spent ten days in arranging his furniture and affairs, and then he began to write. Soon he sped away to Philadelphia to work in the Loganian Library. He completed researches in New York, ransacked the Yale library, and then visited the libraries of Harvard College and the city of Boston. His materials grew into immense proportions, and although he was prostrated for ten weeks at one time with the disease he was describing, he completed in eighteen months without an amanuensis a two-volume work of 712 octavo pages! *A Brief History of Epidemic and Pestilential Diseases; with the Principal Phenomena of the Physical World which Precede and Accompany Them, and Observations Deduced from the Facts Stated* became the world's first historical treatment of this subject.

During its writing, Webster was spurred onward by Dr. Rush: "Go on—go on with your inquiries. Cause Physicians to blush, and instruct mankind to throw off their allegiance to them. Posterity will do you justice. The man who produces truth upon the origin of pestilential fevers, and persuades the world to conform to it, will deserve more of the human race than all the heroes or statesmen that ever lived."

The *History* is not only the best general summary of

epidemiological opinion at the end of the Eighteenth Century, but it is surpassed by few works as a compendium of earlier speculations on this subject. Not only did Webster gather material through library research, but he also wrote to all the prominent men of the day and he sent out circular letters to eminent foreign physicians; he took depositions of patients, sea captains, and sailors. He collected, as Dr. Alfred Scott Warthin has put it, "an enormous amount of material which he arranged systematically and analyzed with that tireless indefatigability which seems the most remarkable characteristic of this remarkable man."

The first volume of the *History* opens with a consideration of the diversity of opinions on the causes and origin of the pestilence, and a series of definitions. The remainder of the volume traces the history of epidemics from Biblical times to 1799. The second volume presents tables of mortality, statistics, and theoretical conclusions on the "pestilential state of the air" as it affects the progress of various diseases. "His essential argument," to quote Dr. C.–E. A. Winslow, "is that epidemics occur in certain periods, generally in widely distributed places; that a pestilential state of air extends, at the same time, over many parts of the world; that if a violent plague is raging in one place, malignant diseases, if not plague, prevail in other places; and that such epidemic periods among human beings are associated with diseases among animals, plagues of locusts, earthquakes, volcanic eruptions and the appearance of comets. . . . Webster is very careful to disclaim direct causal connection between any of the physical phenomena discussed. . . . [He] assumes all epidemic disease to be alike and progressively increasing in seriousness over long periods." He shows that disease is propagated by infection, but that its original source lies in previous diseases of a different sort. His definition of the pestilential state of air is not clear, but he leans heavily to the opinion that it is electrical in origin. In his

chapter "On Contagion and Infection" he heaps scorn on
the importationists and demonstrates the failure of quarantine measures as then practiced. He notes the seasonal char-
acteristics of certain forms of disease, and concludes fatal-
istically: "the pestilence [of non-infectious diseases] which
invades man will be found to arise solely from the uncontrollable laws of the elements; and quarantine will be utterly unavailing." The rat, the flea, and the mosquito had
not then been discovered as the bearers of contagion. These
discoveries have, of course, upset the whole of Webster's
theorizing. But he knew his data was insufficient and his
conclusions unsure: "The reader will consider these opinions rather as *conjectural* than *positive*. No certain conclusions can be drawn from an interrupted and imperfect series
of facts. More materials are necessary to enable us to erect
a theory of epidemics which shall deserve full confidence."
To secure these materials Webster proposed, at the end of
his work, "that all medical and philosophical societies
[should] undertake to register facts and reciprocally to
communicate them by means of general correspondence."
Webster knew the inductive method of science and fostered
it.

The *History* may stand as a monument of immense labor,
dedicated to and illustrating man's age-long groping in the
dark; yet, despite its misdirection, it is a notable piece of
work. The same energy devoted to the use of the micro-
scope might have produced more beneficial results, but it
is foolish to carp at men for using the wrong instruments
when these instruments are the only ones available. The
important contributions of Webster were his historical survey and his emphasis upon facts and statistics. Although
he did not know how to control his data, although his
theories were inadequate, and although his methods of
analysis were unsound, one cannot fail to be thrilled by this
layman's humanitarian zeal to bring "a degree of unanimity

of opinion and measures" to the discussion and treatment of pestilential diseases.

Dr. Currie immediately smiled away Webster's work: "The doctrine of Mr. Webster on this subject, notwithstanding his elaborate researches, appears still more exceptional, and to be as much the creature of the imagination as the tales of the fairies." *The Medical Repository*, with whose editors, Drs. S. L. Mitchill and Edward Miller, Webster had been in almost daily contact in New York from 1794 to 1798, gave this opinion: "In our judgment Mr. Webster has performed a great work. Whether we consider the extent and novelty of the design, the diligence, acuteness, and erudition displayed in the investigations, the ingeniousness and sagacity of the combinations, or the importance of the results: whether we consider the revolution of opinions which it tends to effect, or the range of inquiries which it is adapted to awaken, we must pronounce him entitled to the praise of an instructive and original writer." The reviewer doubted Webster's theory of the electrical basis of the pestilential air, and expressed shock at Webster's atheistical doctrine of equivocal generation. Webster's aversion to bloodletting also was touched upon, since these opinions clashed with Dr. Rush's theories. Dr. Rush, who read Webster's manuscript, was at this time suing Cobbett successfully for libelous publications arising from the physician's fondness for drawing as much as sixty ounces of blood from a patient in a day. On the whole, however, *The Medical Repository* found Webster's work so "astonishing" a scholarly performance, that every layman was advised to purchase the book.

Dr. Joseph Priestley, philosopher, theologian, and scientist who because of his radical opinions had been driven from his home in Birmingham, England, to settle at Northumberland, Pennsylvania, thought Webster deserving of "the thanks of all mankind" for "a most important publication."

Priestley added additional proof of Webster's theory of
the source of disease in noxious vapors issuing from open-
ings in the earth, an idea Webster expanded after his *History* was published. Priestley also expressed much concern
that "a believer in a supreme intelligent author of nature"
should "advance opinions so wild and unphilosophical as
. . . the long exploded doctrine of equivocal generation."

This objection Webster had met in a letter to *The Medical Repository*, dated March 2, 1801. After supplying many
new facts in regard to epidemic history, he defined "equivocal generation" as denoting "doubtful or uncertain origin,"
and he supported this statement with cogent reasoning and
facts. Several paragraphs of this letter showing the quality
of Webster's mind deserve a place here:

> Indeed, Sir, I think it more becoming the limited knowledge of
> man to acknowledge his ignorance, than to be positive on such doubt-
> ful subjects. It is far from being impossible that the principles of
> animal and vegetable life may be radically the same—descending
> from man to the minutest germ of life in grades almost imperceptible
> in the larger species, and in the smaller species wholly beyond the
> reach of optics; and these elementary principles may originate life,
> in the form of vegetables or animals, according to the nidus. But
> hypothesis must not be the basis of system; and when the mode of
> generation is doubtful, I set it down as *equivocal,* which is only an-
> other term for human ignorance. . . .
> As to the atheistical tendency of the doctrine, I am quite un-
> concerned on that score. There is a fashion in opinions as well as
> in dress: each system must have its day. Not many years ago Boer-
> haave was the *omnis homo* of the faculty. He soon yielded his place
> to Cullen: Brown triumphed over Cullen: and now Sydenham, who
> had been cast away as rubbish, has reassumed his station as the
> father of a system, with his occult qualities. Similar is the rotation
> of opinions in chemistry. Opinions even become national—and we
> see Lavoisier arranged against Priestley, as formerly Cassini against
> Newton.
> With respect to the theological consequences of the doubtful
> generation of plants and animals, I have one remark to make—That
> the modern distinction between primary and secondary causes seems

to be carried too far; and, if I mistake not, has been the means of supporting, if not of originating, the usual arguments in favour of materialism. That matter can be endowed with laws, which shall operate uniformly and perpetually, independent of divine agency, may be possible, but appears to me unphilosophical. I can have no belief in permanency of duration in any being but God, and the operations of his power. The opinion that natural effects proceed from laws impressed on matter, without any direct exertion of divine power—and that supernatural effects are produced by the immediate agency of the Supreme Being—appears to me at least unfounded, and even unscriptural. The scripture generally ascribes every event directly to the first cause. It was God who hardened Pharaoh's heart, and who caused it to rain, as well as God who created the world, and arrested the sun in his course. This view of the question is not only more pious, but more philosophical; for I no more comprehend the growth and expansion of the rose in my garden, than the creation of the earth, or the resurrection of Lazarus. The result of my philosophy is to resolve every event and operation in the universe into the direct exertion of omnipotence. And I cannot but think that the modern doctrine of nature and natural laws, which seems to exclude the divine agency from most of the operations in the universe, has furnished the most tenable ground occupied by the materialists. This opinion of mine involves in it the idea that God is the author of evil; but this, in my mind, is no objection to it; for what we call evil is such only to our limited views.

But I am proceeding beyond my depth: it is best to put an end to this desultory letter. I have little leisure for philosophical researches —being engaged in compiling a system of principles for the education of our youth, on a plan new and more comprehensive than has yet appeared. I have an insuperable dislike to metaphysical studies, believing in the utility of plain matter of fact only.

Webster set forth in several articles contributed to *The Medical Repository* additional proofs to his theory of the source of disease in carbonic gas vapors issuing from the earth, to his theory of the electrical origin of pestilential air, and to his theory that influenza or catarrh is a precursor to all epidemic diseases. At the time of the epidemic in 1803 he vigorously denied the importation theory. On October 3, 1803, he wrote a letter "On the Nature of Fever and on the Importance of Remedies applied to the Skin," a startling bit of reasoning in which osteopathic principles are deduced from a simple bite of a worm. Little did it matter to Webster that he upset in this letter many of his earlier notions; he wanted to reach truth. "The proximate cause of fever," he had decided, "is any obstruction of the natural discharge of heat." The cold water cure, therefore, was harmful; heat and exercise should be prescribed. "From my own observations," he concluded, "I am inclined to believe that chronic affections, being occasioned by want of exercise, and a consequent muscular debility, are to be mitigated chiefly by external applications. Nothing will cure them but exercise—action being the natural business of man, and, of course, his natural prophylactic. But friction and the warm bath, by invigorating the muscles and restoring the excretions, relieve the viscera, or rather excite them to perform their functions far better than cathartics, astringents, and chalybeates. The orientals from the highest antiquity have made great use of the warm bath; and the ancients suffused the body with oil, evidently with a view to relax and soften the skin, and keep the excretions free. The modern Turkish practice of rubbing and pinching the skin at the time of bathing is intended for the same purpose. These considerations and many others lead me to believe that in modern practice physicians pay too much attention to the viscera, and too little to the skin and muscles."

This idea was developed still further in a letter of January 30, 1804, presenting critical remarks on Erasmus Darwin's theory of fever as set forth in *Zoonomia*. Webster accepted Darwin's conclusions that "the seat of most chronic affections is primarily in the skin and the subcutaneous vessels," but he objected to much of Darwin's philosophizing as either wrong or irrelevant. Webster concluded that he suspected "that intermittent fevers are, in part, to be ascribed to . . . the diurnal transition from heat to cold, and the torpor of the extreme vessels in consequence of the daily effect of the latter."

If Webster was a "busybody," as Scudder called him, his medical investigations reached no more ridiculous conclusions than those of practicing physicians. Certainly Webster was a "busybody" trying to do good, who most of the time by virtue of his practicality attained as large a measure of truth as any man in his day. But his labors were not rewarded. He lost his time, traveling expenses, and $700 in printing costs on his *History*. Robinsons, who brought out an edition in London, refused to pay one hundred guineas, as promised, because Webster had printed the work in America. One cannot blame Webster for begging the public to purchase his Spelling Book, the utility of which was everywhere recognized, when his really great contributions to social history—*Dissertations on the English Language,* Winthrop's *Journal,* and *A Collection of Essays and Fugitiv Writings,* as well as *A Brief History of Epidemic and Pestilential Diseases*—cost him years of labor and the expense of printing. Few scholars would persist in conducting unrewarded research in this manner and in the face of a hostile, sneering press. Yet Webster went on to even greater projects.

Webster's inquisitive mind wanted information on all sorts of subjects, but the *World Almanac* had not then been established. To meet the deficiency he sent out on May 7, 1798, five weeks after he had settled in New Haven and twenty-seven days after he had begun his *History of Epidemic Diseases,* a circular letter requesting statistical information on the geography, health, agriculture, trade, manufactures, shipping, roads, bridges, churches, schools, mines, and "any curious or important information not falling under any of the foregoing heads." "I have some leisure," he of the Gargantuan stride wrote, "and great inclination to be instrumental in bringing forward a correct view of the civil

and domestic economy of this State." A year later, when
his replies had not been adequate to the desired purpose,
Webster made this ambition a part of the favorite activity of
The Connecticut Academy of Arts and Sciences, of which
society he was an incorporator, if not the leading organizer.
On October 28, 1799, he prepared a similar letter for distribution in the name of the Academy. Sixteen replies were
received, but the response was unsatisfactory.

Webster was active in the Academy until the middle of
1800, when political sniping at his character caused him to
refuse to participate in the meetings. Meantime he read a
lengthy dissertation on the supposed changes of temperature
to refute the idea that winters were becoming warmer. In
January, 1800, he was a member of the committee to take
the census of New Haven. On his lecture tour he had
counted the houses in all the towns he had visited; this
pleasant self-imposed duty was an early manifestation of his
passion for statistics. In the first volume of the *Memoirs* of
the Academy, Webster published four papers: a dissertation
on weather, a table of mortality, a letter on the decom-
position of white-lead paint, and an etymological disquisi-
tion on the origin of mythology. On August 24, 1804, Webster gave "in consideration of my love of letters and a desire
to promote useful science and learning" a grant to the
Academy as follows: fifty cents for every thousand Spelling
Books printed in Connecticut, and two dollars for every
thousand *American Selection* and *Elements of Useful Knowledge*. Political pique had not destroyed his enthusiasm for
furthering the cause he cherished.

Two projects of Webster did not mature. On the death
of President Washington, Webster asked permission of
Bushrod Washington to prepare the official life of the hero.
John Marshall, however, had been chosen; with Senator
Beveridge we can regret that Webster was not given the
task, one for which he was fitted by temperament and ability.

A history of American newspapers also was planned, but only a bare outline of the assembled information was used in *Elements of Useful Knowledge*.

Politics was the be-all and the end-all of the young nation. Nothing else seemed to matter. It was inevitable that Webster in returning to "steady habit" Connecticut should battle against the Jeffersonians and espouse the principles of Federalism, and endure a renewed shower of scurrility.

CHAPTER XIII

The Porpoises of Connecticut

NEW HAVEN was probably the most beautiful small settlement in America in 1798, when Webster moved there. At least he had thought so in 1790, and he had had no reason to change his mind. Rows of elm trees formed Gothic arches over the streets, lending the little city of four thousand inhabitants a natural cathedral appearance in summer. Wide streets led from the harbor to the Green, the public square, where the State House, the Center Church, and the cemetery reminded the citizens of their trinity of obligations. West of the Green were the buildings of Yale College, substantial colonial structures in harmony with the simple beauty of the neighboring homes.

Webster bought the spacious Benedict Arnold House, built by that sturdy apothecary before the Revolution. The house and large garden, in which were many fruit trees, fronted on the harbor and commanded a view of Long Island Sound. Before the door, on what is now Water Street, passed the endless traffic of the Boston Post Road. As Webster pruned trees or experimented with new varieties of seeds and plants, he could keep an eye on the world passing by.

With imperturbable ease Webster carried on many activities at the same time. While he was writing his *History of Epidemic Diseases*, he was contributing more or less regularly to his newspapers, was starting projects for new books, was assisting in founding The Connecticut Academy and the Union School, was entering upon the ladder of preferment in Connecticut politics, was using his energy to keep subversive persons like Priestley and Jefferson from ruining the nation, and was trying to stem the rising tide of democratic sentiment in Connecticut. In this chapter let us examine the acts and thoughts of the politician, and reserve for the next chapter a discussion of the educational and lexicographical activities up 1812, when Webster moved to Amherst, Massachusetts.

No other community appreciated so fully as New Haven the eminent services of Webster to the young nation. Yale took immense pride in her alumni, the students under Timothy Dwight, president since 1795, learning to cherish every manifestation of locally fostered genius. Dwight welcomed Webster as an ally in the great battle for safeguarding the established Congregational Church. Dry, sententious Simeon Baldwin and blustery David Daggett, leaders at the Bar and in the Federalist Party, called on Webster to head the penmen in defense of their common political ideals. Elias Shipman, wealthy shipowner and head of the Chamber of Commerce, looked to Webster for economic advice and assistance in combating legislation hostile to commercial expansion. The influence for which Webster yearned when he resided in Hartford now was his. At forty years of age he was ready to teach his countrymen the philosophy he had learned as a result of extensive travel and study.

On the Fourth of July, 1798, he outlined in a patriotic address the conclusions which he had now reached, conclusions which he would repeat during the forty-five remaining years of his life. The young radical had swung slowly and inevitably toward the right in his political thinking, while he clung tenaciously to his radical notions in language. At one moment he could damn the populace for ignorantly following a set of demagogues, and in the next hour he could write beautiful tributes to the superior mentality of the yeomanry of America whose language habits were more correct than the rules of Bishop Lowth and Dr. Johnson. At forty Webster had fixed ideas; he was already a patriarch moving among his fellows, not quietly like his namesake to save himself from the coming inundation, but rather stridently like Jeremiah, hurling denunciations and pronouncing gloomy prophecies. He was the apologist of the old order, the order of Brother Jonathan Trumbull and the "steady habit" era when old, trusted officers conducted the government until death or infirmities removed them.

Webster had been a pivotal figure in American life for fifteen years. In education, in literature, and in politics, although his position may have been a humble one in comparison with that of any one of six dozen political or military or religious leaders, Webster had made notable contributions. No one else had touched life at more points or had done so much good in so many ways. But the experience was disillusioning. Everywhere he found the popular leaders, only Washington excepted, to be self-seeking, hesitant in espousing good causes, and bent upon personal power rather than national honor. A new spirit had entered the American people, a spirit he could not support, although he had probably done as much as any man to foster it. This was the spirit of democracy, then noisily illustrated by the clubs and by the party tactics of Jefferson.

Webster dreamed dreams of an idealistic Federalist Party. He was not blind to the faults of Adams, Hamilton, Pickering, and Wolcott, but he thought them unfairly treated because of the tumultuous uproar occasioned by the European war. He thought of Washington, of Jay, of King, and of Brother Jonathan, men whose integrity and wisdom had never been questioned. These were the old men, patriots tried and true, and these were the type of men to whom the government should be entrusted. Webster was blind to the faults of Federalism, its insistence upon the property basis of law and the franchise, upon the rights of the few as opposed to the rights of the many, and upon the union of church and state. Too late he realized the error; but no one has stated it better than he did in a letter to King on July 6, 1807:

There is one particular in which, I think, the leading Gentlemen of the Washington School have uniformly erred. They have attempted to resist the force of current popular opinion, instead of falling into the current with a view to direct it. In this they have manifested more integrity than address. They are men of independent minds and unsuspected honor and honesty; and appear to consider it wrong to yield their own opinions in the minutest particular, in favor of such as are more popular. But in this, I think, they err, either from scrupulous regard to *principle*, or from mistaking the means by which all popular governments are to be managed. Between the unbending firmness of an H——n and the obsequiousness of a J——n, there is a way to preserve the confidence of the populace without a sacrifice of integrity. In morality an honest man must make no concessions that violate the laws of right, but political measures are rarely connected with moral right and wrong, at least the greatest proportion are mere matters of expedience, and in these I think *honest, independent men of talents* should yield so far to popular opinion as to *retain the confidence of the people;* for without that confidence they are lost in the scale of political measures; but with it they may *gradually* wean the people from their most foolish schemes and correct their opinions. And it is vastly important that such men should not lose their weight of character, for if they do not lead the people, fools and knaves will. I wish to see our distinguished statesmen regain the public confidence, and I believe they may do it without mean or criminal compliances. Absolute perfection in government is not attainable; and measures not the best may be rendered harmless and even salutary by union of councils. *Union* is of far more consequence than any degree of theoretical perfection in public measures.

King took no comfort in the advice, saying it was impossible to surrender to the will of hordes of recent immigrants who did not either appreciate the "fathers" or the genius of American institutions. Webster himself could not take the advice; he frequently tried to forget politics by energetic scholarship.

In his Fourth of July Oration, 1798, Webster indulged in the usual amount of flag-waving and denunciation of the French XYZ intrigues, and then he turned a discussion of French philosophy into a prophecy of the dangers imminent in America from the rise of the Jeffersonians: "At no period since we become [sic] a nation, have our political affairs been so critical, as at this moment. Ambition, under the specious cover of republicanism, and infidelity, under the deceptive title of reason, have assumed the scepter and the sword, and are stalking over the earth with giant steps, levelling the mounds which wisdom and policy have raised to restrain the vicious propensities of men; turning the physical against the moral force of a nation; dragging from seats of justice the wise and the venerable, and replacing them with bullies and coxcombs; encouraging violence and robbery, under pretence of introducing a factitious equality; plundering states under the name of taking pay for protecting them; dethroning God and trampling on man. . . . Such are the inevitable consequences of that false philosophy which has been preached in the world by Rousseau, Condorcet, Godwin and other visionaries." Therefore, the orator begged his audience, "Never, my fellow citizens, let us exchange our civil and religious institutions for the wild theories of crazy projectors; or the sober, industrious moral habits of our country, for experiments in atheism and lawless democracy. *Experience* is a safe pilot; but *experiment* is a dangerous ocean, full of rocks and shoals!"

Only occasionally did Webster have time amidst his writing of the epidemic history to comment on politics. But when Dr. Priestley published his *Letters to the Inhabitants of Northumberland*, Webster seized his pen and wrote in January, 1800, *Ten Letters to Dr. Joseph Priestly* [sic], a caustic, rude, insulting diatribe against alien theorists lending comfort to the opponents of a government whose protection they enjoyed. Priestley had been drawn forth by William Cobbett, whose antipathy to the chemist amounted almost to a mania. Webster accused Priestley of using Cobbett's attack as a cloak under which to purvey his gratuitious criticisms of the American Constitution and his theoretical notions in support of the French cause and of Jeffersonian democracy, a subterfuge Priestley admitted to Jefferson (April 10, 1801). Webster demonstrated that the French policy had been contradictory, and that Napoleon's seizure of power proved conclusively that republican principles could not prevail in Europe. Webster also rebutted Priestley's objections to the Alien and Sedition Act, to the monarchical tendency of the Federalist leaders, and to the making of a treaty with Britain without consulting an earlier ally, France. Priestley was called "an incorrigible political heretic," and warned "that if you continue to attack the government of the country and excite uneasiness among the people . . . , I shall rejoice to see the alien law extend the arm of justice to you, as I think it ought to have done long ago to your friend Porcupine."

Priestley replied that he had been misunderstood, that he reprobated the conduct of Cobbett, that he loved the American Constitution, and that he had not written on American politics until silence under a stream of abuse had become intolerable. Webster evidently wrote a long letter in reply, now lost, which the old philosopher answered laconically: "I am as confident as I can be of anything that those who think differently from you have not the views which you ascribe to them, viz., 'the complete overthrow of the Constitution.' " He added, "Whatever you think of me, I feel no unfriendly disposition towards you." This sentiment was demonstrated practically some months later when he wrote a long letter to Dr. Rush in approbation of the *History of Epidemic and Pestilential Diseases.*

As fast as treason reared its head, Webster flailed at it. On August 1, 1800, Hamilton inquired of President Adams whether the statement that Hamilton was a member of a "British faction in this country" had emanated from the President. Not receiving an answer, Hamilton on October 1 wrote that he would draw no inference from the silence, but he would assert that the charge "is a base, wicked and cruel calumny, destitute even of a plausible pretext to excuse the folly or mask the depravity which must have dictated it." In this heat he dashed off a long letter, said to have been given circulation by an enemy, in which he stated that Adams did "not possess the talents adapted to the Administration of Government" because of "extreme egotism" and "desultoriness of mind." Obviously the letter had been written to swing the presidential election in favor of Pinckney, but Hamilton had added naively: "Yet with this opinion of Mr. Adams, I have finally resolved not to advise the withholding from him a single vote."

Hamilton's letter was the deathblow to the Federalist Party, as Webster well recognized. The dismissal of Pickering as Secretary of State had foreshadowed the inevitable schism and consequent loss of power. But Webster, with candor akin to rashness, wrote a reply bristling with indignation and charged with the dynamite of inside information. He accused Hamilton of "secret enmity," of fomenting schism, of trying to foist a British offensive and defensive treaty on the American people, of secretly abetting Cobbett in his assault on Adams, of raising an army and trying to destroy the Adams-created navy, of "glaring inconsistencies of conduct and indiscretions," of jesuitism, and of "ambition, pride and overbearing temper [which] have destined you to be the evil genius of this country."

The damage had been done. Not Pinckney, but Jefferson had received the most votes. Webster yielded to the popular will, but he kept a weather eye on the new captain.

Hamilton, relentless in his bitterness, struck at Webster's newspapers, the scholar's chief source of income.

Meantime, too, Webster had become the butt of ridicule in the democratic newspapers. The Philadelphia *Aurora*, Cheetham's New York *American Citizen*, Charles Holt's New London *Bee*, and Elisha Babcock's *American Mercury* were tossing Webster's ideas in the blanket. Particularly distasteful did they find Webster's statement to Priestley: "Whatever may be thought of the position, I am persuaded from extensive reading and twenty years' observation that no truth is more certain than that a republican government can be rendered durable in no other way than by excluding from elections men who have so little property, education, or principle, that they are liable to yield their own opinions to the guidance of unprincipled leaders." In a private letter to Dr. Rush, Webster took this extreme position: "As to mankind, I believe the mass of them to be *copax rationis*. They are ignorant, or what is worse, governed by prejudices and authority,—and the authority of men who flatter them instead of boldly telling them the truth. . . . It would be better for the people; they would be more free and more happy, if all were deprived of the right of suffrage until they were 45 years of age, and if no man was eligible to an important office until he is 50, that is, if all the powers of government were vested in our old men, who have lost their ambition chiefly, and have learnt wisdom by experience, but to tell the people this would be treason. We have grown so wise of late years as to reject the maxims of Moses, Lycurgus, and the patriarchs; we have by our constitutions of government and the preposterous use made of the doctrines of *equality*, stripped *old* men of their dignity and *wise* men of their influence, and long, long are we to feel the mischievous effects of our modern policy."

One of these new "flatterers" was Abraham Bishop, a classmate of Webster at Yale, fresh from European travel and with a fierce passion to destroy the ancient hierarchy of Connecticut Federalism. His father had been the beneficiary of this system, for he had held several offices in the local government for many years. But the son found the rungs of the ladder crowded. Somewhat like Wendell Phillips in later years, Abraham Bishop espoused a cause, and on the wave of popular action rode to preferment and honor. In 1798 Bishop had written a reply to Webster's "milk and water" oration, but this he suppressed. In 1800, however, he organized the Democrats at monster rallies, and called on them to break their galling fetters. Only a small number of the men could vote; to these he appealed for concerted action against the tyranny of the Federalists. To the Baptists and Methodists, who had been forced to go through a legal procedure to escape the payment of rates to the Congregational Church, he shouted about religious bigotry, religious tyranny, and opinions shackled by law. At Wallingford, Connecticut, in September, 1800, Bishop delivered "An Oration on the Extent and Power of Political Delusion," a flaming invective. The essence of his demagogic theme was: "Have mercy upon us! ye well-fed, well-dressed, chariot-rolling, caucus-keeping, levee-revelling federalists; for we are poor, and wretched, and ignorant, and miserable." Jefferson said of this: "It is the best anti-republican eyewater which has ever yet appeared."

Webster immediately responded with *A Rod for a Fool's Back*, in which he characterized the Oration thus: "Much the greatest part is mere rant, declamation, and incongruous sentiments, incapable of being comprehended, much less answered. But such parts of the production as are capable of being understood demonstrate the extreme weakness of the writer's head or the wickedness of his heart." Obviously Webster had lost that earlier patience, that attempt to make reason and the will of God prevail. He thumped Bishop roundly, accusing him of deliberately misleading the people in order to secure the emoluments of office for himself, and of fomenting hostility to the commercial interests of Connecticut. How completely Webster had come round may be gauged by his statement that the debt had been funded to the original holders and had "thus been a principal means of enriching our farmers." Webster evidently had acquired new insight into Connecticut finances, for this story was the opposite of the view he had expressed to Governor Bowdoin in March, 1787.

Bishop, whose pen was no less agile than Webster's, returned the compliment: "But the Oration [1800], though acknowledged by all Federalists to be full of weakness and folly, might do some harm:—So Noah Webster, jun., esq., who is ready to answer every body, and whose head is like a vendue master's room, full of other people's goods, undertook to dub himself *fool-whipper*, and on the succeeding Sunday afternoon, issued from the press, which supports religion and steady habits, a small pamphlet, entitled *Rod for a Fool's Back*, really the best performance of Noah, rather deficient in point of argument and truth, but abounding in his editorial quackery. He confessed that he did not understand the oration; therefore we are not to wonder that his attempt to answer it was feeble indeed; but his father taught him to speak the truth. . . . As Mr. Webster is very apt to give advice to others, I leave him with a word of advice, which is, to prosecute to conviction and sentence of death the man or men who ever told him that he had talents as a writer."

Although his anonymous pamphlet against Bishop descended to mudthrowing, Webster kept the *Commercial Advertiser* and *Spectator* free from such pettiness. On January 17, 1801, he rebuked the Federalists for their sullen, sulky, vengeful mood: "The Federalists, chagrined at the triumph of the opposition, wish further to irritate their opponents by disappointing their wishes and placing Mr. Burr at the head of government. They are now taking the ground which the Democrats have occupied, and descending to the baseness of supporting their cause by railing, abuse, and scurrility. Nothing can be less politic or honorable. It is the duty of good citizens to acquiesce in the election and be tranquil. It is proper that Mr. Jefferson be made Chief Magistrate. . . . Let us have the experiment." Webster also pointed out the weakness of the Federalist strategy in the establishment of new newspapers; Tutor Warren Dutton of Yale was sent to Boston to edit the *Palladium,* and Coleman was establishing the *Post.* Webster had stood almost alone against the rise of Jacobinism from 1794 to 1797. "Their attempts are useless or worse," Webster wrote with that clear insight which makes his writings of superior importance as registers of the social progress of America; "for violent censure, abuse, and ridicule, instead of restraining opposition, will serve only to irritate a victorious party and render them vindictive."

Webster honestly wanted peace. His head frequently ached as he thought of the bitterness of party contention. His anguish arose not only because he was a symbolic figure to be pelted; he had a genuine horror of mobs, of demagogues, and of unsettlers of political tradition. To his editor, Samuel Bayard, he wrote in utter pessimism: "I have no hope of the duration of the Union, but I am sorry to see and hear men talk of *blood.* It is the language of rashness and madness. Let the evils work their own cure. Be calm. Suppress passion. We have on former occasions emerged from equal gloom, and we may do it again, if we will keep our passions bridled."

Webster watched with hawkeyes the experiment Jefferson was conducting. In the Inaugural Address, as printed in the *Courant,* Webster underscored many passages and made two comments: "Modesty" was placed against the President's "The task is above my talents"; and "Did they not before?" against "All will of course arrange themselves under the will of the law." There was a fetching simplicity and harmony-loving quality about Jefferson's suave plea for unity: "We are all Republicans—all Federalists." Webster had little faith in Jefferson, but less in his advisers. Had he not elevated a foreigner, Albert Gallatin, to a Cabinet post? Were not the worst men of Connecticut crying for offices as a reward for wardheeling? Would Jefferson follow his own high principles, or would he yield to his demagogic followers?

The answer came with startling suddenness. President Adams had made a number of last-minute appointments. Some of these Jefferson recalled as an invasion of his prerogatives: the people had turned out the Federalists, but the appointive offices were filled with men of that faith, men known to have slandered the new President. In Washington City, Jefferson withheld from seventeen Justices of the Peace their commissions. In New England several judges and revenue officers were replaced. A precedent was established; the American party spoils system was born. New Haven demanded a showdown, for competent Elizur Goodrich, appointed Collector of the Port late in February, had been tossed overboard in favor of infirm, aged Samuel Bishop, father of Abraham. Obviously the appointment was meant for the spellbinder, who received the portfolio on the death of his father two years later.

The merchants of New Haven, aghast that a profligate should replace by proxy a devoted public servant, sent a letter of remonstrance to Jefferson. The President welcomed the opportunity to declare his principles, for he had long believed that "the first republican President . . . would have a dreadful operation to perform." His reply stated that Samuel Bishop's character was unstained, that the Federalists had monopolized the appointive offices during earlier administrations, and that, if displacements were necessary to put the government in hands sympathetic to the administration installed by the people, removals should "justly begin as with persons appointed in the last moments of an administration."

Webster brooded over the turn of events for several days and then wrote on July 18, 1801, a long letter to Madison, detailing the true state of facts and appealing to him to use his influence to prevent further "irritations." "I submit these facts and reflections to you with a frankness that proceeds from a sincere and honest zeal," Webster concluded, "in hopes that your influence may be exerted to heal the divisions of our country." Madison passed the letter along to Jefferson, then at Monticello, with a request for advice what to do about it. Jefferson replied (August 12, 1801): "Tho' I view Webster as a mere pedagogue of very limited understanding and very strong prejudices and party passions, yet as editor of a paper and as of the Newhaven association, he may be worth striking. His letter leaves two very fair points whereon to answer him." Webster waited in vain for an answer to his letter.

An answer might have staved off the angriest, most incisive, most explosive analysis of the new administration yet made, for Webster sat down late in September and penned eighteen "Letters to the President of the United States" and published them in his papers from September 30 to November 7. The "mere pedagogue" showed again his powers of sustained analysis, forceful reasoning, and ability to judge men and events. If the letters to Priestley were white hot, these were slightly cooler, say red turning white. After all, Jefferson was President and deserved the few amenities his office demanded.

In his *Revolution in France* (1794) Webster had inveighed against the rise of party spirit. The prophecies then made, had now come true: A scheming faction had taken control of the government by force of slander, intrigue, and wanton expenditure of money. Would the trend of events be toward bloody revolution? Webster hoped not. Only a clear explanation of the trickery and deception of Jefferson, he thought, could prevent the coming of chaos. With flaming missionary zeal to instruct the people in the character of their Chief Magistrate, Webster broadcast his letters, not only in his papers, but also in a pamphlet, entitled *Miscellaneous Papers on Political and Commercial Subjects* (1802).

Webster began by stating that he had waited impatiently to see what form the "political millennium," promised by Jefferson's followers, would take, but that in six months adequate demonstration had been given of the "imbecility of mind" from which such notions had come. Webster then went on to comment on "the continued efforts to disguise your [Jefferson's] real intentions" through an analysis of the Inaugural Address, the reply to the New Haven remonstrance, the letter to Mazzei, and the *Notes on Virginia*. He accused the President of "hypocrisy and deception," "imbecility and inconsistency," "vanity," "blind confidence," and an "intolerance despotic as it is wicked." He concluded his seventy-six pages of vitriolic condemnation with this charge against the spoils system:

Your measures, Sir, invert the whole order of society. The natural sentiment of man, is, to respect virtue, religion, grave manners, eminent talents, the wisdom of experience, and the hoary head. Your practices tend to depress eminence of talents, to point the finger of scorn at a veneration for religion; to exalt the young over the head of the old; to discard solid worth, and to dignify with the honors and emoluments of government, the departed, the licentious and profane.

Instead of inviting men of sterling integrity to accept places of trust, with the expectation of a permanent support, your practice, by filling our towns with the ghosts of departed officers, will frighten from offices every man of worth, and leave them a prey to the vile and desperate. Instead of giving stability to government by a judicious use of power and distribution of offices, your practice lends a ready support to opposition, feeds the discontented with new hopes from change, and solicits new proselites to faction. If mankind can long endure this monstrous inversion of principles, of sentiments, and of habits—if they can lay aside their respect for age, wisdom, experience and virtue, and look up with veneration to the illiterate, the debauchee, the blasphemer, the infidel—if they can calmly bear to see the hoary judge driven from the seat of justice, to make way for the beardless tyro—the world has now the opportunity of determining these questions by the experiment; and on the event of this experiment, depends the fate of your official character, and of your administration.

No condemnation of the spoils system has been more vigorous than the one made by its first critic. Webster's whole attiude can be summed up in the indignant sentence: "No, Sir! no individual or party has a *claim* or *right* to any office whatever."

Webster added three other writings to his Letter to Jefferson in the *Miscellaneous Papers,* each of which was a notable contribution. One was a letter to Rufus King, when he was Minister to Great Britain in 1797; in this hitherto unpublished essay Webster pointed out why Great Britain should cease molesting American commerce, since the interests of the two nations were so similar that a maritime league, similar to the old Hanseatic Confederation, should be formed. King evidently did not present the idea to the English leaders, for there is no record of discussions on this subject. The plan was good, however; its adoption might have prevented the War of 1812.

Another of these writings was "A Sketch of the History and Present State of Banks and Insurance Companies in the United States," the first compilation of the kind ever made. An outgrowth of his passion for statistical information, this collection of data demonstrates Webster's interest in economics. Lecky remarked correctly that Webster was one of America's best eighteenth century economists.

The third of these new writings was the immensely learned and careful piece of scholarship, entitled "An Essay on the Rights of Neutral Nations." In 1796 Webster had supported the Jay Treaty with the assumption that the law of nations considered naval stores as contraband of war. To this subject he had given little thought until a writer in the *Boston Palladium* stated that the old American notion of "Free ships make free goods" was erroneous. His patriotism challenged, Webster began an intensive investigation of all the writings on the subject of international law from Polybius to Robert Ward; he collected all the published treaties between princes and between nations, and he studied the practices of nations from Greek times to 1800. The result of his studies was an emphatic vindication of the American doctrine.

In the manner of the epidemic history he approached the problem through chronology, tracing the development of the idea of "Free ships make free goods" to England, where for a century it was propagated. On the rise of the French Revolution, however, England abandoned this doctrine. And Americans, Webster discovered to his horror, had abandoned their own position, as enunciated in the Revolution, in favor of the British. "Were the venerable fathers of the Revolution under a cloud?" he asked.

Webster showed conclusively that there was no such thing as a law of nations, except that which arose from principles of moral justice. On many of these principles all men agree, but on others disputes arise. Consequently, these points are settled by treaties. But in times of war these documents become mere scraps of paper; the belligerent nations simply forget their treaties and by "arbitrary will, supported by superior power" prohibit neutral nations from carrying goods of any kind to an enemy. No nation, Webster declared, until recent times had claimed this right either on the ground of natural law or the general law of nations. Variable and contradictory practices had arisen out of temporary interest, despotic power, or mutual stipulations in conventions. "The present laws of contraband, as they are called, so far from being warranted by the principles of natural and social justice, are no more than the ancient practice of piracy, modified and meliorated by a few humane regulations." From this point he went on to assert: "Instead of saying that 'neutrals have not so good a right to trade as nations to defend themselves,' the true proposition, grounded on fact and principle is, *that neutrals have a better right to trade than nations have to fight and plunder*." In concluding he admitted that England had done the world a service in preventing France from extending her power over Europe, "but it is a fatal mistake to suppose that her depredations on neutral commerce are necessary to that opposition." The principles of a free commerce should be surrendered only with a nation's independence!

It was a high, humanitarian ground on which Webster placed his argument. He opposed the manufacture of laws out of "present exigencies" on the known ground that might always makes right in the eyes of the aggressor. He wanted to substitute the rights of neutrals for the rights of belligerents. Webster's lucid analysis of the complicated mass of materials and subtle principles renders this work the equal of Madison's "Examination of the British Doctrine which subjects to capture a neutral trade not open in time of peace" (1806), a memoir which covers the same ground.

The world was not ready for the adoption of the principles of Webster, nor even yet have nations agreed to subordinate belligerent rights to neutral rights. But had Webster's ideas prevailed, the War of 1812 would never have taken place.

Certainly this essay should have ended all the criticism that Webster leaned over backward in support of England. The diatribe against Jefferson, however, blinded all democratic editors. A renewed cannonade flared about Webster's head. Hungry democrats wanted jobs, and they told the "capacious squirt of federal calumny" to hush. In party warfare minor shades of distinction never temper hostile criticism. Webster was anti-Jeffersonian, and therefore wrong in everything. New Haven was safely Federalist, however, so that Webster received some balm for his wounded spirit. He had been made a common councilman in 1799, an office he held for five years; he was appointed Justice of the Peace annually from 1801 to 1810; he served as Justice of the Quorum from 1806 to 1810; and he was sent to the legislature nine times between 1800 and 1807. By holding legislative and judicial offices at the same time, Webster violated his earlier code of political conduct; however, he was merely falling into the "steady habit" way of conducting the Connecticut government. In all these offices he faithfully performed his duties to the improvement of the community, but his forthrightness antagonized his opponents.

Webster should have become accustomed to political squibs, especially since he had felt free to anathematize Priestley, Hamilton, Bishop, and Jefferson. But he did not. He had, seemingly, a very tender skin. He could give criticism, but he was a poor sport about taking it. And so, when the fusillade became continuous, he sent these paragraphs to Stephen Twining in a letter resigning further duties in the Connecticut Academy (January 22, 1802):

This is the nineteenth year, since, with an ardor bordering on enthusiasm, I have been engaged in some kind of service, either wholly or essentially directed to the interest of my country. In these pursuits, which have not always been guided by discretion, I have made many and great sacrifices of my private interest, without the hope or expectation of reward, except the approbation of my fellow citizens. But amidst the turmoil of parties and passions, even this reward is not to be expected. Either from the structure of my mind, or from my modes of investigation, I am led very often to differ in opinion

from many of my respectable fellow citizens; and difference of
opinion is now a crime not easily overlooked or forgiven. The efforts
which have been made and are now making, to deprive me of the
confidence of my fellow citizens, and of course, of my reputation
and influence—efforts not limited to this town—render it proper and
necessary for me to withdraw myself from every public concern and
confine my attention to private affairs and the education of my children.

If I should survive the enmities and illiberality of the times,
nothing would give me greater pleasure than to unite with my fellow
citizens in any plan of public improvement. But in the present state
of things, my efforts can be of little or no use; as I cannot make
the sacrifices of opinion, either in matters of science or government,
which would probably be necessary to command confidence.

But when called on to make the Fourth of July Oration
in 1802, Webster came out from his library to try again to
instruct the people in the fundamentals of Federalism with
precise, learned definitions of such terms as "republican,"
"democracy," and "representation." With an eye on Bishop
and Jefferson, he denounced the men who seek office as
the ones who corrupt the government: "It is extremely important that this truth should be duly weighed, for popular
jealousy is usually directed exclusively against the officers
of government, when in fact it ought to be employed to
guard against the arts and addresses of office-seekers." In
contrast to these, he praised the old men, "the eminent men,"
who accepted office as a public trust. But Webster went further: he denounced the absurdity that "all men are free, independent, and equal," by showing that for their own protection men must submit to the restraints of a sovereign
power. Most reprehensible had been the propagation of the
doctrine of equality, for herein lay the source of most of the
existent evils of party warfare. He said,

Government is chiefly concerned with the *rights of person* and
rights of property. Personal rights are few, and are not subject to
much difficulty or jealousy. All men are agreed in the *principle* of

protecting *persons*, and differ very little in the *mode*. But the *rights of property*, which are numerous, and form nineteen twentieths of all the objects of government, are beyond measure intricate, and difficult to be regulated with justice. Now if all men have an equal right of suffrage, those who have *little* and those who have *no* property, have the power of making regulations respecting the property of others; that is, an equal right to control the property with those who own it. Thus, as property is *unequally* and suffrages *equally* divided, the principle of *equal* suffrage becomes the basis of *inequality of power*. And this principle, in some of our larger cities, actually gives a *majority of suffrages* to the men who possess not a *twentieth of the property*. Such is the fallacy of abstract proposition in political science! In truth, this principle of *equal suffrage* operates to produce extreme *inequality of rights*; a monstrous inversion of the natural order of society, a species of oppression that will ultimately produce a revolution.

In this oration Webster laid down his fundamental principles as a legislator, principles in harmony with New England Federalism but completely at variance with the Jeffersonian doctrines. Only the October, 1802, session of the Connecticut Legislature was reported in detail in the newspapers; from this record must be generalized the quality of Webster as a lawmaker. With the forensic energy of Daniel Webster, who was still exercising his voice in the classroom, Noah Webster popped out of his seat at the introduction of every bill. No matter whether it concerned the purchase of sounding boards, the stealing of apples by little boys, the reform of workhouses, the quarantine of ports against pestilence, the punishment of adultery, the granting of permission to the Episcopal Academy, Cheshire, for a lottery, or the amendment of the election law, Webster gave an authoritative comment. The "Monarch" of the Philological Society played the same part before the country legislators. And they listened to him. His yea was yea, and his nay was nay.

The session was followed closely by *The American Mercury*, because the bill removing the property qualification

for voters was presented for the fifth time. The Jeffersonians
had great hopes of passing the measure, but Webster ridiculed it out of serious consideration. He told on November 4
an anecdote he had written in his diary at Philadelphia in
1787. Franklin may have told it to him. The substance
of it and Webster's other remarks were reported in the
Mercury for December 2, 1802:

The introduction of this bill reminds me of a circumstance which
took place in Philadelphia while Commodore Truxton and his crew
lay there. The crew were all invited up to Freemen's Meeting, their
votes were handed them, and they voted according to the wishes
of a party. Not long afterwards, when they were returning up the
Delaware from a cruise, they saw a school of Porpoises making
towards Philadelphia. One of them asks the other, where are these
Porpoises going; why damn it replies the other, to freeman's meeting to vote for ——.

I tell this anecdote barely to show the sense which all persons
have of the impropriety of admitting persons to vote who have no
property or families, to attach them to the interest of the states. The
admission of too many persons to the right of suffrage who have no
settled habitation, nothing which can induce them to wish for the
peace of the State, has been the ruin of all popular governments.
When Rome admitted too many strangers to the freedom of the
city, they overturned the Republic. We may be in no danger at
present by extending the right of suffrage; but we are growing
populous, and it is impossible to calculate the evils which will arise
hereafter. We had better adhere to the regulations of our ancestors.

On the following day, November 5, he followed his
earlier statement with a further one. A red rag thrown to
a bull could not have been more productive of rage than
these insufferably aristocratic sentences:

The anecdote which I told was a matter of fact, and showed very
pertinently the ridiculous appearance which the freemen in many
states make in being led up like porpoises to vote as they are told to,
for characters they know nothing about.

The very principle of admitting every body to the right of
suffrage, prostrates the wealth of individuals to the rapaciousness of

a merciless gang who have nothing to lose, and will delight in plundering their neighbors. It opens the door for electioneering, for men of no property are liable to influence, and prostrates our virtuous elections to the ambition of demagogues, who will rise on the ruins of the state. Though we have few citizens now who have not property enough to become freemen, it is probable there will be more hereafter, and we should be careful not to open the avenues which may lead to our destruction.

The observation that the poor have lives, limbs and reputation to be protected, tho' true, does not apply. Our laws principally respect property, that is their great object; and it is very improper that it should be at the direction and disposal of those who have little or no interest in it.

At once a clamor of dissent arose. At every democratic rally a toast was called: "The Porpoises of Connecticut." Bishop accepted the phrase as a substitute for the older one, "the swinish multitude," and the rallying cry of the opposition became "The Porpoises of Connecticut." A writer in the *Mercury* wrote a series of essays under the title, "The Porpoises of Connecticut." He excoriated "Noah Webster, the political Leviathan," who, having established the name, was now made "as immortal as is Monsieur Guillotine." Week after week the ridicule continued, and through the years until the Constitution was adopted in 1818 the phrase reappeared, "The Porpoises of Connecticut."

Webster made an answer or two, but in the end the din of the opposition drummed him into public silence. His textbooks were placed on the index, because they incidently parried the dangers of democracy. Morse's *Geography* was also on the index because that ardent Federalist had written: "The clergy, who are numerous and as a body very respectable, have hitherto preserved a kind of aristocratical balance in the democratical government of the state, which has happily operated as a check to the overbearing spirit of republicanism." This tribute to Pope Dwight and his acolytes grew more and more distasteful, because the Baptists and

Methodists were asking the abolition of church rates. Prose-lyting made slow progress in a state where for one or another reason a man hesitated to demand that his name be stricken from the roll of taxables because of nonconformity. But in this matter, too, Webster had reversed his youthful opinion. Now he considered an established church a necessity in a good government.

Webster believed that "morality is intimately connected with religion, and derives its most essential support from belief in the existence of a Supreme Being. . . . It follows that the moral and religious character of the citizens of a State is an object over which the legislature may rightfully exercise their superintending control. . . . Hence is derived the right of the legislature to organize, encourage, and maintain religious associations, parishes, and churches. . . . On these principles, we are persuaded that the legislature of a state may rightfully require all its citizens to lend their aid in supporting the worship of a Supreme Being, leaving to the choice of every man the right of adopting his own particular tenets and of attaching himself to any external rites, ceremonies, modes of worship, which he shall conscientiously feel." Pope Dwight could not have stated the Congregational case any better. Far from falling in with the current of the times in order to direct it, Webster laid himself across its path. It is no wonder that his garments retained some of the soil that had been carried in suspension.

The conservative of 1802 occasionally went over his radical writings of 1782, and in the margins he wrote: "Charming dreams," "chimerical notions," and "We grow wiser with age." Throughout his career Webster had tried to keep in with the right people, the property class, and his gradual turn to the right resulted from these friendships. But these aristocratic thoughts, being congenial to him, took on the sanction of revelation.

Having failed as an orator, a legislator, and a newspaper

writer to turn the tide against the Jeffersonians, Webster made another effort. *The Prompter* had become the most popular book of maxims ever published in America; it was kept on the tables of inns where travelers might read aloud its wise precepts. Pastors quoted to their parishioners its homely lore. Newspapers reprinted the essays. Webster conceived the idea of adding a new series of Prompter essays to the original twenty-eight. Early in 1803, therefore, he wrote nineteen. But *he did not work it right!* He substituted allegory for the sententious aphorisms of the first series.

The essays, or rather narratives, recounted events in Old Testament history which paralleled the rise of modern Jacobinism, the overthrow of the old men by young schemers, the rise of demagogues, the worship of new idols, and the overthrow of the Christian influence in government. The allegory was perfectly plain, as the following titles indicate: "A Gillotin," "Pride," "Prejudice," "Popular Discontent," "Liberty and Equality," "Inconstancy of the Populace," "Popular Delusion," "The Counsels of Old Men Despised," "Envy, Hatred, and Revenge," and "Charity and Humanity." Jefferson and Bishop are easily recognized as the conspirators, the demagogues misleading the people.

Except among the New England Federalists the new essays attained no popularity. Printers in other parts of the Union continued to pirate the earlier essays as if the later ones had not been written. The author's bitterness hid whatever humor he thought he had employed. The new essays formed a tract for the times, not a book of perennial instruction. Obviously they were received with silence or contempt by democratic readers.

Partly because of his annoyance at the trend of political affairs, partly because his political ideas were being used to undermine the sale and use of his textbooks, partly because he was writing new textbooks, and partly because his new dictionary required much time, Webster withdrew from the public discussion of political questions. Slowly, too, he dropped the offices he held, for his nomination as a candidate for Congress was greeted with jeers by the democratic press throughout the nation. He had to choose between politics and scholarship. On a copy of Joel Barlow's *Letters* he wrote, "Political ambition is as bad as military." And with that thought he resigned any desire to mount the ladder of preferment on which he was rising.

Webster saw Barlow in 1803, but the renegade was beyond hope, as Webster told Stephen Jacob (October 3, 1803): "He is a little convalescent, briefly by means of Bonaparte's harsh remedies for new philosophy, but I think his constitution so much impaired that a radical cure is impossible. He feels himself in an awkward situation: a downcast look, at least when I saw him, marks great depression of mind, or consciousness of something wrong at bottom." Thus Webster mused on the effects of taking a too deep draft of the leveling poison; he thanked God he had recovered from his own youthful indiscretions.

Webster's close connection with politics for twenty years rendered complete severance from his party impossible. With Simeon Baldwin and James Hillhouse, who were in Congress, and with Rufus King, he carried on correspondence. Always he urged renewed vigor in opposing Jefferson and in strengthening the Federalists to arrest popular opinion in support of the President. In 1807 he prepared a new plan for the election of the President of the United States from a standing list of nominees, two names to be presented by each state. At each quadrennial election half of the nominees, chosen by a drawing, would be voted upon by the House of Representatives. By this means, Webster hoped, the raging party spirit might be quelled, because there would not be sufficient time for an alignment of votes between the drawing and the election. It was the best scheme he could propose for preventing the Jeffersonian succession.

The Embargo Act of December 22, 1807, completely destroyed the foreign commercial interests of the United States, then largely in the hands of New Englanders. Although the Act was designed as a retaliatory measure upon Great Britain, Americans suffered more than the British. Nowhere was greater indignation expressed over the Act than in New Haven. Seventy-eight vessels were tied up in the little harbor. Hundreds of sailors, shipwrights, and merchants lounged about the wharves, cursing the "Dambargo" and slowly falling into poverty. In May, 1808, Webster proposed, anonymously through *The Connecticut Herald*, the organization of the American Patriots, a society dedicated to national union and the suspension of the party conflict out of which the Embargo had arisen. It was a program worthy of the proponent of union in 1785.

Webster framed the New Haven resolutions of August 20, 1808, January 28, 1809, and May 1, 1811, directed against the Embargo and Nonimportation Acts. In May, 1811, he also drafted the letter for the New Haven Chamber of Commerce calling upon seaboard merchants to ask their legislatures to seek the repeal of the latter Act. The refrain in each is that the spirit of party has debased and enfeebled the public mind and has permitted an anticommercial policy to menace the best interests of New England. These resolutions reprobate the one-sided animosity toward England, for France had preyed upon American shipping no less than England. Party spirit dominated here, too, and Webster wrote that "a sort of competition in hatred, rather than in attachment, to the rival nations, Great Britain and France," marked the two parties.

Something of the forthrightness of Webster appeared also in a private letter to President-elect James Madison, February 20, 1809, in which Webster explained the importance of his visiting European libraries in order to complete his Dictionary. Webster went on to say that it might be within the power of the President to give him a commission in Europe whereby his expenses might be defrayed by the government. But with no thought of tact he continued: "On political subjects I differ from the present administration, and if the next administration shall pursue a system substantially the same, I must be opposed to it on principle." And he proceeded to give Madison a lecture on the conduct of his office. First, the Embargo must be discontinued. Second, appointments to office should go to worthy, not party, men. And finally, he advised the President to adhere to the Christian religion at least to the extent of appointing Christians to office in New England. Webster had that kind of a New England conscience which not only holds the possessor in rigid conformity to principle, but also anticipates and seeks to correct evil in others.

In all things Webster was the Prompter, the teacher, trying to do good. If in medicine and politics he was less than successful, he achieved greatness in lexicography. And so we will retrace our steps to follow the author as he lays the foundation of An American Dictionary of the English Language.

CHAPTER XIV

The Lexicographer Begins Work

Dictionaries belong in a class with sacred writings, so venerated are these volumes. Disputes are settled by an appeal to their pronouncements, and fanatic devotees guard the honor and extol the virtues of their bible. Paper wars have been fought over the comparative merits of Johnson and Webster, and of Worcester and Webster. Words are dynamite, and a dictionary seems to be concentrated nitroglycerin, if one can judge by its innate combustible power to stir controversy.

Dictionaries developed slowly through the ages. On ancient Latin manuscripts scholars placed annotations opposite hard or unusual words. Later these "hard words" were collected into a *glossarium* or *glossary*. The first use of the word *dictionary* occurs in Sir Thomas Elyot's *Dictionarius Liber* or *Dictionarium* (1538), the literal meaning being "a repertory of *dictiones* or sayings." Until the end of the sixteenth century such collections were of Latin, or another foreign language, words with English equivalents. About 1600 Robert Cawdrey prepared *The Table Alphabeticall of Hard Words*, in which the proper spelling and meaning of some three thousand learned terms were given. Henry Cockham extended *The English Dictionarie* (1623) to include ordinary words and a key to allusions. In the first part, the "hard words," he defined "bubulcitate" as "to cry like a cow-boy," "collocuplicate" as "to enrich," and "garble" as "to clense things from dust." The "ordinary words" were explained by hard equivalents; for example, "youthful babbling" meant "juvenile inaniloquence," and "abound" meant "exuperate."

Nathaniel Bailey in 1721 included all words in his *Universal Etymological English Dictionary*, ten editions of which appeared in twenty-one years. This was the "golden age" of literature and dictionary-making, for it was the desire "to fix the language by means of a Standard Dictionary, which should register the proper sense and use of every word and phrase, from which no polite writer henceforth would be expected to deviate." In 1747 Dr. Samuel Johnson contracted with a syndicate of London booksellers to produce the desired Standard Dictionary within the space of three years for the sum of fifteen hundred guineas. Eight years and considerably more money were required by Johnson and his assistants to produce two massive folios, each seventeen inches long and three and one half inches thick. It was a marvelous achievement. Johnson elevated lexicography into a department of literature. His work had two innovations: it included illustrative quotations, drawn from the best English writers, and it delicately discriminated the senses of words. There were errors, too, but an explanation of these will be deferred until Webster throws a searchlight upon them.

Dr. Johnson's work was not allowed to stand alone. Dr. William Kenrick in 1773, William Perry in 1775, Thomas Sheridan in 1780, and John Walker in 1791 brought out competing tomes. Walker became the supreme arbiter of elegant pronunciation, just as Johnson was pre-eminent in definition and illustration. Walker's affectations won a great following in America, so much so that Webster was frequently advised to alter the pronunciation of his Spelling Book and Dictionary to conform to Walker's. A sample of the stage directions supplied in great quantity in Walker's book may illustrate why Webster went into a towering rage every time the Englishman's name was mentioned. Under *Garden* Walker wrote: "When the *a* in this and similar words is preceded by G or K, polite speakers interpose a sound like the consonant *y* which coalesces with both, and gives a mellowness to the sound; thus *a Garden* pronounced in this manner is nearly similar to the two words *Egg* and *Yarden* united into *eggyarden*, and *a Guard* is almost like *eggyard*."

Imagine the horror with which Anglophiles would receive a book in which the nasal twang of New England was recommended as a better pronunciation than Walker's. Imagine the consternation, too, that would greet the announcement of a spelling-book-maker that he would outdo the learned cham of literature, Samuel Johnson, LL.D., F.R.S. Imagine an American teaching the English anything!

On June 4, 1800, Webster inserted into the New Haven newspapers this indirect statement:

Mr. Webster of this city, we understand, is engaged in completing the system for the instruction of youth, which he began in the year 1783. He has in hand a Dictionary of the American Language, a work long since projected, but which other occupations have delayed till this time. The plan contemplated extends to a small Dictionary for schools, one for the counting-house, and a large one for men of science. The first is nearly ready for the press—the second and third will require the labor of some years.

It is found that a work of this kind is absolutely necessary, on account of considerable differences between the American and English language. New circumstances, new modes of life, new laws, new ideas of various kinds give rise to new words, and have already made many material differences between the language of England and America. Some new words are introduced in America, and many more new significations are annexed to words, which it is necessary to explain. It is probable that the alterations in the tenures of land and the ecclesiastical polity, will dismiss from the language in America several hundred words which belong in the English. The differences in the language of the two countries will continue to multiply, and render it necessary that we should have *Dictionaries* of the *American language.*

Three small American dictionaries had already appeared.
The first had come in 1798 from the hands of Samuel
Johnson, Jr. Caleb Alexander, the Boston textbook maker,
had published the *Columbian Dictionary* in 1800, and Johnson and John Elliott brought out a revised edition of the
first one in 1800. Webster approved "the general plan and
execution" of this work in a testimonial. All of them were
intended "for schools and polite readers," and each promised that "no *low* or indecent word will therefore be found
in the work." This quotation is from the preface of William
Woodbridge's *A Key to the English Language* (Middletown, Connecticut, 1801). Certainly dictionary-making must
have seemed a harmless, yet useful, occupation to these men.
And to Webster. But the American press thought otherwise.

Be it remembered that in 1800 Webster was the butt of
ridicule for his political and medical opinions and his theories of language. The announcement of the forthcoming
American Dictionary speeded the tempo of criticism. Naturally one would expect the pitch pipe of the Democrats, the
Aurora, to poke fun at the lexicographer; it did in this editorial:

Noah Webster

There are some beings whose fate it seems to be to run counter
from reason and propriety on all occasions. In every attempt which
this oddity of literature has made, he appears not only to have made
himself ridiculous, but to have rendered what he attempted to elucidate more obscure, and to injure or deface what he has intended to
improve.

His spelling-book has done more injury in the common schools of
the country than the genius of ignorance herself could have conceived a hope of, by his ridiculous attempts to alter the *syllable* division of words and to *new model* the spelling, by a capricious but
utterly incompetent attempt of his own weak conception.

After involving the question of the yellow fever in deeper obscurity,
and producing nothing but the profit by the sale of the work, he now

appears as a legislator and municipal magistrate of Connecticut; writes nonsense pseudo-political and pseudo-philosophical for his newspaper at New York, and proposes to give to the American world no less than three dictionaries!

This man, who ought to go to school for the regulation of his understanding, has, it appears, undertaken to complete a *system of education,* and as a part of these, we are told, is to give us a dictionary for *schools,* a dictionary for the *counting-house,* and a dictionary for the *learned!*

His motives, for they are truly *Gothic,* it appears are that a number of English words have been misapplied—new words introduced—and a considerable number exploded in America; for this reason he says it is necessary to make a new Dictionary. The plain truth is, for the reason given is preposterous, that he means to *make money* by a scheme which ought to be and will be discountenanced by every man who admires the classic English writers, who has sense enough to see the confusion which must arise from such a silly project—and the incapacity of a man who thus undertakes a work which, if it were at all necessary or eligible, would require the labor of a number of learned and competent men to accomplish it.

"The Colossus of Federalism" no doubt expected his fellow editors to support him or at least to be silent. Not a bit of it. They vied with each other to damn the editor whose essays they pilfered. In the van was Joseph Dennie, now editing the *Gazette of the United States* in Philadelphia, the very same man who had told Webster *The Prompter* had taught him the value of the Franklin style. This fawning timeserver had a habit of clinging to the coattails of the great. Cobbett had lavished a few kind words and had won Dennie as his only American apologist. Timothy Pickering gave Dennie a minor clerkship just before that statesman was dropped for insubordination. And now, in Philadelphia among the Jeffersonians, Dennie curried favor by pelting Webster in the *Gazette* and the *Portfolio,* a weekly magazine. With Coleman, editor of Hamilton's *Evening Post,* Dennie conducted for years a mutual admiration society, one of the earliest examples of the puffery and log rolling

Poe despised. Dennie set the fashion of sneering at Webster's Dictionary. Within six days of the announcement Dennie called Webster an absurd, vain innovator, and trusted the dictionary would "meet with the contempt it deserves from all the friends of literature." Two weeks later Dennie wrote: "In a word, I would compare the present labors of Mr. Webster to that of a maniac gardener, who, instead of endeavoring to clear his garden of weeds, in opposing to reason, entwines them with his flowers!" He printed (June 12) the following squibs, too, as samples of the orthography that would be required by the polyglot American commoners:

To Mr. *noab* Wabstur

Sur,

by rading all ovur the nusspaper I find you are after meaking a nue Merrykin Dikshunary; your rite, Sir; for ofter lookin all over the anglish Books, you wont find a bit of Shillaly big enuf to beat a dog wid. so I hope you'll take a hint, and put enuff of rem in yours, for Och 'tis a nate little bit of furniture for any Man's house so it 'tis.

PAT O'DOGERTY

As I find der ish no DONDER and BLIXSUM in de English Dikshonere I hope you put both in yours to oblige a Subscrybur

HANS BUBBLEBLOWER

Massa Webser plese put sum HOMMANY and sum GOOD POSSUM fat and sum two tree good BANJOE in your new what-you-call-um Book for your fello Cytzen.

CUFFEE

Mr. Webster,

As I'm a lad of spirit, I loves all new things, & should like to coin new words, vastly; tother day as Jack Trotter and I were twigging an Old Codger with our Puns & Jokes. out came a develish keen thing from Jack—dang it, Thats a dagger says I.

Jack says this is a new application of the word Dagger; if so, it is at your servis.

DICK SPLASHAWAY

Mistur Webstur

being told as how you wants a word maker to help you fill a new diksonery, with the consent of my good man, I offer my servis, please to let me know whether you buy words by the hundred or by the dozen, &c your price, I unclose your a certificat from my husband of my billyties

and am at your servis

MARTHA O'GABBLE

I hereby certufy that my wife martha has the best knack at coining new words of any I ever knew—& with the aid of a comforting drop she'll fill you two dictonerys in an hour if you please,—before she had worn out the drum of my ear with her tongue you might have had it for nothing, but as I am now quite deaf & she a usefull body in other respects I shall expect something for service in her way

DERMOT O'GABBLE

Brother noab

Instead of *I keant keatch the keow,* an English man *or a town bred american* would say. *I cannot Catch the Cow,* but you being a *brother Yankey* will be sure to spell right in your new Yankey dictionary

yours, &c. *Brother Jonathan*

N.B. *mind and give us true deffinition of bundling.*

To NOAH WEBSTER

When Noah perceiving his trade he mistook;
By straining his noodle at making a Book;
Altho' retrograding he took rather hard,
He again try'd his hand at framing a Word.
But to suit the extent of thy talent much better,
Try again, honest Noah, to make a good Letter.

ROUND O

Tutor Warren Dutton, editor of the Boston *Palladium,* official gazette of New England Federalism and Congregationalism, took up (October 2 and November 6, 1801) the fight against Webster's "absurd orthographical doctrines" in a column, entitled "Restorator." As to Webster himself: "I am willing to allow this gentleman the praise of industry and of good intentions, and sincerely wish I could acquit him of the charges of vanity and presumption. But modesty, most certainly, is not the leading feature in his literary character. . . . I turn in disgust from the pert hyper-critic whose pages, dull, cold, and formal, are never illuminated with a single ray of genius." The folly of preparing a new dictionary was thus explained: "A language, arrived at its zenith, like ours, and copious and expressive in the extreme, requires no introduction of new words. . . . Colloquial barbarisms abound in all countries, but among no civilized people are they admitted with impunity into books. . . . Now, in what can a Columbian dictionary differ from an English one, but in these barbarisms? Who are the Columbian authors who do not write in the English language and spell in the English manner except Noah Webster, junior, Esq.? The embryo dictionary, then, must either be a dictionary of pure English words, and, in that case, superfluous, as we already possess the admirable lexicon of Johnson, or else must contain vulgar, provincial words, unauthorized by good writers, and, in this case, must surely be the just object of ridicule and censure." Further to dignify his remarks, Dutton offered a final suggestion to Webster: "But, if he will persist, in spite of common sense, to furnish us with a dictionary which we do not want, in return for his generosity I will furnish him with a title for it. Let, then, the projected volume of *foul* and *unclean* things bear his own christian name and be called Noah's Ark."

Webster's reply covers the ground so well and with such good humor, that its length must not be an excuse for omitting it:

When the design of an improved paper, to be denominated the *New-England Palladium*, and destined to protect our moral, political and religious rights was first announced, it was little suspected that, in less than one year from its first publication, it would be permitted to degenerate into a vehicle of personal abuse. Much less could it be supposed that the assistant editor of the paper [Warren Dutton], a man of reputation and letters, would become accessary to an attempt to vilify a fellow citizen, who has never been charged with a crime, and whose whole life has been devoted to promote the honor, and defend the rights, of his country. How much the essential interests of morality, religion and good government will ultimately suffer, by dissensions among their defenders, incautiously provoked and wantonly inflamed, is left for your own good sense to determine. It is sufficient for me to remark, that whatever evils may result from the intemperance of indiscrete [*sic*] party men, the blame must eventually rest on the aggressor. When the citadel of all we hold dear, as men, as citizens and as christians, is assaulted on every side, it is folly and madness for the garrison to weaken their strength, by wrangling among themselves about the loss of the outworks, or about trifling points unconnected with the defence.

In two or three late numbers of the RESTORATOR, many illiberal remarks have appeared upon my proposed dictionary. Whether that work, if ever published, will have merit or not, is a point about which the gentleman may make himself very easy; as it would be as difficult for *me* to *corrupt* and *debase* the language, as it is for *him* to *improve* it. If the work should be a real improvement on those before published, my fellow citizens would find it useful, as they have some of my other publications. If not, the loss would rest on myself or the printer, and the work would descend quietly into oblivion, accompanied perhaps by the RESTORATOR.

It might not perhaps be amiss for an American to take the liberty (if the audacious wretch can be found to hazard an improvement on an *English Book!*) to publish a Dictionary, for the purpose of introducing and defining some words not found in any *English* Dictionary, but which are authorized by *English* Authors—and even by the RESTORATOR himself—such, for instance, as *appreciate, disorganizer, editorial, sentimentalist,* and especially RESTORATOR. English lexicons leave us in obscurity in regard to these and many well-established words; and really it is difficult to see the crime of adding them to a dictionary, with correct definitions. Should I ever venture upon such a license, it would afford me no small satisfaction to introduce these words and be able to cite the authority of the RESTORATOR. As the word RESTORATOR is the least known in this country, I might take the liberty of defining it according to the sense it bears in the gentleman's own writings, viz. *a man who keeps an ordinary, or retails ordinary fare.*

As to any scheme of making innovations in the orthography or construction of our language, the gentleman's apprehensions are groundless. He has raised a bug-bear to frighten himself, and I shall leave him to combat the phantom, and enjoy the honor of a triumph.

But what connection has this subject with a general charge of "dullness" against all my writings, which, it seems, "are not illuminated by a single ray of genius"? Admit the fact; yet dull plodding fellows sometimes accomplish more by industry, than the sprightly and fanciful by the flashes of wit, the fire of genius, or the glow of animated period. The field of exertion is open to every man, and if *dullness itself* is honestly engaged in *trying* to do good, it may lay credit to the claim of "good intentions," and cite the RESTORATOR as a precedent in point.

Wishing, by all convenient means, to improve my mind, I have regularly read the RESTORATOR; and although I have not been able to discover in it much elegance of style or originality of remark, yet this may be ascribed rather to *my* want of capacity, than the author's want of genius. However vast his resources of genius and erudition, it would be unreasonable to require of him to furnish his composition with ideas, and his readers with understanding to comprehend them. Some beauties, I think I *have* discovered; such, for instance, as *"hitting the taste"*—the *"scanning of dishes"*—*"a brace of vixens"*—*"fires and darts, flames and arrows*, played off in fearful *corruscations"*—*"elegant* and substantial *food,"* &c., which are probably specimens of the sublime or "rays of genius."

I am determined still to be in the way of improvement, by reading the future numbers of the RESTORATOR; and altho' the invigorating warmth of the author's "rays of genius" may not be powerful enough to quicken and animate my "dull" faculties, the world will doubtless give me credit for my *patience.*

As I shall not proceed to a newspaper contest with the RESTORATOR or any other writer on the subject of plans not yet matured, I will only say that it would be very becoming in a gentleman not to prejudice a question and condemn a fellow citizen without a hearing. Percipitation is the vice of youth; but hopeless indeed is the condition of a man who, at the age of forty, has not become *"too wise to write"* on what he cannot have the means to understand.

N. WEBSTER

New-Haven, Nov. 10, 1801

Dutton replied that he respected "the purity and excellence of Mr. W's principles and conduct" and gave full credit for "the variety and extent of his erudition, the solidarity of his talents and the utility of his labors," but he begged leave to "give publicity to strictures upon proposed publications in accordance with those just and liberal principles upon which a journal ought to be conducted." In his column he added a very arrogant, unfair, disingenuous attack in which he compared Webster with Blackmore, "incomparably the worst and at the same time the vainest writer in England." He went on: "Sometimes vanity appears among us in the shape of a new spelling-book, which, ornamented with a wooden engraving of its author, fondly hopes, together with its own merits, to transmit his features to posterity. Sometimes it appears in proposals for publishing a *Columbian* dictionary, in which the vulgar provincialisms of uneducated *Americans* are to be quoted as authorities for language." Worse was Webster's opinion that he was a greater man than Dr. Johnson. Obviously prejudice could not sink a man's reasoning faculties to a lower level than Dutton's.

Webster maintained silence on the subject of his dictionary, adding only this dialogue to the new Prompter series:

An American Dictionary! Impossible! Who has the effrontery to attempt such a thing!

But perhaps some improvement can be made—

Improvement! What, improvement on Bailey, Johnson, Walker, Sheridan, Ash, Kenrick, and other English authors! Ridiculous! None but a blockhead would ever think of such a project! An American, a native of this God-forsaken country, where horses degenerate to palfreys, and man dwindles to a pigmy—an American harbor the audacious opinion that he can improve upon the works of British authors! I turn from the wretch with disgust and contempt!

But be quiet a little. Perhaps we have a few words not used in England.

Not used in England! Then banish them from the language. They are corruptions and must be rejected.

But suppose we have some new ideas, originating from new objects, new laws, new customs, new inventions; must we not use new words to express them?

New words! New ideas! What, Americans have *new* ideas! Why the man is mad!

But suppose this continent peopled with a hundred millions of inhabitants, must they have have no ideas, nor words, nor books, but what come from Great Britain? Perhaps the British nation may hereafter learn something from America.

Pshaw! What nonsense. No, no. Keep to the authorities; never try to mend them. Let us have none of your improvements!

Webster's first dictionary, *A Compendious Dictionary of the English Language,* did not appear until 1806. Let us turn, therefore, to examine the new plan of "a system of principles for the education of our youth," which Webster had announced in *The Medical Repository.*

After his marriage, Webster had practical opportunity to test in the training of his own children his theory of education, the keyword of which was utility. In the few extant letters of these youngsters one reads not only the affectionate words of loving children, but also an eagerness to receive the rewards promised for improvement. Emily Scholten, born on August 4, 1790; Frances Juliana, born February 5, 1793; Harriet, born April 6, 1797; Mary, born January 7, 1799; William Greenleaf, born September 15, 1801; Eliza, born December 21, 1803; and Louisa, born April 12, 1808, all survived their father. Henry Bradford, born November 20, 1806, died shortly after his birth. The family was a happy one, the girls joining with the parents in indulging William, of whom Webster often said, "He is my only son, and you know I love him."

Much of the children's early instruction was given at home. The girls learned to sew, knit, and cook, to sing, and to play the harpsichord. William borrowed his father's flute as a youth and became a proficient musician. Indeed, the Webster family took the responsibility for the music at the Center Church. Webster himself directed the choir, and the children joined the chorus as soon as they were old enough. In the little details of household management, too, all were initiated. Each had a set of duties, and each was held strictly accountable for prompt performance.

Webster frequently journeyed from home on business and research trips; from 1783 to 1843 he regularly toured New York and New England to increase the sale of his books. On returning he would catechize the children on their conduct, test their accuracy as students, and then reward them with useful gifts and new coins. Strict obedience to parental orders was always demanded, Webster having felt that a general slackening in this respect had done much damage to the character of American youth. A happy, noisy, busy-bee group, the Webster children were the pride of their Pa and Ma.

Upon his arrival in New Haven Webster was appointed a member of the school visiting committee. At once he was impressed with the fact that no secondary school suitable for his daughter Emily was conducted. He called together a group of leading citizens and organized The Union School. One hundred shares of stock were issued, Webster serving as treasurer of the company. In 1799 a brick schoolhouse with two rooms, one for boys and one for girls, was built. Within two years, when Webster became president of the organization, fifty-two boys and sixty-three girls were in attendance.

Adequate books for advanced instruction in the liberal arts had not yet been prepared in America, the children finding little else to do, besides Latin, than to study arithmetic, Morse's *Geography*, Webster's *Grammar* and *American Selection*, books which they had already used in elementary school. To remedy this deficiency Webster framed a new series of four textbooks under the general title, *Elements of Useful Knowledge.*

The chief purpose of these books was to present systematically a survey of the sciences and a history of the United States. In addition to elementary principles or ascertained facts, Webster gave brief moral or pious reflections; at the conclusion of his survey of the solar system, for example, he wrote: "All is order, harmony, beauty and grandeur, manifesting the infinite wisdom, power and goodness of the glorious creator."

The first volume contained a "Historical and Geographical Account of the United States," the history being carried down to the beginning of the Revolution. Washington's Farewell Address, an abridgment of the federal Constitution and of each state constitution, and a chronology were included. The second volume carried the discussion down to 1789. The third gave "A Historical and Geographical Account of Europe, Asia and Africa." The fourth contained "A History of Animals," a simplified textbook on biology. The books appeared in 1802, 1804, 1806, and 1812 respectively. They enjoyed only a short-lived popularity, other books on the same model soon replacing Webster's.

Although Webster was not a pioneer in this field, his books carried the old burden of nationalistic and patriotic pride, and here, as in language instruction, his imitators and successors adopted his manner. The *Elements* was auxiliary to the main design of the original American system of education, the beginning of which was the Spelling Book and the end, the Dictionary. *Elements of Useful Knowledge* in a sense replaced *An American Selection,* the Reader, because "it is so easy to make books of this sort, and so difficult to make one better than others." Webster thought the *Elements* the more valuable work, because, as its title indicated, it had "utility" for its aim.

In 1804 the original copyright, under the Act of 1790,

expired on Webster's books. In anticipation of a revision of the law, he requested Simeon Baldwin, the Congressman, to initiate legislation which would improve the conditions under which the copyright was renewed. If an author died before the first right expired, his heirs were deprived of the property, so that it might become "an object of universal plunder" at the very time it was most needed by the author's family. "I do not see," Webster explained, "why an interest in original literary composition should stand on different ground from all other personal property. . . . Literary composition [is] a species of property more peculiarly a man's own than any other, being the production of his mind or inventive faculties, . . . while a horse or an acre of land, which a fool may obtain by muscular exertions, is a permanent inheritable estate."

At the same time the contracts with the publishers expired. Webster, therefore, spent the months of November and December, 1803, and part of January, 1804, in making new arrangements in visits to Philadelphia, New York, Hartford, and Boston. Everywhere he heard that his Spelling Book had been printed without license by unethical publishers. Samuel Campbell, with whom Webster had had an earlier skirmish, and the Merriams of Brookfield, Massachusetts, were the chief known offenders in this respect. A pirated edition appeared at Edenton, North Carolina. It was difficult to secure evidence, however, because these men rented the forms from less scrupulous copyright holders and printed huge impressions without changing the imprint. In making his own returns, the lender could more or less truthfully say that he had printed only a certain number of thousands and pay the royalty thereon. Bonsal and Niles of Wilmington, Delaware, like Campbell at the expiration of his contract, threw off a vast impression. These copies they sold at a reduced price on long-time notes to country merchants. Every species of trickery was used to defraud Webster; new purchasers, like Jacob Johnson in Philadelphia, haggled a good bit over the price because of the vast supply already in the field and because of the underselling tactics of country printers.

In his new contracts, therefore, Webster specified that he would improve the Spelling Book so that the older edition would be rendered out-of-date. He also specified the price at which copies should be sold: ten cents for each copy in quires or sheets in lots of one thousand or more; sixteen cents five mills for each copy "in common binding with scale board and covered with blue paper"; and twenty-five cents for each copy retail. Jacob Johnson, December 28, 1803, agreed to pay $10.50 a thousand royalty. When Webster was hard pressed for cash in 1808, he sold his right for the remaining ten years of the grant for $2365, although the average royalty paid by Johnson had amounted to about $500 a year. Thus necessity drove Webster time and again to take a fraction of the income he might have had.

Thomas and Andrews in Boston refused to renew their contract on the old basis; they thought the price should be reduced, since the work had already given Webster a larger income than most authors ever received. They threatened Webster, too, that if he did not accede to their wishes, they would publish a competing book and drive his from the field. Webster stood his ground. They brought out Alden's Spelling Book, the pronunciation of which followed the outmoded style of Sheridan's Dictionary. Through their newspaper and magazine, as well as their contacts in Massachusetts, they made some headway in displacing Webster. In New York Picket's Spelling Book, based on Walker's pronunciation, was issued. Lindley Murray's Spelling Book, with the old fashioned syllabication, was being pushed by the Quakers in Philadelphia. Against the new books Webster successfully used the argument: "If our citizens are to imitate all the changes of English authors, there will be no end to innovations. . . . Every effort to establish a particular English book as a standard will serve to defeat that national uniformity which is desirable and which, I am persuaded, all good Americans will agree to be useful and necessary."

In his revised edition of *The American Spelling Book* (1804) Webster attempted to reach perfection, as he told Barlow: "To this end I have done what is not done by any other book of the kind. I have collected and classed all the more difficult words, so that after leading the child through tables of easy words, I present him, in short tables, all the varieties of anomaly; and when he has mastered this little book he has overcome the chief difficulties in learning the language; and as our books should have special reference to the local knowledge most necessary for us, I have introduced the names of places in this country. No English compilation can answer our purpose for want of such tables." It was the passion for nationality, for national unity, that drove Webster's pen in his textbook writing as in his political argumentation.

The new book vastly improved the older one. For one thing, the type was larger and the printing was better. New reading selections increased the student's pleasure in using the book. In conformity with the trend of the times Webster added religious and moralizing passages, although the main body of the new bits of prose and verse was of the Franklinian type. A few sentences will illustrate how topical some of these remarks were:

A wise man will consider, not so much the present pleasure and advantage of a measure, as its future consequences.
Sudden and violent passions are seldom durable.
Faction seldom leaves a man honest, however it may find him.
Small parties make up in diligence what they want in numbers.

The following sentence sums up Webster's creed as an author:

The basis of all excellence in writing and conversation is truth—truth is intellectual gold, which is as durable as it is splendid and valuable.

With fatherly pride Webster included his children's activities in this book. William recites the money table and talks about fruits and berries. Pa adds: "You must not eat too many and make yourself sick." The four daughters, Emily, Julia, Harriet, and Mary, are represented in their favorite occupations, and each sings a little song composed by Webster. Emily and Julia are in the garden watering the flowers and weeding the beds. Harriet reads a book of poems, and Mary is sewing. "Your little fingers are very handy with the needle," Pa fondly remarks; "Very pretty indeed; very pretty work. What small stitches. You shall hem and mark all your Papa's handkerchiefs, and very soon you shall work a muslin frock for yourself."

Something of the upright quality of Webster's mind can be gleaned from this selection:

PRECEPTS CONCERNING THE SOCIAL RELATIONS

Art thou a young man, seeking for a partner for life? Obey the ordinance of God, and become a useful member of society. But be not in haste to marry, and let thy choice be directed by wisdom.

Is a woman devoted to dress and amusement? Is she delighted with her own praise, or an admirer of her own beauty? Is she given to much talking and loud laughter? If her feet abide not at home, and her eyes rove with boldness on the faces of men—turn thy feet from her, and suffer not thy heart to be ensnared by thy fancy.

But when thou findest sensibility of heart joined with softness of manners; an accomplished mind and religion, united with sweetness of temper, modest deportment, and a love of domestic life—Such is the woman who will divide the sorrows, and double the joys of thy life. Take her to thyself; she is worthy to be thy nearest friend, thy companion, the wife of thy bosom.

Art thou a young woman, wishing to know thy future destiny?

Be cautious in listening to the addresses of men. Art thou pleased with smiles and flattering words? Remember that man often smiles and flatters most, when he would betray thee.

Listen to no soft persuasion, till a long acquaintance and a steady respectful conduct have given thee proof of the pure attachment and honorable views of thy lover. Is thy suitor addicted to low vices? is he profane? is he a gambler? a tipler? a spendthrift? a haunter of taverns? has he lived in idleness and pleasure? has he acquired a contempt for thy sex in vile company? and above all, is he a scoffer at religion?—Banish such a man from thy presence; his heart is false, and his hand would lead thee to wretchedness and ruin. . . .

Simplified spelling theories never corrupted the accepted orthography in *The American Spelling Book,* for Webster was too wise to experiment in a popular elementary school book. Only in the *Dissertations* and the *Fugitiv Essays* did he lay before the public his notions, but some critics have erroneously accused Webster of misleading American youth by a textbook use of the truncated forms. Not so. The final *e*'s remained, and so did all the other letters, the *u* in *favour* and *k* in *musick,* etc., excepted. In the *Compendious Dictionary* he would again set forth his theories and partially exemplify them, but he did not foist his newfangled notions on helpless children. Had he attempted to do so, his book would have disappeared from the schools with the celerity of leaves falling in autumn. In his effort to attain perfection, he occasionally fell into error; for example, in attempting to set suffixes apart on his analogical principle, he achieved *clas-sic-al, an-im-al, droll-e-ry* (by analogy with *chiv-al-ry*), *nu-trim-ent* and *ru-dim-ent.* Consistency is not the jewel of English spelling, and soon Webster departed from this unifying device by framing more acceptable and now generally held rules for syllabication.

The American Spelling Book was safely established; not even political opposition could dislodge it from the schools. Sales mounted steadily; in 1804 more than two hundred thousand copies annually were contracted for by authorized publishers. No estimate can be made of the thousands slipped into the market by dishonest printers.

Webster's seriousness as a grammarian can be better understood when it is realized that he refused (June 14, 1805) to allow Mathew Carey to make further impressions of Part II of the *Institute* "on the ground of its imperfections. Not that I think it more imperfect than most of the English Grammars now used—rather less so." A study of Anglo-Saxon had unfolded new principles, and until he could refashion his Grammar in accordance with truth, he would not countenance further dissemination of error under his signature. This is the first instance on record of the operation of this type of scholarly conscience; a precious example of integrity, it deserves to be written large in the history of American scholarship.

It was the Dictionary, however, to which Webster gave his best thought and time. Here was to be made his great gift to scholarship, a solemn declaration to this effect having given caution, if not sloth, to his progress. Where the sciolist rushed to print after a few weeks' work in compilation, Webster scanned his sources, tested etymologies, and investigated definitions. Much was wrong. Johnson, whose Dictionary had been pilfered by all successors, did not know law, medicine, and the physical sciences. His imitators knew less. Rapidly growing vocabularies in chemistry, botany, and geology found no record in the new books. Webster set out to correct this deficiency.

What qualifications did Webster have for this task of writing a new Dictionary? First, he had literally taken all knowledge for his province, and he had achieved distinction as a contributor in many departments. In law he had not only practiced before local courts, but he had served as legislator and judge, and had written essays and treatises of great merit. In medicine he had made adequate studies for the preparation of the first history of epidemic diseases. His experiments in science had kept him abreast of the developments in these fields, and his writings on scientific subjects in *Elements of Useful Knowledge* had required a complete survey of these topics. A keen student of economics, he had written wise words on American business conditions. As a New Englander he was by inheritance a theologian, a field in which he would soon distinguish himself. As an itinerant lecturer, schoolmaster, and editor, Webster had touched life at many points; his clear, gray eye missed nothing.

Second, Webster may have been "a born definer of words," as James A. H. Murray has said, but the fact is that he was called by his experiences to exercise and develop whatever native talent he possessed. In every essay he took time to define carefully each important term he used; by this means, as in his distinction between impost and excise, he carried conviction. Fuzzy thinking, arising from fuzzy terminology, had led astray legislators and people alike. From the day he entered the newspaper scribbling contest in 1782 until his death, he was writing definitions to help his countrymen think straight. The meaning of meaning was no idle pun with him; it was fundamental that the root meaning of every word be fixed and that all additional radiations be understood in relation to that root.

Third, Webster delighted in etymological investigations; language study afforded pleasureful relaxation from other duties. He kept his Greek fresh by comparing the English translation of the New Testament with the original. He learned German, Danish, and Anglo-Saxon in order to trace the relationship between English and its ancestors. Horne Tooke had mentioned Celtic as the parent of English; Webster studied Welsh and Old Irish. Old Testament study required Hebrew; Webster studied it. Hebrew had connections with Persian; Webster studied it. Soon there were twenty alphabets from as many languages which had

revealed their secrets to him. It became a fascinating study
to put together the same root word, like *father*, in its twenty
different language forms. Startling results appeared. Consonants and vowels squirmed like protean snakes. *Father*
doesn't look much like Latin *pater*, or Greek *patar*, or German *vater*. But see: the *p* became *v* in German, and this in
turn became *f* in English. Try it again: *foot*, Latin *pes*,
pedis, German *fusz*. It doesn't always happen the same way,
but still that Latin (and Greek) *p* became *f*. The labials,
the letters formed by the lips, had a sequence in the progres-
sion of time. How about that *t* in *pater* becoming *th* in
father. Let's try again: *tres* becomes *three*. And so on.
There were many exceptions, many anomalous cases. But
the consonants seemed to shift from language to language
with a fixed regularity. Likewise the vowels, though here
the problem was more complicated. It all resolved itself to
consonantal groups or radicals, Webster decided, and on
this ground he proceeded. It all may seem like a game, but
Webster found in it guidance through the daedalian maze
of etymology.

Fourth, Webster's curiosity was fortified by the scholar's
greatest asset, patience. Unhurriedly, imperturbably he
pushed forward on a work which would take, he thought,
three to five years. Only his awareness that one is not immortal, allowed him to stop investigating at the end of
twenty years and bring his work to a temporary close.

By comparison with all other earlier lexicographers, even
Johnson, Webster stands out the superior in qualifications.
But he was wont to be touchy, arrogant if you will, about
his unique possession of truth; he turned friends against
him and forever alienated others by constantly harping on
his discoveries and on the errors of Johnson. It was Webster's old trick, this of denouncing all competitors, but it
served to get him nowhere. The more he talked, the more
his opponents ridiculed him. The mocking screech of the

charivari horsefiddle, scraped since 1783, continued its harassing music.

A Compendious Dictionary of the English Language, in
which "compendious" was defined as "short, brief, concise,
summary," came from Sidney Babcock's press, New Haven,
on February 11, 1806, price $1.50. The title page boasted
the addition of five thousand words to the "best English
compends," and further promised, "for the benefit of the
merchant, the student, and the traveller," tables of moneys,
tables of weights and measures, the divisions of times among
all nations, an official list of post-offices in the United
States, the number of inhabitants in the United States and
the value of exports, and "new and interesting chronological
tables of remarkable events and discoveries." This was
not the first time a dictionary was made the bearer of useful information of this variety; but Webster's example
caused other compilers to add similar encyclopedic material.

This duodecimo of 408 pages, plus a 24-page Preface,
was avowedly an improvement upon Entick's Spelling Dictionary, a small work of wide use in the United States. Had
it not been for the Preface, Webster's book might have
sneaked into circulation without much ado. In microscopically fine type, Webster set forth his linguistic discoveries
and theories. His study of Anglo-Saxon convinced him that
Johnson and Lowth—"it may appear at first incredible"—
had "mistaken many of the fundamentals of language."
Their ignorance was proved by many examples, and the
gusty American plunged his pen through his predecessors'
books! "How would the elegant Addison," Webster asked,
"that pre-eminent writer of unadulterated English, smile,
were he to rise from the grave and see this genuine idiom
in the Spectator ['Charm he never so wisely'], stigmatized
by a hypercritical editor [Lowth] as bad grammar and
printed in Italics!" Further, Johnson mistook the sense of
many words; his errors are "so obvious that it is not easy

to number them with the effects of ordinary negligence."

As to orthography, Webster said that he was inclined to take the mean between the extreme of Franklin and the do-nothings. The irregularity of the English language demanded attention, but the addition of new characters seemed "impracticable and not at all necessary." Failure to make any changes would destroy the benefits of an alphabet and reduce "our language to the barbarism of Chinese characters insted [*sic*] of letters." "No great changes," he went on, "should be made at once, nor should any change be made which violates established principles, creates great inconvenience, or obliterates the radicals of the language." This doctrine seemed sensible enough and reasonable. Suggested changes included the rejection of the final *k* in words like *musick,* and the final *e* in *determine, examine,* and other words with a short vowel in the last syllable. He proposed the use of *s* instead of *c*, as in *pretense* and *defense*. The *u* in *honour* and similar words was again rejected. Johnson had changed all Greek derivatives in *sk* to *sc* in English, as *scene*, except *skeptic*. This anomalous form Webster proposed bringing into harmony with the whole group by making it *sceptic*. The last change proposed was the use of *er* endings for all words, whether *re* or *er* in the original language, as *theater, luster,* etc. Everyone of these reforms, with the exception of the dropping of the final *e*, has been adopted in America, although *skeptic* still appears. The *-our* ending prevails in England and among those American authors or publishers who hope to sell their books in England. Nothing indicates more clearly America's kowtowing to England at the present time than this deviation from standard American spelling.

Most controverted early in the nineteenth century was the manner of pronouncing English words. We have already seen that some American spelling books copied Sheridan's and Walker's different notations, while Webster clung

A

Compendious Dictionary

OF THE

English Language.

In which FIVE THOUSAND Words are added
to the number found in the BEST ENGLISH COMPENDS;

The ORTHOGRAPHY is, in some instances, corrected;

The PRONUNCIATION marked by an Accent or other suitable Direction;

And the DEFINITIONS of many Words amended and improved.

TO WHICH ARE ADDED FOR THE BENEFIT OF THE

MERCHANT, the STUDENT and the TRAVELLER,

I.——TABLES of the MONEYS of most of the commercial Nations in the world, with the value expressed in Sterling and Cents.

II.——TABLES of WEIGHTS and MEASURES, ancient and modern, with the proportion between the several weights used in the principal cities of Europe.

III.——The DIVISIONS of TIME among the Jews, Greeks and Romans, with a Table exhibiting the Roman manner of dating.

IV.——An official List of the POST-OFFICES in the UNITED STATES, with the States and Counties in which they are respectively situated, and the distance of each from the seat of Government.

V.——The NUMBER of INHABITANTS in the United States, with the amount of EXPORTS.

IV.——New and interesting CHRONOLOGICAL TABLES of remarkable Events and Discoveries.

By NOAH WEBSTER, Esq.

From Sidney's Press,

FOR HUDSON & GOODWIN, BOOK-SELLERS, HARTFORD, AND INCREASE COOKE & CO.
BOOKSELLERS, NEW-HAVEN.

1806.

WEBSTER'S FIRST DICTIONARY (1806).

to the New England style. In his Preface to *A Compendious Dictionary*, therefore, Webster despaired of attaining a universally satisfactory standard, because "a living language admits of no fixed state," and because each compiler adds a few forms peculiar to his native locality or to his mental habits. The guiding rule, therefore, should be that one laid down by Dr. Johnson: "Those are the most elegant speakers who deviate least from the written language." In New England this rule had been obeyed since the first settlement, so that "the common unadulterated pronunciation of the New England gentlemen is almost uniformly the pronunciation" of the golden age of Addison and Pope. For this reason American pronunciation seemed a more satisfactory standard than the affected theatrical elegance of Sheridan and Walker. Webster's notions rested on a solid foundation of fact:

Real improvements should never be checked; but the changes which are made by the fashionable part of a nation, who are sometimes ignorant and often capricious and proud of singularity, prove not unfrequently to be gross improprieties, which, like modes of dress, have a temporary currency, and are then condemned to neglect and oblivion. Hence from the practice of the gay and fashionable world, there is always an appeal to a higher tribunal, the great body of literary and well informed men in a nation, whose opinion of propriety is not to be seduced, nor their judgment perverted by the influence of names and fashion. Hence the established popular usages of a nation are rarely changed but by a conquest or great revolution among the inhabitants of a country. Custom among a whole people erects an impregnable bulwark against the preservation of many English idioms, which writers and critics, from an affectation of refinement, have most injudiciously attempted to banish. It is a curious fact . . . that the principal corruptions of our language, within the last five hundred years, are the work, not of the vulgar as is commonly supposed, but of authors and writers pretending to purify and refine the language.

Real improvements in pronunciation arise from a popular tendency to abridge words which are of difficult pronunciation; to soften or reject harsh letters and syllables; and to give to letters and syllables such sounds, and to words such a disposition of accent as best suit the organs of utterance and of hearing. Any alteration in pronunciation which is not recommended by these advantages will never become general.

In support of these remarks Webster offered two illustrations. *Came,* the past tense, had been introduced late into the language by refiners, but the common people everywhere say *come:* "I *come* home last night." *Ask* is pronounced *aks;* "The latter is the true pronunciation of the word, the Saxon verb being written *acsian* or *axian.*" Here was heresy, indeed; yeomen were given preference over scholars!

Mason in his preface to the supplement of Dr. Johnson's Dictionary had remarked: "That lexicographer's etymologies are deservedly reckoned the most erroneous part of his Dictionary." Building on this statement, Webster wrote: "Johnson, who, when correctness depended solely on the exertions of his vast intellectual powers, seldom made a mistake, was often betrayed into errors by his natural indolence which led him to write often without investigation, or he must have been pressed by disease and poverty to send his papers to the press in an unfinished state." Johnson had depended upon older etymologists, and Webster readily found many errors. To this department of lexicography, therefore, Webster intended to devote much attention.

In the last section of his Preface Webster explained how he chose the new words he was adding to Entick, and why new words and new meanings of words, arising out of the situation of America, demanded an American dictionary. "In each of the countries peopled by Englishmen," he wrote, "a distinct dialect of the language will gradually be formed, the principal of which will be that of the United States." This notion, so commonly expressed at the turn of the century, was one of the leading tenets of the American nationalistic credo. "In fifty years from this time," Webster continued, "the *American English* will be spoken by more people than all the other dialects of the language, and in one hundred and thirty years by more people than any other language on the globe, not excepting the Chinese." The year 1936 has brought to fulfillment this prophecy, if we agree that no other group of people to the number of one hundred and twenty million speak and write the same language in the same fundamental way. Russia, India, and China have many dialects, some of which are unintelligible in distant sections of each country. "Those words," to conclude Webster's statement, "which express ideas common to the several nations [using English] will remain so nearly the same in all dialects as to render mutual intercourse easy —a circumstance for which the citizens of each country will be much indebted to the art of printing, which will retard the progress of variations. But those terms in Great Britain which express local ideas only will be lost in the dialects of India and America, while local circumstances among the descendants of the English in their new settlements will originate new words or give to old words new significations, which will never be received or generally known in Great Britain."

With these extensive views of the subject, Webster announced his intention of "compiling for my fellow citizens a dictionary which shall exhibit a far more correct state of the language than any work of this kind." And he concluded his Preface with this solemn dedication to the great task before him: "However arduous the task, and however feeble my powers of body and mind, a thorough conviction of the necessity and importance of the undertaking, has overcome my fears and objections, and determined me to make one effort to dissolve the charm of veneration for foreign authorities which fascinates the mind of men in this country and holds them in the chains of illusion. In the investigation of this subject great labor is to be sustained and numerous difficulties encountered; but with a humble dependence on Divine favor for the preservation of my life and health I shall prosecute the work with diligence and execute it with a fidelity suited to its importance."

Here spoke the nationalistic schoolmaster in tones less strident but more perfervid than those of 1785 when he called upon the thirteen republics to cease their squabbling and unite under one banner and under one chief executive. Few men have been driven by so consistent a patriotic passion continuously striving to render a nation independent, united, and great. Few men under so many adverse and hostile conditions have kept burning brightly the candles on the altar of nationality. In this respect one can find suitable confreres for Webster, the scholar and schoolmaster, only among national political and military leaders. But he brought the pen and not the sword; he brought understanding and clarity to disputes, not vengeful power or personal ambition; he brought the hope of peace through unity, the unity of a common language.

The tide of party passions was running full, however, and Webster was spurned as he knelt at the altar of dedication. The Jeffersonians, the Hamiltonians, and the Unitarians sneered at him, caricatured his vanity and effrontery, and impeded his progress. Why? Because he had spoken bluntly the truth about party passions and because he was a Congregationalist with courage to defend his faith in Calvinistic fundamentals. And because he dared to say Dr. Johnson was not the only god, the true god, of English lexicography.

Webster's detractors disliked not only the Preface, but also some few of the innovations in *A Compendious Dictionary*. The *u* was dropped, of course, from *honour*, and the *e* was omitted thus: *ax, imagin, medicin, doctrin,* but by a curious error *fugitive* slipped in. The final *k* did not disfigure

music, logic. etc. Other silent letters disappeared, as in *catcal,
etiquet, farewel, benum, thum* (as verb), *crum, fether, lether,
wether, tung,* and *wo.* On analogical principles he developed
ake, skreen, soop, troop, cloke, mold, and *spunge.* He unified
all *-re* and *-er* endings as *-er: center, theater,* etc. He preferred *apprise* to *appraise,* and *epitomy, catastrophy, apostro-
phy,* but let *synecdoche* slip in. He admitted the *-y* adverbial
suffix, much to the disgust of critics, as in *soapy, haily,
streamy, strawy, squally,* and *dozy,* by analogy with *drowsy.*
Localisms like *dreen* (*v.* to draw off water; *n.* drain), *yux*
(*n.* the hickup), and *swosh* (*n.* a narrow or shallow channel
[carolina]) were included. He declared that *wimman* and
wimmen were "the old and true spelling," that *hainous* was
better than *heinous,* and *tho* than *though,* and that *sley* was
preferable to *sleigh.*

Webster admitted cant words like *caucus,* but purged the
vocabulary of Johnsonian words like *decumbiture, repas-
ture, deuteroscopy, fishefy, jacalent,* and *thingumbob.* He
also enriched the vocabulary with *accompaniment, adjutancy,
advisory, ascertainable, insubordination,* and the only word
he ever created, *demoralize.* His brief, generally synonymous, definitions prevented completeness, but he corrected
Johnson's erroneous legal terminology, and he gave for the
first time in a popular, cheap compend the new terms of science. The Jeffersonians immediately pounced on *Federal,
Federalist n. A friend to the Constitution of the U. States.*
The implication, they said, was evident. This one definition
placed Webster in a class with Jedidiah Morse, who prated of
the Connecticut clergy's preservation of an "aristocratical balance" in that state.

Morse reviewed the book favorably in *The Panoplist;*
the London reviewers objected to an American's dabbling
in etymology; Coleman sneered at it in the *Evening Post;*
and here and there other papers printed squibs about "Noah's
Ark." In Boston the editors of *The Monthly Anthology*

passed the book from member to member in an effort to
secure a slashing review. Three years of effort brought the
desired butcher into the business. Dennie shot spiteful arrows at "The American Language" in the *Portfolio*. Even
Webster's closest friends grew alarmed, his brother-in-law,
Thomas Dawes, writing, "I ain't yet quite ripe for your
orthography." President Smith of Princeton wrote: "I think
you will meet with more success if you do not too strenuously attempt to maintain the peculiarities of what is called
the New England pronunciation."

Despite this almost universal annoyance at Webster's
vanity in attempting to overgo Dr. Johnson, the lexicographer daily labored in his library. In December, 1807,
he published his second dictionary, an abridgment of the
first, with the title, *A Dictionary of the English Language;
compiled for the use of common schools in the United States.*
In this book obsolete, improper or vulgar, and learned terms
found no place, although words of everyday use in the home,
factory, and farm were included. This collection of thirty
thousand words and their brief definitions sold for a dollar
a copy. In order to keep the price down, Webster gave
John West, the Boston printer, the right to print an edition
of three thousand copies in return for twenty-five copies.
This book sold well, several editions being called for. But
Webster's income from it, as from *A Compendious Dictionary*, was small.

On February 25, 1807, Webster mailed to all his friends
and to bookstores throughout the country a circular letter,
setting forth his aims, present achievement, and plans for
completing the large dictionary. He asked the assistance
of scholars and men of wealth, the former to give etymologies and the latter to contribute to his support during the
coming years. All might help by extending the use of his
schoolbooks. In England similar undertakings were supported by contributions; the plan was novel in America,

and of course much ridicule was heaped on the ambitious scholar. Rufus King, John Jay, Oliver Wolcott, Chancellor James Kent, among others, sent Webster contributions, but not one of these encouraged Webster to look either for general support or public approbation. King wrote: "I am sorry to remark that I am able to discover but little probability of your receiving adequate encouragement to continue to devote your time and talents to the important and laborious investigation in which, for so many years, you have been engaged. Neither learning, morals, nor wisdom seem any longer to be regarded as objects of public esteem and favour." He followed these remarks with a gloomy description of American "prejudice against learning." Oliver Wolcott, then president of a bank in New York, wrote: "I cannot encourage you to expect success." These paralyzing statements came despite the fact that the circular contained an "unqualified approbation of the design" by the faculties of Yale, Princeton, Dartmouth, Williams, and Middlebury colleges.

Something of the grand conception Webster held in mind may be gleaned from this paragraph:

From an examination of all the radical words in the Hebrew, and a great part of those in the Celtic and Teutonic languages, I can assure the friends of learning, that much new light may be thrown on this subject. The wonderful structure of language, and its progress from a few simple terms, expressive of natural objects, which supplied the wants or affected the senses of unlettered men, thro a series of ingenious combinations, to express new ideas, growing with the growth of the human mind, to its highest state of refinement, are yet to be charted and elucidated; numerous facts respecting the origin, migration and intermixture of nations are to be unfolded or illustrated; and the origin of all the nations of Europe, and those of Asia, at least on the west of the Ganges, may be confirmed beyond the possibility of a reasonable doubt by the affinity of their languages. Equally useful are these inquiries in disentangling the difficulties of the heathen mythology, which have perplexed and confounded the ablest writers.

Webster here planned to put his linguistic researches to the full test; he wished not merely to elucidate word meanings, but also to throw upon ethnography the light which language history gives. Few, however, were the men able to understand the profundity of the scholar; they assessed him in terms of political party affiliation.

In August, 1807, Webster published a second circular, but the response to this was no better than to that of the first. He realized that his was to be an independent task, and yet at no time did he quite surrender his hope that help might come from his countrymen. The ardor with which he contemplated his nationalistic ideal prevented his appreciating to the full the public apathy. To Daniel Webster, the young orator, he stated: "It will be proper that every subscriber should understand that this application is addressed more to his patriotism than most others of a like kind, and that he advances his money on the risk of my *life*, *health*, and *fidelity*."

Dr. David Ramsay had written from Charleston: "Prejudices against American attempts to improve Dr. Johnson are very strong in this city." Webster thought over this too frequently expressed reverence for Johnson, and then in October, 1807, published a twenty-eight-page pamphlet, entitled *A Letter to Dr. David Ramsay . . . respecting the Errors of Johnson's Dictionary*. Ramsay's statements, Webster wrote, did not surprise him, for similar prejudices had been manifested in other parts of the nation. Something of the experience of Galileo was being re-enacted in principle, if not in degree, in America. After this remark, Webster quoted from Tooke, who said of Johnson's Dictionary that nearly one third of it was "as much the language of the Hottentots as the English." Tooke also had opined, "I could never read his preface without shedding a tear." Seven specific charges were leveled by Webster against Johnson:

1. Johnson inserted a multitude of words in his Dictionary which did not belong to the English language.

2. The selection of authorities was injudicious.

3. Johnson's Dictionary "contains more of the lowest of all vulgar words than any other now extant, Ash excepted."

4. There is "a want of just discrimination" in the different senses of words.

5. Johnson failed to discriminate carefully in defining words nearly synonymous.

6. Illustrations were chosen from authors who did not write English with purity; these examples "throw not the least light on his definitions." "One half of the whole bulk of Johnson's Dictionary is composed of quotations equally useless."

7. The etymologies are inaccurate. "On this subject, therefore, almost every thing remains to be done."

In closing, Webster quoted Mason: "This muddiness of [Johnson's] intellect defaces almost every page." And Webster added for himself that the errors were ten times more numerous than his friends supposed. In favor of Johnson Webster could say little more than that the great cham had added many words to older lists. As to patronage, Webster expressed unconcern: "I therefore rely upon my own resources, and am not without a belief that I shall be able, with these alone, to accomplish my design. If I should succeed, my opposers will certainly regret their premature expressions of disapprobation. I ask no favors: the undertaking is Herculean, but it is of far less consequence to *me* than to *my country*. . . . I shall pursue [the task] with zeal—and undoubtedly with success."

Harvard College had refused to approve the project; a painfully precise letter from Professor John Quincy Adams, later President of the United States, had praised Webster's "genius and learning," but had carried this opinion as to Webster's standard of pronunciation: "Now if I deemed a new standard necessary, I know not where I could find one which I should prefer to yours. But I am not entirely convinced that a new one is necessary." And as to new words:

"Your liberality of admission in the compendious Dictionary extends so far, that I should prefer to find in the larger work a restriction rather than an enlargement of it." Harvard's Boylston Professor of Rhetoric had spoken. Harvard again denied that any good could come from Yale. A definite anti-Webster sentiment was propagated among the Harvard alumni.

During a revival meeting in April, 1808, Webster's daughters felt the workings of grace as they listened night after night to the sermons of the Reverend Moses Stuart, pastor of the Center Church. Webster leaned toward the Episcopalian form more than the Congregational; he suggested that the family unite with Trinity Church. Mrs. Webster and the girls objected. Webster, who had retained all the prejudices and beliefs of his father's church, had not tested its creed. The revival forced him to do so, and when conviction flashed across his mind, bringing that peace which passeth understanding, he yielded wholeheartedly. With the fervor of a new convert, he wrote letters to all his relatives, enjoining them to find equally sweet joy. Dawes replied (October 25, 1808), "I am no disbeliever," but he added, "I have thought that to exercise our talents, such as we have, to obtain knowledge and honestly to abide by the dictates thereof, was all that could be expected by our master." With care Webster formulated a statement of his belief on December 20, 1808, and sent it to Dawes. Dr. Moses Stuart procured it for publication in *The Panoplist*, and soon a pamphlet was made of it, entitled *Peculiar Doctrines of the Gospel, Explained and Defended*. The Reverend Abiel Holmes, father of Oliver Wendell Holmes, wrote from his Brattle Street Church, Cambridge:

We have been much gratified in the perusal of your Letter in explanation and defence of the "Peculiar Doctrines of the Gospel." I hope the publication of it will promote the interests of pure Christianity. Arguments used by *us*, who are *set for the defence of the gospel,* are often inefficacious, because we are considered as merely "labouring in our vocation." When men of learning and talents, in *other* professions, voluntarily engage in the defence of our holy religion, the world is less apt to suppose them *interested,* and therefore more ready to listen to their arguments. I rejoice to find you defending, not the outworks merely, but the citadel; not the truth of Christianity in general, but the peculiar doctrines of it—*the truth as it is in Jesus.*

Abiel Holmes, a Yale graduate, could not alter the attitude of Unitarian Harvard and Boston. Webster's pamphlet aroused increased animosity. *The Monthly Anthology,* among whose founders was Ralph Waldo Emerson's father, now demanded a review of *A Compendious Dictionary* that would annihilate the New Haven philologist. In issue after issue appeared "cruel and wanton attacks." Moses Stuart wrote from Andover, whither he had gone as professor: "The *Anthology* is outrageous against you. I believe it will do good, and promote the very cause it is meant to destroy. May the Lord turn their haughty and unfriendly designs into foolishness! Be assured, the object of their vengeance is more against your religion than against you."

Webster bearded the lions in their den, carrying his sample pages directly to a meeting of his opposers. They promised support, but as soon as Webster's back was turned, they renewed their jibing comments. A young Yale graduate, Simeon Colton, was living in Salem at this time, and he, for the honor of his Alma Mater, wrote (September 8, 1809) these excited sentences to his uncle, Simeon Baldwin:

Mr. Webster has just been in this town and in the neighboring towns soliciting patronage for his Dictionary to be published at some future day. In this town he applied to John Pickering, jun., son of the Colonel. . . . I know him and through him the opinion of the literary men in the neighborhood concerning Mr. Webster. . . .

In this quarter every thing contrary to the opinion of Cambridge [Harvard] University is rejected by the principal characters; consequently, Mr. Webster would be much less popular here than if

he paid more respect to that institution. Again Mr. Webster seems
determined to run down Johnson and build upon his ruin; nothing
could be more fatal to him in this quarter, for our *litterati* will never
believe that he is superior to this great English lexicographer, and by
this means will withhold the support they would grant were he more
modest in his pretensions.

But there is another capital defect in Mr. Webster's proposition.
He proposes that the subscribers should advance 10 dollars each. This
I am certain will never succeed in this quarter, for their opinion of
the man is not good enough to induce them, *hardly*, to become
obligated to take his books after they are printed. He must devise
some other plan or he will get but few subscribers within the atmosphere of Cambridge.

Another thing which has been noticed is his peddling his own production in person; had he addressed the public thro the medium
of the papers, or in handbills, with a specimen of his work, he would
have been more successful, and nothing would be more efficacious
than the publication of a specimen. But the great and capital defect
is the unbounded vanity of the man, (Perhaps I use a hard expression, but I use such as I hear, and such as I am inclined to think is
proper from his publications and conversation which I have heard
related) which is so great as to excite ridicule. Many of the principal characters here have visited or corresponded with men in England, and when they hear Webster say that he has more knowledge
than any European they are rather disposed to laugh than to admire.

I will however state what I believe to be true, that the people
here are willing to see his Dictionary, tho they have no great opinion of it, from the great prejudice they have against the man. These
are facts which I have collected chiefly thro Mr. Pickering and his
father, the Colonel, the latter of whom, I know, has a low idea of
Mr. Webster. I write these things to give you a statement of what
I think to be the opinion concerning Mr. Webster here; and I wish
for the honor of our Alma Mater, for the good of the public, and
the credit of the man himself, he were not so confident in his own
merit, but would be content to address the public as though there
were some equal to himself. I suppose Dr. Morse and friends encouraged him, but their opinion would not weigh much with the
greater part of the people in Boston and other large towns this way.
I would not be censorious on this subject, for I wish the man success,
but I wish he would be content to use the ordinary means to obtain it.

Joel Barlow had responded cordially to Webster's circular, so that Webster wrote long letters about his literary plans. But, unhappily, *The Columbiad* reached Webster shortly after he had been converted. The "atheistical principles" avowed in the epic were distasteful. With forthrightness typically Websterian, he wrote: "No man on earth not allied to me by nature or by marriage had so large a share in my affections as Joel Barlow until you renounced the religion which you once preached and which I believe." With this letter ended the correspondence between them. Curiously, Webster could not understand why religious sentiments should have led the Bostonians to pillory him, and yet he himself lacked sympathy for another's point of view.

In 1810 Webster gave up his last public office in Connecticut, the judgeship of the local county court. His name had been bandied about so much that he desired to escape to the solitude of his own study chamber. Two daughters were now being courted by Yale students; he did not want to spoil their chances. His income had been so sharply cut by the Embargo and Nonimportation Acts, that in 1811 he was ready to move to the country. His energy in writing remonstrances arose from the threat of poverty. Friends came forward with an offer of a loan each year until his great work could be completed. In 1812, however, these men refused to advance more money. He sold printing rights of his books for a fraction of their value to raise ready cash. The mounting cost of living occasioned by the War of 1812 forced him to admit that he could no longer maintain his family in New Haven. He sold his house, and in September moved to Amherst, Massachusetts.

CHAPTER XV

FOUNDER OF AMHERST COLLEGE

THE village of Amherst spreads over the crest and sides of one of the foothills of the Green Mountains. Broad views over the lower hills to the Connecticut River, eight miles to the west, and to the more rugged hills and peaks on the other three quarters of the compass, give the inhabitants an enviable outlook. The fat river-bottom land, yielding rich harvests, still makes farming the chief occupation.

From the bustling trading and college city of New Haven, Webster moved with his family of seven children to the country village in the exact center of Old Hampshire County. In the whole town there were about 250 houses and 1600 inhabitants. These people, according to one commentator, were all avaricious: "they want to get as much property as they can; they are generally honest, but tight in their dealings." Two distilleries were in operation; their product, unfortunately, gave good deacons many extra hours of work in their attempts to check the appetites of less temperate neighbors. It was a season of religious revivals throughout America; conscience-searching, such as Webster had experienced in 1808, was going on in Amherst. The First Church had viewed with grief the low state of religion among the people, the backslidings of some of the members, and, by report, the criminality of others. A committee of seven was diligently conversing with the fallen ones; William Dickinson, for example, confessed to intemperance, but neither prayer nor promise aided him. Finally he was suspended from communion.

Webster had bought a large double house at the east end of Phoenix Row; about it were ten acres of meadowland. He set out an orchard and annually raised the family supply of vegetables. His experiments continued. To *The Hampshire Gazette* he sent communications on his experiments with potatoes, fertilizers, and varieties of crops not generally grown in Massachusetts; he restated for his new neighbors his ideas on the conservation of forests, a topic he had been bringing up for more than twenty years. He became a member and officer of the local agricultural society and before one of its meetings pronounced a Prompter-like dissertation on farming, "the first, best, and most useful" occupation. Webster's enthusiasm for general ownership of land among all the people, as the bulwark of a republican government, gave urgency to his remarks. He was not a dilettante farmer; he delved in the earth, gathered his own hay, fed his cattle, and milked the cows. His philosophy was well stated in the final paragraph of an article in the *Gazette* (December 3, 1817):

It is very gratifying to observe the increasing disposition and taste for agriculture in this country, and more particularly to see men of property and distinction in our large towns turning their attention to this subject. For five and twenty years past, our citizens have been so occupied with the great events in Europe and with the means of acquiring property by commercial speculations, that they seem to have forgotten that almost all the food, and clothing, and riches of men are primarily drawn from the earth. It would be a happy thing for our country if a hundred millions of capital now vested in stocks, producing an income to the proprietors which is expended or wasted in luxurious enjoyments, could be drawn into the service of agriculture, in which it might contribute to improvements of great value to the community. Wealth is one of the talents entrusted to men for use and employment, and a severe account must be rendered by those who hide it in a napkin. And in regard to the pleasures of life, how little do men enjoy who lounge away day after day and year after year in the same dull round of eating, drinking, and sleeping, without an object to call forth mental exertion—strangers to all the operations and beauties of the vegetable world, and to the satisfaction which useful improvements afford to the generous mind of a philanthropist.

Webster's credo as a citizen was given in his Address in 1818: "The proper business of man is to enlarge the powers of the mind by knowledge, and refine it by the culture of moral habits; to increase the means of subsistence and comfort; to supply the wants and alleviate the distresses of his brethren; to cherish the virtues and restrain the vices of society; to multiply the rational enjoyments of life; to diffuse the means of education and the blessings of religion; and to extend his benevolence and charities to the whole human family. In a word, the duty, the whole business of man is, to yield obedience to his Maker; and just in proportion to that obedience will be the private happiness and the public prosperity of the nation."

The older daughters had joined the flitting to Amherst under protest. They recognized the inability of Webster to bear the expenses of the family in New Haven, and yet their own plans were in jeopardy by the removal. Emily had had an understanding with William Wolcott Ellsworth, the son of Chief Justice Oliver Ellsworth, the man under whom Webster had first studied law. Julia had been receiving visits from Chauncey A. Goodrich, a fellow member with Ellsworth of Yale's Class of 1810. Goodrich was in September, 1812, entering upon a tutorship at his Alma Mater. It was difficult to be good-humored about a retreat one hundred miles into the wilderness when there had been dreams of being within a whistle's sound of one's beau. Julia hid her dissatisfaction with great effort. She was thinking of herself when she wrote to Goodrich of her mother's thoughts dwelling "with painful regret on the blessings she has left. It is impossible for her to find any substitute for them, at least for many of them—inward peace and all the enjoyments of devotion are still hers—but the affectionate friends whose habits of thinking accorded with her own, such as partook of her confidence with the highest degree—with whom she experienced the pleasures of religious converse without restraint—these are denied her; for these she can find no substitute."

The Webster family brought new vigor to the First Church, then under the pastoral care of Dr. David Parsons, learned, jovial, and witty, who, when rebuked for a too free indulgence in wit, remarked, "I know it and it has been a burden to me, but grace does not cure squint eyes." Webster and his three elder daughters organized a choir, and during the revivals the girls were active in seeking out their companions and guiding them into the new life. The Webster home became a focal point for visiting ministers, the hospitality of Mrs. Webster winning praise from all. Whatever lack the family may have felt in the narrow range of activity in the rural community, was made up in energetic support of worthy causes. In 1820 Webster organized a Sunday School and became a member of the Board of Managers. As moderator in the the church meetings he was called upon to bring harmony to measures. To him was entrusted the unpleasant task of telling Dr. Parsons's successor, Daniel A. Clark, how he might mend his ways. Webster also took the lead in attempting to unite the First and Second churches, but for his pains won only the ill will of the "East-streeters."

One by one four of the Webster "angels," as they have been repeatedly described by commentators on Amherst, left the parental home. On September 14, 1813, Ellsworth claimed Emily and took her to Hartford, where she would share his political triumphs as congressman, governor, and supreme court justice. Harriet married Edward H. Cobb, son of a wealthy West India merchant of Portsmouth, New Hampshire, on May 22, 1816. Julia captured her little minister on October 1, 1816. Goodrich at this time was a pastor at Middletown, Connecticut, but within a year he accepted the professorship of rhetoric at Yale, where for forty years his learning lent luster to his Alma Mater. In 1818, Mary, the bright, irrepressible favorite of all, married the widower Horatio Southgate of Portland, Maine. Her death in childbirth a year later prostrated the whole family with grief; the marks of Webster's sorrow never dimmed with time. The babe survived, and Webster adopted it, giving little Mary the affectionate place in his heart which the mother had held. Harriet had lost her babe and her husband, and she returned to the Amherst home. A buoyant faith in Providence sustained them all during these sorrows and another trial equally shocking: little Louisa as a result of an illness lost full command of her faculties. Tenderly Webster and his wife did everything humanly possible to mend the broken fortunes of their dear children. William, the apple of his father's eye, confessed "a native imbecility of mind" and blundered from one school to another and from one occupation to another. But always Webster would relent after casting the boy on his own resources, take him home again, supply him with an income for a time, and then put the fledgling out anew to test his strength. To the sisters' objections at this continuous indulgence Webster would always remark, "He is my only son, and you know I love him." Yet William was a jolly companion, whose boyish exuberance and teasing ways delighted his sisters.

Webster carried himself with extreme dignity, both abroad and at home. The children, Mary excepted, were somewhat in awe of him, and the sons-in-law squirmed under the rising patriarchal rule. Webster had a way of swooping down upon his daughters and carrying them away on carriage rides through New England and New York while he was furthering the sale of his books. The Old Testament code lost none of its authority in his family. Yet he was affec-

tionate and devoted to all. He showered gifts on the grandchildren, carried them to his home for long visits, wrote
them letters, and demanded letters in return. "Let units
be tens," he proposed at a family dinner; that is, let there
be ten children for every parent, and he rejoiced as each
new child was announced. But always he refused to allow
his name to be given to male children: he wrote again and
again, "I do not like my name, Noah."

Webster's erudition and public spirit gave him the leading
position in the community. As soon as he was established
in Amherst, the local political leaders called him into service. The American dissidence of dissent was probably no
stronger in New Haven than in Western Massachusetts.
The Webster pioneer, Governor John Webster, had led his
little band of democrats to this community in 1659, and the
tradition of independence had never died. Shays had raised
his revolt here. And now as the War of 1812 continued to
place harassing restrictions upon New England trade, these
inlanders, provoked to wrath that their voice in the national
council had been drowned by Madison's southern followers,
called for a redress of grievances. Plans were laid for the
Hartford Convention. In the early negotiations Webster
played a leading part.

By January, 1814, the war had rumbled fitfully for nearly
two years, and public affairs had been reduced to a deplorable condition. The troops raised to defend the seacoast
had been transferred to the Canadian battlefields. A British squadron patrolled Long Island Sound to prevent the
escape of frigates and to intercept coasting trade. One town
in Maine, then a territory of Massachusetts, was in the possession of the British, and it appeared that the war would be
carried on in Massachusetts itself. Trade had been dis-
rupted. Ships were tied up in harbors, embargoed, dis-
mantled, and rotting. The banks south of New England
had stopped the payment of specie; the national treasury

was empty. A pall of gloom smothered New England.

Along the coast, especially in Boston, there was much talk but no action. Joseph Lyman, lawyer, ardent patriot, and Federalist, talked the matter over with his friends in Northampton, and then sent out letters of invitation to "some few of the most discreet and intelligent" Old Hampshire citizens "for the purpose of a free and dispassionate discussion touching our public concerns." The Massachusetts Legislature would soon be in session, and recommendations from such a group might have weight. On January 19, 1814, came together General Maltby, Major General Hoyt, E. Williams, Lewis Strong, Col. Porter, General Mattoon (who left the meeting before the close), Webster, Lyman, and some gentlemen of Northampton. After a lengthy consultation, Webster proposed that a convention of delegates from the legislatures of the northern states, to agree upon and urge certain amendments to the Constitution, should be requested by the several towns. This motion carried and Webster was appointed, with Williams and Strong, to draft a circular letter. With that same prompt command of the situation he had demonstrated in New Haven, Webster prepared the letter, and this, with minor changes, was sent out on the very day of meeting.

The writers asserted that "the evils we suffer under are not of a wholly temporary nature springing from the war, but some of them are of a permanent character resulting from a perverse construction of the Constitution of the United States. . . . By means of the representation of slaves, the southern states have an influence in our national councils altogether disproportioned to their wealth, strength, and resources; and we presume it to be a fact capable of demonstration that for about twenty years past the United States have been governed by a representation of about two fifths of the actual property of the country." Further evils were found in the formation of new states in the South and in the power assumed by Congress to lay a permanent embargo. By the latter act the rights of the states had been usurped, and the President had been made a dictator with military power to control persons and property. Therefore the committee invited their fellow citizens "to consider whether peace will remedy our public evils without some amendments to the Constitution which shall secure to the northern states their due weight and influence in our national councils."

Here certainly nothing subversive to the government or the best interests of the American people was projected. By the party system of government inaugurated by Jefferson, New England had lost not only the shaping destiny of legislation, but also a voice in it. On strict party votes the northern measures always failed. Webster, who detested party spirit, for this reason entered energetically into the support of the proposed convention. He wrote long letters to his friends in Boston, and he talked to his neighbors. The measure failed in the January meeting of the Massachusetts Legislature. Webster, therefore, let it be known that he would stand for election to that assembly in May, and that he would use his strength in the enterprise. He had presided over the Amherst town meeting, January 3, 1814, when this outspoken resolution which savors of his style was adopted:

That the representatives of this town in the General Court [Assembly] are desired to use their influence to induce that honorable body to take the most vigorous and decisive measures compatible with the Constitution to put an end to this hopeless war, and to restore to us the blessings of peace. What measures it will be proper to take, we pretend not to prescribe; but whatever measures they shall think it expedient to adopt, either separately or in conjunction with their neighboring States, they may rely upon faithful support.

On this platform Webster stood for nomination and election. On May 2, 1814, on the first ballot Webster was given ninety votes and Simeon Strong, one. This honor came to him, although he had barely fulfilled the legal residence requirements. On February 1, 1814, he had been appointed a Justice of the Peace and of the Quorum, an office he held continuously until 1822.

At the meeting of the Legislature, Mr. Webb of Weymouth objected that the proposal to secure amendments to the federal Constitution by the resolution of a Convention was unconstitutional, for "no state shall enter into any agreement or compact with another state." Webster replied that such a construction would prohibit two contiguous states from settling their boundary lines, and that the true meaning of the clause was, that two or more states should not combine to resist or thwart the national government. To other objections that the Convention would be an unconstitutional body, Webster said, "This sort of stuff has been very current at taverns and shops among the wiser ones who leave their business to settle the national concerns, which they are more ready to do than settle their grog-score." Further, he showed that in *The Federalist,* No. XL, Madison had upheld the legality of conventions. But neither precedent nor ridicule subserved Webster. The measure was lost, partly because negotiations looking toward peace had been undertaken by President Madison, and it was felt that interference might adversely affect their progress.

In October Governor Caleb Strong called a special meeting of the Legislature to consult on the state of affairs, "so threatening and destructive." The motion was put by Mr. Low of Lyman: "That a committee be appointed to confer with the New England States, and see if they will agree to appoint a committee to join with them, and repair to the city of Washington immediately . . . to make known to the President the general opinion of all the New England States in regard to the present war and the manner in which it was conducted, and inform him that he must either resign his office as President or remove those of his Ministers and other officers of the General Government who have, by their nefarious plans, ruined the nation." A less outspoken resolution was adopted, after a long debate in which Webster supported the measure. A committee of twelve was authorized to meet with similar committees from other states to request a revision of the Constitution "more effectually to secure the support and attachment of the people, by placing *all* upon the basis of fair representation."

Webster was not given membership on this committee, which carried through its task. The Convention met, passed a number of resolutions, sent its delegates to Washington, and then returned home to be assaulted by the opposition with cries of "traitor." Although the Convention hastened the treaty of peace, it was long represented as a subversive conspiracy against the safety of the nation. Theodore Dwight wrote in 1833 an elaborate history of the events leading up to the meeting, but odium clung to it. Two years later Webster attempted to tell the truth, but he succeeded no better. Harrison Gray Otis, who had suffered under the lash of criticism as much as any man, good-humoredly wrote Webster (May 6, 1840): "The adoption of [the resolution] was the consequence, not the source, of a popular sentiment, and it was intended by those who voted for it as a safety valve by which the steam arising from the fermentation of the times might escape, not as a boiler in which it should be generated. . . . We at Boston played only second fiddle to our country friends. . . . My impression is that the County of Hampshire was always foremost in these matters, and that if I had been hanged as a ringleader, you and your friends had been bound in honor to maintain my family." Webster, modestly omitting his part in the early preceedings, published his account of the origin of the Convention in his *Collection of Papers* (1843). In the May, 1815, meeting of the Legislature Webster was made chairman of the com-

mittee to distribute 5000 copies of the Hartford resolutions.
He was in at the beginning and end, even if he did not sit
in the Convention.

Webster was re-elected to the Legislature in 1815 and
1819. In these sessions he performed very much as he had
in the Connecticut Legislature. He served on many committees, spoke freely on every subject, and won for himself
a good deal of disfavor among his Boston enemies. Again
his political activities were used against him as a lexicographer. In the 1819 session he vigorously insisted that
Maine should be a sovereign state, although he seems not
to have used the argument which must have been uppermost
in his mind: if the North was to gain an equality of representation, it was necessary to create as many new states in
that region as had been formed in the South. Rather, he
spoke tenderly of his daughter Mary's grave in that distant
soil, and of the economic advantages which would accrue
from a separation. Scornfully he noted that many representatives fled before the final vote in order to prevent a
quorum from meeting. In the following session the Act
of Separation was passed, February 5, 1820. At this session
Webster pressed charges of graft against the State Printer.
When his evidence was tabled and when his plans for improved schools and state hospitals were shelved, Webster
surrendered any further desire to take part in Massachusetts
politics. Forthrightly he wrote to Solomon Smead of Green-
field: "The State of Massachusetts possesses a great deal of
talent, enterprize, and wealth, and individuals distinguish
themselves by many noble enterprizes of great public utility.
But, to be plain, Sir, I do not discover in this Commonwealth those comprehensive views of public interest and those
prospective measures which tend gradually to augment the
resources, the dignity, and prosperity of the State, which char-
acterize the proceedings of some other States. An immense
effect may be produced by small powers wisely and steadily

directed. But whatever may be my wishes, my efforts can have no effect. I have had so many intimations I am yet a stranger in the Commonwealth that I shall henceforth cease to concern myself with public affairs."

In the fall of 1816 Webster was nominated for Congress from his district. Immediately a hue and cry went up about electing an outsider, a newcomer, a man who was so unpopular in the State Legislature that he was not returned that year. A reply to these charges was made by "Hancock" in *The Hampshire Gazette,* October 30, 1816, but Webster failed of election.

On one subject Webster never lost an opportunity to press his opinions on his fellows: that was education. In the Legislature he constantly attempted to secure for Massachusetts a school fund similar to that which had been achieved in Connecticut by the sale of the Western Reserve. He proposed that small sums be appropriated annually and then be put out to accumulate by compound interest. "It is no less obvious from experience, than from the declaration of inspired Truth," he said, "that the training of children in the path of integrity and virtue is the best method of securing their future rectitude of conduct, their reputation, their influence, and their usefulness. . . . To draw from the obscure retreats of poverty the miserable victims of ignorance and vice; to enlighten their minds and correct their evil habits; to raise them to the rank of intelligent, industrious, and useful members of society, will ever be the object of deep solicitude with a wise legislature." At another time he stated: "I should rejoice to see a system adopted that should lay a foundation for a permanent fund for public schools, and to have more pains taken to discipline our youth in early life in sound maxims of moral, political, and religious duties. I believe more than is commonly believed may be done in this way towards correcting the vices and disorders of society." Webster's proposals were not adopted, but he initiated the movement that culminated so gloriously in the work of Horace Mann after 1837.

If at Boston he was not entirely successful, he redoubled his efforts in behalf of Amherst educational projects. In July, 1812, subscriptions were started for the establishment of an academy in Amherst. Dr. Parsons donated a plot of ground, and friends contributed a total of five thousand dollars with which a spacious, three-story brick building was erected in 1814. Samuel Fowler Dickinson, grandfather of Emily Dickinson, and Hezekiah Wright Strong circulated the lists and were largely instrumental in founding the institution. Webster was much interested in the new school, not only because he wished to send his children there, but also because of his immense enthusiasm for education. He could not contribute in a pecuniary way, but he lent all the aid he could by his pen and influence. He prepared many of the legal papers and labored in the Legislature of January, 1816, to secure an Act of Incorporation. When it was objected that four such institutions were already in existence in Old Hampshire, some of them suffering from the want of students, Webster replied: "The Academy at Amherst is in a prosperous condition; above five thousand dollars have been expended in a building. In the present county of Hampshire there is no other academy. Such seminaries, between the common school and the university, are useful and necessary." So successful was Webster that the Act was passed and signed on February 13, 1816; he became a charter member of the Board of Trustees.

Webster took a very active part in the Academy, visiting the school statedly, speaking to the students, and opening the doors of his spacious home for receptions and parties. Soon one hundred students were in attendance, this hearty support of the academy outdistancing the founders' expectations.

At the meeting of the Trustees on November 18, 1817,

Rufus Graves, Esq., proposed that a permanent fund be raised "in order to afford its instructions gratuitously to indigent young men of promising talents and hopeful piety, who shall manifest a desire to obtain a liberal education with the sole view to the Christian ministry, and who, on a reasonable probation, shall be adjudged worthy of the benefactions of the seminary." At the same time it was decided to found a professorship of languages. Friends were loath to give funds on so inadequate plan; consequently, according to Webster, "it was found necessary to form a plan for the education of young men for the ministry on a more extensive scale." On August 18, 1818, was adopted a "Constitution and System of By-Laws, for the raising and managing of a permanent Charitable Fund, as the basis of an Institution in Amherst, in the County of Hampshire, for the Classical Education of indigent young men of piety and talents, for the Christian Ministry."

Williams College in the northwest corner of Massachusetts had not prospered satisfactorily because of its distance from centers of population; it had been proposed, therefore, that the College be moved. A delegation of Amherst trustees visited Williamstown and presented the advantages of moving to Amherst. Silence greeting their proposal, the Amherst trustees determined to proceed by inviting a convention of Congregational and Presbyterian clergymen and laymen to approve and patronize the contemplated institution. As chairman of the committee, Webster sent out on September 11, 1818, a call for the convention. Sixty-nine men attended from Hampshire, Franklin, Hampden, and Worcester counties. The Reverend Joseph Lyman was chosen president. Webster read the proposed constitution. A committee reported favorably, but with the provision that the door be left open for "a union of interests with Williams College." Webster was appointed a member of the Amherst committee to wait upon the Williams trustees at their meeting in November, where were given a copy of the proceedings and resolutions of the convention, and such verbal representations of facts as were deemed useful and proper. Again the Williams trustees gave no answer.

The trustees of Amherst Academy on November 17, 1818, again appointed Webster as a member of a committee to present the claims of the town of Amherst to be the new seat of Williams College. He drew up a four-point address in which were stated the convenience of Amherst's situation, the salubrity of the climate, the cheapness of subsistence, and the advantages for literary and moral improvement in this and in future ages. An impartial committee chose Northampton as the most favorable site. Since this adverse decision rendered union impossible, the Amherst trustees voted on November 18, 1818, to proceed with their own project. Webster, now vice-chairman of the Board, was appointed chairman of the committee "to solicit subscriptions to the charitable fund and also for the foundation and support of a college." On July 6, 1819, Webster reported that the contributions in money and other property amounted to $51,404. Further negotiations with Williams College were attempted, but when the Legislature failed to permit the removal of that college, the Amherst trustees on March 15, 1820, carried out their plans by erecting a college building.

Webster had attempted to resign as a trustee because of illness. He had written to his daughter Harriet: "My nervous affections and the irregular action of the heart which I have had for forty years, seem to increase with age, and the inactive state of my stomach probably tends to increase those affections. These complaints are partly constitutional and partly induced by a sedentary and studious life. At times I have not thought it improbable that they may speedily end my earthly career." His colleagues smiled away Webster's notions that the age of sixty-two was an adequate excuse for retiring from the important undertaking. He continued, therefore, and energetically called upon all to redouble their efforts to provide funds. From Stephen Van Rensselaer he secured a gift of $150, and doubtless from many others he received smaller sums. When construction was stopped for want of funds, he wrote (June 27, 1820) to Jeremiah Evarts: "As I deem this a *very important* object, I take the liberty in my private capacity to ask you whether in this exigency we can find a few friends in Boston who will send us aid."

At the laying of the cornerstone of South College on August 9, 1820, Webster closed the ceremonies with an address, in which he again repeated the creed of education in the task of regenerating mankind:

The object of this institution . . . is one of the noblest which can occupy the attention and claim the contributions of the Christian public. It is to second the efforts of the apostles themselves, in extending and establishing the Redeemer's empire—the empire of truth. It is to aid in the important work of raising the human race from ignorance and debasement; to enlighten their minds; to exalt their character; and to teach them the way to happiness and to glory. Too long have men been engaged in the barbarous works of multiplying the miseries of human life. Too long have their exertions and resources been devoted to war and plunder; to the destruction of lives and property; to the ravage of cities; to the unnatural, the monstrous employment of enslaving and degrading their own species. Blessed be *our* lot! We live to see a new era in the history of man —an era when reason and religion begin to resume their sway, and to impress the heavenly truth, that the appropriate business of men, is to imitate the Savior; to serve their God; and bless their fellow men.

Mindful of the need for funds to forward the work of building and instruction, Webster called for increased gifts. The reward to the contributors he thus described:

And should success attend this establishment, how delightful to the friend of religion must be the thought, that he has thrown his mite into this treasury of the Lord! With what satisfaction will the sons of its benefactors hereafter hear it related, that a missionary, educated by their fathers' charity, has planted a church of Christ on the burning sand of Africa, or in the cheerless wilds of Siberia— that he has been the instrument of converting a family, a province, perhaps a kingdom of pagans, and bringing them within the pale of the Christian church! Who that duly appreciates the influence of the gospel in civilizing the savage, and in preventing or restrain- ing the disorders of civilized society, can hesitate a moment, even on motives of temporal advantage, to enrol his name among the benefactors of such an institution! No, my friends; the man who loves the peace and security *in this life*, must lend his aid to the propagation of the *gospel*, and contribute to give efficacy to its prin- ciples. The *gospel* only can convert swords into ploughshares and spears into pruning hooks—the gospel only can supersede the neces- sity of bolts and bars—the gospel only can dispeople the state prison and the penitentiary!

Following the ceremony of laying the cornerstone, Dr. David Parsons resigned his seat as president of the Board of Trustees of Amherst Academy, and Noah Webster was elected in his place. Dr. Parsons, because of his great age and infirmities, had been unable to meet with the trustees, so that the duties had fallen upon Webster long before his elevation to the presiding office.

As head of the trustees, Webster wrote many letters re- questing financial assistance in completing South College. To William Leffingwell, Webster explained (September 27, 1820) why the Calvinists urgently required a college to com- bat the Unitarian doctrines as taught at Harvard: "We want our Christian friends in this and the neighboring states to take an interest in this Great Enterprise, which has for its object the common benefit of the world; and we do hope that this infant institution will grow up to a size which will con- tribute to check the progress of errors which are propagated from Cambridge. The influence of the University of Cam- bridge, supported by great wealth and talents, seems to call on all the friends of truth to unite in circumscribing it. This is a cause of common concern, and we beseech our prosperous

Amherst, Massachusetts, in 1820. The white building on the right is Amherst Academy.

Amherst Church and Old South College, 1821.

friends in Connecticut, who love to do good, not to forget us. Any contribution however small will be gratefully received and soundly applied."

In 1821 Zephaniah Swift Moore of Williams College accepted the presidency of the new college; Gamaliel S. Olds and Joseph Estabrook became professors. The building was dedicated and the new officers inaugurated on September 18, 1821. Webster, as president of the trustees, made the introductory remarks and charged the officers. On the following day Amherst College opened with an enrolment of forty-seven students, and on this day Webster resigned. He was satisfied that the institution was well established; he had worked so faithfully for Amherst College that he had fallen behind schedule in his lexicographical work. At sixty-three, with a heart that cut capers, Webster had to think of the great, unfinished book. His letter of resignation frankly assigned this reason: "Experience has long since convinced me that a faithful discharge of my duties as a member of the Board is not compatible with my private pursuits; and nothing but a sincere desire to assist in giving some stability to the collegiate institution and insuring its success has for a long time prevented a resignation of my seat." Webster had looked upon his office as a call to active duty; that duty he performed wholeheartedly. He did not retain the office as a mark of honor, as he might have done; utility was the keyword in his philosophy: and when in justice to his own work he could not be useful he refused to be ornamental. In accepting his resignation, the Board of Trustees voted this resolution, "That the thanks of this Board be presented to him for his faithful services rendered to this Academy, both as a member and as President of the Board of Trustees, and also for his indefatigable exertions for the benefit of the Collegiate Institution."

In this service, as in all others, he had been "indefatigable," an adjective properly belonging to Webster. In the years following it was felt by some, Lucius Boltwood for example, that Webster had not been given due credit as "the master spirit in all these improvements." Another said that Webster's speech on inducting the first officers was the "confession of faith of Amherst College," and then added, "In the body corporate Webster might be called the brain and the mouthpiece, and the other ardent Christian projectors, the heart and hands and the feet which carried this daring visionary project into effect and gave it bodily shape and substance." Today there stands on the Amherst campus a heroic memorial monument to Webster as a symbol of that early youthful aspiration which carried him to success in so many activities. Or it may be a symbol of the spirit of pious and humane youth, a spirit Webster cherished.

As an educator Webster had now run the whole gamut. He had fostered improvements in elementary schools and had taught the wisdom of instructing each child in the classroom. He had assisted in founding two middle schools, Union School in New Haven and Amherst Academy. Now he had crowned his work with indefatigable labors in establishing a college. His Spelling Book everywhere was opening blinded eyes. The movement for the reform of American education was on. Now an elderly man with a monumental book to prepare, he could not take active part in the work which he had initiated. Others could do that, and others did. But he alone could compile An American Dictionary of the English Language.

The lexicographer had completed the work so far as he could with his own library facilities. It was necessary for him to be near a good library; a trip to Europe was inevitable. After a season of indecision as to whether the family should move to Boston or New Haven, Mrs. Webster elected New Haven. There were her dearest friends and her daughter Julia. During Webster's long absence abroad, Professor Goodrich could look after the business affairs of Webster and provide comfort for Mrs. Webster. In the summer of 1822, therefore, the Websters moved to New Haven where they took a small house at College and Wall Streets. From James Hillhouse a plot was purchased at the southwest corner of Temple and Grove Streets, and here Webster erected a commodious house the following year.

As avocations from his steady pursuit of philological investigations Webster proposed in 1822 to publish a collection of sermons, but this project failed. In 1823 he brought out *Letters to a Young Gentleman Commencing His Education: To which is subjoined a brief History of the United States.* This book combines Webster's conclusions on the subjects of government, religion, and philology, a curious compend filled with crotchets now familiar. Goethe said, "The best that a man can know cannot be told to youth." Webster, however, attempted in this book to give his "best" to college students. Another work was projected, an American version of the Bible, but theological professors were not yet ready for the innovation.

In 1823 Samuel F. B. Morse, son of Jedidiah Morse, was in New Haven painting portraits of the celebrities, among whom were Webster and James Gates Percival, the young poet whose works had just been acclaimed in England and America as the best yet written in America. At this time Percival, serving as editor of the *Herald,* a New Haven newspaper, was entering upon philological studies which would bring him into union with Webster. The portrait of Webster, photographically reproduced in the frontispiece of this book, is vastly superior in accuracy to the etchings commonly published.

At the annual commencement in 1823 Yale did itself honor by conferring the honorary degree of Doctor of Laws upon Webster. He had proved himself in the forty-five years since his graduation worthy of highest academic distinction by virtue of his political and literary activities. Today the Harkness Memorial Tower at Yale University is adorned with eight statues of eminent sons of that institution. On the north side in company with Nathan Hale, stands a marble portrait of Webster by the eminent American sculptor, Lee Lawrie. In memory as in life Yale reveres her patriot-scholar.

In June, 1824, Webster placed his affairs in order and with the loan of a thousand dollars from his daughter Harriet, who had also paid for the Morse portrait, Webster departed for a year's study in France and England. With his son William as a companion and amanuensis he sailed from New York on the ship Edward Quesnel for Havre on June 15, 1824. William's diary describes the twenty-one passengers, four of whom were ladies; unhappily for William, three of these were "old and ugly as Macbeth's witches." On the Fourth of July Webster gave a short address to his fellow passengers, "dwelling chiefly on the advantages that have actually accrued to both England and France since the separation of America from the old country, and closing with an invitation to the ladies and gentlemen of both those nations to join us in celebrating the glorious event." The old patriot carried his enthusiasm for America with him to Europe, just as in 1785 he had preached to the South the glories of New England.

Let us catch up the fallen strand of the lexicographer's activity and follow it to Webster's glorious triumph.

CHAPTER XVI

An American Dictionary of the English Language

Language is the only art which affects all people. Human beings can and do get long without money, dress, and ornament, but not without communication. Probably the greatest achievement of man was his discovery and improvement of language, for with that tool he has been able to report his knowledge and to codify his behavior. Although language study is considered by some persons a tasteless, boring, disagreeable, profitless occupation, it has always held a noble place in the history of scholarship. Aristotle, Quintilian, and Cicero prepared rhetorical treatises. Greek and Latin words were brought under comparison in ancient Rome, and a primitive type of comparative linguistics was begun. During the dark years of the Middle Ages linguistic study helped keep alight the flickering torch of learning. Early modern scholarship introduced the study of Hebrew as a means of interpreting the Old Testament correctly. Until the end of the eighteenth century, Greek, Latin, and Hebrew were the languages studied in the western world. Latin was considered decayed Greek, and no relationship between Hebrew and these other two languages was discoverable, although philosophers debated the question.

Late in the eighteenth century, through English officers stationed in India, interest arose in the Oriental languages; slowly the sacred books of the East were translated for the benefit of Europeans. In 1786 Sir William Jones declared that Sanskrit in relation to Greek and Latin "bears a stronger affinity, both in the roots of verbs and in the forms of grammar, than could possibly have been produced by accident; so strong, indeed, that no philologer could examine all three without believing them to have sprung from some common source, which, perhaps, no longer exists; there is a similar reason, though not quite so forcible, for supposing that the Gothick and the Celtick, though blended with a different idiom, had the same origin with the Sanskrit." Here was laid down a remarkable thesis of the unity of western languages. Jones found few converts to his theory, but Noah Webster, the itinerant lecturer on language and education, was one of them. The biblical version of the origin of language and the confusion of tongues had never been proved by philologists. Jones moved one step nearer proof; Webster determined to verify the narrative of the Tower of Babel by demonstrating the affinities of the languages of Western Asia with those of Europe.

Sanskrit remained an almost unknown language until after Webster had completed his Dictionary. In 1808 Friedrich von Schlegel published *Ueber die Sprache und Weisheit der Indier* [*On the Language and Wisdom of the Hindus*], the first work to evoke a lively interest in Hindu culture. In this book he first used the term "comparative grammar," which he said would give "entirely new information on the genealogy of languages, in exactly the same way as comparative anatomy has thrown light on natural history." As we have already seen, Webster in 1807 had enunciated a similar idea, although far more comprehensive because he included ethnography. Franz Bopp published in 1816 a treatise on the Sanskrit system of conjugations, but still no complete grammar nor any dictionary had come forth. Webster was, therefore, shut out of the knowledge of the most important new information yet revealed in linguistics, for the ancient Hindu grammarians had derived correctly the stems of words from the inflectional forms, and they had ascertained the laws of derivation and composition. Most im-

Two pages of Webster's manuscript of *An American Dictionary of the English Language* (1828).

portant of all, they had observed the vowel changes which took place in inflection and derivation. What had been misty in such forms as *sing, sang, sung; write, wrote, written,* now became clear. But in spite of the fact that this information did not reach Webster, he was right more times in his etymologies than he was wrong.

Modern linguistic science really dates from 1818, the year of the publication of Rasmus Kristian Rask's *Investigation of the Old Norse or Icelandic Language.* In this work the significance of the laws of sound was first recorded, but Rask did not perceive a complete regularity of development. Jacob Grimm, one of the two brothers noted for their fairy tales, gave in his *Deutsche Grammatik* [*German Grammar*] (1822–1837) the first clear explanation and systemization of consonant and vowel changes. He, too, erred, though "even where he erred he exerted inspiring influence." Bopp's *Vergleichende Grammatik* [*Comparative Grammar*] (1833) reached the high point of achievement in that bright morning season of philology. But none of these investigators attained any clear idea of the life and development of language. All of them erred at many points; particularly faulty was the exaggerated importance assigned to Sanskrit. Rask denied the relationship of the Celtic and Germanic languages, a point on which Webster supplied contrary evidence in his Dictionary; Bopp's definitive proof of kinship came in 1833.

The German universities took the leadership in these studies in comparative linguistics. The English dons clung to the three ancient languages and sneered at "dabblers in etymology" who were insisting that Dr. Samuel Johnson was an ignoramus. Noah Webster may have been tactless in the way he besmirched England's lexicographical saint, but the fact remains that the American schoolmaster was correct. It may seem an idle bit of guesswork to say that in 1817, when Webster completed his still unpublished Synopsis, the American philologist had penetrated more deeply into language problems—the hidden Sanskrit excepted,—and that he was more nearly correct in his theories and conclusions, than any Englishman and many Teutons. But the fact is capable of proof.

Rival groups, devotees of Johnson, Walker, Worcester, Richardson, and other lexicographers, poured out their scornful remarks against Webster. His book was said to have been defaced with pedantic ignorance and a tyro's errors. Webster erred, of course; but why Grimm's errors should be inspiring and Webster's the result of ignorance, must be left for unprejudiced minds to solve. Suffice it to say that Webster—that hidden mine of Sanskrit remembered—not only is America's first eminent lexicographer but also her first notable comparative philologist.

In his lexicographical creed, published in *The Panoplist* (July and August, 1807), Webster wrote: "The lexicographer's business is to search for truth, to proscribe error, and repress anomaly. . . . The compilers of dictionaries should not be 'dabblers in etymology," as many of them have been, but men of deep research and accurate philological knowledge. . . . The lexicographer should not be misled by his habits, nor biased by the caprices of eminent men." To this creed Webster remained faithful.

In 1807 Webster had mastered twelve languages. Steadily as grammars and dictionaries were made available, he penetrated the secrets of new languages or dialects. By 1813 he had learned twenty languages, seven of them being Asiatic or dialects of the Assyrian; these were: Chaldaic, Syriac, Arabic, Samaritan, Hebrew, Ethopic, Persian, Irish (Hiberno Celtic), Armoric, Anglo-Saxon, German, Dutch, Swedish, Danish, Greek, Latin, Italian, Spanish, French, Russian, and, of course, English. Later he added Portuguese, Welsh, Gothic, and the early dialects of English and German.

As soon as *A Compendious Dictionary* was printed, Webster set to work to complete his unabridged dictionary, which he had begun as early as 1800. His ambition was merely to correct such errors as had escaped former compilers and to supply such new terms as had sprung from modern improvements in science. But in searching the originals of English words, he found that the field of etymology had been very imperfectly explored. One discovery succeeding another, his curiosity was excited to persevere in the pursuit. Finding no safe clue through the labyrinth, he wrote, "I adopted a new plan of investigating, that of examining and comparing the primary elements, articulations or consonants of words in twenty different languages." After completing two letters of the alphabet, he turned aside to prepare a synopsis of the affinities of these twenty languages.

The Synopsis, which never reached publication, required ten years of steady labor. Webster's method of work was this: On a semicircular table, two feet wide, he placed his books; beginning at the right end of the table, he would thumb grammars and dictionaries while tracing a given word through the twenty languages, making notes of his discoveries. Many times a day did he follow this pendulum movement. At four o'clock Mrs. Webster brought him fruit or nuts and cake, a signal that the lexicographer should remove his eyeglasses and relax. Much caustic humor has been printed about Webster's Synopsis, the manuscript of which is in the New York Public Library. An examination of it reveals a mine of philological lore. It is not mere guesswork, but a serious effort to bring together words whose form might throw light on the affinities of languages and on the primary sense in each word. In this work may be seen Webster's knowledge of the interchange of consonants, since he based all his work on consonantal radicals. Often, too, his groupings indicate a clear understanding of the vexed problems of the relationships of vowels. The results of his research were embodied in his Dictionary; the Synopsis gave him the great grasp necessary for defining well the basic meaning of each word.

In comparing the Synopsis with the writings of other philologists, it must be remembered that Webster was interested in word relationships only so far as they clarified root meaning. Rask, Grimm, and the Teutonic scholars were at first engaged in morphological studies, in the similarities or differences in the forms of words, their inflections, etc. Later they followed the Hindu philologists into the laws of sound change. Although it is ideally true that complete morphological studies should have preceded the search for affinities, it is likewise true that Webster antedated in his own investigations the researches of the first great comparative grammarians. It is also true that Webster did not study the literatures of the languages he mastered; at times he erred in a meaning because he adopted a dictionary definition rather than the subtle nuance which literature supplies. But when it is remembered that Webster became a pioneer in this subject at the age of fifty, and that he prosecuted his lonely task in a land with few facilities for research and amid sneering detractors, the achievement of worthy results at all is marvelous.

Just as Webster was completing the Synopsis, John Pickering, who as a small boy had been brought up on the first edition of Webster's Spelling Book and who in 1809 had castigated Webster violently to Simeon Colton, published *A Vocabulary, or Collection to the Words and Phrases which have been supposed to be peculiar to the United States* (1816), in which he indirectly referred to Webster thus: "In this country, as in England, we have thirsty reformers and presumptuous sciolists, who would unsettle the whole of our admirable language, for the purpose of making it conform to their whimsical notions of propriety." Webster had endured patiently and quietly for five years the recurring newspaper and magazine squibs directed against him. This charge, however, came from too high a source to be ignored; with the bludgeoning power of his own integrity and high purpose behind his words, he mocked Pickering's amateur philology and made that man of prejudice wince.

"This is a heavy accusation, Sir, from a gentleman of your talents, liberality, and candor," Webster wrote. "It certainly becomes you, and the character you maintain in society, to learn the distinction between an attempt to find what the language is, and an attempt to unsettle its principles. Whether you number me with the thirsty reformers and presumptuous sciolists is a fact which I shall take no pains to discover, nor, if known, would the fact give me the smallest concern." On the animus of men in Massachusetts he wrote: "The unfriendly dispositions manifested towards me by men of high standing in the republic of letters, and particularly in this Commonwealth, and the virulence with which every effort to detect errors in long received opinions has hitherto been assailed; a virulence by no means compatible with a candid desire of improvement, and probably not warranted by the low estimate which even my opposers have formed of my talents, labors and public services; these dispositions, affording little ground to expect that any remarks of mine would have a salutary influence upon public opinion, have, at times, disposed me to withhold all strictures upon philological subjects, till I can prepare a more critical and extended treatise, than has yet been exhibited to the public. To a man who seeks his own tranquillity, and whose sole object is to enlighten and benefit his fellow-citizens, controversy, even when conducted with liberality, is extremely irksome; and, rather than be engaged in it, I would spend the small portion of life that remains to me in the humble walks of obscurity. In controversy with my fellow-citizens on any subject I will not be engaged. "

Webster picked apart Pickering's *Vocabulary*, again attacked Johnson and Lowth, defended the right of Americans to make and accept changes of language which grow out of their own conditions, and deprecated "the effects of a blind acquiescence in the opinions of men, and the passive reception of everything that comes from a foreign press." He repeated his declaration of independence: "My mind revolts at the reverence for foreign authors, which stifles inquiry, restrains investigation, benums the vigor of the intellectual faculties, subdues and debases the mind. I regret to see the young Hercules of genius in America chained to his cradle. . . . I will be neither frowned nor ridiculed into error and a servile imitation of practices which I know or believe to be corrupt. I will examine subjects for myself, and endeavor to find the truth, and to defend it, whether it accords with English opinions or not. . . . I trust the time will come when the English will be convinced that the intellectual faculties of their descendants have not degenerated in America; and that we can contend with them in LETTERS with as much success as upon the OCEAN."

Webster closed his sixty-four-page pamphlet, entitled *A Letter to the Honorable John Pickering*, with this disarmingly frank statement of his own estimate of his position among American writers: "I am not ignorant, Sir, of the narrowness of the sphere which I now occupy. Secluded, in a great measure, from the world, with small means and no adventitious aid from men of science; with little patronage to extend my influence and powerful enmities to circumscribe it; what can my efforts avail in attempting to counteract a current of opinion? Yet I am not accustomed to despondence. I have contributed in a small degree to the instruction of at least four millions of the rising generation; and it is not unreasonable to expect that a few seeds of improvement, planted by my hand, may germinate and grow and ripen into valuable fruit, when my remains shall be mingled with the dust."

It was not vanity that sustained Webster in his lonely task amid jeering catcalls. Nor was his work merely a scholarly avocation indulged in by an old man for something to do. The fiery patriotism of the days of '76 still burned brightly; Webster still cherished the old faith in America's power to equal England in literary achievement. Webster's conversion to fundamental Congregationalism deepened, almost sanctified, this long-standing nationalistic ambition. To the inner drive of patriotism was added the tremendously energizing force of religious purpose. Webster's zeal and stamina during the period between his sixtieth and eighty-fourth years cannot be understood without a reference to the buoyant power of these two concurrent impulses.

Webster had been an essentially religious man throughout his early life. His conversion in 1808, far from being a sudden acceptation of a sense of guilt as some writers have asserted, was in reality a symbol of the attainment of mental peace. All his life he had been changing his mind; at fifty he made up his mind and never changed it again. Like Lyman Beecher, Ralph Waldo Emerson, and Theodore Parker, younger contemporaries, Webster found religion to be the center of life's experience. To the great evangelistic movement of the first half of the nineteenth century, Webster lent his voice and pen: Each of his books fostered morality and piety. Even in the Dictionary he wrote, as illustrative examples of the use of words, many maxims or sentiments in religion, morality, law, or civil policy. The aging Yankee schoolmaster dwelt in a fortress not easily shaken by windy doubt or criticism.

In November, 1821, Webster had reached the letter H in his Dictionary, and he correctly estimated that he would complete the whole work in four years. Since America afforded inadequate materials, he and his son William set out in June, 1824, for France and England, as has been stated earlier.

Webster carried to Europe the same sharp eyes which he had taken to the South in 1785. With a geographer's care he noted every detail of the new scene; what he failed to state in his letters, William recorded in a diary. They complained of miserable hotel rooms, wretched food, and bad attendants. At Rouen, William wrote, "We were surrounded by a crowd of porters, all eager to get hold of our baggage, and it was with extreme difficulty that we could prevent them from taking it separate ways. Seven of these followers accompanied us to the Hôtel de France and had the impudence to demand thirty-five francs, or five francs each for about ten minutes' service! an imposition we could not submit to. After a severe wrangling with them, we summoned the Maîtresse d'Hôtel and requested her to give them eleven francs and dismiss them from the house." The diligence to Paris, a large clumsy wagon, had six horses, "not fit for a plough and with harnesses which would have disgraced the poorest beggars in America." In the great city board and lodgings were taken at Madame Rivieres, 19 Rue Bergère, at one hundred and eighty francs a month.

American friends immediately were sought out by the newcomers. On July 17 Samuel G. Goodrich, the "Peter Parley" of publishing fame, walked into the Hotel Montmorency, where he was staying, and there he saw a familiar figure: "I saw," he wrote in his *Recollections,* "a tall slender form, with a black coat, black small-clothes, black silk stockings, moving back and forth, with its hands behind it, and evidently in a state of meditation. It was a curious, quaint, Connecticut-looking apparition, strangely in contrast to the prevailing forms and aspects in this gay metropolis. I said to myself—'If it were possible, I should say that was Noah Webster!' I went up to him, and found it was indeed he. At the age of sixty-six, he had come to Europe to perfect his Dictionary!"

At the Bibliotheque du Roi, where he went on July 24,

Webster gasped at the sight of 800,000 books and 80,000 manuscripts in one collection. American college libraries owned a tenth of this number. Steadily he pursued his task of recording terms in science, taking time off to visit William who was studying French and with him to visit the opera, famous shrines, public buildings, and sites of interest. They dined with the American minister and consul, and with other American friends. William reported that the Church of St. Etienne du Mont, where Pascal and Racine lie buried, offered the place "in which I have seen the only appearance of genuine religious feeling, altho so enveloped in superstition." But when it was decided to leave Paris on September 13, William wrote: "I leave it with regret. If man were not an accountable being, I know of no spot under Heaven where one could pass an earthly existence with more delight."

After waiting three days in Dieppe for a packet, the Websters sailed to Brighton on September 17; two days later they were in London. By correspondence with Samuel Lee, Professor of Arabic at Cambridge University, Webster had made arrangements to spend the winter in Cambridge and to work in the University library. On September 21 they hired a chariot and a pair of horses, "preferring a private conveyance in this interesting country to a hasty ride in a crowded stage coach." William's account of Cambridge is worth recording: "My father is almost discouraged on account of the character Professor Lee gives of the inhabitants of Cambridge. According to his description of the people, and his account is confirmed by other respectable inhabitants, the morals of the greater part of the population are wretchedly depraved. Those families particularly who let lodgings know no distinction between *meum* and *tuum*. If the servant can find no opportunity to pilfer and cheat, the mistress will. This filching disposition is increased continually by the carelessness of the gownsmen of the University, who have no regard to expense, and to whom it is a matter of indifference whether they throw away their money or whether it is stolen. However, in spite of these discouragements, we have engaged a set of rooms, consisting of a parlor and bed rooms and dressing rooms for eight months. . . . The lady is rather prepossessing in her appearance and, trusting to her physiognomy, she is free from the vices so common here, and will be obliging and attentive to our wants." Of the University Webster wrote: "The colleges are mostly old stone buildings, which look very heavy, cold, and gloomy to an American accustomed to the new public buildings in our country."

Webster remained close to business in Cambridge. Only occasionally did he withdraw from his lexicographical labors, and then to support a worthy cause. On November 23 he attended a meeting of the Cambridge Bible Society. "As soon as I arrived," he wrote to his wife, "I had a written motion put into my hand, which I was to second and then make a speech. This was rather embarrassing, as I was a stranger and not prepared, but I did as well as I could. I told the Society what our people are doing in America for spreading the gospel, and among other things I told them that my fair countrywomen far outstrip the men in all works of Charity. The substance of my speech, with *half a dozen gross mistakes*, is published in the Gazette of this day. So you see, my name has gone abroad—how it will sound I do not know."

Because Professor Lee was ill at this time, Webster did not meet many of the Cambridge dons, but as time wore on his acquaintance widened. Lee examined the Synopsis and wrote that he was "much interested in the ingenuity of [Webster's] remarks." Thomas Musgrave wrote, when Webster left Cambridge on February 13, 1825, that he and his friends were "so sorry not to have formed an earlier acquaintance with a gentleman of such attainments and character." On leaving Cambridge, William noted in his diary: It is "a place endeared to us during a residence of five months by an acquaintance with some interesting families and some gentlemen of the University, whose uniform kindness to us will form a pleasurable source of recollections of this venerable seat of literature and science."

One statement of Webster shows with what excitement he, then in his sixty-seventh year with a heart that cut didoes and an over-active mind that often caused nightmares, reached the end of his gigantic research task: "I finished writing my dictionary in January, 1825, at my lodgings in Cambridge, England. When I had come to the last word, I was seized with a trembling, which made it somewhat difficult to hold my pen steady for writing. The cause seems to have been the thought that I might not then live to finish the work, or the thought that I was so near the end of my labors. But I summoned strength to finish the last word, and then walking about the room a few minutes, I recovered."

If the European visit brought to successful completion the manuscript of the Dictionary, it failed to achieve two other goals. Just as Webster had sought to bring a degree of unanimity in the treatment of yellow fever, so he had gone to England to achieve a similar agreement in the matter of the pronunciation of the English language. Letters were dispatched to Oxford University with an invitation to members of that institution to meet with Lee and other Cambridge professors and Webster, in an effort to adjust the principles of spelling and pronunciation so that both nations might follow a single code. Here might have been founded an international academy, but Oxford, unable to endure the cool effrontery of a Yankee schoolmaster's dabbling in affairs peculiarly English, did not reply.

In London Webster attempted through William E. Woodbridge, an American friend, and Richard Rush, the American minister, to secure a publisher for his Dictionary and Synopsis. Todd's Johnson was being prepared for a second edition at this time, and Charles Richardson, with the aid of many unpublished Horne Tooke manuscripts, was at work on his Dictionary; many of the booksellers were engaged in these enterprises. Publishers like Longman and Co. refused the offer of the manuscript. Webster had felt so sanguine about English publication, that he had procured through Daniel Webster a special Act of Congress by which the English edition might be imported into America free of duty. Nothing daunted by his failure, Webster placed his manuscripts in his trunk and engaged passage home. After a short tour through southern England, Webster and William embarked on May 8 on the ship Hudson. They landed at New York on June 18 and the next day were in New Haven.

A spontaneous celebration of the scholar's return took place at the Webster home. Members of the family had come to New Haven to greet their "dear Pa," and the Yale faculty and the townsmen turned out to greet him. Honor was given where it is most cherished, in one's own home.

For a time it appeared that Webster would have to finance the publication of the Dictionary himself. Early in 1826, however, Sherman Converse assumed responsibility for the publication, although Webster endorsed a large note. A prospectus was issued on March 3. James Madison, atoning for his failure to lend a friendly hand in 1809, immediately commended Webster's "learned research, elaborate discrimination, and taste for careful definition." In Boston, however, the old animus was revived by *The American Quarterly Review*, which denounced Webster's heretical notions about Johnson and Walker. Converse procured oriental types from Germany, but "everything else about the work," Webster told Madison proudly, "will be *American*."

A page from Webster's manuscript of *An American Dictionary of the English Language* (1828), in which seventy thousand words were defined. The entire manuscript is in Webster's own handwriting.

359

To assist in the gigantic task of reading proof and checking details, Webster secured the assistance of his son-in-law
William C. Fowler, who had married Harriet Webster
Cobb on July 26, 1825. Fowler, who had been preaching,
came to New Haven to prepare himself for a professorship
at Middlebury College. Denison Olmsted, later a Yale professor, checked the scientific terms, and James Gates Percival, the timid, eccentric, much buffeted poet, read proof.
On May 8, 1827, the printing was begun by Hezekiah
Howe; the last pages came from the printers in November,
1828. Percival, who had entered upon a study of the writings of Bopp, Grimm, and the other German philologists,
became a sore trial to Webster. And yet, because Percival
felt that he was the best fitted to see the work through the
press, he clung to this position as he had clung to no other.
As the printing progressed, he called errors to Webster's
attention; frequently their arguments ran deep into the
night. Percival wished to delay publication until every
etymology was correct, but Webster, seeing the sand run out
of the glass, went forward with the feeling that absolute
perfection was impossible. In later years it was said that
Percival had contributed much to the accuracy of Webster's
Dictionary, but his work is hidden. The moody poet represented the new order of linguistic students whose work was
piling up new proofs of the relationships of languages, but
their incomplete investigations had not yet upset Webster's
conclusions. Webster was correct in pushing his work
through the press; had he listened to Percival, the work
would have remained unfinished.

When the two bulky quarto volumes of *An American
Dictionary of the English Language* were delivered to the
subscribers, a swelling chorus of praise greeted the ears of
the seventy-year-old lexicographer. Praised were the successful etymological researches, the great vocabulary of 70,-
000 words (12,000 more than Todd's Johnson), the per-

spicuity of the definitions, and the careful distinctions in the many radiations of meaning in common words. There remained no doubt about Webster's success in surpassing Johnson. Here and there, however, especially among the English booksellers and publishers supporting Todd and Richardson, efforts were made to minimize the work. But E. H. Barker, an English scholar, promptly applied for permission to bring out an English edition. This appeared in parts between 1830 and 1832. Soon Webster became the standard in England, as he had become the standard in America by the adoption of the Dictionary in the halls of Congress and in the various American courts of law. In Germany "the profound learning" of Webster was acclaimed: Heinrich Meidinger paid a fine tribute to Webster in *Vergleichendes etymologisches Wörterbuch* (1833), and as late as 1852 the noted scholar, Felix Flügel, wrote appreciatively of Webster's superb work.

Webster's Introduction briefly outlined some of the discoveries he had made. Beginning with the assumption that the Genesis version of the origin of speech was correct, Webster explained how the nations were dispersed and how the original parent language disappeared into numerous dialects. But he insisted that a supernatural event was not necessary to produce the resulting confusion of tongues. While admitting that no satisfactory explanation had been made of the relationship between the Semitic and Japhetic families of languages, Webster tried to find points of contact. In this attempt to prove the correctness of the scriptural narrative, Webster laid himself open to criticism, because scholars poopoohed every suggestion that Hebrew had affinities with English. Webster also pursued to its end his theory of the origin of all words in verbs. Proudly he declared that his discovery of the radical significations of words constituted "an era in philology," and yet he also recognized that "some of the most important principles or rudiments of language have hitherto escaped observation, and that philology is yet in its infancy."

In spelling and pronunciation Webster followed in his great book the principles which he had laid down in *A Compendious Dictionary*. Some minor changes in the interests of regularity were made, and on the whole he became more conservative in pushing eccentric spellings like *lether*, *wo*, etc.

The nationalism of Webster appeared not only on the title page in the adjective "American" but also at length in the Preface. "The chief glory of a nation," Webster quoted Dr. Johnson, "arises from its authors"; and just as Johnson had expressed a wish to give celebrity to Bacon, Hooker, Milton, and Boyle, so Webster had the same ambition to honor Franklin, Washington, Adams, Madison, Jay, Kent, Irving, and others. "It is with pride and satisfaction," Webster wrote, "that I can place them, as authorities, on the same page with those of Boyle, Hooker, Milton, Dryden, Addison." Webster also declared that "the genuine English idiom is as well preserved by the unmixed English of this country, as it is by the best English writers. . . . I may go further and affirm with truth that our country has produced some of the best models of composition. The style of President [Samuel S.] Smith [of Princeton]; of the authors of the Federalist; . . . of Chancellor [James] Kent; the prose of Mr. [Joel] Barlow; of Dr. William [Ellery] Channing; of Washington Irving; of the legal decisions of the Supreme Court of the United States; of the reports of legal decisions in some of the particular states; and many other writings; in purity, in elegance, and in technical precision, is equalled only by that of the best British authors, and surpassed by that of no English compositions of a similar kind." This statement was literally slapped in the teeth of those Britishers and American Anglophiles who were then echoing Sydney Smith's disparaging remarks about American

AN

AMERICAN DICTIONARY

OF THE

ENGLISH LANGUAGE:

INTENDED TO EXHIBIT,

I. The origin, affinities and primary signification of English words, as far as they have been ascertained.
II. The genuine orthography and pronunciation of words, according to general usage, or to just principles of analogy.
III. Accurate and discriminating definitions, with numerous authorities and illustrations.

TO WHICH ARE PREFIXED,

AN INTRODUCTORY DISSERTATION

ON THE

ORIGIN, HISTORY AND CONNECTION OF THE

LANGUAGES OF WESTERN ASIA AND OF EUROPE,

AND A CONCISE GRAMMAR

OF THE

ENGLISH LANGUAGE.

BY NOAH WEBSTER, LL. D.

IN TWO VOLUMES.
VOL. I.

He that wishes to be counted among the benefactors of posterity, must add, by his own toil, to the acquisitions of his ancestors.—*Rambler.*

NEW YORK:
PUBLISHED BY S. CONVERSE.
PRINTED BY HEZEKIAH HOWE—NEW HAVEN.
1828.

Title page of Webster's great dictionary.

363

culture. In concluding his Preface Webster wrote: "It satisfies my mind that I have done all that my health, my talents, and my pecuniary means, would enable me to accomplish. I present it to my fellow citizens, not with frigid indifference, but with my ardent wishes for their improvement and happiness; and for the continued increase of the wealth, the learning, the moral and religious elevation of character, and the glory, of my country."

And finally this thankful prayer: "To that great and benevolent Being, who, during the preparation of this work, has sustained a feeble constitution, amidst obstacles and toils, disappointments, infirmities, and depression; who has borne me and my manuscripts in safety across the Atlantic, and given me strength and resolution to bring the work to a close, I would present the tribute of my most grateful acknowledgments. And if the talent which he entrusted to my care, has not been put to the most profitable use in his service, I hope it has not been 'kept laid up in a napkin,' and that any misapplication of it may be forgiven."

"And now, Dear Pod," Mrs. Webster wrote to Harriet on February 16, 1829, "I must tell a little about your Father and the babe which he had dandled twenty years and more. Mr. Converse writes that it is everywhere well received and the expectations of the public are fully answered. Letters are flowing in from every quarter to your father, praising the work with encomiums that amount almost to hyperbole." Among the first to eulogize the scholar and his work was Chancellor James Kent, who rapturously extolled the Dictionary as a monument to American genius. Webster modestly wrote to Harriet: "I have just been reading Chancellor Kent's flights of fancy." Webster appreciated the firm friendship of Kent, now of some thirty years' duration, and that of John Jay, too, for Jay had frequently sent Webster gifts of money to speed the work. As soon as the Dictionary was completed, Webster, despite the raw late

November winds, rode in his carriage to Jay's home in Westchester, New York, and there presented to the aged Justice the first two completed sets.

The edition of 2500, at twenty dollars a set, moved quite rapidly, but Converse went bankrupt as a result of speculations, and the work became tied up in litigation. A new issue became impossible, and the market really remained unsupplied. Webster made very little profit from the work, his receipts prior to Converse's failure having been barely sufficient to pay the editorial assistants. For a time the English edition was imported, but this recourse hurt Webster's pride. Other books appeared, too. Joseph E. Worcester, who in 1829 had prepared for Webster an octavo abridgment of the great dictionary, shoveled together a large book in 1835, and Richardson's two volumes appeared in 1836–7. English compilers took Webster verbatim and by a slight reshuffling made new books. In self-defence at the age of eighty, Webster mortgaged his home and brought out a second edition in 1841. He saw the work through the press, his undimmed gray eyes still holding up under the terrific strain of proofreading. The first signature was impressed on October 22, 1839, and the work was completed on January 30, 1841. The title page and Advertisement give the year as 1840; this error resulted from the unusually long period required in printing the work.

The history of Webster's Dictionaries and the cultural history surrounding them, would require a volume to detail, but the main facts deserve a summary here. On Webster's death in 1843 George and Charles Merriam purchased the unsold stock of the 1840 edition, and determined to make this work their sole object in business. They engaged Webster's son-in-law, Professor Chauncey A. Goodrich, to edit an edition in 1847. Marketed in one volume at six dollars a copy, this work took immediate hold, and the presence of a Webster Dictionary in almost every literate

household dates from this year. Dr. Noah Porter, later
president of Yale, edited the 1864 edition, the famous *Unabridged*. In 1890 came *Webster's International Dictionary*
in which the vocabulary was increased to 175,000 entries. In
1909 came *Webster's New International Dictionary*, and in
1934 appeared the Second Edition, completely rewritten and
revised. This latest work, the result of many years' preparation by a permanent staff and several hundred consultant
specialists, has carried to perfection those ideas of lexicography which Webster enunciated in 1807 and exemplified
twice during his lifetime. It is a far cry from the lonely
schoolmaster's 70,000 entries to the 600,000 in the latest
edition. The honor of this great achievement, of course,
belongs to the publishers for their scholarly ideals in continuously correcting and improving the original. This is
exactly what Webster wished.

Meantime there had come many editions of smaller
works drawn from the large books. Of the hundreds of
such issues, many of them pilfered compilations or abridgments, it is not necessary to speak. One finds them everywhere in the world. Large dictionaries also grew out of
Webster's original quartos. About 1850 there was edited
by John Ogilvie, a Scottish schoolmaster, *The Imperial Dictionary of the English Language*. This dictionary was Webster's 1828 edition plus a large amount of new material.
Later came the immense *Century Dictionary*, edited by Professor William Dwight Whitney of Yale. This work was
founded on Ogilvie's *Imperial*. *The Standard Dictionary*
was begun on the plan of the 1847 Webster, but the characteristic features of Webster's work were abandoned. Late
in the nineteenth century a printer reproduced the 1847
edition by means of photoengraving and sold vast quantities
at a low price. Webster, even in the original editions, has
been the mark of perfection aimed at by all succeeding lexicographers.

The Dictionary War, mention of which has been made

several times, deserves a special monograph, so interesting is it as a manifestation of American culture in the 1850's and 1860's. Indeed, this topic vied with the Civil War as material for argumentation. This inky war arose from the publication in England in 1853 of Joseph E. Worcester's *Universal and Critical Dictionary of the English Language* with the following statement on the title page: "Compiled from the Materials of Noah Webster, LL.D., by Joseph E. Worcester." In the American edition Worcester had specifically stated in his Preface that he had not used Webster's work at all, but this portion of the Preface was elided in the English edition. Merriams published a pamphlet, entitled *A Gross Literary Fraud Detected,* in which the brazenness of their competitors was handled roughly. Jenks, Hinckling, and Swan, publishers of Worcester's Dictionary, responded with the charge that the trick had been perpetrated by Merriams in order to manufacture a reputation for Noah Webster, who, it was alleged, "was a vain, weak, plodding Yankee, ambitious to be an American Johnson, without one substantial qualification for the undertaking, and the American public has ignored his pretensions!" Pamphlet echoed pamphlet in a discussion of the relative merits of Webster and Worcester. Magazines and newspapers took sides in the contest. *The Atlantic Monthly* declared in favor of the Bostonian, Worcester: "We believe Dr. Worcester's Dictionary to be the most complete and accurate of any hitherto published. He intrudes no theories of his own as to pronunciation or orthography, but cites the opinions of the best authorities, and briefly adds his own where there is occasion. He is no bigot for the spelling of certain words." College faculties threshed over the matter, and Legislatures debated the question. Massachusetts gave each school its choice; Webster was chosen by an overwhelming majority. The New York Legislature voted to put Webster in every school. Congress retained Webster.

A good bit of heat had been generated. Testimonials by

the acre were broadcast. Washington Irving found himself endorsing both works, although he had noncommittally written that he followed British spelling because of the vogue of his books in England. In his *Life of Washington* he referred to Worcester as the author of "the pugnacious Dictionary." William Cullen Bryant, as editor of *The New York Evening Post* and inheritor of Coleman's hostility to Webster, reprinted a caustic article from *The Democratic Review* and added these remarks: "We would gladly contribute toward the expense of having it read twice a year in every school-house in the United States, until every trace of Websterian spelling disappears from the land. It is a melancholy proof of the amount of mischief one man of learning can do to society, that Webster's system of orthography is adopted and propagated by the largest publishing houses, through the columns of the most widely circulated monthly magazine, and through one of the ablest and most widely circulated newspapers in the United States."

It was melancholy, indeed, that Grub Street compilers were not given precedence over the scholar who had spent sixty years in studying the English language. In the end, however, Webster's mode prevailed, partly because of the widespread use of the Spelling Book, and partly because the 1864 *Unabridged* became unmistakably the best English dictionary in the world.

There is much that might be said about the 1828 Dictionary to explain its lasting qualities. In the final analysis the definitions can be said to have made it supreme in its own day. After all, a dictionary is designed to give word meanings; anything else is a gift from the author or publisher. Webster had included much encyclopedic material, and the latest large Webster, in continuing the tradition, has brought within one set of covers, a vast array of reference material. But fundamentally the definitions are most important. In this department Webster was supreme and unequalled. James A. H. Murray, editor of the Oxford *New English Dictionary on Historical Principles,* a monumental work requiring nearly fifty years for its completion, said Webster was "a born definer of words."

Webster believed that "There is a primary sense of every word, from which all others have proceeded; and whenever this can be discovered, this sense should stand first in order." Here the Synopsis brought results. And here he surpassed Johnson, who placed synonyms and definitions of a single word in haphazard array. Further, Webster took great pains to discriminate the various senses in which a word was used. These he illustrated with great care. The following explanations, under *clever* and *lend,* will show how the difference between English and American usage was made clear:

Clever, *a.* 4. In *New England,* good-natured, possessing an agreeable mind or disposition. In *Great Britain,* this word is applied to the body or the intellect, in respect to adroitness of action; in *America,* it is applied chiefly to the temper or disposition. In *Great Britain,* a clever man is a man of a pleasing, obliging disposition, and amiable manners, but often implying a moderate share of talents.

Lend, *v.t.* 6. To let for hire or compensation; as, to *lend* a horse or gig. [This sense is used by Paley, and probably may be common in England. But in the United States, I believe, the word is never thus used, except in reference to money. We *lend* money upon interest, but never *lend* a coach or horse for a compensation. We use *let.*]

Colloquialisms were included, and *New England* was flaunted bravely as authority for the correctness of such words as *spell,* "a short time," and *whittle:*

Whittle, *v.t.* To pare, or cut off the surface of a thing with a small knife. Some persons have a habit of *whittling,* and are rarely seen without a penknife in their hands for that purpose. [*This is, I believe, the only use of this word in New England.*]

Particularly painstaking was Webster in annotating idiomatic expressions. Under *make* he defined among others, *to make port, to make a difference, to make a bed, to make amends, to make good, to make free with, to make love, to make merry, to make suit, to make over, to make out,* and *to make of.* Similar distinctions were made throughout the whole work.

Few "naughty" words were admitted. The American code in this respect had been established by the first native dictionaries. Whether it is an act of squeamishness to exclude unmentionables and unprintables, the fact is that recent dictionaries are as fastidious in this respect as was Webster. Certain words in Shakespeare's *Henry V*, for example, have had to depend upon an oral transmission of pronunciation and explication. Even Dennie's request that "bundling" be defined, was refused.

To Webster the Dictionary was, next to the Bible, the great schoolbook. He wanted a copy placed on the desk of every schoolmaster where students might consult it freely without permission. Like a lodestar it might guide youth, not only to accuracy, but also to correct thoughts on the fundamentals of religion and morality. Cautiously he labored to eliminate sectarian bias, but just as actively he wrote into his illustrations such sententious wisdom as his wide experience had given him. How well the Dictionary supported the cause of religion, can be gleaned from the following illustrations from Webster's own pen; it must be remembered that Webster also drew a multitude of illustrative remarks from the precepts of the Bible and of writers like Franklin and Bacon:

Fanatic, *n.* A person affected by execessive enthusiasm, particularly on religious subjects; one who indulges wild and extravagant notions of religion, and exhibits strange motions and postures, and vehement vociferation in religious worship. Fanatics sometimes affect to be inspired, or to have intercourse with superior beings.

Happy, *a*.2. . . . The pleasurable sensations derived from the gratification of sensual appetites render a person temporarily *happy;* but he only can be esteemed really and permanently *happy,* who enjoys a peace of mind in the favor of God.

Hope, *n*.2. . . . A well founded scriptural *hope* is, in our religion, the source of ineffable happiness.

Improve, *v.i.* . . . It is the duty, as it is the desire, of a good man to *improve* in grace and piety.

Indebted, *a*.2. . . . We are *indebted to* our parents *for* their care of us in infancy and youth; we are *indebted to* God for life; we are *indebted to* the Christian religion *for* many of the advantages, and much of the refinement, of modern times.

Instrument, *n*.2. . . . Bad men are often *instruments* of ruin to others. The distribution of the Scriptures may be the *instrument* of a vastly extensive reformation in morals and religion.

Internal, *a*. . . . The *internal* evidence of the divine origin of the Scriptures is the evidence which arises from the excellence of its precepts, and their adaptation to the condition of man, or from other peculiarities.

Interposition, *n*.2. . . . How many evidences we have of divine *interposition* in favor of good men.

Knowledge, *n*.1. . . . We can have no *knowledge* of that which does not exist. God has a perfect *knowledge* of all his works. Human *knowledge* is very limited, and is mostly gained by observation and experience.

Love, *n*.1. . . . The *love* of God is the first duty of man, and this springs from just views of his attributes or excellences of character, which afford the highest delight to the sanctified heart. Esteem and reverence constitute ingredients in this affection, and a fear of offending him is its inseparable effect.

Love, *v.t*.1. . . . The Christian *loves* his Bible. . . . If our hearts are right, we *love* God above all things, as the sum of all excellence, and all the attributes which can communicate happiness to intelligent beings. In other words, the Christian *loves* God with the *love* of complacency in his attributes, the *love* of benevolence toward the interests of his kingdom, and the *love* of gratitude for favors received.

Marriage, *n.* . . . *Marriage* was instituted by God himself, for the purpose of preventing promiscuous intercourse of the sexes, for promoting domestic felicity and for securing the maintenance and education of children.

Meritorious, *a.* . . . We rely for salvation on the *meritorious* obedience and sufferings of Christ.

Offensive, *a.* . . . All sin is *offensive* to God; rude behavior is *offensive* to men; good breeding forbids us to use *offensive* words.

Prepare, *v.t.* . . . Holiness of heart is necessary to *prepare* men for the enjoyment of happiness with holy beings.

Profane, *a.*1. . . . A man is *profane* when he takes the name of God in vain, or treats sacred things with abuse and irreverence.

Rectitude, *n.* . . . *Perfect rectitude* belongs only to the Supreme Being. The more nearly the *rectitude* of men approaches to the standard of the divine law, the more exalted and dignified is their character. Want of *rectitude* is not only sinful, but debasing.

Reverence, *v.t.* . . . We *reverence* superiors for their age, their authority, and their virtues. We ought to *reverence* parents and upright judges and magistrates. We ought to *reverence* the Supreme Being, his word, and his ordinances.

Sabbath-breaking, *n.* . . . All unnecessary secular labor, visiting, traveling, sports, amusements, and the like, are considered as *Sabbath-breaking*.

On the subject of education the Schoolmaster to America had much to say; indeed, one can trace through the Dictionary his whole theory of education. Here are some of the thoughts which by now are quite familiar to the readers of this biography:

Government, *n.*4. . . . Children are often ruined by a neglect of *government* in parents.

Habit, *n.*4. A disposition or condition of the mind or body, a tendency or aptitude for the performance of certain actions, acquired by custom, or a frequent repetition of the same act. *Habit* is that which is held or retained, the effect of custom or frequent repetition. Hence we speak of *good habits* and *bad habits*. Frequent drinking of spirits leads to a *habit* of intemperance. We should endeavor to correct evil *habits* by a change of practice. A great point in the education of children, is to prevent the formation of bad *habits*.

Incapacity, *n.* . . . . There is a *natural incapacity* in children to comprehend difficult propositions in logic or metaphysics, and a *natural incapacity* in men to comprehend the nature of spiritual beings.

Increase, *v.i.* . . . . Knowledge *increases* with age and study; passion and enmity *increase* by irritation, and misery *increases* with vice.

Indulgence, *n.* . . . . How many children are ruined by *indulgence!* *Indulgence* is not kindness or tenderness, but it may be the effect of one or the other, or of negligence.

Inferior, *a.2.* . . . . Pay due respect to those who are superior in station, and due civility to those who are *inferior.*

Ingredient, *n.* . . . . Addison wondered that learning was not thought a proper *ingredient* in the education of a woman of quality or fortune.

Instruct, *v.t.* . . . . The first duty of parents is to *instruct* their children in the principles of religion and morality.

Learn, *v.t.* . . . . It is much easier to *learn* what is right, than to unlearn what is wrong.

Parent, *n.* . . . . The duties of *parents* to their children are to maintain, protect, and educate them.

Prejudice, *n.* . . . . Innumerable are the *prejudices* of education; we are accustomed to believe what we are taught, and to receive opinions from others without examining the grounds by which they can be supported. . . . . A judge should disabuse himself of *prejudice* in favor of either party in a suit.

Prerogative, *n.* . . . . It is the *prerogative* of a father to govern his children.

Hundreds of other definitions or illustrative sentences might be given to show how thoroughly Webster wrote the best elements of his philosophy into his book. Here are twenty-eight, some curious, some weighted with the author's crotchets, and some rich in Franklinian common sense:

Cow, *n.* The female of the bovine species of animals; a quadruped with cloven hoofs, whose milk furnishes an abundance of food and profit to the farmer.

Dandy, *n.* [Fr. *dandin,* a ninny, a silly fellow.] A fop, a coxcomb; one who dresses himself like a doll, and who carries his character on his back.

Friendship, *n.* . . . *True* friendship is a noble and virtuous attachment, springing from a pure source, a respect for worth or amiable qualities. *False* friendship may subsist between bad men, as between thieves and pirates. This is a temporary attachment, springing from interest, and may change in a moment to enmity and rancor.

Generally, *adv.* . . . Men are *generally* more disposed to censure than to praise, as they *generally* suppose it easier to depress excellence in others than to equal or surpass it by elevating themselves.

Happiness, *n.* . . . Perfect *happiness,* or pleasure unalloyed with pain, is not attainable in this life.

Have, *v.*6. . . . We *have* to encounter strong prejudice.

Hoist, *v.*3. To lift and move the leg backward; a word of command used by milkmaids to cows, when they wish them to lift and set back the right leg.

Honor, *n.*6. True nobleness of mind; magnanimity; dignified respect for character, springing from probity, principle, or moral rectitude; *a distinguishing trait in the character of good men.*

Impudence, *n.* . . . Let a man of sixty attempt to enumerate the evils which his *impudence* has brought on himself, his family, or his neighbors.

Impunity, *n.* . . . No person should be permitted to violate the laws with *impunity. Impunity* encourages men in crimes.

Inducement, *n.* . . . The love of money is an *inducement* to industry in good men, and to the perpetration of crimes in the bad.

Inestimable, *a.*2. . . . The privileges of American citizens, civil and religious, are *inestimable.*

Infatuation, *n.*2. . . . All men who waste their substance in gaming, intemperance, or any other vice, are *chargeable* with infatuation.

Kill, *v.t.* . . . A strong solution of salt will *kill* plants.

Modesty, *n.* . . . Unaffected *modesty* is the sweetest charm of female excellence, the richest gem in the diadem of their honor.

Neglect, n. . . . The *neglect* of business is the cause of many failures; but *neglect* of economy is more frequent and injurious.

Patriotism, *n.* . . . *Patriotism* is the characteristic of a good citizen, the noblest passion that animates a man in the character of a citizen.

Press, *n.*3. . . . A free *press* is a great blessing to a free people; a licentious *press* is a curse to society.

Property, *n.*11. *Literary property;* the exclusive right of printing, publishing, and making profit by one's own writings. No right or title to a thing can be so perfect as that which is created by a man's own labor and invention. The exclusive right of a man to his literary productions, and to the use of them for his own profit, is entire and perfect, as the faculties employed and labor bestowed are entirely and perfectly his own. On what principle, then, can a legislature or a court determine that an author can enjoy only a *temporary property* in his own productions? If a man's right to his own *productions in writing* is as perfect as to the *productions* of his farm or his shop, how can the former be abridged or limited, while the latter is held without limitation? Why do the *productions* of *manual labor* rank higher in the scale of rights or *property*, than the *productions* of the *intellect?*

Promise, *n.*3. . . . An *expressed promise* is one expressed in words or writing. An *implied promise* is one which reason and justice dictate. If I hire a man to perform a day's labor, without any declaration that I will pay him, the law presumes a *promise* on my part that I will give him a reasonable reward, and will enforce such *implied promise.*

Sauce, *n.* . . . *Sauce*, consisting of stewed apples, is a great article in some parts of New England; but cranberries make the most delicious *sauce.*

Scold, *v.i.* . . . A *scolding* tongue, a *scolding* wife, a *scolding* husband, a *scolding* master, who can endure?

Stove, *n.*2. A small box with an iron pan, used for holding coals to warm the feet. It is a bad practice for young persons to accustom themselves to sit with a warm *stove* under the feet.

Swear, *v.i.*4. To be profane; to practice profaneness. Certain classes of men are accustomed to *swear*. For men to *swear* is sinful, disreputable, and odious; but for females or ladies to *swear* appears more abominable and scandalous.

Swine, *n.* . . . . The swine is a heavy, stupid animal, and delights to wallow in the mire.

Taste, *v.i.*2. . . . . Apples boiled in a brass kettle, sometimes *taste* of brass.

Vice, *n.*2. . . . . *Vice* is rarely a solitary invader; it usually brings with it a frightful train of followers.

Vice-gerent, *n.* . . . . Kings are sometimes called *God's vice-gerents.* It is to be wished they would always deserve the appellation.

Obviously, Webster's Dictionary was a highly personalized volume, despite the great care with which he suppressed Johnsonian prejudice and animosity. None of his own writings was drawn on for illustrative examples, and, vain though he was said to be, he frequently expressed doubts about his etymologies, about his success in linking languages, and about the exact sense of a word. Only once did Webster insert the first person:

Witness, *v.t.* To see or know by personal experience. I *witnessed* the ceremonies in New York, with which the ratification of the constitution was celebrated in 1788.

Yes, not only did Webster *witness* the procession in New York in 1788, he also *witnessed* the procession of English words in the process of formation from the time of the dispersion to 1828. And just as he described the 1788 parade, so he described with amazing accuracy, fullness, and discrimination the marshaled columns of English and American words. The completion of the Dictionary was the feat of a pre-eminent scholar who had not forgotten his days of schoolmastering, and who therefore continued to instruct his fellow citizens through the world's most important secular book.

CHAPTER XVII

The Spelling Book War

THE long drama, in which Webster exhibited heroic courage while battling against prejudice to produce America's first work of monumental scholarship, *An American Dictionary of the English Language,* was not without its subplots and minor villains. The ideal for which Webster had fought during the whole of his career was American national unity. He preached nationalism in politics, nationalism in education, and nationalism in literature. "Literature," be it remembered, in Webster's day embraced the whole of the liberal arts as well as belles lettres. Although his campaign for nationalism succeeded, there were detractors and opponents always spewing invectives against the first consistent advocate for national advancement by means of scholarly and literary enterprise. Before entering into detail in the controversy that arose in 1827 over the Websterian and Walkerian modes of spelling, let us examine the forces which conflicted in the establishment of nationality, and the various manifestations of the national spirit which achieved successful goals.

The American aristocrats, some of whom haltingly supported the American Revolution, retained an inveterate love of royal splendor and English modes of thought, fashions, and manners. It was believed by some persons that even President Washington affected royal prerogatives and a too courtly manner. President John Adams, similarly and to a greater degree, was accused of subserviency to England and of a fondness for monarchical notions. Even Joel

Barlow, as we have seen, rushed off to Boston in 1785 to unite the Massachusetts military leaders with those of Connecticut to give a monarchical government to this country by force. A few years later Barlow, converted to the principles of the French Revolution, emitted caustic denunciations of England and of the English faction in America. Jefferson, with identical notions, assailed Hamilton as leader of the British faction. But as Webster so clearly pointed out, the two political parties, the Federalists and Democrats, vied with each other in professing greater and greater love for a foreign country rather than love for America. If the Federalists erred in loving England too much, the Democrats erred similarly in their blind love of France. Webster had taken his position between these two groups; he demanded the destruction of the hegemony of Europe and the establishment of a native tradition based on high principles of political neutrality and intellectual independence.

The French Revolution passed from a glorious civil war, fought for the enfranchisement of downtrodden humanity, into terroristic butchery and a means of Napoleon's personal aggrandizement. Love of France receded in this country, except among the hardiest Jeffersonians, and even they hated England more than they loved France. On this ground alone the War of 1812 could have been fought. These Francophiles, however, did not attempt to substitute the French language or French books for American; they operated chiefly in politics. Although Jefferson wrote privately in 1813 about the need for an American language, he himself hired foreign teachers for his University in 1826, rejecting applications from such men as Josiah Meigs, who had lost his position at Yale for espousing the Jeffersonian party. It was not until after the War of 1812 that the Democrats grew at all noisy about a national American literature, but everything they wrote had been stated and restated by New Englanders for thirty and more years. It was as much

the defeat of France as the victory of America in 1815 that
created the shift in attachment. Possibly, too, British reviewers' continuous mocking of America and popular American sentiment in the lower strata of society helped to bring
about this zest for nativism.

The Anglophiles loved England for more subtle reasons
than the Democrats loved France. The Bostonians, with
Harvard College as the inspiring agent, looked back to "Our
Old Home," as England was affectionately called, and
sighed for a nod of approval of their imitative manners.
They gossiped about England, avidly read letters describing English styles and mannerisms, imported English books,
diligently incorporated into their speech the affectations
of Cockney stage players, and swore by Johnson as the only
true god among lexicographers and by Walker as the only
authority on pronunciation. Joseph Dennie, lifted into ecstasy by Tom Moore's friendliness on an American visit in
1804, redoubled his efforts to make *The Portfolio* the organ
of English thought and manners and language in America.
John Pickering, too, adopted the same tone, as did the best
citizens of Charleston, South Carolina. This was an aristocratic manifestation, emanating from a powerful small group,
powerful in the sense that they controlled a university or
two, and many schools, or that they pontificated from pulpit
or court of law. Essentially, however, they were not hostile
to American nationalism, except as they wished it to imitate English example.

There were equally powerful aristocratic groups fighting
for thorough nationalism in American art, literature (in its
original broad signification), and science. It was lamented
that Benjamin West, an American, should have to go to
England, where he became president of the Royal Academy;
and George Clymer attempted to establish an art gallery
and an outlet for artistic production in this country. Webster wrote and talked for improved music instruction and

appreciation, particularly in the vocal department; he taught music at Baltimore in 1785, and he supported Adgate in Philadelphia in 1786–1787. *The Royal American Magazine* as early as 1774 in Boston had called upon Harvard graduates to prove that America could produce a worthy literature. This call was echoed by Hugh Henry Brackenridge in his *United States Magazine* in Philadelphia in 1779. Brackenridge was particularly incensed at the remarks of Abbé Raynal, Buffon, and Robertson, who declared that all things degenerated in America and that soon Americans would be little better than orangutans. Webster repeated the nationalistic call in *The American Magazine*. Among the members of the Philological Society was William Dunlap, who set to work on plays with native themes. James Nelson Barker wrote strident nationalistic dramas. Charles Brockden Brown espoused the cause of a native literature in his various magazines and in the Preface to his novel, *Edgar Huntly*. "American Tales" crowded the magazines, and a unanimous plea for native authorship came from writers in newspapers and magazines. Newspaper Parnassian columns invited the native muse to strum its lyre. The call for an American bard echoed through American poetry and criticism, finding expression in the writings, among others, of Freneau, Bryant, Whittier, Emerson, Thoreau, Lowell, and Whitman. There is no more clearly defined and more consistently reiterated subject in American literature than this.

The American Philosophical Society announced a prize award in 1796 for "the best system of liberal Education and literary instruction, adapted to the genius of the Government of the United States," and the Society printed the two best essays. The Society also furthered the collection of materials relating to America and encouraged native research and writing. The Massachusetts Historical Society and the Connecticut Academy of Arts and Sciences similarly called for the advancement of American historical and scientific investigations. Samuel Latham Mitchill, voluminous writer on miscellaneous and scientific subjects, proposed American chemical and geographical terminologies, and his magazine, *The Medical Repository*, lent a helping hand to every manifestation of American genius. He supported Webster, and to the harassed lexicographer wrote a letter proposing the name of "Fredonia" for this country, since we lacked, and still do lack, a generic name. "There is scarcely anything for which we are suffering more, in our public and national capacity," declared Mitchill on April 13, 1803, "than for want of a 'name.' Without it we cannot be completely national, nor properly express national feelings, concerns, relations of any kind." The usurpation of the name "America" by the inhabitants of the United States is at present a source of irritation to our Central and South American neighbors.

A definite intention of developing an American common law, departing in many respects from the findings of English law courts and Blackstone, animated American legal thinkers, because American democratic institutions varied so greatly from the monarchical English forms. James Kent's *Commentaries* did for the law what Webster's *American Dictionary* did for language. The religious and missionary magazines fostered a nationalistic spirit in the cause of saving the world for Christ. Comparisons were made between the work of oversea and local agencies in the conversion of Indians and Negroes; even Webster made such a comparison tacitly in his talk at Cambridge, England, in 1824. The nationalism of this work may be read large in the romanticized achievement of Marcus Whitman, who was said to have saved the Northwest Territory for the United States.

If among many intellectuals there was a strongly expressed nationalistic feeling, among the lower strata of American society the feeling was even more intense. Webster's text-books had set the tone of American instruction in 1783, and few books departed in spirit from his patriotic nativism. Jedidiah Morse had prefaced *The American Geography* (1789) with this remark: "It is calculated early to impress the minds of American youth with the idea of the superior importance of their own country, as well as to attach them to its interest." Little children, whether of native or foreign birth, imbibed American ideals and American dreams as they read the works of Washington and Jefferson, the speeches of the great orators of the Revolution, the verses of our patriotic poets, and the narratives of military glory in primers, spellers, and readers. These children taught their parents to sing "Yankee Doodle," "Columbia, Columbia, to glory arise" by Timothy Dwight, and other inspiriting lyrics. The newspapers and the preachers taught lessons of national pride. Mason Weems's *Life of Washington*, with its fabulous lore of the cherry tree and its bitter denuncia-tion of Benedict Arnold, gave many patriotic texts to Fourth of July speakers, nearly all of whom referred to our gallery of heroes on each successive national festival. Wirt's *Life of Patrick Henry* and Ramsay's *Life of Washington* gave similar materials. A veritable patriotic mythology arose, and this became the unifying American hagiology. James Gates Percival's patriotic lyrics, Bryant's nature poems, Irv-ing's legends of the Catskills, and Cooper's Indian and American heroes, all very popular in the early 1820's in textbooks, gave a literary aura to popular prejudices. These writers were accorded praise in England, and, despite the sneering British travelers and reviewers, Americans literally patted their own backs in self-satisfaction.

It was in the midst of all these nationalistic manifesta-tions that Webster worked; it is evident, of course, that he had much to do with developing them. If he was only com-paratively solitary, there being so many other patriots around him, he was essentially alone, because he fought almost singlehanded the battle for the retention of native pronunciation and American spelling. Even if the spelling was his own, it nonetheless was American. The Anglophiles disliked Webster's choice of the drawling, nasal dialect of New Englanders as his basic pronunciation. These uncouth Yankee rustics dwelt apart from the refining influences of university society; they lacked grace, polish, and urbanity. Naturally, Webster's adoption of this seemingly degenerate patois as standard shocked the would-be Brahmins, who assailed the schoolmaster for soiling American children's minds and tongues with American words and pronunciation. Essentially, therefore, so far as Webster's linguistic ideas were concerned, it was class hostility that opposed the adoption of his dictionaries and Spelling Book.

The earlier books competing with Webster's Spelling Book took over wholesale Dilworth's or Walker's or Johnson's or Sheridan's orthography and orthoëpy. Gradually all others except Walker faded as authoritative, and, partly because the Bostonian group accepted Walker, new textbooks followed Walker. The battle for the lucrative spelling book textbook trade settled down to a conflict between Walker and Webster as authorities. Walker possessed the awesome respectability of having taught Edmund Burke's son, as Edward Everett reminded Webster. Essentially the battle of 1784 was to be refought: should Americans send to England for books to teach their children the abc's?

Some three dozen books had been published to give Webster's the deathblow. Three were British in origin. Dilworth lingered for a time, but even such an active undercutter as Patten in Hartford had been unable to push it successfully. William Perry's *The Only Sure Guide to the English Tongue* gave Webster the most competition until about 1815. Lindley Murray, Pennsylvania born, captured the market with his Reader, but his Spelling Book, though popular for a time, did not take firm hold. Here and there an American author won a local market, the cities almost uniformly refusing to use Webster. Three books, each using Walker as a base, came out in 1825 in upper New York State. Each was prefaced with a denunciation of Webster, and each praised Walker. Webster noted the new opponents, but trusted they would fail as had all others. His own book had not been altered since 1804. Meantime he had spelled many words in a new way in *A Compendious Dictionary*, but had retained his Spelling Book orthography in his *School Dictionary*. Slightly different would be his spellings in *An American Dictionary*. Shrewdly he had let the Spelling Book alone, knowing that innovations and changes would destroy the sale or invite competitors to supplant the old book. Not until 1827 did a competitor sense the sales value of an attack based on Websterian inconsistency.

Rumblings of vigorous opposition sounded over the Catskills to New Haven in 1826. Webster, with his ear always to the ground, detected in the New York books a threat of destruction, not only to the income by which he was enabled to compile his great book, but also to American self-determinism in language. His hands were tied by the immense labor of putting his Dictionary manuscript into shape for the printer; also, the copyright and printing licenses would not expire for several years. To stem the rising tide of Walkerian enthusiasm, Webster broadcast a statement of his nationalistic ambitions on March 14, 1826:

As I was an ardent republican in principle [in 1783], and had exposed myself as a volunteer to the hardships of the field in defense of my country, I felt a peculiar pride and a degree of enthusiasm in contributing my feeble efforts to detach my country from an undue dependence on our mother country for our opinions and books. . . . I desired to see my countrymen disposed to give a due preference to all their native productions, to promote all efforts to exalt the literary character of their country, and to disengage themselves from the thraldom of an overweening reverence for foreign opinions and authority—*a species of slavery that hangs like a mill-stone about the neck of all literary enterprize in the United States.*

Having repeated his declaration of literary independence, Webster went on to state that his efforts had succeeded for some years, but that recently the current of opinion had changed. "Nothing now will be received and counte-nanced which is not *British,* or sanctioned by British au-thority. . . . Whenever we manifest a disposition to re-volt from their authority, the reviewers apply the lash freely and whip us into the ranks. Whether this species of despotism is to be exercised over us till we really lose all literary ambition and national spirit and become as despicable as they would represent us—despicable at least in the view of others, if not in our own—cannot be certainly foreseen. One thing is obvious—the false opinion respecting the su-periority of British erudition, is to us a national calamity of no ordinary magnitude."

Then Webster launched into a renewed attack upon John-son's deficiencies as a lexicographer and upon Walker's inaccuracy as an orthoëpist. He had spent six months in England to settle this very problem, Webster declared, and he had been assured by eminent scholars that Walker en-joyed no critical standing at all. "You know," Webster wrote to W. C. Fowler, "that the utterance of many Walkerisms operates on me like a box on the ears." Of his latest com-petitors he wrote:

In order to accomplish their object, it has been found expedient to depreciate my work, and to charge me with *innovation* and with *introducing a system of orthography and pronunciation, in many re-spects, vain and pedantic.* Surely, if this is true, if my book is really a bad one, I have been very much deceived, and I have done not only injury, but great and extensive injury to my country. If this is true, I should deeply regret my zeal and my labors, for I have certainly loved my country and have cordially devoted myself to its best interests. But I have examined some of the books which are

sent into the world to correct the evil I have done. One of them
[by Elihu H. Marshall] is little less than a copy of mine—it contains *almost all my tables,* with no alteration except the transposition
of a few words. Not less than sixty or seventy pages of it are wholly
mine—and what is more, the *pronunciation is mine,* with the exception of a few words. And this work is ushered into the world
under a different name and recommended by distinguished characters, who probably did not know they were recommending *my*
book as the work of another man, and a book published in violation
of the copy-right law of the United States!

Although the chief plagiarist had been Marshall, Lyman
Cobb alone responded. He sent items to the newspapers,
spoke to teachers, and initiated an active campaign, not only
in support of his own book, but also against all others. He
offered a prize through *The Albany Argus* for the best dissertation on spelling books used in American schools. When
no manuscript appeared to claim the reward, he himself
meticulously examined all the published writings of spelling-
book-makers and broadcast his findings in *A Critical Review of Noah Webster's Spelling-Book* (1828) and in the
Preface to a new edition of his own Spelling Book. In the
Advertisement to his pamphlet, Cobb asked his readers to
con thirty-six pages of microscopically fine type and then "to
decide whether Mr. Webster's book with all its evident
defects ought to be retained longer in use," and, if not,
which of the other books should replace it.

Cobb predicated his assault on the ground that the recent
efforts of legislatures and societies to improve common
school education made it necessary "that correct systems of
education be adopted." First in importance is the spelling
book: "It is the first elementary work placed in the hands
of the scholar. From this he derives his earliest impressions of the nature and utility of the language in which he
is to speak and write. From this book he acquires habits of
thought and expression; the tone and modulation of voice
which distinguish him generally throughout life: from this

he is to acquire the practice of spelling and pronouncing
correctly; qualifications which give great force and effect
to whatever is spoken and written." Then Cobb proceeded
to his analysis of Webster's book, first paying this compliment:

Webster's spelling book was founded upon and succeeded Dilworth's. It was so superior to its predecessor, in many respects, as
to acquire an immediate and unparalleled popularity, which it has
sustained with little interruption for more than *forty years*. So
magical indeed has been the charm of popularity woven around it,
that all desire for, or efforts to improvement, seem to have been
paralyzed; and it is not until within a few years, that any successful
attempts have been made to improve upon this popular system. The
merits of Mr. Webster's book have been duly considered by me; and
while I would award to him the just meed of praise for timely efforts in the cause of education, I am not disposed to deny, that,
since our systems of instruction have undergone much change, and
the elements of our language have been more closely investigated
and more clearly defined, useful improvements in the department in
which Mr. Webster was so successful may be made, if they be not,
in fact, from circumstances and the spirit of the age absolutely
required.

In his analysis Cobb pointed out every inconsistency in
Webster's book, both in respect to the earlier dictionaries
and the editions prior to 1827. It was a convincing indict-
ment, but it protested too much. The captious quality of
the investigator, too anxious to find all wrong, and the small
type of the pamphlet gave the author less success than he
merited. Webster in replying could merely admit the presence of inconsistencies and to regret that "No English book
is consistent with itself," a truthful statement, but one that
could not exculpate the creator of "an American standard."
Cobb shot right back: "Hence, it must be admitted that
Mr. Webster's zeal for something different from English
led him to adopt innovations without regard to their defects,
propriety, consistency, or uniformity; for he has not carried

a single innovation through the language; and, instead of producing arguments to convince the American people of the utility of his innovations in orthography, he has adopted an easier method, that of condemning every English lexicographer, without reserve, who has been so presumptuous and unfortunate as to disagree with his (Webster's) favourite notion of innovations in orthography."

Elihu H. Marshall, who had been reproved similarly but less strenuously by Cobb, noted in his Preface (Rochester, 1829): "Many of the words, the orthography or pronunciation of which he considers erroneous, are in strict accordance with the text of Walker. I cannot better illustrate the difficulty of attaining to perfect accuracy than by mentioning the fact, that even the sagacious author above alluded to [Cobb] had left a far greater number of errours in his own work, than he has discovered in mine." E. Hazen ridiculed the controversy in the Preface to his *Speller and Definer* (Philadelphia, 1829), by showing that deviations from Walker were found chiefly in such words as *honor* and *public*. "But the friends of literature need not be alarmed at the few deviations from their favorite author, whether he be John Walker or Noah Webster; since, with the exceptions just mentioned, they will be hardly perceived, or but slightly regarded, except by the hypercritical."

Cobb was not to be shaken off quite so easily as this. He carried his criticism to teachers' meetings, made exhibits of parallel pages, and secured long lists of recommendations. In the summer of 1827 Webster toured the whole of New York State, partly as a vacation from the grinding labor of reading proof on the Dictionary and partly to see his aging brother Abraham, but in every city and village he took time to answer Cobb. In the following summer he again made the tour, and he also made a hurried trip through New England. Indeed, every summer until his death, he took his horse and carriage and spent at least two months on the road. He lectured teachers' meetings, addressed Dartmouth and Amherst college students, and on one occasion spoke to an audience at seven thirty in the morning.

When *An American Dictionary* was published, Cobb secured a copy and ran through it as meticulously as he had examined the Spelling Book. He discovered that Webster had been more inconsistent than any other lexicographer, that his book was "particularly objectionable" as a standard of orthography, and that "Mr. Webster has exhibited a greater want of decision than any of his predecessors." In the definitions words were spelled differently from the main entries. Similarly scrutinized was the Octavo Dictionary, abridged by Joseph E. Worcester, who departed from Websterian forms on occasion. Daniel Barnes, a New York City schoolmaster, flew to the support of Webster in *The Red Book* with a highly encomiastic review of all of Webster's works. Barnes had been employed by Webster to edit *The American Spelling Book* in order to bring it into conformity with the great dictionary, and to fit it to the needs of the New York City teachers. Barnes died in an accident before he had executed his commission, and the task was handed to another New Yorker, Aaron Ely, who for a thousand dollars helped to build *The Elementary Spelling Book*. How much he actually did on the book, it now cannot be learned. To Cobb's assertions that Ely actually compiled the whole work, Webster answered merely by saying, "It is a palpable falsehood I will not notice." The base of the book is so obviously *The American Spelling Book*, that Ely's work must have consisted largely of rearranging and reclassifying certain elements. He may have added some of the many new sententious and proverbial passages. Cobb had so thoroughly pointed out the changes needed in the book, that he himself might have taken credit for all improvements. Webster spent two months of the summer of 1829 in New York City working on the book, so that at most Ely worked as a collaborator. In his Preface Webster acknowledged "the advice and assistance of some of the most experienced instructors in New York."

Cobb rested his case until 1831. Meantime Webster had been busy abridging his Octavo Dictionary into a Duodecimo for the use of schools. He worked daily for six hours at this task during several months in 1829. He engaged no amanuensis, but wrote out the whole manuscript in his flowing longhand style.

The problem of copyright annoyed Webster, too; he had asked Daniel Webster in 1826 to secure a better law than the existing one which gave protection only for fourteen years, with the right of one renewal by the author himself for fourteen years. Noah Webster wanted perpetual copyright, but Daniel Webster could not sponsor such a law. He wrote: "I confess frankly that I see, or think I see, objections to make it perpetual. At the same time I am willing to extend it further than at present." A law was not produced, nor indeed was one enacted until 1831.

In December, 1830, when William W. Ellsworth, Webster's son-in-law, was unable to force a bill through the Judiciary Committee of the House of Representatives, of which he was a member, Webster moved down to Washington to lend his presence in the cause. Everywhere he was greeted cordially. Although the members of Congress felt little interest in such a law, they told Webster, as he wrote to Harriet, "They had learned in my books—they were glad to see me, and ready to do me any kindness in their power. They all seemed to think also that my great labors deserve some uncommon reward. Indeed," Webster went on, "I know of nothing that has given me more pleasure in my journeys, the last summer and this winter, than the respect and kindness manifested towards me in consequence of the use of my books. It convinces me that my fellow citizens consider me as their benefactor and the benefactor of my

country." On December 28, 1830, he called upon President
Andrew Jackson, who insisted that Webster dine with him.
The old Federalist felt slightly uncomfortable at the dinner table of the leading American Democrat. His description of the event shows how nationalistic were his New England prejudices:

"We sat down at six o'clock and rose at eight. The President was very sociable and placed me, as a stranger, at his
right hand. The party, mostly members of the two houses,
consisted of about thirty. The table was garnished with artificial flowers placed in gilt urns, supported by female figures
on gilt waiters. We had a great variety of dishes, French
and Italian cooking. I do not know the name of one of
them. I wonder at our great men who introduce foreign customs, to the great annoyance of American guests. To avoid
annoyance as much as possible, the practice is to dine at
home, and go to the President's to see and be seen, to talk
and to nibble fruit, and to drink very good wines. As to
dining at the President's table in the true sense of the word,
there is no such thing." Having written this much, Webster
thought what a tidbit this item might be for the anti-
Jackson papers, and so he scratched large quotations marks
around the passage from "We had" to the end, and then
went on: "The foregoing passage in commas might well
appear in the prints, but the writer must not be known!"

On the evening of January 3, 1831, Webster lectured
for an hour in the House of Representatives "before a respectable number of ladies and gentlemen. It was," Emily
Webster Ellsworth wrote, "an interesting lecture to all who
heard it. Some complained it was too short. He spoke
nearly an hour. The darkness and humidity of the weather
prevented some from attending. I think, however, enough
were present to get the bill through. All I believe who
heard him were convinced. He said nothing by way of self-
praise—perfectly indirect. He urged no claims. He said,

should the bill for extending the copyright law be carried successfully, he should rejoice for himself, for his family, for his country. I think it will succeed."

Early in February, largely through the efforts of Daniel Webster and Ellsworth, the bill passed both Houses. By its provisions copyright protection was extended in the first instance to twenty-eight years, and fourteen more on a renewal by children or widows. By an error "to him" was omitted, so that an author could not secure the renewal himself. To remedy this defect, Noah Webster asked Daniel Webster at a later session to amend the Act. The lexicographer was quite correct in stating, "I have reason to think my presence here has been very useful in this affair," for it was his white-haired presence in Washington during ten weeks that gave urgency to the proposition. Of his efforts, beginning in 1782, Webster wrote in *A Collection of Papers* (1843): "In my journeys to effect this object, and in my long attendance in Washington, I have expended nearly a year of time. Of my expenses in money I have no account; but it is a satisfaction to me that a liberal statute for securing to authors the fruits of their labors has been obtained."

While he was in Washington, Webster secured from more than one hundred members of the Judiciary and of both Houses signatures endorsing the whole Websterian series of books, from the great Dictionary to the Spelling Book. This testimonial, together with a great number of others, was published in a small pamphlet and scattered the length and breadth of the nation.

Cobb flew into a tantrum at the sight of the new leaflet. Converse, as publisher of the Dictionary, had made several slighting allusions to Cobb, "recently a schoolmaster in one of our western villages, who has had the misfortune to compile a Spelling-Book and small Dictionary." On October 10, 1831, therefore, he wrote a new "emphatic" Introduction to all his anti-Webster articles and published the whole series, in still smaller type, in a fifty-six-page pamphlet. Not only did he repeat the old catalogue of errors, but he secured affidavits to the effect that Ely had compiled the Spelling Book. In conclusion, Cobb commented on Webster's business methods:

> I regret, in closing this Introduction, the necessity of animadverting upon the malevolent and unwarrantable aspersions in which Mr. Webster has thought proper to indulge, in a pamphlet recently published by him, containing the recommendations of his Series of Books, accusing others of plagiarism, and stigmatizing them with the appellation of "Peddling Compilers," when it is notorious that for the last three years he has been making tours through the country, and by appeals to the sympathies of individuals, has succeeded in procuring for his works an introduction to which their comparative merits would never have entitled them. The propriety of such a course for proselyting, and for procuring the names of individuals, as recommendatory, whose opportunity and business totally disqualify them for giving an opinion founded upon knowledge, may reasonably be questioned, a course which it is humbly conceived would never be resorted to, where personal feelings had not usurped the reins of reason and candour.

Cobb secured for his books an immense popularity by this continuous assault upon Webster. Several millions of copies of his various books were sold before they lost the market because of their Walkerian spelling. But at no time did he successfully challenge the supremacy of Webster's book. Webster's reply to Cobb's pamphlet exhibited some of the acidulousness of the earlier years of journalism: "The tenor of his remarks discovers indeed a degree of persevering malevolence rarely exhibited even in this world of evil; but the weakness of the man must be equal to his malevolence, if he supposes that twenty wagon loads of such pamphlets distributed by the mail would do me any harm or himself any good." *The New York Daily Advertiser* remarked editorially: "Mr. Webster's reputation as a philologist cannot be materially affected by such small criticism."

One by one the newer books adopted Websterian spelling, even as they plagiarized the Spelling Book. Nathan Guilford's *The Western Spelling Book* (Cincinnati, 1831) took over many of Webster's tables, two of the fables (The Country Maid and The Partial Judge), and the Familiar Lessons of Harriet and Mary and of William reciting the table of coins. The number of such examples of plagiarism is too large to detail here, but it is evident that Webster, the spelling-book-maker, was the object of imitation as much as Webster, the lexicographer. Schäfer and Koradi, Philadelphia publishers of German textbooks, took over the four Fables remaining in *The Elementary Spelling Book* and turned them into German slightly tinged with "Pennsylvania Dutch." William Holmes McGuffey adopted Webster's spelling in his universally used Readers. Charles Sanders, in adopting Websterian spelling, wrote (*Spelling Book*, Andover, 1839): "It is important, therefore, that the youthful learner should acquire a knowledge of that orthography and pronunciation which he is to meet in almost every book which he subsequently peruses." John G. M'Call prefaced his *New English Spelling Book* (Norwich, Conn., 1844) with both an objection to Walker and this comment on Webster: "It is regarded, however, as a matter of gratulation to teachers, that Webster's Dictionary has become so generally acknowledged as a standard work in this country. On this basis, it is believed, a good degree of uniformity in the spelling and pronunciation of our language will, at no distant day, be attained." The controversy dragged along for years, however. Worcester's Dictionary (1835) gave rise to a host of spelling books with his orthography, some by Worcester himself. These writers also warred on Websterian innovations. Joseph Griffin published in 1836 *A Summary of Some of the Most Prominent Defects in Webster's Elementary Spelling-Book*, largely a restatement of Cobb's strictures. Alonzo B. Chapin of New Haven intro-

duced in 1841 his new book with such a violent denunciation of his neighbor, that *The Hampshire Gazette* remarked:
"It is sad to see that the veteran of letters, the venerable Dr.
Webster, compelled, on the wintry verge of the autumn of
life, to turn literary constable and endeavor almost single-
handed to drive the multifarious herd of poachers from his
ancient and rightful province in literature." In the 1850's
the Spelling Book war coalesced with the Worcester-Webster
Dictionary War and continued until the end of the century.

The Elementary Spelling Book gained momentum during the years. Webster corrected errors as he found them,
and several times after his death the pronunciation was more
rigidly determined by diacritical marks. In this department Webster himself had been weakest; he despaired of
securing uniformity, although that goal had been aimed at.
Probably the chief criticism that can be leveled against him,
was a failure to study methods of notation and to perfect a
satisfactory phonetic system. By 1859 *The Elementary* was
called the "National Standard," and the publishers, who
had purchased the highest speed steam press available for
the work, thus described their activity: "They print at the
rate of 484 copies per hour, during 10 hours of each of the
310 working days of the year: or 4,840 copies per day. Being over 1,500,000 per annum." And they closed their
Advertisement with this comment from Jefferson Davis:
"Above all other people we are one, and above all books
which have united us in the bond of common language,
I place the good old Spelling-Book of Noah Webster. We
have a unity of language no other people possesses, and we
owe this unity, above all else, to Noah Webster's Yankee
Spelling-Book."

With that itching desire to do good as long as his life
lasted, Webster prepared seven more schoolbooks. Two
were introductions to *The Elementary Spelling Book*. The
first of these, *The Elementary Primer* (1831), was a small

paper-bound pamphlet of thirty-six pages, highly illustrated with pictures of familiar things. Webster objected to the tendency to use many pictures in the larger works, so that this book was a compromise for the benefit of children. Stereotyped, it passed through many editions. Among its poems was the ever popular "Twinkle, twinkle, little star." The second, put forth because many printers continued to print against his wishes the old spelling book, was *The New American Spelling Book for the Use of Primary Schools in the United States* (1833). This contained much of the old material, although many new sententious passages were added.

In *The Teacher; a Supplement to the Elementary Spelling Book* (1836) Webster organized thousands of words under their respective subject headings and gave simple definitions. He began with human relations, and then worked through anatomical, biological, geological, religious, publishing, political, etc., terms. Then he listed prefixes and suffixes, and placed words under their Latin and Greek roots. At the end he placed "A Moral Catechism" and "Wisdom and Benevolence of God Manifested in the Works of Creation," two compositions which he himself believed of importance to the newer schools as was "The Shorter Catechism" to the earlier. The book, a handy guide for teachers, was similar to recent publications designed to increase one's vocabulary.

Three reading books were among the seven new publications. *Biography, for the Use of Schools* (1830) contained thirty-seven brief biographies of characters from Homer to Cowper. Twenty-one Americans were honored, including Governor John Webster. Seven scriptural heroes, including Jesus, were characterized. *The Little Franklin: Teaching Children to read what they daily speak, and to learn what they ought to know* (1836) presented in words of one and two syllables lessons and truths which might be useful in the common affairs of life. It was in a sense *The Prompter*, rewritten for children. The old Part III of the *Institute*, the Reader, had long been out of print. Many schoolmasters remembered its nationalistic lore and urged that it be reprinted. In 1835 Webster refurbished it by adding a number of interesting items of the "wonders of the universe" type, selections illustrative of the newly opened West, and a new group of patriotic pieces. In his own new writings Webster stressed again his Federalistic political notions.

Most important, since it was widely used, was the *History of the United States* (1832). Webster had been first to include American history in schoolbooks, but not until 1832 did he publish a work under this title. First had been his brief statement in *An American Selection* (1787); this statement had been amplified and improved for Jedidiah Morse's *The American Geography* (1789) and, with some changes, for *A Collection of Essays and Fugitiv Writings* (1790). A more extensive account of American history, with much geographical and constitutional lore, was given in the first two volumes of *Elements of Useful Knowledge* (1802–1804). Considerably abridged, these historical passages were reprinted in *Letters to a Young Gentleman* (1823). The preparation of the *History* seemed imperative to Webster, because most of the new writers, Abiel Holmes, Emma Willard, Salma Hale, John Marshall, Jessie Olney, and Charles A. Goodrich, had either omitted much pertinent material in political history or had prepared "jacobinical things," to use Webster's phrase. Some of these authors, too, had lifted passages from Webster's earlier publications.

The *History* began with a discussion of the origin of the human race, and proceeded through descriptions of the Teutonic race, the settling of the Saxons in England, the peopling of America by aboriginals, the settlement of Mexico, and the discovery and settlement of America. Webster traced the hand of God and the influence of Christianity in the wonderful work of establishing the new western nation. His paragraph on the origin of civil liberty is notable:

Almost all the civil liberty now enjoyed in the world owes its origin to the principles of the Christian religion. Men began to understand their natural rights, as soon as the reformation from popery began to dawn in the sixteenth century; and civil liberty has been gradually advancing and improving, as genuine Christianity has prevailed. By the principles of the Christian religion we are not to understand the decisions of ecclesiastical councils, for these are the opinions of mere men; nor are we to suppose that religion to be any particular church established by law, with numerous dignitaries, living in stately palaces, arrayed in gorgeous attire, and rioting in luxury and wealth, squeezed from the scanty earnings of the laboring poor; nor is it a religion which consists in a round of forms, and in pompous rites and ceremonies. No; the religion which has introduced civil liberty, is the religion of Christ and his apostles, which enjoins humility, piety, and benevolence; which acknowledges in every person a brother, or a sister, and a citizen with equal rights. This is genuine Christianity, and to this we owe our free constitutions of government.

No less remarkable, because the interpretation has been offered as novel in recent histories, are the following two paragraphs, in which Webster honored the Puritans as the founders of the first genuine republics in the world:

For the progress and enjoyment of civil and religious liberty, in modern times, the world is more indebted to the Puritans in Great Britain and America, than to any other body of men, or to any other cause. They were not without their failings and errors. Emerging from the darkness of despotism, they did not at once see the full light of Christian liberty; their notions of civil and religious rights were narrow and confined, and their principles and behavior were too rigid. These were the errors of the age. But they were pious and devout; they endeavored to model their conduct by the principles of the Bible and by the example of Christ and his apostles. They avoided all crimes, vices, and corrupting amusements; they read the scriptures with care, observed the sabbath, and attended public and private worship. They rejected all ostentatious forms and rites; they were industrious in their callings, and plain in their apparel.

They rejected all distinctions among men, which are not warranted by the scriptures, or which are created by powers or policy, to exalt one class of men over another, in rights or property.

The Puritans who planted the first colonies in New England, established institutions on republican principles. They admitted no superiority in ecclesiastical orders, but formed churches on the plan of the independence of each church. They distributed the land among all persons, in free hold, by which every man, lord of his own soil, enjoyed independence of opinion and of rights. They founded governments on the principle that the people are the sources of power; the representatives being elected annually, and of course responsible to their constituents. And especially they made early provision for schools for diffusing knowledge among all their members of their communities, that the people might learn their rights and their duties. Their liberal and wise institutions, which were then novelties in the world, have been the foundation of our republican governments.

To this work, as to several others, Webster subjoined "Advice to the Young," a series of precepts on moral, social, business, and political conduct. Webster's ambition in preparing his textbooks—and in this he succeeded—was: "I endeavor that all my books for schools should contain valuable matter and truths that will last." No schoolmaster labored more continuously than Webster to elevate the moral tone of society. With a sense of finality he wrote in the Preface to the *History:* "Republican government loses half its value, where the moral and social duties are imperfectly understood, or negligently practiced. To exterminate our popular vices is a work of far more importance to the character and happiness of our citizens, than any other improvements in our system of education."

CHAPTER XVIII

AN AMERICAN VERSION OF THE BIBLE

"WHEN my maker has nothing further for me to do, I hope I may be prepared cheerfully to obey the summons that shall separate me from all that I love in this world," Webster wrote to Harriet on May 6, 1833. At the moment he was busily engaged in reading proofs on his amended version of the King James' Bible, a work which he had had in contemplation for many years and for which he had sought advice from Moses Stuart in 1822.

If the Dictionary was the pre-eminent secular reference book, the Holy Bible was the single textbook by which all people might be guided into a knowledge of revelation and divine truth. This book and the newspaper formed the library of the average citizen. From these he culled wisdom and knowledge. The Bible was read at family prayers and in schools, as well as at church services. The vigorous Anglo-Saxon base had become the warp and woof of English speech, and biblical characterizations and narratives had become familiar allusions in daily speech and in writing. There were regrettable faults in the language, however, faults of grammar, of archaism, of geography, and of immodesty. These had long been deplored. Webster determined to climax his philological studies with "the most important undertaking" of his career, the improvement of the only book which rivaled his Spelling Book in popularity.

Even in the original edition of the Grammar (1784), Webster had tucked into a footnote an item indicating his dissatisfaction with the use of "strain *at* a gnat" in Matthew, XXIII, 24. Doubtless Dr. Ezra Stiles had pointed out this error in a classroom discussion, and the young student never forgot the notebook entry. A few years later Webster had diligently gone through the New Testament and had compared the Greek original with the translation to test the grammatical rules of Lowth by the received version; on the basis of this investigation the doctrine of the subjunctive mood was overthrown. Still later, after he had learned Hebrew, Webster tested the Old Testament translation of 1611 for accuracy. In *Letters to a Young Gentleman* (1823) he proved as a result of these inquiries that Moses was not the author of the Pentateuch, but at the same time he insisted that the Scriptures were of divine origin. In citing passages from the Bible as illustrative of his Dictionary entries, he again made a word for word investigation. He had read the chief critical works, and he had noted in the margin of his own Bible such suggestions as seemed correct. A biblical scholar could not have kept the English text under longer or much greater surveillance than had Webster.

Webster had objected to the Bible as a textbook because of its "uniform antique style" and the tendency of children to treat with freedom, if not contempt, sacred names and objects. It was not so much his purpose to keep the Bible from children, as it was to increase their respect for it. The use of holy names in anathemas or in cursing or as mild expletives jarred his nerves. It was a sign that moral chaos had laid its foundation of irreverence on Holy Writ itself. There was also a good deal of freedom used in quoting words, generally unmentionable or grown impolite through the wear and tear of centuries, because they were countenanced in the Bible. If the restraining of vices is the most important part of education, the suggestion or sources of these sins certainly should not come to children from the "good book." Essentially, therefore, it was the old schoolmaster who went to work to amend the language of the Bible, the schoolmaster who wished to do good in all things. Although Webster laid himself open anew to the charge of arrogance in attempting this work alone, he was not the first to "improve" the common version. Forty and more years were required to bring the 1611 version into general use, and by that time other translations had been proposed. The Long Parliament of 1653 and Cromwell's parliament of 1656 voted favorably on motions to make "a new translation out of the original tongues." In 1729 came the "vulgar and ludicrous" translation of W. Mace, and in 1764 Antony Purver published a Quaker Bible, with amendments in language and statement to support the doctrines of his church. Dr. Alexander Geddes produced a translation for English Catholics (1792–1797), in which, said a critic, he attacked "the credit of Moses in every part of his character." The Unitarians, not permitted to adopt Gilbert Wakefield's translation (1791), took over Archbishop Newcome's New Testament (1800), in which the readings were altered to establish the doctrine that Jesus was a man and not a member of the godhead. Nathaniel Scarlett and others conformed their translation (1798) to the tenets of the Universalists. Alexander Campbell, who founded the Disciples of Christ Church in Kentucky, amended Dr. George Campbell's version of the Gospels, MacKnight's translation of the Epistles, and Doddridge's translation of the Acts and Revelation. To the third edition (1832) Campbell added a Preface, pluming himself upon his qualifications as reviser thus: "We stand on the shoulders of giants, and, though of less stature, we can see as far as they; or like the wren on the back of the eagle, we have as large a horizon as the eagle, which has carried us above the clouds."

In Boston, where Webster suffered continuously from the barbed arrows of linguistic criticism, Rodolphus Dickinson illustrated in his translation of the New Testament (1833) what the grand style might do to the Bible. He wrote for "accomplished and refined persons," men who, one might suppose, were hostile to the New Haven lexicographer. Dickinson's Preface is an unconsciously humorous reflection of the toploftical notions of the followers of Walker:

Why should the inestimable gift of God to man, be proffered in a mode that is unnecessarily repulsive? Why should the received translation be permitted to perpetuate, to legalize, and almost to sanctify, many and unquestionable defects? While various other works, and especially those of the most trivial attainment, are diligently adorned with a splendid and sweetly flowing diction, why should the mere, uninteresting identity and paucity of language be so exclusively employed, in rendering the word of God? Why should the Christian scriptures be divested even of decent ornament? Why should not an edition of the heavenly institutes be furnished for the reading-room, saloon [salon], and toilet, as well as for the church, school, and nursery? for the literary and accomplished gentleman, as well as for the plain and unlettered citizen?

The quality of Dickinson's "beautified" version appears in the following rendering of Matthew, XXV, 14–21: ". . . a man, who intending to take a distant journey, called his own servants, and delivered to them his effects. . . . And his master said to him, Well-done, good and provident servant! you was [sic] faithful in a limited sphere. I will give you a more extensive superintendence; participate in the happiness of your master." Although the translation was not irreverent, as some critics thought, the spirit of the original, so familiar to the ears and eyes of every English speaking Christian, was utterly lost in this dandification.

Webster, whose edition was published in October, 1833, certainly did not fall either into the arrogance of Campbell or the singularity of Dickinson. Yet there were many objections raised to Webster's modest corrections, partly from prejudice against the man and partly from principle. The Troy, New York, *Press* attempted to excite odium against

Webster's scheme by linking his version with an account of the falsification of the Scriptures. James Milnor, chairman of the American Tract Society, doubted the expediency of the undertaking (January 30, 1832): "It is feared that any private attempt at emendation would only encourage others with less honorable motives to attempt improved versions, so as at length to bring in disrepute and hinder the circulation of the received translation."

Now that the American Revised Version is quite universally used in the United States, and now that we have become accustomed to the modern translations of Weymouth, Moffatt, Ballentine, and Goodspeed, great excitement no longer is occasioned by new translations or revisions. In the nineteenth century, however, objections were raised on principles readily understood and appreciated. First, there were those men who believed that the King James' Version had reached the ultimate in verbal beauty, idiom, and rhythm. Nor can this conclusion be attacked merely as the result of prejudiced familiarity, for the 1611 translators certainly did achieve marvelous felicity of expression. Second, the sanctity attaching to the divine inspiration of the original gave rise to a belief in the divine nature of the translation. The alteration of a single word, it was believed, destroyed the authority of the whole Scriptures. Third, many men who had learned the vocabulary of the Bible possessed a secret reluctance to admit unscholarly people to the fellowship of those who might know, at first sight, what the Bible means. The explication of the Scriptures, to these men, was analogous to the explication of abstruse legal terminology, a vocabulary reserved for a specially educated group. In more recent days we have had a further parallel in the attitude of scientists who insist that their knowledge cannot be popularized. Finally, there was a large group of people who in their secret hearts felt that the Bible was not meant to be understood; they distrusted

all attempts to make it understood. This idea existed despite the declared word, "All is written for our understanding."

The reasons for a revision were equally compelling, and
Webster set forth most of them in his Preface and Introduction. Because he recognized the value of continuing, so
far as possible, traditional readings where these were acceptable, he thought the "general style" of the 1611 Version ought not be departed from. This opinion prevailed
among the English revisers of 1884, who in their emendations accepted no word not in the language before 1611.
Since it was felt, even in the seventeenth century, that
archaisms and vulgar phrases had been admitted needlessly
in the King James' Version, all critics attacked these two
faults. Webster, of course, was threshing old straw in re-
peating them, but he first weeded the garden without destroying the flowers.

"Some words have fallen into disuse," Webster wrote on
the necessity for clarifying the meaning of many passages, "and the signification of others in current popular
use is not the same now as it was when they were introduced
into the version. The effect of these changes is that some
words are not understood by common readers who have no
access to commentaries and who will always compose a great
proportion of readers; while other words, being now used
in a sense different from that which they had when the
translation was made, present a wrong signification or false
ideas." With a lexicographer's desire to make every term
precise, he went on: "Whenever words are understood in a
sense different from that which they had when introduced,
and different from that of the original languages, they do
not present to the reader the *Word of God*. . . . A version
of the scriptures for popular use should consist of words
expressing the sense which is most common in popular
usage, so that the *first ideas* suggested to the reader should

be the true meaning of such words according to the original languages. . . . My principal aim is to remedy this evil."

Many words in the Bible were offensive to delicacy and even to decency, Webster thought. "Language which cannot be uttered in company without a violation of decorum or the rules of good breeding, exposes the scriptures to the scoffs of unbelievers, impairs their authority, and multiplies or confirms the enemies of our holy religion." At another time he insisted that these objectionable words "fortify and extend infidelity." Of those hesitant to approve his revision he asked, "How can the neglect to correct and purify the language be reconciled either to expedience or morality? Is it not sinful?"

The grammatical errors, though not so reprehensible, needed correction, because men gained a predilection for scriptural phrases and insisted upon using them. Thus dual standards of language arose, the one from ordinary usage and the other from a reverence for the antique locutions of the Bible. To a man whose passion for uniformity amounted almost to a religion in itself, as with Webster, this duality seemed most wrong. The universal textbook required the language of common people in 1833, even as the language of commoners had been adopted in 1611. Few others recognized the living development and change of language as did Webster, and consequently his notions seemed quite wrong to many critics.

Naturally Webster tied up his revision with his nationalistic linguistic program. "The language of the Bible," he declared, "has no inconsiderable influence in preserving our national language." On this account the language of the common version ought to conform to the grammatical and semantic rules generally traceable in speech in the United States. He admitted that it would require some effort to subdue the prevailing predilection for the older version and to arouse enthusiasm for a newer set of readings, but, he

said, "for the sake of the rising generation it is desirable.
The language of the scriptures ought to be pure, chaste,
simple, and perspicuous, free from any words or phrases
which may excite observation by their singularity; and neither
debased by vulgarisms, nor tricked out with the ornaments
of affected elegance."

Webster recognized that there was no general principle
which would control all cases of amendment. He sinned on
the side of too little change, rather than too much. But he
studiously avoided, as he did in the Dictionary illustrations, the introduction of sectarian bias. Indeed, just as he
had prepared his great Dictionary for the use of all English-speaking people, so he hoped his Bible might serve
similarly for all denominations of Christians.

With scholarly conscience, Webster stated in his Introduction exactly what changes he had made and why he had
made them. A few illustrations will suffice to indicate
these emendations. He substituted *hinder* for the Elizabethan *let*, *button* for *tache*, *advanced* for *stricken* in years,
boiled for *sodden*, *interest* for *usury*, *insane* for *mad*, *cows*
for *kine*, and so on. Easy as it is for the scholar to translate
these terms, or Shakespeare's "Fear boys with bugs," few
lay readers bother to learn the older meaning and to feel
the surprise of Shakespeare's use of the verb "fear" in the
sense of "frighten," an interpretation which wholly changes
the modern meaning of Petruchio's speech.

Webster made many grammatical changes, particularly
in the use of the articles, in the agreement of subject and
verb, and in the pronouns. *Who* was substituted for *which*,
when the reference was to persons. This change was designed to avoid the pitfalls into which children, trained
to say "Our Father which art in Heaven," fell when they
recited in school. The personality of the deity seemed to
have been destroyed by the older usage. However small
this point may seem to be, the psychological factor demand-

ing the change is tremendous, as any schoolteacher knows. *My* and *thy* replaced *mine* and *thine*, Webster not going the whole road by using the common second person forms. *Its* was uniformly substituted for *his*, when the reference was to plants and things without life. One improvement of this kind appears in the First Psalm:

1611	Webster
3. And he shalbe like a tree . . . that bringeth forth his fruit in his season, his leafe also shall not wither, and whatsoever he doeth, shall prosper.	3. And he shall be like a tree . . . that bringeth forth its fruit in its season; its leaf also shall not wither; and whatsoever he doeth shall prosper.

Here the almost hopeless confusion of the man and tree was quickly and simply clarified. It is an interesting fact that the American revisers thrice requested this same change of the English revisers of 1884 before the emendation was allowed.

The frequently reprobated error of the accusative in the position of the predicate nominative, as in Matthew, XVI, 13, was corrected:

1611	Webster
whom doe men say, that I, the sonne of man, am?	Who do men say that I the Son of man am?

Although Webster succeeded pretty well in laundering the grammar of the 1611 Version, occasionally he slipped into an inconsistency. "Save [meaning "except"] we two" in I Kings, III, 18 was properly altered to "Save us two"; but when he came to John, VI, 46, Webster corrected two forms and allowed "save" to have its old-fashioned nominative:

1611	Webster
Save he which is of God.	Save he who is from God.

And in Genesis, XXIV, 14, he retained: "Let the same be she." But if he failed occasionally, he straightened out tenses, particularly the pasts and perfects, and set the controverted present subjunctives into the future indicatives where they rightfully belonged. He also regularized *shall* and *will*, *should* and *would*. In this part of the work the "New England Grammarian" did yeoman service, and it is interesting to note that the Revised Versions took over nearly every one of his changes, although no credit for his previous labors was given.

In his *Institute*, Part I (1783), Webster eliminated all but one of Dilworth's many citations of God, and he eliminated all other references to the deity and Christ. For fifty years he had clung tenaciously to the idea that a too frequent repetition of sacred names led to their defilement on youthful lips. In his Bible, therefore, he exchanged *O that* for *Would God* or *Would to God*, because the original passages did not contain the name of the Supreme Being, and because the insertion of them in the 1611 Version had given countenance to their introduction into discourse and popular speech with a levity that was incompatible with a due veneration for the name of God. *God forbid*, likewise, was changed, following MacKnight, to *By no means*.

Webster's euphemistic changes have been ridiculed as excessive and as the result of a supersensitively squeamish mind. Not necessarily so. The old schoolmaster had had his ear to the ground to hear common speech for sixty-odd years; even though he did not learn how to record this patois phonetically, he knew what he heard. He thought he heard, and he probably did in legislative halls as well as in taverns, too much vulgarity, too much obscenity, and too much license in the use of unmentionables. Children picked up these phrases, even as first grade children do now as they venture from home alone on the quest for knowledge. "The wicked world," as Webster was wont to call it, uses the great books and great instruments for teaching its perversity.

There is a show of bravery in quoting Shakespeare's
2 Henry IV,

> *'Tis needful that the most immodest word*
> *Be look'd upon and learn'd,*

but what is meat for the scholar can be poison for the child.
Webster reiterated the point that such expressions become,
in the hands of unbelievers, weapons which are used "with
no inconsiderable effect" in casting contempt on the sacred
oracles. But even worse, "many words and phrases are so
offensive, especially to females, as to create a reluctance
in young persons to attend bible classes and schools, in
which they are required to read passages which cannot be
repeated without a blush; and containing words which on
other occasions a child could not utter without rebuke. The
effect is to divert the mind from the *matter* to the *language*
of the Scriptures, and thus, in a degree, frustrate the purpose of giving instruction." As he brought up six daughters
and one granddaughter, Webster knew whereof he wrote.
He was not the first to soften harshnesses or remove ugli-
ness, but his restrained use of circumlocution was followed
quite generally in the Revised Version.

Although Webster's aim was to preserve the sense of the
1611 Version by expressing it in clearer language, he did
not hesitate to correct other than verbal errors. Thus,
"Ye blind guides, which strain *at* a gnat, and swallow a
camel," became "strain *out* a gnat." In this emendation
Webster for the first time in an English Bible rendered
Jesus's saying as He said it, and corrected the figure of
speech. "For I know nothing *by* myself" (I Cor. IV, 4)
was correctly altered to "For I know nothing *against* myself." Some geographical names were corrected, such as
Ethiopia (Gen. II, 13) and the Red Sea (Deut. I, 1), which
became Cush and Suf, respectively. These improvements,

as well as a host of others, were adopted by the authors of
the Revised Version, and it is not without reason that Webster's work, though slow to gain a footing, helped to make
the success of the later work possible.

In his alterations Webster proceeded with conservative
caution, for he approached the Bible with deep reverence
and with the assurance of its inspired character. A pious
probity, akin to John Woolman's, had guided his steps since
youth. The moral and religious precepts, scattered through
his textbooks and great Dictionary, were not craftily sown
seeds to increase his sales. They sprang from a mind convinced of the truths of New England Calvinism. "The
longer I live," he wrote on January 7, 1835, to his daughter Harriet, "the stronger is my faith in the truth of the
Scriptures, and in the truth of that creed in which I have
been educated. I am perfectly well satisfied that what is
denominated 'moderate Calvinism' is the genuine religion
preached by Christ and his apostles, and that there is no
other genuine religion. I rest all my hope on the doctrines
of that system, and commit myself cheerfully to that savior
who preached them."

Many preachers objected strenuously to Webster's emendations. On April 6, 1835, he wrote: "I do not know that
any person has yet hazarded a commendation of the work.
I stand alone and unsupported, even by gentlemen who
agree with me in the importance of the revision. In this,
as in some other efforts of mine at real improvements, I am
either not supported, or opposed by men who claim to be
the directors of public instruction." On November 16 he
returned to the subject: "I wish a few clergymen would
summon courage to commend my Bible to the public. It
wounds my feelings to observe how indifferent the public
are, and especially clergymen, to the correction of faults
in the common version." In December the Yale faculty
approved the Bible, and thereafter its use spread through

the schools and churches of Connecticut, until it became almost the standard text in the Congregational Church. President Theodore D. Woolsey, President Timothy Dwight, II, and Dr. George E. Day, Yale members of the American Bible Revision Company, may well have derived their insistence on Webster-like emendations from their use of Webster's edition. In 1835 Dr. Woolsey signed the Yale faculty testimonial recommending Webster's Bible to the public. So great was the demand for more and cheaper copies, that a duodecimo New Testament was published in 1839, and a 64mo Bible was stereotyped after the second Quarto Dictionary was completed in 1841. "With this work my literary labors must close," Webster declared, but he labored daily at his desk, adding new words to his Dictionary, and writing letters advertising or defending his books. And he added another book to his long list of volumes as late as 1843.

Although Webster's last labors were directed toward the revision of his Spelling Book and Dictionary, *The Holy Bible . . . with Amendments to the Language* was the crowning work of his career, because it brought to completion his learned philological studies and because it rounded out fully his cherished plan for giving to the United States a body of literature from which correct language could be derived. Just as his own enthusiasm had effected improvements in education from the elementary school to the college, so his books embodied useful innovations from the humblest primer to the majestic Bible.

In the winter of 1833–1834 Webster wrote a companion work for his edition of the Bible, a small duodecimo of one hundred eighty pages with the title, *Value of the Bible, and Excellence of the Christian Religion: For the Use of Families and Schools.* This little handbook on the nature, contents, and value of the Bible set out to present "the evidence of purpose or design in the works of creation, thus proving the wisdom and benevolence of the Creator, no less than His unlimited power." Again Webster suppressed his Calvinistic bias in his effort to reach all men and to bring them into the great Christian brotherhood. The pious, humanitarian character of Webster's philosophy becomes apparent in these four brief quotations: "The existence of the human intellect is by itself absolute demonstration of the being of an infinite God, and of his exclusive agency in the creation." "The form of the continents is fitted to favor commerce. . . . Commerce is made the handmaid of civilization, and the instrument of evangelizing pagan nations." "God has so formed the moral system of this world, that a conformity to his will by men produces peace, prosperity, and happiness; and disobedience to his will or laws inevitably produces misery." "The first and most important duty of man is to furnish his mind with correct notions respecting God, his laws, and human duty; and then to exert his faculties, and direct his knowledge, to the benevolent design of making others wiser and better."

Finally, the very last paragraph of the book may serve not only as a summary of Webster's purpose in writing *Value of the Bible*, but also as a clear reflection of his own lifelong dedication to Truth: *"Genuine religion*. We must be careful to distinguish the real religion taught by Christ and his apostles, from those systems which interested men have established. We find the true religion of Christ in the Bible only. It is a scheme wonderfully simple, the principles of which are all comprehended in two short phrases, *love to God* and *love to men*. Supreme love to God, the source and model of all excellence, is the foundation of the whole system of Christianity; and from this principle in the heart flow all the benevolent affections and exercises which constitute practical piety. The person who loves God supremely will reverence His character and laws, and will extend his benevolent affections and charities to all his creatures. From this source will proceed love to man, and the careful performance of all moral and social duties."

The Hartford Prompter of 1791 had mellowed with the years, and at the age of seventy-five he promulgated universal truths rather than practical devices for enlarging man's happiness. Yet always he was the teacher, the monitor, the public conscience—a white-haired patriarch with a bit of the earlier Jeremiah quality still left, but also with the bolder Isaiah note, if not poetic surge, hymning the innate power of man to rise to perfection. A lay preacher, Noah Webster taught patriotic nationalism supported by a fundamental, humanitarian Christian faith.

CHAPTER XIX

PATRIARCH

NOAH WEBSTER and his wife passed imperceptibly into a Quaker-like, pious, industrious, useful old age. Since their marriage day they had lived happily as devoted companions and lovers, proud of their children and eager in their attempts to do good. Sickness seldom marred their lives; yet Mrs. Webster, though the younger, felt the strain of age more than her husband. Always she wrote of being "feeble," but always her letters recounted domestic exploits, the making of quilts, comforters, dresses, and caps for her children or grandchildren, or the putting down of food for a later season, or deeds of charity. To the end, her daughters complained, she maintained a "tenacity of superintending rule." Freed from the cares of rearing her family, she assisted her husband in his literary labors. To Harriet she wrote in 1833 with an unfailing twinkle in her eye and pen: "Your Papa . . . bids me say that his Bible is progressing. I must go now and read what Louisa calls a pious proofsheet, which will close the prophet Isaiah. So you see, dear Pod, after helping your father make his Dictionary, I am still assisting him in his literary pursuits. You doubtless remember the fable of the fly on the coach." Mrs. Webster's sweet, kind face mirrored a lively, cheerful, hopeful temperament. In a sense she and her husband were complementary in nature; he was taciturn in private, with a brow wrinkled in thoughtful concentration, while she was joyous, animated, talkative, and whimsical in her gay moods. Each looked after the other with tender solicitude; their life together was a poem of domestic bliss.

"I love my children," Webster frequently wrote; and Mrs. Webster once recorded, "Papa longs to see you all. I heard someone conversing in the drawing room the other day and found him standing before your portraits. . . . We often talk together (your father and myself) of our singular happiness in our sons-in-law and daughters and such a promising batch of grandchildren. . . . Your father says there is not a lovelier bunch of grandchildren than ours." When Mary Southgate, the granddaughter whom he adopted, was married to Henry Trowbridge, Jr., on July 24, 1838, Webster wrote to Harriet: "We have parted with our last child in matrimony. Although Mary has good prospects, still when I think that a child leaves my house for life and forever, the painful thought affects me, and as I sit alone a tear is stealing down my cheek." The Websters demanded visits from their children and grandchildren, and every summer Webster, and on several occasions Mrs. Webster, toured New England to visit each daughter in her home. To each he wrote frequently, giving advice of one sort or another, and always he maintained his patriarchal privilege of directing their activities.

"We are treated like boys and girls," Emily Webster Ellsworth once petulantly wrote to her sister Harriet, but it was a momentary grievance and not a settled conviction that found utterance. All the children loved in an awesome manner their dignified, high-souled father; they expected him to yield authority to them and to surrender his business concerns into their hands, but until the very end he conducted his affairs without deferring to them. When the homestead was mortgaged to bring out the 1840 Dictionary, a flurry of agitation ran through the whole family. But Webster was unperturbed by their remonstrance. With inflexible courage he risked all to continue in usefulness the books he had spent his life to prepare.

Professor Chauncey A. Goodrich, Julia's husband, had

secured the copyright on the Octavo Dictionary, and, although he had vowed on his knees to dedicate his profits to the propagation of the gospel, the other men in the family were not very happy over his success. When he secured the editorship of the great Dictionary in 1843, a quarrel with W. C. Fowler, Harriet's husband, developed. Goodrich was quietly foxlike, while Fowler was brusque, pompous, and leonine in his rages. Both had prepared themselves for the task of succeeding Webster, but Goodrich had the higher claim by position and by long association with the lexicographer in his publishing ventures.

Henry Jones, whom Eliza had wed on September 5, 1825, had surrendered his pulpit as a result of ill health, and had founded a school at Bridgeport, Connecticut. Both he and his wife were ingenuous, unaffected, and self-reliant. Neither asked parental favors or expected fortune to wave its wand over their heads. Eliza became the confidante of Webster, because she supported his plans.

William W. Ellsworth, Emily's husband, rose steadily in Connecticut politics until he reached the governorship. Early he had shaken off the patriarchal rule; never did he assist Webster in his plans, the copyright legislation excepted. Webster respected the achievements of Ellsworth, but often lamented his son-in-law's unwillingness to aid financially in bringing out the 1840 Dictionary.

Webster's only son, William, was a Greenleaf in temperament. His gaiety of disposition and elasticity of spirit, he wrote, alone kept his heart buoyant in an ocean of troubles. Failure dogged his steps. He had been forced to leave Yale and Middlebury colleges and he had been bankrupted in several business ventures. Always his father had rescued him by purchasing his debts. William married Rosalie Stuart of Fairfax, Virginia, daughter of the same Dr. David Stuart who had assisted Webster in securing copyright legislation in Virginia in 1784; she was allied

Painted by Flagg, 1832

REBECCA GREENLEAF WEBSTER

Aged 66

with the Washington family. Business failures forced them
to depend upon Webster for support for many years; the
other children took little comfort in this parental generosity.
But Eliza always wrote calming letters to her sisters, advising them that William's presence at home gave their
father great pleasure.

If Webster's children chafed under a parental rule which
excluded them from the right to shape their father's actions, the grandchildren on their long visits frisked and
frolicked in the Temple Street home with keen joy. When
Webster's study hour ended, they pattered into his room,
claimed affectionate tokens of love, and listened to his narratives and advice. He heard their lessons, reproved their
carelessness, and rewarded industry. Always a box of raisins
and a plate of candy lay on the mantle awaiting their coming. The old schoolmaster never forgot the art of winning
children's love. Mary Southgate was of even age with many
of the other grandchildren; she bridged the gap for them
and destroyed the starched stiffness so common when children visit their grandparents. Emily Fowler, "with quick-
silver in her veins," was Webster's favorite. During her
long visit, while her parents went South for the benefit of
Harriet who was racked with illness, she became Webster's
companion. She trotted twice daily to the post office with
him, helped him market for groceries, and rode about the
country on his tours. A good pianist and vocalist, she
played and sang the old favorites he had taught her mother.
Often "he would strike in with a very true, sweet, quaver-
ing voice." The love of music never left him.

Mrs. Webster marshaled the youngsters about her like
a hen with a brood of chicks. She taught them stories and
games, whispered advice on love and matrimony, and tutored
them in tickling the fancy of their grandfather. Always
she was their confidante, a tribute to her youthful spirit.
When the older Ellsworth and Goodrich boys were students

in Yale, she arranged delightful musical parties. Once she planned "an old times frolic." She wrote to Harriet: "I am watching for a time of peculiar *begassity* on the Patriarchal side of the house. The boys are to bring their costumes from college and dress in the drawing room here. The girls will dress in their own room and then meet in grand style. They will speak dialogues the first part of the evening and then make a call on William and Rosalie and perhaps go over to Uncle [Professor] Goodrich. They have promised to be very still about it, but I own I have some misgivings. Henry will represent an Italian nobleman; Chauncey a priest; Harriet a nun; Emily a high-born lady, the mother of the nun; Mary the heiress or eldest daughter; Pinckney has not decided what part to take—something great no doubt."

There were parties for the grownups, too. "Since I wrote you last," Mrs. Webster wrote one November, "I have had a large party which I call my Woolsey party, taking in the Dwight and Whitney connections and as many of the faculty as we could *cram* in. The party went off well, for all seemed happy, especially Mrs. Leverett when she got alongside your father. This week I shall make a Temple Street and take in the Brintnalls, Mr. and Mrs. Elliot; and the day after a few of us meet here to quilt a charity bed quilt, and then I shall shut up for the winter which is fast approaching."

Many visitors crowded through the Webster door. The lexicographer sat in a high-backed arm chair on one side of the fire in the south front parlor which was their sitting room, and his wife in a rocking chair on the other, receiving their friends as they happened in, often without the ceremony of knocking at the front door. The Yale professors regularly made calls; the old line Connecticut Federalists stopped in for a rebirth of enthusiasm; visiting clergymen paid homage to the reviser of the Scriptures; and travelers stopped to shake hands with the illustrious lexicographer. Basil Hall recorded a long philological discussion, as did Jared Sparks, who jotted in his diary: "I am glad to have seen Noah Webster, for I respect him for his great attainments, and for the noble, untiring zeal with which he has devoted a whole life to the investigation of an important though neglected subject. The example is worthy all praise. Let those who condemn, first do as much, and do it better."

Anne Royall, the spitfire feminist author and traveler, etched a portrait with vitriol, the only substance which seemed to flow easily from her pen: "I knocked at the door with more than common enthusiasm; for, though we backwoods folks are not learned ourselves, we have a warm liking for learned people. In a few minutes, a low chubby man with a haughty air stepped into the room; his face was round and red and by no means literary looking. He was dressed in black broadcloth, in dandy style; in short, he comes nearer the description of a London cockney than any character I can think of. He eyed me with ineffable scorn and scarcely deigned to speak at all. I am sorry for his sake I ever saw the man, as it gave me infinite pain to rescind an opinion I had long entertained of him." Doubtless Mrs. Royall had touched off one of Webster's prejudices, and he chose dignified silence as the best defensive weapon.

Webster's "refinement of nature and innate modesty were feminine," says Mrs. Ford; a spotlessness of thought and utterance, a Quaker-like purity of mind, and an ambition to model his life on those of the grave biblical elders, gave Webster a strait-laced appearance and a dour countenance. Yet deep set under his beetling brows were eyes filled with sentiment and good humor. His severity arose from unrelaxed principles of noble thought and action. He winced at vulgarity and obscenity as if he had been lashed with a blacksnake whip. Indelicacy in his children aroused flaming anger, and his rebuke made an evil-doer "shiver like a top." Though his common mood was grave, reticent, and kindly, he grew very animated in discussing history, education, philology, and politics.

Webster had found his warmest advocates in New Haven when on his youthful tour he peddled his Spelling Book and his nationalistic language notions. In old age he found this friendliness increasing; his venerable presence enjoyed universal respect. When President Andrew Jackson visited New Haven in 1833, an incident illustrated this popular opinion. Webster called on the President, and, while waiting to be ushered into his presence, as Mrs. Webster wrote Harriet, "several strangers took him by the hand, supposing that he was the great man himself. This was very amusing to the bystanders, and some of them remarked that those who were so eager to do honor to Jackson took the hand of a much better man."

Webster's calling on Jackson was not intended to indicate an approval of the Democrat's political policies, for the old patriot saw in Jackson a lesser Jefferson. Let Mrs. Webster report the family opinion: "Your Papa is sitting in his rocking chair with a paper in his hand, and a large pile before him. Once in a while a deep groan escapes from him at the critical state of our country. What a dark cloud hangs over us and how will it end? In a dreadful hurricane I fear. We are now experiencing as a nation the curse of having 'a wicked man placed over us, with Satan standing at his right hand.' The wicked man is so *weak* that he could not do much of himself, if he had not seven others, if possible, more wicked to instigate and spur him on to try their hateful experiments which will ruin our once flourishing and happy land. Our good people hope much from the approaching election, but your father says that he has been so often disappointed in his expectations, that he does not predict a happy result. The Jackson men are secretly at work, and yesterday three hundred new freemen were qualified to vote. Barber, the Jackson editor, qualified sixty of the baser sort to vote on the government side."

Webster frequently commented on Jackson's acts: on December 27, 1832, he wrote: "All heads are puzzled and all hearts solicitous for the fate of our Constitution and public peace." On April 17, 1834: "We are indeed in a singular condition. President Jackson has his foot upon our necks, and a great portion of the people of New England justify him. What is our republicanism worth? . . . We depart from the precepts of the Bible. We depart from the Constitution, and how can we prosper?" To Daniel Webster, he wrote, February 9, 1835: "I see by the proceedings of Congress that measures are taken to destroy the independence of the judiciary and to give the people a full swing in other things. Thus we shall be able to give a full trial of a republican government to the people of the United States. On this gloomy subject I must forbear comment." In the preceding September he had addressed a long letter to the Massachusetts Senator to explain the virulence of party spirit, as demonstrated in the times of the Middletown and Hartford conventions. It was a gloomy letter, designed to cheer Daniel Webster in a moment when distorted remarks were used against him.

Editor Barber alluded to Webster's "spirit of aristocracy." The old Federalist scalded his youthful critic with a letter outlining his services to the young republic. "And you are not to suppose," he stated (February 17, 1835) with controlled anger, "that I feel no indignation at the base ingratitude which would charge me and my companions with principles or designs unfriendly to the government of my country. . . . I am a farmer's son and have collected all the small portion of property which I possess by untiring efforts and labors to promote the literary improvement

of my fellow citizens, and to establish the freedom and
tranquillity of my country. If I have any other aristocracy
about me, it must be my *old age*, an aristocracy resulting
from God's appointment, with a reference doubtless to the
advantages which society may derive from the wisdom,
prudence, and correct judgment which age only can give."

When it was apparent that President Jackson had killed
the United States Bank, Webster told his daughter (April 6,
1835), "I have labored in vain and spent my strength for
naught. This is particularly the case with my labor to support
the government and the sound principles of the Constitution. In that business I expended years and probably wrote
more than other private person now living or that has lived.
But the true principles of republican government are now
abandoned by all parties, and elections are a mere scramble
for offices; and instead of expecting things to grow better,
I am confident they will grow worse. I have lost all hope
of amendment. The intrigues of ambitious men and the
collision of parties will not abate but increase; and to all
our other evils we may add the excitements arising from
the questions respecting slavery and the increase of Roman-
ism. The latter evil is alarming, and is not improbable
that the inquisition may, at some future time, be established in the West. But we deserve chastisement, and must
expect it. I look forward with gloomy apprehensions, and
have no consolation except in the government of a righteous
Sovereign, who will make our sins and follies subservient
to his design." On June 10, 1835, he was ready to move
in order "to be forever delivered from the *democracy of
Connecticut*. This is now," he went on, "the *rankest despotism* which I have ever known; it goes far beyond the
despotism in Jefferson's days. Constitutional principles are
trampled under foot, and arbitrary will is the only rule of
action. Had the Washingtons, the Jays, and the Rutledges
of revolutionary times forseen the strides of corruption and

tyranny which our country has already made, I believe they would never have opposed the British government. I believe no state under heaven has ever experienced such determined efforts to *destroy* every thing good and *debase* every thing exalted and honorable, as we now experience. . . . The measures now pursued must inevitably end in changing the *form*, as they have already corrupted the *principles* of a genuine republican government." On November 16, 1835, he returned to the theme: "If *one state* shall maintain the good old republican principle of the Federalists who formed the government and for some years administered it, while all the rest are subjected to popular licentiousness, endangering life, liberty, and property, I would remove to that state, wherever it may be. I wish to be in a state where *constitution* and *law* and *wisdom* have the control." "If I could be certain," he wrote on April 29, 1836, "that Vermont would remain firm to the old Federal principles, I should be tempted to remove into that state, to be freed from our *democracy*. As to the cold of the winters, I would, if necessary, become a troglodyte and live in a cave in winter, rather than be under the tyranny of our desperate rulers. But the worst of tyrannies I submit to the righteous dispensations of Providence. We deserve all our public evils. We are a degenerate and wicked people. That a kind Providence may watch over you and all of us, is [my] prayer."

In August, 1837, after Van Buren had demonstrated his willingness to continue the Jacksonian tradition, Webster sent to William Leete Stone, editor of the *New York Commercial Advertiser* and *Spectator*, the papers Webster had founded, a short essay over the pseudonym "Sidney":

In the Spectator of August 29 you have given a brief account of the police of London, which I have read with pleasure. You then contrast the condition of London with that of New York, where the police is miserably inefficient. This inefficiency you ascribe to the true cause, the *democracy of the country*. You call it *ultra-*

democracy. To this denomination I must object. It is not *ultra;* it is *common democracy;* such as formerly existed in Greece and occasionally in Rome.

It has been a prevailing opinion, even with many of our greatest men, that the *people* can govern themselves, and that a *democracy* is of course a *free government.* Such language as this has been in the mouths of our patriots, and in the columns of newspapers for thirty or forty years, until it is considered as expressing political axioms of unquestionable truth. The men who have preached these doctrines have never defined what they mean by the *people,* or what they mean by *democracy,* nor how the *people* are to govern themselves, and how *democracy* is to carry on the functions of government. But in practice the word *people* denotes any collection of individuals either in meetings legally assembled, or in mobs, collected suddenly, no matter how, for any purpose good or bad.

Now I appeal to history for the fact, that there has never yet been a democratic government, that is, a government in which the whole populace have exercised the whole power of making laws and of choosing executive officers, which has been a free government. On the other hand, the annals of history show beyond contradiction, that such governments have ever been furious and implacable despotisms.

Our writers have uniformly charged the tyranny of civil government to *Kings,* and true it is that Kings have often been tyrants. But it seems never to have occurred to such writers that the people, so called, are just as bad as Kings. By nature, all men have the same passions as Kings—they are all selfish—all ambitious—*all,* from the King or President down to the corporal of a militia company, aspiring to power, and striving for superiority over their fellow men. Give the people the *power,* and they are *all tyrants* as much as Kings. They are even more tyrannical; as they are less restrained by a sense of propriety or by principles of honor; more under the control of violent passions, exasperated by envy and hatred of the rich; stimulated to action by numbers; and subject to no responsibility.

These are undeniable facts. Why then do men wonder at the outbreakings of popular violence? Many men and good citizens, too, appear to be *surprised* at the scenes which have taken place in Charleston, New York, Philadelphia, Baltimore, Vicksburg, Cincinnati, and St. Louis. Why, Gentlemen, these scenes do not surprise those who have studied history and mankind. These outrages were foreseen and distinctly foretold by our ablest statesmen forty and fifty years ago. The whole sin of the old Washington federalists consisted in attempting to incorporate into our government, or establish by law, some power which should effectually control or prevent such popular violence. It was perfectly well foreseen that, without some provision of this kind, the *people* would, whenever they please, break over the constitution and laws, and trample them under their feet. In what has taken place, nothing strange or unexpected by sound statesmen has taken place. Such scenes have characterized democratic governments in every country where they have existed. They proceed from the universal depravity of man, and they will be repeated whenever occasions of excitement occur. The people will in their cool moments ask, "Is thy servant a dog, that he should do this great thing?" But the people do it—they have always done it, and they will always do it, when they have the power. And it is a melancholy truth that fills us with alarm, that the people will not create a power which shall effectually defend their own personal rights and safety.

SIDNEY

An enraged Jacksonian press went into convulsions over this article in the same way that the "Porpoises of Connecticut" allusion had agitated the Jeffersonians in 1802. *The Daily Albany Argus,* November 30, 1837, declared editorially: "It is the essence of the Federal doctrines, which have been 'scotched,' not killed. Here is the same innate distrust and hatred of the people—the old habit of depreciating their intelligence and integrity—the same longing for a 'strong' federal government, for an hereditary executive, and for elections and responsibility so remote as to be little else than power in perpetuity." *The Albany Evening Journal* remarked: "Stone calls this a voice of wisdom. It sounds to us like the hoarse voice of treason." The article was reprinted in a pamphlet, entitled *Voice of Wisdom.* Down in Washington Caleb Cushing decided something had to be done about the "very shallow and very weak" essay; he prepared a series of answers under the pseudonym "Poplicola." *The Montreal Gazette* (November 20, 1837) called it "a very interesting, if not important communication, in relation to the present aspect of public affairs in the United States." The *Montreal Herald* (November 25, 1837) averred it was "one of the very best articles that we have read for many years." Stone (December 7, 1837) smiled away the Albany panic by asserting: "It is an essay glowing with the genial warmth of chastened patriotism, and rich in the counsels of ripened experience—and delightful in the calm spirit of political philosophy which it breathes." The Whigs, of whom Stone was a leader, feared the aristocratic "Sidney" might mar their campaign, and so the General Committee of the Whig Young Men of New York on December 15, 1837, formally voted that they "do utterly and absolutely disclaim, repudiate, and condemn the anti-republican doctrines of Sidney." Webster responded, December 21, 1837, with the following

NOTE FROM SIDNEY

In the year 1777, when a British army was marching from the north toward Albany, Sidney volunteered his services, shouldered the best musket he could find, marched up the Hudson, in sight of the flames and smoking ruins of Kingston, encountering the hardships of a soldier's life, to which he had not been inured, to lend his feeble aid in checking the enemy. This he did for the purpose of defending the country, in the hope of establishing *Independence* and a *free republican government.* Had he foreseen that a generation would have passed before this republican government would be changed into the *tyranny of a party;* a tyranny which has inflicted on the community, more losses, more distress, more calamity than any monarch in Europe has inflicted on his subjects in half a century, and all this under the hypocritical pretext of republicanism; had Sidney foreseen all this, with the prostration, or imbecility of law, the popular outrages upon life, liberty and prosperity; the direct violations of constitution and law, and of the ordinances of God, in authorizing secular employments on the Sabbath, and all the baneful effects of party spirit and usurpation; he would not have moved a step to oppose the enemy. Sidney knows no difference in tyranny; the authors of it may be monarchs or republicans, but *tyranny* is the *same thing* and is to be resisted by every man who

values his rights, and loves his family and his country. The men of
the revolution did not fight for an *oligarchy;* they fought for a
commonwealth.

For four years the Sidney article was trotted out as the
bugaboo with which to frighten the populace into supporting the Jacksonians. And therefore at eighty, Webster,
whose authorship of Sidney was not generally known,
smiled to see swirling about his head the political brickbats
he had first experienced at the age of twenty-five. His
gloomy views of American democracy led him to write to
various papers in 1838 to reprobate the editors' "ignorance
of our political history." Always he showed that Jefferson
had first claimed "the supreme and uncontrollable right or
power to interpret the Constitution as he understood it,"
and by his acts and those of his successors had made "a five
or six headed monster [of] our government." The party
spirit initiated by Jefferson had paved the way to national
ruin, and in a paper under the pseudonym of "Rutledge"
Webster begged that party strife cease: "The men who
exasperate parties now are the worst enemies of the country. Healing and wise measures now are indispensable to
our safety."

When *The Hartford Times* (February 15, 1840) called
in question some of Webster's opinions, largely because he
was supposedly directing Governor Ellsworth's policies,
Webster defined his political position thus: "I belonged
to the school of Washington, but sometimes differed from
the Federalists on particular points, as I did from their
opposers. That Washington's policy was in general correct,
I firmly believe, and, when the citizens of this country
abandoned that policy, I foresaw and foretold the evils which
would follow with nearly the same certainty as we now know
them, from history and from present sufferings. I belong
to no party but to the class of citizens who love their country and strive to promote its interests, political, moral, liter-

ary, and religious. For many years past I have attended no
political meetings; I have no communication with either
party in public measures, and rarely give my vote at the
polls. I speak and write my sentiments with freedom whenever occasion offers, and this I shall continue to do without
fear or affection. With the same freedom I now predict
that, if the supporters of either party rely on the measures
they are now pursuing to restore *harmony* and *prosperity*
to our afflicted country, they will be grievously disappointed."

Webster's heart bled for the underprivileged in America.
He objected to the ruthlessness with which the Cherokee
Indians were driven from Florida. He disliked the employment of girls in factories, and he frequently urged
that domestic service was superior as an occupation if not as
an income producer. On the slavery question Webster grew
very warm. His earliest books had carried abolition pleas,
and one of his best pamphlets had dealt wisely with the
problem. William Lloyd Garrison and his followers
seemed quite wrong in method and principle. "What the
abolitionists mean," he wrote Harriet (November 5, 1835),
"I do not know. They have exasperated the South, so that
their preaching can do no good—they may as well whistle
against the west wind. It would be well for the North if
they were all in straitjackets." A month later he thought
an excess of zeal "may yet bring the Northern states into
serious trouble." On January 9, 1838, he wrote: "The
abolitionists will probably dissolve the Union. Oh, for the
times when the people had some respect for elders and wise
men." Two weeks later: "The conduct of Congress in not
receiving petitions on the subject of slavery increases abolitionism, but this is what pleases the party; they seek opposition and persecution. It is obvious to me that the leaders
intend to work up commotion. They complain of the article
in the Constitution which obliges the States to suppress
information. This I see in some of their publications. But

this article cannot be altered. Their intention then is to make a majority of the northern people abolitionists, so that in case of insurrection of the blacks the militia will not aid in suppressing it. Then, the way is clear for the slaves to rise and emancipate themselves. It is said openly that, were it not for the North, the slaves would soon free themselves. I know not what is to be the issue of our difficulties."

It was the lecturer on American union in 1785 who viewed with alarm the schismatic tendency of abolitionism and of party spirit. "I love my country," Webster repeated over and over; his head ached as he contemplated the ruinous party or reforming zeal at work in undermining those firm foundations of nationality to which he had devoted his life. Well might he sound the Jeremiah note, because no American held higher ideals of civic duty than Webster, and none had been so persevering in teaching them to millions of school children and to the few calm minds which cherished the advice of their elders.

The 1830's saw the beginning of many reforming projects, the curious manifestations of which Emerson described in his "New England Reformers." Probably of them all, in immediate and in permanent good, the public school reformers achieved most. Horace Mann pushed through the Massachusetts Legislature various bills for the improvement of common schools. These were similar in type to those which Webster a decade and more earlier had presented. A Public School Law was passed in Pennsylvania in 1834, and soon other states placed state-wide systems of public instruction under the direction of a State Superintendent. In teachers' meetings and by his writings Webster lent the support of his aged, but still vigorous, pen. There was no unanimity of opinion to support the proposals. Factions preached against colleges and public instruction with as much virulence as the abolitionists fomented rebellion

among the slaves. Webster sighed (December 13, 1835):
"Our factions would bring all learning down to a level
with common people. Men must not improve their intellect beyond the standard of common men, although I had
always supposed God intended our souls to be enlarging
their powers and capacities to eternity."

Webster found too much zeal, too much haste hurrying forward the reformers. "The excitements which exist
in this country," he wrote, "drive our people, in all their
undertakings, to do every thing in a hurry. The abolitionists
are in a hurry for the emancipation of the slaves in the
South. The missionary societies are in a hurry to Christian-
ize all nations, and urge their operations too fast for their
resources, making no allowance for unforseen disappointments. Men are every where in a hurry to get rich, and
this hurry often drives them into folly, excess, and poverty.
From five hundred to a thousand lives are annually sacrificed to hurry in making and managing railroads and steam-
ers. Even learning and education can not escape the contagion. . . . Children are no longer to learn the first
rudiments of language; they are to bound over their horn-
books at a leap, and plunge at once into geometry, trigonome-
try, conic sections, botany, chemistry, mineralogy, geology,
logic, intellectual philosophy, and other sciences. Instead of
learning to *spell*, they are to learn the *properties* of matter.
This leaping over the elements of language, or only giving
them a brush, is the principal cause of the inferiority of American scholars in the languages to European scholars. Our
characteristic hurry in learning is well adapted to fill the
country with smatterers, and it is very successful." Webster
reprobated the failure of colleges to teach English grammar, since the English language will be "of more use and
consequence to the English and American nations, and
perhaps to the gospel and the world, than any other language on the globe."

Always, too, he stressed the importance of utility as the educational goal. He repeated the ideas of his earlier papers on education, pointing out in an article, entitled "To the Young of Both Sexes," the futility of crowding into professions already well-supplied and urging perseverance in business and agriculture, where "books and learning can not supply the want of labor and experience." In 1839 he published, at the age of eighty-one, his last wholly new textbook, *Manual of Useful Studies,* a compend on the arts and sciences with which a student might learn simple fundamentals. Just as "uniformity" was his keyword in language, so "utility" was the keyword of his whole educational philosophy.

It was to religion that Webster looked for an amelioration of the unhappy plight of America. "I consider the Christian religion as our sheet anchor during our political storms," he wrote Harriet on July 24, 1832. "If we can not maintain that, we have no hope for our free institutions. I wish some of the Boston zeal to improve education in letters and arts, might be directed to reform our morals and political opinions. Without religion, good morals, and sound principles of government, letters and erudition will not save us from conclusions of a serious nature." But it was religion of the heart and mind, not of the emotions, which he supported. Against the revivalistic fervor of the times he repeated again and again the substance of his Dictionary definition of "fanatic": for example (January 3, 1836), "Genuine religion has little to do with physical excitement. Excited passions or feelings may, for a moment or a short period, produce grief and tears; but these are no certain signs of true repentance. Genuine repentance must proceed from a firm conviction of guilt incurred by transgressions; this conviction must be the dictate of a well informed understanding, not the sudden burst of feeling nor of fear. The impressions made on sinners by vociferation, violent agitations of the body, and excited feeling may be and usually are evanescent and transient; they pass away without producing genuine repentance and faith, without which no person can become a real Christian. . . . I have little confidence in what are denominated *conversions* under such violent excitements." To William Miller, leader of the millennialists who announced the end of the world as ordained for the year 1843, Webster addressed an open letter of rebuke: "Your preaching can be of no use to society but it is a great annoyance. If you expect to frighten men and women into religion, you are probably mistaken. . . . If your preaching drives people into despair or insanity, you are responsible for the consequences. I advise you to abandon your preaching; you are doing no good, but you may do a great deal of harm."

In behalf of the propagation of his own ideas of the methodology best adapted to moral and religious culture, Webster circulated through the newspapers a "Form of Association for Young Men," the suggested pledge of a society similar to the Christian Endeavor Society of today. It began: "We, firmly believing the revealed will of God, as delivered in the Scriptures, to be the standard of moral rectitude, and moral rectitude to be the only basis of true honor and dignity of character, do associate for the purpose of giving efficacy to those principles, and for discountenancing, as far as our influence may extend, the operation of principles which tend to render vice respectable or diminish its infamy." Then followed specific pledges to conform to the character of the Supreme Being; to avoid duelling, lewdness, intemperance, seduction, gaming, violations of holy time, fraud, overreaching in trade, falsehood, deception, or other vice, however common or sanctioned by fashion; to abstain from uniting with secret organizations; to consider respect for religion and its institutions as indispensable qualifications for aspirants to political office; and "to give no countenance or support to persons whose occupation is to furnish amusements which tend to demoralize society." Again, the aged schoolmaster was attempting to marshal the forces of righteousness in the perennial warfare against sin.

Never were Webster's days idle. He did not enter upon fretful, peevish, disgruntled old age, but through work the roses in his cheeks bloomed to the end. At eighty his hair was but slightly "silvered o'er with age." Asked if his remarkable health, mental vigor, and his longevity could be traced to assignable causes, he responded quickly, "Certainly. I always accustomed myself to retire at an early hour, and to make it a point to lay aside my cares with my clothes. In the second place, though I had but a feeble constitution, I have made it an invariable rule to rise with the lark. In the third place, I have, even to my present advanced age, uniformly combined mental labor with considerable bodily exercise, without remitting it even for a day. And in the fourth and last place, I have studiously endeavored to keep a conscience void of offense toward God and man."

On April 21, 1840, Webster delivered at Hartford the historical address on the occasion of the celebration of the two hundredth anniversary of the founding of Connecticut. A slight hoarseness, occasioned by a cold, caused him to abridge his remarks. Yet he spoke for an hour and a half; "his voice was so clear and distinct as to be heard from all parts of the Center Church."

At eighty, as has been already stated, Webster mortgaged his home to publish the second edition of his great quarto Dictionary. Until early in 1841 he labored daily in reading proof and in revising his definitions. In 1842 he gathered many of his fugitive essays and prepared some new ones for *A Collection of Papers on Political, Literary and Moral Subjects*, a 373-page octavo volume which went to press in April, 1843. Early in May he finished correcting a new edition of the Spelling Book. "My literary labors are now completed," he remarked again; this statement, though it had been repeated through the ten years which had seen ten books published since the amended version of the Bible, at last came true. The patriot, lexicographer, and schoolmaster entered upon the immortal journey.

On Sunday, May 21, 1843, Webster attended church all day, and in the evening he spent an hour at the home of his neighbor, Professor James Luce Kingsley. Here he remarked that his "literary labors were all ended" and that during the remnant of his days "the cultivation of his garden and the contemplation of the works of God would afford him sufficient employment and recreation." On Monday he walked twice to the post office, but, on returning the second time, he noticed a chill, the forerunner of pleurisy. Until Friday his condition seemed to warrant no fear. Then his lungs began to fill, and on Sunday, May 28, 1843, he knew the end was nigh. In his last hours he spoke of his willingness to enter his ageless rest. "I'm ready to go," he whispered; "my work is all done; I know in whom I have believed." And then, the future having no fears for him, his thoughts ran back to the past: "I have struggled with many difficulties. Some I have been able to overcome, and by some I have been overcome. I have made many mistakes, but I love my country, and have labored for the youth of my country, and I trust no precept of mine has taught any dear youth to sin." At five minutes before eight in the evening, without apparent pain, without one struggle or groan, he ceased to breathe.

Impressive memorial services were held in the Center Church, New Haven, and at Amherst College, places where to this day the memory of his long, useful life is cherished. Professor Benjamin Silliman, the eminent Yale scientist, jotted a brief tribute in his diary: "He died in the fulness of reputation, of health, of mental power, and of Christian faith. He has left a brilliant fame. Millions have been instructed by his writings, and millions more will study them in years to come. He encountered no small opposition, which was due quite as much to his personal peculiarities as to the boldness and novelty of some of his speculations. His Dictionary surpasses all others in the fulness of its alphabet and in the excellence of its definitions. His elementary works for schools have received a universal sanction and many other works remain to instruct mankind while their learned and virtuous author is in his grace or rather while his spirit is with God."

Mrs. Webster lived until June 25, 1847, when she passed away as the result of a paralytic stroke occasioned by a fall while hanging curtains in her parlor. In her hours of pain she looked forward, eyes shining, to a reunion with the stouthearted Christian warrior and patriot whose battles she had shared for fifty-four years.

SOURCES AND BIBLIOGRAPHY

I

MANUSCRIPTS

SOME six hundred new letters were found in the possession of the following named institutions and individuals, to whom my appreciation is again extended. The Noah Webster Papers, presented through J. P. Morgan, Esq., are in the Gordon L. Ford Collection at the New York Public Library. These include most of the extant letters to Webster and many of Webster's letters, papers, the manuscript of the Synopsis, and the diaries. In the same place are the papers and diary of William Greenleaf Webster. The Pierpont Morgan Library possesses about a hundred letters of Webster, chiefly to Hudson and Goodwin, and the main portion of the manuscript of the Dictionary. Other good collections of Webster letters are in the Massachusetts Historical Society (many published by the Society), the Historical Society of Pennsylvania, the New York Historical Society, the Jones Memorial Library of Amherst, Massachusets, the Library of Congress, and the Yale University Library. Letters also are in Haverford College Library, Lehigh University Library, Henry Huntington Library and Art Gallery, American Philosophical Society, Library Company of Philadelphia, Connecticut Historical Society, Rutgers University Library, Columbia University Library, New Haven Colony Historical Society, Rosenberg Library of Galveston, Texas, Pequot Library of Southport, Connecticut, Burton Collection of the Detroit Public Library, Dartmouth College Library, and Boston Public Library. The Connecticut Historical Society has a large collection of William Wolcott Ellsworth correspondence, in which are many letters concerning the editing and publication of the Dictionary after 1843, and letters to Webster from Norman White, last publisher of the Spelling Book during Webster's lifetime. The Connecticut Academy of Arts and Sciences has deposited its papers in the Yale University Library; several letters and manuscripts of Webster are there preserved. The most notable collection of Webster family papers is in the possession of William Chauncey Fowler, Durham Center, Connecticut. These include hundreds of letters to Mrs. Harriet Webster Cobb Fowler from her father, mother, sisters, and brother. Other private collections having Webster manuscripts are those of Carroll A. Wilson, Stuart W. Jackson, Mrs. Roswell Skeel, Jr., Mrs. Julia B. Farrar, Miss Fannie H. Boltwood, Mr. and Mrs. Theodore Bailey, G. A. Plimpton, Mrs. Hildegarde E. Taylor, F. L. Pleadwell, and the author.

Mrs. Roswell Skeel, Jr., permitted me to examine parts of her extensive Webster bibliography, soon to be published, and to make use of her notes on the issues of the three parts of *A Grammatical Institute* and of her list of Webster's newspaper contributions.

II

CHIEF BIOGRAPHICAL WORKS

THE work indispensable to a study of the life and times of Webster is *Notes on the Life of Noah Webster* (two volumes, privately printed, 1912), compiled by Emily Ellsworth Fowler Ford, Webster's favorite granddaughter, and edited by her daughter, Emily Ellsworth Ford Skeel (Mrs. Roswell Skeel, Jr.). Here are reproduced with scholarly accuracy Webster's diary and all the important letters to and by Webster, found in 1912 in the New York Public Library, the Library of Congress, the Library Company of Philadelphia, the American Philosophical Society, the Connecticut Historical Society, the Yale University Library, the Massachusetts Historical Society, and the Historical Society of Pennsylvania. A check list of Webster's books is added. Horace E. Scudder's *Noah Webster (American Men of Letters;* Boston, 1881) is a jaunty critical sketch in which the author achieves admiration for Webster despite an evident prejudice against him. Allen Oscar Hansen's *Liberalism and American Education in the Eighteenth Century* (New York, 1926) presents a useful classification of Webster's political and educational ideas, as recorded in his books and pamphlets before 1801. James Herring, who painted Webster's portrait in 1833, gave the first brief, authorized biography in *The National*

Portrait Gallery of Distinguished Americans (New York, 1834–1839). The brief sketch by William Chauncey Fowler in *A Dictionary of the English Language* (University edition, New York, 1846) gives illuminating details of Webster's youth. The basic sketch, to which all other biographies and articles have been indebted, was written by Professor Chauncey A. Goodrich; it appeared first in the 1847 edition of *An American Dictionary of the English Language,* and then in an expanded form in *The American Literary Magazine* (January, 1848).

III

ADDITIONAL SOURCES FOR PARTICULAR CHAPTERS

(not including Webster's own publications)

CHAPTER I

Daniel Steele Durrie, *Steele Family. A Genealogical History of John and George Steele (Settlers of Hartford, Conn.) 1635–6, and their Descendants* (Albany, 1859).

Alice Morse Earle, *Child Life in Colonial Days* (New York, 1899).

William H. Webster and Melville R. Webster, *History and Genealogy of the Gov. John Webster Family of Connecticut* (Rochester, N. Y., 1915).

The Connecticut Courant (Hartford, 1764–1774).

Webster's comment on Connecticut's "singular machinery" is from *The Herald* (New York, September 28, 1796).

CHAPTER II

Franklin Bowditch Dexter, *Biographical Sketches of the Graduates of Yale College* (Vol. III, New York, 1903).

Henry P. Johnston, *Yale and Her Honor-Roll in the Revolution, 1775–1783* (New York, 1888).

Anson Phelps Stokes, *Memorials of Eminent Yale Men* (Vol. I, New Haven, 1914).

Theodore A. Zunder, *The Early Days of Joel Barlow* (New Haven, 1934).

The letter of President Daggett, dated New Haven, April 10, 1778, is preserved in the Yale University Library.

CHAPTER III

Joel Benton, "An Unpublished Chapter in Noah Webster's Life. Love and the Spelling-Book," *The Magazine of American History* (x, 52; July, 1883).

Helen Evertson Smith, *Colonial Days and Ways as Gathered from Family Papers* (New York, 1900).

Charles Burr Todd, *Life and Letters of Joel Barlow* (New York and London, 1886).

The New-York Packet (Fishkill, 1782).

The Freeman's Chronicle (Hartford, 1783).

The letter of Henry Wisner is in the New York Historical Society.

CHAPTER IV

Rev. A. M. Colton, *The Old Meeting House and Vacation Papers, Humorous and Other* (New York, 1890).

Clifton Johnson, *Old-Time Schools and School-Books* (New York, 1904).

Weekly Monitor (Litchfield, Conn., 1785).

The letter to John Canfield, January 6, 1783; the Memorial to the Legislature of Connecticut, October 24, 1782; and the Memorial to the Legislature of New York, January 18, 1783, are preserved in the New York Public Library.

CHAPTER V

American Mercury (Hartford, Conn., February 21, 1785) contains Webster's remarks about illiterate schoolmasters.

CHAPTER VI

The charge that "Dilworth's Ghost" rose because of politics is in the *New-York Journal* (September 23, 1784) and in the *Connecticut Journal* (New Haven, December 15, 1784).

Chapter VII

J. E. P. Boulden, *The Presbyterians of Baltimore; Their Churches and Historic Grave-Yards* (Baltimore, 1785).

John Pendleton Kennedy, "Baltimore Long Ago" in Mrs. Lincoln Phelps's *Our Country, in its Relations to the Past, Present and Future* (Baltimore, 1864).

The "friendly critic's" remarks are in *The Daily Advertiser* (New York, April 11, 1786). Six days later appeared Childs's puff.

Webster's letter of April 14, 1786, is in the Pierpont Morgan Library.

Chapter VIII

William Cobbett, *The Rushlight,* February 28, 1800 (New York, 1800).

Catharine Van Cortlandt Mathews, *Andrew Ellicott, His Life and Letters* (New York, 1908).

Rush's comment on New Englanders is in *Massachusetts Historical Society Collections* (IV, 474; 1891).

Thomas Fitzsimmons's letter of September 15, 1787, is preserved in the New York Public Library.

Chapter IX

[Dorothy C. Burck, ed.], *Diary of William Dunlap* (three volumes, New York, 1930).

Allen Walker Read, "The Philological Society of New York, 1788," *American Speech* (IX, 131–136, April, 1934).

Webster's letter to Dr. Cogswell, dated Boston, January 31, 1789, is preserved in the Jones Memorial Library, Amherst, Mass.

Chapter X

Francis Parsons, *The Friendly Club and Other Portraits* (Hartford, Conn., 1922).

The American Mercury (Hartford, 1789–1793).

The Connecticut Courant (Hartford, 1789–1793).

Chapter XI

Claude G. Bowers, *Jefferson and Hamilton: The Struggle for Democracy in America* (Boston and New York, 1925).

Bernard Faÿ, *The Two Franklins: Fathers of American Democracy* (Boston, 1933).

Meade Minnegerode, *Jefferson, Friend of France: 1793; The Career of Edmond Charles Genêt* (New York and London, 1928).

Aurora (Philadelphia, 1793–1800).

Greenleaf's New-York Journal (1793–1800).

Porcupine's Gazette (Philadelphia, 1797–1799).

The American Minerva (New York, 1793–1797) and its semi-weekly edition, *The Herald* (New York, 1794–1797).

The Commercial Advertiser (New York, 1797–1803) and its semi-weekly edition, *The Spectator* (New York, 1797–1803).

For further abuse of Webster, see James Thompson Callender, *American Annual Register . . . for 1796* (Philadelphia, 1797).

Chapter XII

Nathan G. Goodman, *Benjamin Rush, Physician and Citizen: 1746–1813* (Philadelphia, 1934).

Allen Walker Read, "Noah Webster's Project in 1801 for a History of American Newspapers," *Journalism Quarterly* (XI, 258–275, September, 1934).

Aldred Scott Warthin, "Noah Webster as Epidemiologist," *The Journal of the American Medical Association* (LXXX, 755–764, March 17, 1923).

C.-E. A. Winslow, "The Epidemiology of Noah Webster," *Transactions of the Connecticut Academy of Arts and Sciences* (XXXII, 21–109, January, 1934).

The Medical Repository (New York, 1797–1810).

Reviews of *A Brief History of Epidemic and Pestilential Diseases* may also be found in *The Monthly Magazine, and American Review* (New York, II, 30–36, 108–115, 208–213, 289–296; 1800); *The Monthly Review; or Literary Journal* (London, XXXVII, 404–407, April, 1802); and *The Critical Review; or, Annals of Literature* (London, XXXI, 260–268, March, 1801).

Chapter XIII

Edgar F. Smith, *Priestley in America, 1794–1804* (Philadelphia, 1920).

Thomas R. Trowbridge, Jr., *History of the Ancient Maritime Interests of New Haven* (New Haven, 1882).

The letter to Rufus King, July 6, 1807, is in the New York Historical Society. The letter to Samuel Bayard, March 2, 1802, is in the Library of Congress. The letter to Stephen Twining, January 22, 1802, is in the Connecticut Academy deposit in the Yale University Library.

Chapter XIV

F. Sturges Allen, *Noah Webster's Place among English Lexicographers* (Springfield, [1909]).

Simeon E. Baldwin, *Life and Letters of Simeon Baldwin* (New Haven, 1919).

M. M. Mathews, *A Survey of English Dictionaries* (London, 1933).

James A. H. Murray, *The Evolution of English Lexicography* (Oxford, 1900).

The letter to John West, January 18, 1805, is in the Jones Memorial Library, Amherst, Mass.

Chapter XV

An Historical Review. One hundred and fiftieth Anniversary of the First Church of Christ in Amherst, Massachusetts. November 7, 1889 (Amherst, Mass., 1890).

Claude Moore Fuess. *Amherst, the Story of a New England College* (Boston, 1935).

Frederick H. Hitchcock, *The Handbook of Amherst, Massachusetts* (Amherst, Mass., 1891).

Genevieve Taggard, *The Life and Mind of Emily Dickinson* (New York and London, 1930).

Everett E. Thompson, "Noah Webster and Amherst College," *Amherst Graduates' Quarterly* (August, 1933).

Frederick Tuckerman, *Amherst Academy, A New England School of the Past: 1814–1861* (Amherst, Mass., 1929).

W. S. Tyler, *History of Amherst College during its First Half Century* (Springfield, Mass., 1873).

The letter to William Leffingwell is owned by G. A. Plimpton.

Chapter XVI

[William C. Fowler], *Printed but not Published* [1854?]

Felix Flügel, "Die Englische Philologie in Nordamerica," Separatausdruck aus E. G. Gersdorfs *Reportorium der deutschen und ausländischen Literatur* (Bd. 4, Heft 4, 1852).

John Pickering, *A Vocabulary, or Collection of Words and Phrases which have been supposed to be peculiar to the United States of America* (Boston, 1816).

Chapter XVII

[Lyman Cobb], *A Critical Review of Noah Webster's Spelling-Book . . .* by Examinator ([Albany], 1828).

Lyman Cobb, *A Critical Review of the Orthography of Dr. Webster's Series of Books for Systematick Instruction in the English Language* (New York, 1831).

George Philip Krapp, *The English Language in America* (two volumes, New York, 1925).

H. L. Mencken, *The American Language* (third edition, New York, 1923).

The letter of Jefferson to Josiah Meigs is owned by W. C. Fowler.

Chapter XVIII

Blackford Condit, *The History of the English Bible* (second edition, New York, [1896]).

Allen Walker Read, "Noah Webster as a Euphemist," *Dialect Notes* (VI, 385–391).

Harry R. Warfel, "Centenary of Noah Webster's Bible," *The New England Quarterly* (VII, 578–582, September, 1934). I have taken a few sentences from this article without using quotation marks.

Henry M. Whitney, "The Latest Translation of the Bible," *Bibliotheca Sacra* (April, July, and October, 1902; January and April, 1903; January and April, 1905; and July, 1907).

CHAPTER XIX

Herbert B. Adams, *The Life and Writings of Jared Sparks* (two volumes, Boston and New York, 1893).

Basil Hall, *Travels in North America, in the Years 1827 and 1828* (Philadelphia, 1829).

[Anne Royall], *Sketches of History, Life, and Manners in the United States* (New Haven, 1826).

Webster's letter to *The Hartford Times*, dated February 15, 1840, is owned by Mrs. Hildegarde E. Taylor.

The family correspondence on which much of this chapter is based, is in the possession of William Chauncey Fowler.

INDEX